The Second Addendum of

Victorian Staffordshire Figures

1835-1875

Book Four

Schiffer Publishing Ltd

4880 Lower Valley Road Atglen, Pennsylvania 19310

A. & N. Harding

Dedication

This book is dedicated to the life and memory of
The Reverend Harry Bloomfield
Whose passion for Staffordshire lives on in us all
24th May 1929 – 2nd January 1999
The Vicar of Kennington
1984 – 1998

'Open the windows wide, there is nothing to fear'
Jim Winskill, Dorset Farmer
Dying Words

Other Schiffer Books by A. & N. Harding
Victorian Staffordshire Figures 1835-1875, Book One: Portraits, Naval & Military, Theatrical & Literary Characters.
Victorian Staffordshire Figures 1835-1875, Book Two: Religious, Hunters, Pastoral, Occupations, Children & Animals, Dogs, Animals, Cottages & Castles, Sport & Miscellaneous.
Victorian Staffordshire Figures 1835-1875, Book Three.
Victorian Staffordshire Figures 1875-1962
Victorian Staffordshire Dogs.

Other Schiffer Books on Related Subjects
Staffordshire Animals: A Collector's Guide to History, Style, and Value. Adele Kenny.
Staffordshire Figures. Adele Kenny & Veronica Moriarty.
Staffordshire Spaniels. Adele Kenny.

Copyright © 2007 by A. & N. Harding
Library of Congress Control Number: 2007930643

Designed by Mark David Bowyer
Type set in Bodoni Bd BT / Arrus BT

ISBN: 978-0-7643-2762-9
Printed in China

Published by Schiffer Publishing Ltd.
4880 Lower Valley Road
Atglen, PA 19310
Phone: (610) 593-1777; Fax: (610) 593-2002
E-mail: Info@schifferbooks.com

For the largest selection of fine reference books on this and related subjects, please visit our web site at
www.schifferbooks.com
We are always looking for people to write books on new and related subjects. If you have an idea for a book please contact us at the above address.

This book may be purchased from the publisher.
Include $3.95 for shipping.
Please try your bookstore first.
You may write for a free catalog.

In Europe, Schiffer books are distributed by
Bushwood Books
6 Marksbury Ave.
Kew Gardens
Surrey TW9 4JF England
Phone: 44 (0) 20 8392-8585; Fax: 44 (0) 20 8392-9876
E-mail: info@bushwoodbooks.co.uk
Website: www.bushwoodbooks.co.uk
Free postage in the U.K., Europe; air mail at cost.

Contents

Acknowledgments

The authors wish to thank those collectors and dealers who imparted their knowledge and allowed their collections and stock to be photographed; without their help this book would not have been so comprehensive.

In particular we would like to thank Mr. Ray Walker, Mr. Harry Ryans, and we would also like to thank Mrs. Sara Hales, Crows Auction Rooms, Mr. A. Wood, Mr. J Waters, Lambrays of Wadebridge, Cornwall, Russell Baldwin & Bright of Leominster, and Allison Moore, Mr. G. & Mrs. J. Brealey, Mr. D. & Mrs. J. Prentice & Mr. R. Elsey, John Howard, Mr. A. Anderson. Professor.

R. Edwards CBE, Mr. K. Gomersall, Bonhams Chelsea and Millers Publications for allowing us access to their picture libraries.

We would also wish to thank the museums who gave us access to their collections, which included Ms. M. Goodby at The City Museum and Art Gallery, Hanley, Stoke-on-Trent, the home of one of the finest collections not in private hands. The Brighton Art Gallery and Museum and The Balston Collection, Bantock House Museum, Wolverhampton.

I, the N. in A. & N. Harding, would particularly like to give the utmost thanks to the collectors I visited on my trips to the United States, whose collections are some of the finest I have seen. I extend my gratitude to Elinor Penna, Arnold Berlin, Carrol Barnes, Sheila Ferguson, and Susan Bishop, whose collections and stock feature prominently in these volumes.

We would also wish to thank the many collectors who, for security reasons, wish to remain anonymous, which is a sad reflection of the times we live in. We are indebted to them for allowing us into their homes to photograph their collections, even though we are unable to acknowledge them personally.

Even after cataloguing over 5000 figures we know that there are some that have escaped us, and hope that this book will encourage collectors and dealers alike who own figures not included to contact us, so that a third edition may contain them.

We can be contacted by E-mail.
Or you can visit our website at:
www.staffordshirefigures.com
Or E-mail us at nick@staffordshirefigures.com

A. & N. Harding

Preface to the Second Addendum

In 1998 *Victorian Staffordshire Figures 1835-1875* was published in two volumes; in 2000 Book Three The Addendum was published. In the acknowledgments it was stated that *'we knew that there were a lot more figures out there'* and we asked collectors and dealers to contact us, so that a second addendum might contain them.

The response we have had has been overwhelming, collectors and dealers from all over the world have contacted us. S. J. Hales and Crows of Dorking, whom both hold sales devoted almost entirely to Staffordshire Figures, have allowed us to photograph all the figures in their sales, and where we have asked, most other auction houses have been just as helpful.

We have taken the opportunity in this addendum to correct any errors discovered in the first three Volumes and have also included photographs of many figures that were listed in the first two Volumes but 'not illustrated'. We have also illustrated pairs of figures, where only one was previously shown.

We have also added over 1400 figures that did not appear in the first three volumes; these four volumes now contain photographs of over 5000 figures. Whilst there are still some figures of which we have been unable to obtain a photograph, these are now in the minority. Should, some time in the future, a further edition be printed, we will do our best to include them.

Whilst the vast majority of the photographs in this second addendum are of studio quality, due either to their location or the fact that we have been supplied with a photograph, some are not. The authors apologise for this lesser quality but are of the opinion that it is better to have any sort of photograph of a figure, rather than none at all.

Introduction

From the early 1900s up until the 1950s, the collecting of Victorian Staffordshire figures was unheard of and would have been deemed an eccentric pastime. For a long time the realisation that they were one of the last English folk arts was sadly overlooked.

At the end of the Second World War, when the visiting sailors, soldiers, and air crews returned home, it was to America that thousands of these figures were taken as mementoes of their stay in England. The exodus of figures continued when American tourists returned after the war. At that time they were very inexpensive and recognised as typical, unique of an age that had long since past, and many of these figures have stayed in America and some of the finest collections are there.

It was not long before the situation changed in this country and by the 1960s collections were starting to be formed; Victorian Staffordshire figures had finally achieved the appreciation that they so justly deserved in their own homeland.

The collecting of Victorian Staffordshire figures is now firmly established, and never again will we see them dismissed as mere 'pottery chimney ornaments'. The prices now realised for the rarest and the best compare to and exceed the prices paid for porcelain figures made at the same time. The prices for our unknown potters' work often exceeds that of marked Dresden, Meissen, and other Continental factories' figures.

Books

In 1955 Mr. R. Hagger's book, 'Staffordshire Chimney Ornaments', was published. This text was followed closely in 1958 by Mr. Thomas Balston's book entitled 'Staffordshire Portrait Figures of the Victorian age'. This book illustrated, for the first time, a quite comprehensive catalogue of the Portrait figures that had been made.

These two publications led to an increased interest and awareness of this forgotten art. Soon articles on the figures began to appear in magazines, and periodicals, and other smaller books on specific themes were also published.

These books and periodicals revived interest in Victorian Staffordshire as an art form and, in 1970, P. D. Gordon Pugh's 'Staffordshire Figures of the Victorian Era' was published. It contained comprehensive pictures and information on over 1300 portrait figures. This publication was complimented in 1971 by Anthony Oliver's book 'The Victorian Staffordshire Figure'. And in 1981 Anthony Oliver followed the success of his first book with another titled 'Staffordshire Pottery The Tribal Art of England'

Due in part to the revived interest in Victorian Staffordshire figures and the ever increasing prices, auction houses began to hold regular sales devoted entirely to Staffordshire figures, whereas previously, unless a particularly large collection was for sale, these figures were included with the general pottery and porcelain sales.

In 1990 the late Clive Mason Pope published privately 'A – Z of Staffordshire Dogs'. This was the first time any attempt had been made to catalogue items other than portrait figures.

With the publication in 1998 in two volumes of 'Victorian Staffordshire Figures 1835-1875' we attempted to catalogue all aspects of Victorian Staffordshire figure production, concentrating not just on portraiture or dogs, but including the many other categories which had been made. The entire range of figures were included, which had in the past been neglected, including Animals, Cottages, Religious, and the many types of Decorative figures.

The year 2000 saw the publication of our 'Book Three The Addendum' which supplemented the first two volumes and added a further 1100 or so figures to the catalogues.

The year 2003 saw the publication of 'Victorian Staffordshire Figures 1875-1962', which catalogued all the later figures until the last pottery making these figures closed down in 1962.

The year 2006 saw our specialist publication 'Victorian Staffordshire Dogs' which extracted from all the volumes those figures in which dogs were the only or main part of the figure, and added another 300 or so which had not previously been catalogued.

This year also saw the publication of 'Dudson Staffordshire Figures 1815 – 1865' by Audrey Dudson and Alison Morgan, which is the first time a book dedicated to the production at one particular pottery making Victorian Staffordshire figures has been published. This book has laid claim to a single pottery making a substantial diverse range of figures, which have never before been identified with any pottery.

Since the publication of our previous four volumes, we have been able to photograph many new figures, and photograph figures that were listed in our previous publications, but 'not illustrated'. We have also included new sources and attributions to figures that have come to light, and we have corrected all known errors.

Every book published on this nineteenth century folk art should add to our knowledge and understanding; knowledge which is still surprisingly scant. The potters kept few written records of their work, and virtually none have survived the past one hundred and fifty years.

Throughout this book where we have referred to 'Book One, Book Two, and Book Three, these relate to our previous publications, Victorian Staffordshire Figures 1835-1875: Book One, Two, and Three.

Figures Included

This book, as with the previous four volumes, is in the main a catalogue of all aspects of Victorian Staffordshire Figures. What has been confirmed in the compiling of this book is the absence of Portrait figures of personalities previously unrecorded.

This lack of new Portrait figures is, we believe, because they are all now included in these books, any that subsequently come to light will be extremely rare, though new examples of existing personalities may yet be found.

What we have found however in abundance, and are still finding, are previously unrecorded animal and decorative figures of hunters, musicians, dancers, and actors as well as figures of pastoral scenes, pastimes, and occupations

We have been able to identify a few of the figures illustrated in the previous books, but we are sure that there are many sources still out there undiscovered, which in time will identify more.

The task of compiling a comprehensive catalogue of items other than the Portrait figures may never be completed, as we are still finding new examples. We do believe that with this second edition, the majority of collectable figures that have survived the last 150 years have now been catalogued.

This still leaves the minority, whilst difficult to be precise, from our experience and knowledge we would estimate, and we would emphasize that it is an estimate, that there are between 400 and 500 collectable figures still to be found and photographed and with the help of collectors and dealers alike some time in the future the second edition may contain them.

The above figures do not include the many pairs of which only one have we been able to photograph and catalogue.

There are many small figures of two to five inches in height which were made in their thousands: probably made as fairings to be given away at fairs as prizes, all of little merit, usually poorly coloured, if coloured at all, generally badly modelled, often because the potter used the mould for too many figures, thus producing inferior ones. Many of these figures have survived and can be purchased for relatively small sums.

Figures such as these have not been included in this book as most collectors avoid them. The Victorians created many thousands of wonderful oil paintings, but also painted thousands of little or no quality, the same applies to Staffordshire figures.

Prices

As with most antiques, the quality and condition of a Staffordshire figure does vary, and no two are exactly alike. The price paid for a piece will not only reflect this, but also where it was bought. A figure is likely to be more expensive if it is purchased from a specialist dealer, with a large stock from which to choose, and willing to offer advice and detail any repair or restoration, rather than if it was purchased from a market stall where the figure is part of a general stock, the trader knowing little or nothing about it.

In the authors opinion auction prices are not a reliable guide. In the past there have been numerous occasions when figures at auction have realised high prices, which have not been sustained.

There are a number of reasons for this situation:

- Private purchasers may not realise that they are bidding against a high or unrealistic reserve.
- It takes only two bidders intent on acquiring a particular figure for the price to escalate.

- 'Auction fever' can occur when bidders drawn by the occasion and a persuasive auctioneer pay a price that is later regretted. As an example of Auction fever, about six years ago a figure of Van Amburgh, Fig. 336 see Book One, sold at a provincial auction room for over £6000.00. In September 2006 this very same figure sold in another provincial auction room for under £4000.00.

Prices at Auction continue to reach record levels, levels that if sustained, and carried through to other figures of equal merit will take many figures beyond the means of most. This trend, whilst disturbing, and cold comfort to collectors wishing to add to their collections, will no doubt be of great satisfaction to those who collected figures whilst prices were relatively low.

As examples of the prices presently being paid and obtained we would instance the following.

A pair of lop eared Rabbits eating lettuces	Figs. 3071/3072	£13500-00 ($27000) plus premium
A pair of walking Leopards	Figs. 3002/3003	£ 5600-00 ($11200) plus premium
A pair of Lion and Lioness	Figs. 3025/3026	£ 3700-00 ($7400) plus premium
A pair of Lions with lambs	Figs. 3027/3028	£ 3600-00 ($7200) plus premium
A pair of Lions with lambs	Figs. 3013/3014	£ 7000-00 ($14000) plus premium
Mr. Van Amburgh	Fig. 336	£ 4600-00 ($9200) plus premium
A group of Military cricketers	Fig. 880	£5000-00 ($10000) plus premium
Sir R. Peel on horseback	Fig. 263	£4750-00 ($9500)
Lion and tiger group	Fig. a3034	£3650-00 ($7300)
Napoleon Bonaparte	Fig. 42	£7000-00 ($14000) plus premium
The Victory	Fig. 801	£3400-00 ($6800) plus premium

The price for the pair of Rabbits remains, to the best of our knowledge, the highest price ever paid for Victorian Staffordshire figures. Had the purchaser contacted a specialist dealer at the time, a pair very similar could have been purchased for under half the price paid at auction. And at a later auction a single, similar Rabbit sold for £1500-00, ($3000) whilst the price for the rabbits is an exception, prices over £2000-00 ($4000) are now commonplace.

Wild animals, figures with sporting connections, very rare portrait figures, and rare dog groups and Pairs are now at the top of the market with four figure prices being paid. In most instances they are at last realising what most Staffordshire collectors knew to be their true value when compared to other equivalent antiques.

There are however, in the author's opinion, still bargains to be found. Decorative figures of huntsmen, gardeners, and musicians either singularly or in Pairs can all still be purchased for less than £1000-00 ($2000) and most for less than £500-00 ($1000) and at this price they can be found perfect and extremely rare. For those who like cottages and houses, a very good example can be purchased for under £400-00. ($800) It is unlikely that this situation will remain and very soon these too will have found their true price level.

As a footnote to the above prices, in September 1999 a major auction sale was held in Newbury, England. It consisted of over 600 figures in nearly 450 lots, the bulk of the collection of the late Reverend Harry Bloomfield. The Reverend Bloomfield had been an avid collector for nearly fifty years, and this auction was the first time in twenty years that a collection of this quality and quantity had been offered for sale.

The media coverage of the event was unlike anything seen before in the world of Staffordshire, with articles appearing in magazines and national newspapers, even on local TV. Cameras were there on the day of the sale. The interest for this sale was immense, with over 2500 catalogues distributed, and record numbers of people attending the viewing days. On the day of the sale, the number of bidders present was so large that there was not enough room for all in the main saleroom and bidding had to be conducted through a porter in an adjoining room, for those unable to get a seat in the auction room. The sale itself was a resounding success with all lots sold and many record prices paid. The majority of figures exceeded the top estimate, this not being the fault of the auctioneers acting on the prudent side, but because of the sheer volume of bidders present not only in the saleroom, but bids left on the book, and bidders on the telephone. It had been anticipated that the figures would sell for up to £120000-00, in the event nearly £200000-00 was achieved.

Listed below are a selection of figures, with their guide price, and final selling price.

Description	Fig. No.	Estimate Paid	Price
A pair of figures of Moody & Sankey	209/307	£600-£900	£2470-00
A standing figure of Wallace	1142	£250-£350	£882-00
A figure of Uncle Tom & Eva	1090	£180-£220	£705-00
A pair of figures Returning home – Going to Market	2172/2173	£200-£300	£610-00
A figure of First Ride	2201	£500-£700	£2352-00
A pair of spill vases of a lioness with Cubs	3021/3022	£1500-£2000	£2352-00
A theatrical group of Lucrezia Borgia & Gennaro	1312	£500-£700	£1410-00
A figure of three squirrels around a Clock face	3101	£300-£400	£4940-00
A pair of pointers	2698/2699	£500-£800	£3646-00
A pair of seated pugs	2779/2780	£200-£300	£1152-00
A pair of lions with lambs	3013/3014	£2000-£3000	£6433-00
A pair of cricketers	3032/3033	£2000-£3000	£5175-00
A pair of zebras	3120/3121	£400-£600	£1300-00
A pair of walking lions	3015/3016	£1500-£2000	£3175-00
A pair of seated spaniels on malachite bases	2530/2531	£1200-£1800	£2940-00
A pair of figures of shepherds	1964/1965	£250-£350	£1823-00

There was a degree of 'Auction fever' about many of the prices; the pair of shepherds (Figs. 1964/1965) had been bought in the same sale rooms by The Reverend Bloomfield not much more than a year before for under £300, and two similar groups of the squirrels (Fig. 3101) had been sold by dealers in the previous year for between £600 and £900.

Within This Price Guide

Against each figure a GUIDE price has been given; we must EMPHASISE that this is not necessarily for the figure illustrated, as many of the figures illustrated are of the finest figures and collections existing.

- If the figure is pristine or unique it is likely to be **ABOVE** the higher guide price.
- A figure of good quality, in reasonable condition with minor restoration, or minor repair should be found **WITHIN** the price guide.
- A heavily restored figure or one of poor quality should be purchased **BELOW** the lower price guide.

The **GUIDE** price below has been given in two currencies, Pounds Sterling and U.S. Dollars.

Prices for Staffordshire figures in the United Kingdom are generally lower than prices in the United States, so it is difficult to give a direct price conversion. There are exceptions to this rule, Portrait figures whilst eagerly sought after in Britain, are not so commercial in America, whereas Decorative and Animal figures have always been more popular and in turn more expensive in the United States.

We have now updated the scales below, allowing for the change in the U.S. Dollar and the general price trends of the current marketplace. Over the last ten years since publishing our first Volumes, many prices have remained steady but on the lesser pieces there has, if anything, been a reduction in price. We have made changes to the D/E/F/G/H price bands to reflect this. The more expensive pieces have generally held their value.

These scales should now be used in conjunction with our previous books to get a more accurate value.

Pounds Sterling £			U.S. Dollars $		
A+	£4000.00+		A+	$8000.00+	
A	£3000.00 to £4000-00		A	$6000.00 to $8000.00	
B	£2000.00 to £3000-00		B	$4000.00 to $6000.00	
C	£1000.00 to £2000-00		C	$2000.00 to $4000.00	
D	£400.00 to £1000-00		D	$800.00 to $2000.00	
E	£200.00 to £400-00		E	$400.00 to $800.00	
F	£100.00 to £200-00		F	$200.00 to $400.00	
G	£50.00 to £100-00		G	$100.00 to $200.00	
H	Below £50		H	Below $100.00	

Sizes

The size of each figure is given to the nearest quarter inch, but the same figure can vary in size, up to half an inch, usually due to the size of the base. Where the authors are aware of more than one size, each measurement has been given. **But this is not definitive and other sizes of figures do exist.** When the larger size is substantially different, it has been given a separate figure number see for instance Figs. 1813/1814

Buying and Selling

Over the course of 150 years, for most of which Staffordshire figures were not regarded as anything other than cheap decorations and for the most part treated with contempt, it is therefore surprising that so many figures have survived. Many if not most of the figures have suffered degrees of damage; in particular, the overglaze enamels are prone to flaking, so examples that have survived in pristine condition are a rarity. When figures of this nature are offered for sale they do command a premium.

The other fake that has been recorded was of a titled figure of a 'Whaler', originally a figure of William Shakespeare, his manuscript had been replaced by a concertina, a cap applied to his head, and his left leg was now a peg leg.

In 1998 the faking of dogs with baskets in their mouths occurred. The price of these figures has escalated in the past few years and it seems that a faker realised a profitable market. The dogs themselves are original, but what is happening is that baskets are being applied carefully to their mouths. As a general rule the best course of action is to look very carefully at their mouths and baskets, look for over painting and any join marks.

Another faker realising the high prices that pairs of cats can realise has made pairs of seated cats with and without kittens, as fakes go they are very good and have fooled auction houses into cataloguing them as '19th century', underglaze blue has been applied to the base of some of these and it is this aspect of the figures that is the least convincing.

Misattributions and the Identification of Figures

It is in the field of misattributions that the greatest care should be taken. Over the years many figures have, on little if no evidence, been attributed to a particular person or production. Dealers have not always done this with a profit in mind.

The majority of Staffordshire figures were modelled and made with no particular person in mind. The hundreds of decorative figures are just that, decorative, their purpose for a mass market was to brighten up a shelf or mantelpiece.

The difference in price has caused many of the figures of children with dogs to be passed off as 'The Royal Children'. Many figures are said to be of actors or actresses in specific roles and it is possible that a portion of them are, but unless there is definite proof, (i.e., a music front, engraving, etc,) care should be taken.

A number of the earliest collectors were actors or others connected to or with a love of the theatre, and we have them to thank for some of the attributions that we have today. They spent many hours trawling through early music fronts, playbills, and prints. Though in some cases, over enthusiasm has led to decorative figures being given theatrical attributions.

If the potters titled the Queen, who would have been identifiable to nearly all of her subjects, they would, if they were portraying an actor, have titled such figures, as the actor would have been identifiable to very few. The reason they did not is that they were portraying, at best, the dramatic moment and the actor was of little consequence.

The Parr factory produced a number of figures based on engravings from Tallis's 'Shakespeare Gallery'. These figures were all titled with the character or play, the engravings all had details of the actor or actress portraying the parts; but the figures are never, with one exception, found titled with the names of the actor or actress. They were unimportant, for it was the dramatic moment that was being portrayed.

There are a very few figures with the actual actor/actress's name included in the title. These include: a figure of William Charles Macready in the role of James V of Scotland, titled 'Macready' (Figure 1156); a figure of the Cushman sisters in the role of Romeo and Juliet, titled 'Miss Cushmans in character of Romeo and Juliet' (Figure 1072); a figure of Van Amburgh as himself, titled 'Van Amburgh' (Figure 336); a figure of 'Julien' the conductor (Figure 178); and a pair of figures of a standing horse and attendant that can be found titled 'Rarey' (Figures 1367/1368), however this pair of figures bears little resemblance to him, and the last three were not actors but performers.

The only other exceptions are the figures of 'The Swedish Nightingale', Jenny Lind. Some may be found titled 'Jenny Lind' (Figures 184, 185, 186, 187, 1300, 1301, 1330, 1332, 1335 Book One). These are figures which either have her as a 'Portrait' figure, or titled in a specific production.

We have only included figures in the Portrait Chapter of which we are virtually sure are Portraits. All the other figures will be found in other Chapters. We would advise collectors never to pay a premium for untitled Portrait figures unless there is a titled equivalent or a known incontrovertible source. We would urge that figures be judged on their quality and not their identity, if this advice is followed there would be no reason for the imaginative attributions that have been made to continue.

Identifiable Sources

When writing this book, we have tried to include illustrations of as many identifiable sources next to the figure as possible. When this has not been possible, we have given details of the source.

The volumes contain illustrations and details on over 5000 figures, the sources that have been found amount to less than 200. This is not because they have all been lost over time, although many will have, but because the majority of figures were from the modeller's imagination.

The potters did however use a variety of sources for their figures, and included are drawings from 'The London Illustrated News', 'Cassell's Illustrated Family Paper', and 'Punch'. Other sources include the figures based on engravings from Tallis' 'Shakespeare Gallery', produced by the Parr factory, and The Illustrated Bible, which was the source or inspiration for some of the religious groups.

Penny plain and Tuppenny coloured prints may have influenced the potters to a degree, although very few of them are exact copies of the figure, quite a surprising number are very similar to known figures.

PLATE 7
Mr. G. Clair as Matthioli, London, Published by J. Redington. 208 Horton Old Town & and sold by J. Webb, 75 Brick Lane, St Lukes.

This print is similar in respects to a number of the Brigand figures made, in particular See Figures 1415 & 1415A

PLATE 8

Skelt's, late Webb's Four Favourite Positions in the Lost Ship as performed at the Royal Surrey Theatre Nov 13th 1843. Mr. T. P. Cooke as Ben Treenant, Mr. N. T. Hicks as Ned Martin, Mr. R. Honnor as Jan Dowsterswyvel, and Mrs. R. Honnor as Rose Linden. Jersey Published by G. Skelt, 24 Clearview, St. Helier.

There are a number of figures reminiscent of this print; however, very few figures were made with arms outstretched as they would have been difficult to produce and very prone to damage, and the potters would have altered them accordingly. See Figures 1114/1115.

History

The county of Staffordshire has been producing pottery of all types for many years. The area in which the majority of it was produced was, geographically, quite small, made up of seven villages covering a mere thirty square miles. What these villages had in common was an abundance of coal to fuel the kilns, and a more than sufficient supply of clay to make the figures.

These seven villages of Stoke, Fenton, Longton, Tunstall, Burslem, Hanley, and Shelton grew into towns and finally into The County Borough of Stoke on Trent. The scale of production of pottery and porcelain in these towns was immense, for it was not just figures that were produced, but every conceivable item, from candlesnuffers to lavatory pans, from jardinières to dinner services. It is likely that even today each home in Great Britain possesses at least one article of domestic or decorative ware that was produced in the potteries.

Decorative, animal, and religious figures have been produced in Staffordshire since the early 1700s. This book concentrates on the specific type of figure design known as

Victorian Staffordshire flatbacks. There was of course an overlapping period during which both pre-Victorian and Victorian figures were made. Attributed to one Obadiah Sherratt, who was born in about 1775, is a whole host of figures, and in particular figures with 'Table bases', having either four or six feet, with titles such as 'Ale Bench' and its pair 'Tee Total', depicting either a happy or unhappy family depending on whether or not alcohol was consumed. Bull baiting was avidly watched and a group of bull, dogs, and attendant was made titled 'Bull Baiting, Now Captain Lad'. Obadiah was illiterate, he had signed his wedding certificate with a cross, and thus the spelling on many of his titles was less than accurate, for instance, a spectacular figure of a standing lion with one foot on a ball is titled 'Roran Lion'.

The most sought after and the most expensive of Sherratt's figures are the menagerie figures. Polito's touring menagerie had visited Staffordshire in 1808, and to commemorate the event, a large figure was made titled 'Polito's Menagerie'. It must have been successful, for shortly thereafter an even larger, more elaborate version was made. Polito died in 1814 and he was succeeded by a Mr. Wombwell and this second version can also be found titled 'Wombwell's Menagerie'. A third, even more elaborate version was made that is only ever found titled 'Wombwell's Menagerie'.

Obadiah died in the mid-to late 1830s and was succeeded by his son Hamlet. By the 1850s the business was being run by Obadiah's widow, Martha. The business appears to have ceased in about 1860. None of Sherratt's figures have ever been found factory marked and most are impossible to date within ten to twenty years of manufacture. So it is possible that these pre-Victorian figures continued being manufactured up to 1860, or alternatively, perhaps the son changed his methods of production and started to make flatbacks, which would have meant changing from often up to fifty separate handmade moulds to as few as three. Other potters who were in production both before and after 1835 would either have continued with the pre-Victorian style, or changed to meet the demand for the newer, more simplified figures of the Victorian era.

This new style of figure was a simplified version of pre-Victorian figures, which had used many handmade subsidiary parts. These new figures were very simple to produce, the majority of them needing only three moulds, a front, a back, and a base. Because of the extreme heat of the glost oven only two colours could withstand this heat and remain unchanged, the prime colour was Cobalt blue, a hallmark of this period, a derivative black or purple could also be produced, but this was rarely used.

The other colours seen on figures were added after and refired at a lower temperature. These colours are overglaze enamels. Whilst these overglaze enamels can flake, the blue and black cannot. The darker the colour, the more likely it is to flake. Overglaze black that was used much more frequently than underglaze black is the most likely to suffer.

There were numerous pot banks at this time in Staffordshire, some employing many hundreds of people, others working on a much smaller scale. This was the early part of the Victorian era, when there were no real worker's rights or effective trade unions. Workers were employed in near slave labour conditions. Children as young as five years of age were expected to work twelve hours a day, six days a week. They were used for the menial tasks, carrying the clay, pressing the moulds, and painting and decorating the figures.

When and which pot bank produced the first 'flatback' will never be known, but what is certain is that it did not take other potteries too long to realise the commercialism of this style of figure.

It would be inaccurate to suggest that styles of production changed on a particular date at the beginning of the Victorian period, and it is more than probable that the early style of figure carried on in tandem with the 'flatbacks' for a number of years. The ease and cheapness of producing these figures would have eventually forced the demise of the earlier hand modelled figures.

There were exceptions to this, and even though the style of the figure changed, a few potteries did continue to produce figures in the round. These figures had moved on from their pre-Victorian counterparts, having the look and feel of Victorian Staffordshire, the difference being that they were still modelled and decorated all around. The perceived wisdom has been that the Parr factory produced the majority of these figures, although during recent excavations of the Dudson factory site, a number of shards found were similar to figures at present described as Parr figures.

To the majority of collectors of Staffordshire figures, which pottery produced which figure is unimportant, probably due to the fact that the vast majority of figures are unmarked. Refreshingly, Staffordshire figure collectors are not afflicted by the need to have a mark or a stamp on the bottom of a figure, a condition suffered by so many collectors of other pottery and porcelain. The bottom of a figure is usually the last place a collector or a dealer will look when deciding whether or not to buy a Victorian Staffordshire figure.

The legacies left by the Victorian potters are the wonderful figures we have today. For about forty years a standard was maintained. After that time, with a few exceptions, debased cheaper versions appeared, decorating ended, and if the figures were coloured at all, they were coated rather than decorated. The best gold that had been used for the gilding was abandoned and a bright, brassy, cheaper method applied. The production continued but the heyday was over and the quality was never to be seen again.

The Makers and the Modellers

The Modellers

The true Staffordshire artist was not the factory that produced the figures, but the modeller who made the original and produced the first moulds. There were a large number of small pot banks. It would not have been economically viable for each and every factory to employ their own full time modeller, and for the small family pot banks it would have been impossible. So unless that talent existed within the family, they would have to buy models. So it would be to the travelling self-employed modeller that these pot banks would go for their figures.

We have no documented evidence to prove this, but there is evidence in the form of signed work. In the Pugh collection, housed at The City Museum and Art Gallery, Hanley, Stoke-on-Trent, there is a finely modelled figure of Admiral Sir Charles Napier, the base of which is inscribed 'John Carr 1857'. No records of any factory bearing this name are recorded in Staffordshire, and the figure is not a product of the Parr factory, so we must assume this is a signature of the artist himself.

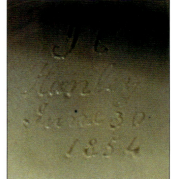

PLATE 9/10
Illustrated are a pair of seated whippets with hares, and on the base of one of these figures is inscribed, J. C. Hanley June 30 1854.

Plate 9 illustrates this point. These whippets are products of the Parr factory, bearing all the recognised hallmarks; the bases are inscribed 'J. C. Hanley June 30 1854' and the writing is similar to the hand of the Napier figure. This would seem to prove that one modeller had been identified, who had worked for at least two different factories. As Mr. John Carr signed two of his works, it is likely that he has signed more, as he was working at the height of production. It will be interesting to see whether any more of his work is discovered.

It would appear from the above that not only did the modeller design the figure, but that he would have also overseen the first stages of production, signing his pieces prior to firing. Only the very first figures would have been signed, and this would explain their rarity.

With the above exception, we are unable to attribute figures to a particular modeller and indeed their names remain obscure. Mr. Haggar, in his 1955 book 'Staffordshire Chimney Ornaments', said that he had been told by an old pottery printer that Sampson Smiths' figures were modelled by 'Edwards of East Vale' but that he had been unable to discover any modeller of that name. He also said that the unusual pseudo-baroque figures, which were made by Sampson Smith, were the work of a Giovanni Meli, a Sicilian trade modeller who worked in Rome Street, Stoke from about 1845 until 1865. He did not however attribute any particular figure to Mr. Meli.

The Alpha Factory/Modeller

It is possible to attribute a number of figures to a modeller, albeit un-named. Since Mr. Balston's 1958 book, a group of figures have been known as 'Alpha figures'. These are quite recognisable. They, like Parr figures, are modelled and decorated all around; if they are titled, it is with indented capitals, somewhat like printers would have used, although a few were titled with gilt script. What is apparent is the similarity of the facial features and design; as their features are so similar to each other, it is unlikely that they were a true likeness of the person portrayed.

PLATE 11
An 'Alpha' figure of Lord Byron with indented gilt capitals.

The following figures are all from 'The Alpha Factory/Modeller':

Fig. 80 Lord Byron	Figs. 84/85 Lord Byron and The Maid of Athens
Fig. 108 Cobden	Fig. 115 Captain Cook
Fig. 178 Jullien	Fig. 182 Kossuth
Fig. 187 Jenny Lind	Figs. 237/238 William and Lucy O'Brien
Fig. 272 Peel	Figs. 310/311 Shaftsbury and Fry
Fig. 493 Victoria	Figs. 565/566 Prince of Wales and Princess Royal
Fig. 1091 Uncle Tom's Cabin	Fig. 1313 Bloomers
Figs. 1687/1688/1689/ 1690 The Apostles	Figs.1715/1716 Christ and The Virgin Mary

There are also quite a number of untitled figures that are by the same hand.

The Green Factory/Modeller

Other modellers can be identified by their handiwork, in Plate 12 there are illustrated a pair of figures of a boy and girl at water fountains. This particular modeller's work was always to a very high standard. He appeared to concentrate mainly on decorative figures, although he did produce a figure of The Prince of Wales and The Princess Royal in a pony cart. (See Fig. 604 Book One)

The figures are always very well modelled, usually in full colour, and the facial features have a slightly Oriental look about them. Plumed hats and separate moulds also distinguish these figures, but what is so very distinctive is the use of a vibrant green colour on the base of many of the figures. Alternatively, this is sometimes replaced with an equally vibrant yellow/gold.

The following figures were all made by, 'The Green modeller':

Figs. 604 The Prince of Wales and the Princess Royal

Fig. 1481, A man and woman standing above a boat

Figs. 1535/1536 A pair of figures of a man dancing and woman with children

Fig. 1743 Joseph and Mary

Fig. 1771 Samuel anointing David

Fig. 1855 A group of two hunters

Fig. 1874A A group of a falconer and family

Fig. 1454 A man and two girls in an arbour

Figs. 1519/1520 A pair of figures of a boy and girl dancing

Fig. 1544 A group of three girls

Fig. 1758 Rebekah at the well

Figs. 1823/1824 A hunter

Figs. 1871/1872 A pair of equestrian falconers

Once seen it is relatively easy to recognise this modellers work.

of many Victorian men and women. He was extremely prolific and the list below is by no means comprehensive.

The following figures are all by 'The Beta modeller':

Figs. 632 The Prince of Wales

Fig. 633 The Prince of Wales

Fig. 836 The Sailors Return

Fig. 837 The Sailors Return

Fig. 889 The Soldiers farewell

Fig. 890 The Soldiers Return

Fig. 907 A Scottish soldier

Figs. 1862/1863 Huntsman & wife

Fig. 1814A Fairground entertainer

Fig. 1849A Hunter with Stag and dog

Fig. 1904 The Lion slayer

Fig. 1961 A standing shepherd

Figs. 1964/1965A shepherd & shepherdess

Figs. 1985A/1985B A shepherd & shepherdess

Fig. 2103 A Highland couple

PLATE 12.
A pair of 'Green Factory/Modeller's' figures of a boy and girl standing by water fountains.

The Beta Factory/Modeller

With the next modeller, it is not only by the facial features that he can be identified, but also by the particular and unique way the back of the figure is designed. Plates 13/14 illustrate the front and back of two figures. The head of the man in two very different subjects is almost the same. The features that this modeller gives his subjects are usually very full faced, but it is the back of a figure that will unfailingly identify him. The use of lines of indentations in random patterns is not seen on other figures in any such manner. For want of a better name we have called this modeller 'The Beta modeller'; he specialised in groups of a Jingoistic nature, appealing to the patriotic nature

PLATES 13/14
An example of two 'Beta Factory/Modeller's' figures.

Mr. Haggar's book in his appendix lists over twenty modellers who work at the relevant times. Even after this publication of nearly fifty years ago, figures have still not been able to be attributed to named modellers and it is extremely unlikely now, that they ever will be.

The Makers

Unlike the modellers, there is some documentary evidence as to which factory made figures, and in some instances particular figures can be attributed to a particular potter. What is surprising is that Mintons, which was by far the largest employer with over 1500 people employed and for which records survive, has no evidence that they produced flatbacks. The same can also be said of another major potter and employer, Wedgwood. Doulton of Lambeth did produce a pair of figures of Albert and Victoria that were titled, but these were in stoneware and they did not move to the potteries until 1877. It was not until then Doulton diversified into earthenware, and their products from that date are well documented and not all flatbacks. So if the major potters did not, then who did?

James Dudson

This pottery was one of the few that worked throughout the Victorian period covered by this book. Their factory was in Hope & Hanover Streets, Hanley and was operational from 1838 until 1888. It continued as J.T. Dudson from 1888 until 1898 and then changed its name to Dudson Bros (Ltd.) and has continued ever since.

They advertised that they made 'Earthenwares, Figures etc.' Most of their marked work is of jasper ware in the Wedgwood style. A recent book on the pottery has stated that they first made figures in 1815, finally phasing out production in 1865. They were the only company to exhibit Staffordshire figures at the 1851 Great Exhibition at the Crystal Palace. They also traded as colour makers and it is likely that other potteries bought their colours. As colour makers they had access to underglaze enamels not generally used and underglaze green and brown can be found on some of their earlier figures.

Relatively recent excavations at the factory have turned up shards that in a number of respects are similar to figures believed to have been made at The Parr - Kent factory.

Fig. 3321C, a tobacco jar in the form of a Turks head, is marked on the base 'DUDSON' and Figure. 2834, a parrot perched on a tree stump, has been identified by Miss A. Dudson as having been made in the Dudson factory.

The book 'Dudson Staffordshire Figures 1815 – 1865' has now laid claim, amongst others, to the following figures as having been made by Dudson: Fig. 3346C The Fox and Goose; Figs. 1132/1133 Ali Baba and Morgiana, in which green and brown underglaze enamel has been used; Figs. 1232/1233 Artabanes and Mandane, which appear to have been produced in a number of variations, the later ones not using such lavish decoration; Figs. 1011/1012 Mr. Pickwick and Sam Weller, a range of spaniel figures; Figs. 2540/2541, 2560, & 2560A, a pair of hunters; Figs. 1893E/1893F, in which case they almost certainly made a number of figures that were by the same modeller and used the same rococo base. See Figs. 627, 628, 628A, 1601/1602, a pair featuring a man and woman with peacocks.

Many of the figures claimed are of the highest quality but they also produced a cheaper range, which is detailed in the book.

PLATE 15
A 'Dudson' figure of a Turk, in the form of a tobacco jar, with the impressed mark on the base 'DUDSON'.

Lloyd, John & Rebecca

This partnership commenced in 1834 and continued until 1852. It is believed that John Lloyd died in 1850 and that his wife, Rebecca, continued for two years after his death. The pottery was at Shelton, Hanley, and unlike most of the Staffordshire potters they did factory mark some of their figures. In particular, a pair of figures of Victoria with a baby and Albert can be found marked 'LLOYD SHELTON' (see Figs. 526/527). Many of their figures are more porcelain than pottery and they continued to model in the round with many separate moulds, a particular example being the group of Van Amburgh (see Fig. 336). Their figures are usually of very good quality, but they do not appear to have made any 'flatbacks', probably because they ceased production before these figures were in their heyday.

The Parr - Kent Factory

This pottery commenced at 34 Church St., Burslem under the auspices of Mr. Thomas Parr in 1852. It continued under this name until 1870 when the name and address changed to Mr. John Parr at Wellington St., Burslem.

A Mr. William Kent had been in partnership with Gaskell and Parr in Burslem and this partnership was dissolved in 1878. At that time Mr. Kent built a factory at Auckland St., Burslem and traded from that date until 1894 under the name Kent & Parr, which name survived until 1894 when the pottery became William Kent. Finally, in 1944 it became William Kent (Porcelains) Ltd. Production of figures ceased at the end of 1962.

As late as 1955 William Kent issued a coloured catalogue of their range of figures. Many of these figures can be identified as having first been produced in the 1850s to 1860s. It is certain that a number of the figures in the catalogue were not originally made by The Parr - Kent factory, for as other potteries went out of business Parr - Kent acquired the moulds and continued production.

This company of potters started at the beginning of production of Victorian Staffordshire and continued late into the twentieth century. They were amongst the first and were certainly the last to produce figures; their range was enormous, partly due to buying other potter's moulds.

When most other potteries were making flatbacks, Parr-Kent had to a major extent ignored the mainstream and continued to make figures in the round. For whatever reason they were successful and continued long after their competitors had ceased. Their earlier production is superior to that made later. Gradually the decoration, which in the earlier figures of the 1850s and 1860s is a delicate combing of colours, particularly on the base, becomes in the 1880s and 1890s a coating of paint in a block of colour. The modelling remains quite good throughout and it is from the palette used that the figures can best be dated.

The following figures are amongst many that were produced by The Parr - Kent Factory:

Fig. 117 Archbishop Cranmer	Fig. 838 The Sailors return	Fig. 1147 The Fortune Teller
Fig. 139 Garibaldi	Fig. 857 Naval gunners	Fig. 1163 Little Red Riding Hood
Fig. 141 Garibaldi	Figs. 898/899 French & Scottish soldiers	Fig. 1177 Mother Goose
Fig. 142 Garibaldi	Fig. 1043 Titania	Fig. 1190 Paul and Virginia
Fig. 143 Garibaldi	Fig. 1044 Hamlet	Figs. 1384/1385 Standing pair Eastern man and woman
Fig. 149 Garibaldi	Fig. 1046 Ophelia	Fig. 1456 Eastern man standing with horse
Fig. 156 Garibaldi	Fig. 1049 Macbeth	Figs. 1532 Harlequin and Columbine
Fig. 216 Napier	Fig. 1050 Lady MacBeth	Fig. 1637 Girl musician with attendant man
Fig. 249 Omar Pasha	Fig. 1059 Shylock	Fig. 1832 A Scottish hunter
Fig. 299 Ridley & Latimer	Fig. 1061 Falstaff	Figs. 1873/1874. A pair of equestrian falconers
Figs. 580/581. The Prince of Wales & The Princess Royal	Figs. 1068/1069 Romeo & Juliet	Fig. 2272 Beg Sir
Figs. A602/a603. The Prince of Wales & The Princess Royal	Fig. 1073 Romeo & Juliet	Figs. 2710/2711 pair of standing Newfoundland dogs
Figs. 629/630 Prince Alfred & The Prince of Wales	Figs. 1074/1075/1076/1077 Romeo & Juliet	Fig. 2738 A Bloodhound & Pointer
Fig. 635 The Prince of Wales	Fig. 1086. Winters Tale	Figs. 3351/3352/3353/3354 The four Seasons
Figs. 665/666 The Prince of Wales & Princess Alexandra	Figs. 1088/1089/1093 Uncle Tom & Eva	Fig. 755 Victor Emmanuel II

This is by no means a comprehensive list and many more figures are illustrated within the four volumes.

PLATE 16
A typical pair of Parr figures, modelled in the round, delicately coloured and decorated with 'combing' to the colours on the base.

Poole & Unwin

This pottery started in 1871 at the Cornhill Works, Longton. By 1877 it had changed its name to Joseph Unwin & Co. A figure of two harvesters, Fig. 2019, has been recorded with two different marks. One example bears the mark 'Unwin' in a diamond on the back of the figure, the other the initials 'P & U' on the base. The figure bears some resemblance to figures known to have been made by Sampson Smith, so possibly the same modeller was used by both potteries.

PLATE 17
A group figure of two harvesters by the Poole & Unwin factory.

Ridgway & Robey

Little is known of this partnership as they only existed for less than two years. Their works were in Hanley and the partners were William Ridgway and Ralph Mayer Robey. Their claim to fame was that they produced a series of Dickensian figures and marked them fully with 'Published June 15 1839 by Ridgway & Robey Hanley Staffordshire Potteries'

The figures are very rare and owe more to Pre–Victorian figures in their style as they are modelled in the round, decorated back and front, and have a number of subsidiary moulds.

William Ridgway also appeared to have another factory with his son for a period of ten years from 1838 to 1848 but no figures from this Company are known.

PLATE 18
Two figures by Ridgway & Robey, Kate Nickleby and Wackford Squeers (part of a series of six) see Figs. 1007/1008/100 9/1010/1010A/1010B.

Sampson Smith

Sampson Smith was born in 1813 and died in 1878. He is recorded as a pottery decorator; his obituary notice described him as 'a well-known and highly respected china manufacturer carrying on business in Barker St. The funeral was at St. James Church Longton and was attended by a great throng of people. There were twenty coaches; the crowd in the churchyard were dispersed by a bull that had broken loose.'

Not the proverbial Bull in the china shop!

It is not known for certain when the pottery first started, but a number of figures have been recorded with a mark of either 'Sampson Smith 1851 Longton' or 'S Smith Longton 1851', these were not the dates of the figures, so it could be safely assumed that the pottery had put the date of its inception on the figures.

Until 1859 Sampson Smith was making these figures at The Garfield Pottery, High St., Longton and from 1859 until his death at The Sutherland Pottery.

What made this pottery important to Staffordshire figure history was that in 1948 in a disused part of the factory about sixty old press moulds were discovered in good condition. This find enabled the attribution of not only the moulds found but of many other figures that were recorded and were clearly by the same hand. Many of these related to post 1875, but a number were from the 1850s and 1860s

Shortly after this find a number of the moulds were put into production. Care should be taken as the resulting figures now have fifty years of age and either through intent or ignorance can be passed off as nineteenth century figures.

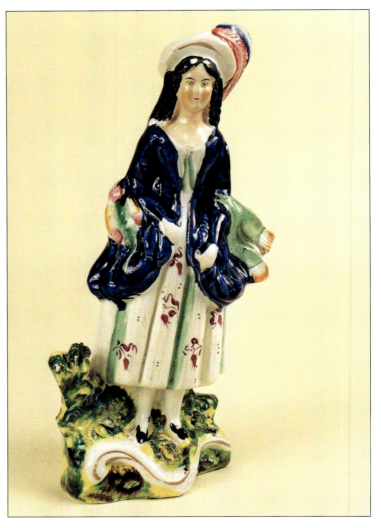

PLATE 19
The mould from which this figure was produced was one of those found in a dis-used part of the Sampson Smith factory and in 1949 a number of figures were made from the moulds. The figure illustrated is a genuine nineteenth century version; the reproductions were well modelled and coloured.

The following are figures known to have been made in 1949 from nineteenth century moulds:

Fig. 62, Burns and Highland Mary
Figs. 2348/2349, a pair of Goat herders
(In original versions the boy has a drum, in the reproductions this has been simplified and becomes a bag.)
Fig. 1710, a figure of Christ on the Cross
(In original versions, this is a Holy waterstoup, the cup of which is decorated with an angel, in the reproductions the cup, which was a separate mould has been left off completely.)

Figs. 1568A/1568B, a pair of figures of a man and woman, both with birds and musical instruments
Figs. 2348/2349, a pair of figures of Goat herders
(In original versions, the boy has a drum. In the reproductions, this has been simplified and becomes a bag.)
Figs. 3314/3315, a pair of mounted Jockeys

A monumental pair over sixteen inches high of Wellington and Napoleon, each seated astride a horse which is standing above a clock face and both titled, were also reproduced.

What is interesting is that no original versions of this pair at that time were known, though one pair and two singles have subsequently been recorded.

The Sampson Smith pottery was also very prolific, and amongst the figures known to have been made at this factory are the following:

Fig. 152 Garibaldi	Fig. 631. The Prince of Wales
Fig. 183 Abraham Lincoln,	Fig. 683. Louis of Hesse and Princess Alice
Fig. 198 Cardinal Manning	Figs. 713/714 The Duke and Duchess of Edinburgh
Fig. 209 Moody	Fig. 835 A group of a Sailor and Girl,
Fig. 235 Florence Nightingale	Fig. 883 Volunteer Rifles
Fig. 242 O'Connell	Fig. 922 Highland Jessie
Fig. 261 Peard	Figs. 945/946 Dick Turpin and Tom King
Fig. 307 Sankey	Figs. 3302/3303 A pair of standing Cricketers
Fig. 351 Wellington	
Figs. 551/552 Prince of Wales & Queen Victoria	

It is also known that Sampson Smith made comforter dogs in great quantities and it is believed that they produced the dogs numbered 1 to 6, Figs. 2416 to 2427.

Many other potters of this period are known by name, and it is certain that many were producing 'Toys' or 'images', as Staffordshire figures were called. However it has proved impossible to allocate particular figures to any of them, and after such a lapse of time it is very doubtful if it ever will.

We have written of a few of the factories that made the figures, but what of the actual people who produced them? In the early 1840s Mr. Samuel Scriven was Her Majesty's Commissioner and was allocated the task of reporting to Parliament the condition, both moral and physical, of the children working in the potteries. He took statements from well over one hundred workers in a number of potteries. Their statements survive. They make harrowing reading and a number are here reproduced.

Earthenware Factory of Messrs Minton and Boyle, Eldon Place, Stoke, December 1840

Statement from **Benjamin Taylor Aged 12 Years Employed in the Press Room, temperature in room 98F, in open-air 42F**

I have worked in the press-room for 2 years; I come at half past 6 in the morning, and leave at 6 at night. I have half an hour for breakfast, 1 hour for dinner. I make cockspurs to place ware upon when it is baked; have one brother working in the same room. I get 4 shillings a week; don't know what brother gets, he is older; got a mother but no father: father has been dead 10 years; he was a presser working here he died of consumption; he was 49 when he died, I give my money to my mother; get nothing for myself; never work over hours. I go to Sunday school down to Methody's; can read, can write, can cipher a little; can tell how much 5 times 7 is, 21 and 4 times 9 is 30 (sic) my health is pretty good; can eat, drink and sleep pretty well. I find it hot in the workroom and very cold when I go out. I make no difference in clothing, summer or winter; believe there are no boys or girls in the works who do night work. I get meat for dinner three or four times a week; other day's milk and tatoes. Sometimes open the windows, but can't stand the draught.

Statement from **Thomas Kay Aged 46 Employed in Hot House and Throwing Room, temperature in room 94F, open-air 42F**

I have worked for Mr. Minton 18 years next Christmas. Slip making in the fore part of my service, that is making the clay for use; I now look to the ware in the hot house, besides that I beat the clay in the adjoining room; beating clay is tremendous hard work; I stand near the open door to do that, the hottest work is in the hot house, don't keep a thermometer there, heat rises from 90F to 120F tis not so hot now by a deal as in the morning we cool it now for the ware. I am paid by the quantity of work done; my average wages are about 15 shillings per week. I have a wife and 7 children, only one is a potter. I come to work at 6 in the morning sometimes 5, it depends upon what goods are in heat, leave at 3, 4, 5, and 6 and afterwards do a little job work for another master and earn 4 or 3 shillings a week. Don't find the great change of heat affects my health, it sometimes affects others, very few live to any age in such an employment, tis the hardest business of potting. I live at Harford Bridge, do not go home to dinner. I take my dinner in the throwing house get bread and cheese, no ale, but get some meat at home at night, can't read or write.

Statement from **Herbert Bell Aged 12 Employed in Handlers Room (looks very pale and phthisical) (sic), temperature in room 62F, in open-air 44F**

I have worked in this room 4 years as handle presser; I come at 6 and leave at 6 in the evening, I live about a mile off, I do not go home to breakfast, I go home to dinner, am allowed half an hour for breakfast and 1 hour for dinner, I work in the same room as my father, father gets so much a week piece making, does not know what father earns, all I get goes to him and mother, have a mother and sister, one works at the china works. I get no holidays remember now, that I get about five weeks in a year, a week at Martilmas, 2 weeks in August and 1 at Whitsuntide, all the other boys get the same and a day at Christmas. I get meat at home and have clothes enough; I get a strapping sometimes; think I deserve it; father is good to me; have got a cough, have had it 3 or 4 years; feel it more in winter; I do not think the jumping on the moulds hurts me; feel no pain from it; I do not like it; I want to go into another room; I like potting would rather be a potter than a tailor or shoemaker; I never do night work. Master and overseer are very good to me, they never beat me.

Statement from **George Burton Aged 9 Employed in the Oven, Temperature 96F, open-air 42F**

I work in the oven as a stoker, and carry coal to the fires; begin work at 6 o'clock and leave at 5; I do not attend at night; the oven man, Henry Reach, does that from 9 o'clock at night to 5 in the morning: he then goes home, and comes again at 9, and remains all day till 5 again. He's the fireman; there are six as takes it in turn, so that one man only sits up two nights a week. His father does the same work as him. I don't know how much wages I get a week; all goes to father;

he sometimes gives me a penny, sometimes two pence. I can't read, can't write. I went to Sunday school don't go now; there is no school belonging to the works, I am in good health, I have a good appetite; I get bread and cheese for dinner, sometimes tatoes and bacon; never get ale. I feel the cold on coming out of the oven; tis very hot in there, I get very thirsty there. This is all the clothes I got; I have no change at home for Sunday. Overseer very kind to me so is master. I never get a strapping, except from father sometimes.

Statement from **William Hell Aged 13 Employed in the Oven Room, Temperature 100F, open-air 42F**

    I have worked for Messrs. Minton and Boyle 2 years, first at the other bank where I ran moulds, then came here and worked in the dipping house for better than 12 months; I received there 1s. 6d per week; was never ill from that work, but some of the boys were, and one of the dippers. I left that work to work in the oven, where I am now and get 2s per week. I come about 6 in the morning, and leave about 3, because we than have nothing else to do. I find it pretty hot in the oven; we bake the ware there after it is printed. I feel the cold very much when I leave work and go home. Samuel Jones is the man who works with me; he is very good to me, never scolds or straps me. I give my money to my mother, my father is a plumber, and gets often drunk, and my mother is often in great distress, she has 10 of us to support; 4 do no work, they are too young. Can't read; can't write; don't go to a Sunday school; never went to day school; don't know the reason why; except that mother's so poor and haven't got no clothes. I am very happy in my work, but don't get enough to eat and drink. I get mostly dry tatoes and salt; I have had no dinner today; never get meat, never get bread. Father works at Burslem, but seldom brings home any money for mother.

Statement of **James Watson Aged 42 Employed in The Dipping House, Temperature 56F, open-air 32F**

    I have been a dipper a dozen years with this firm; come at 8 leave at 4; sometimes 5 or 6. I am a fireman too and work in the gloss oven; I then sit up one night a week; as a dipper and firer I make 4s 8d per day. The nature of my employment has affected my health formerly, but has not these last two years; it is always reckoned very injurious. Three men work with me and one boy; he is 12 years of age last July and is my son; no women. There is a small portion of lead in the dipping, but it is worse elsewhere, don't think the change of heat in the ovens affects me much.

Statement of **Ann Dishly Aged 9 Employed by Mr. Joseph Clementson, High Street Shelton (Earthenware), as a painter**

    I have been a painter for 12 months last Martinmas. There are eight little girls work in the same room with me. Mary Worrelow looks after us; we all come to work at six o'clock in the morning, and go home at six, some go home to dinner, an hour is allowed us for dinner, and half an hour for breakfast. I can read very well but can't write; I go to Bethesda Sunday school and went two years to day school, they didn't teach me to write. Ann Dishly is very good to us, she never flogs us, or master either; she is my mother. We get holidays altogether perhaps a month.

Method of Production

Press Moulds

    The majority of Staffordshire figures during the Victorian era were produced using press moulds, this process was as follows:

- The potter would firstly make or have made a model of the figure out of clay. Once this was done the model would then be encased in a mould of plaster of Paris. This mould would then be divided into three parts, the front, back, and base.
- Once the parts had been separated from the original model, this 'master mould' would then be placed back together, the opening filled with plaster of Paris, and then left to set.
- Once set, the mould was opened the solid figure inside would appear. This solid figure was called the 'block mould', which was kept, if other moulds were needed to be made.
- The master mould was then encased in a further mould of plaster of Paris, and once set separated into two pieces, which were then used as the working mould. The master mould was then kept in case extra working moulds were needed.

    It is possible that, in some cases, if a figure were for a small limited number, then the figures would be made from the master mould.

- Each of the moulds were then laid out and a flat sheet of clay, known as a 'bat', was placed on them. The clay was then pressed into the mould (it is interesting to see, quite often, on a broken figure the actual finger prints of the person who had pressed the clay into the mould). Any surplus was then trimmed off and the edges were then painted with liquid clay. The moulds were then placed together and thin rolls of clay were inserted to seal the seams inside. This was then left to dry.
- Once dry the figure was then removed from the mould and the base was applied. Any excess clay on the seams was now removed, any other moulds, i.e., separate arms, legs, etc. applied, also any shredded clay for decoration, i.e., ermine edged coats or foliage on the base.
- A small hole was then made; this was so the air was able to escape during firing (this hole would not be necessary in the case of spill vase figures). Then the figure was placed in the kiln, receiving its first firing at around 1100 C. (2000F.)
- The figure now emerged in 'biscuit' form. Underglaze blue, if used, would now be painted on with fat oil and hardened by a further firing at 600C (1100F.) to 700C (1300F). This was done as underglaze colour was very expensive and without this further firing the colour was likely to come off when dipped in the glaze.
- The figure would then be 'dipped' into a liquid glaze, always containing lead, often arsenic (such glazes causing the early death of the 'dipper') and refired in the 'glost' oven at about 950C (1750F).
- The figure now emerged from the kiln glazed with the blue firmly fixed under the glaze and was painted with enamel (overglaze) colours and any gilding required. For the last time the figure was fired in the kiln at between 750C to 850C. At this heat the enamel colours that had been mixed with a flux which vitrifies at a lower temperature would fuse with the previous glaze.
- When the figure now came from the kiln all that was required was the burnishing of the gilding, usually with an agate stone, and the figure was complete.

    Not more than three figures a day could be made from one mould, depending on the detail of the figure they were making and how many hours the factory worked. There could have been many working moulds of the same figure all being made at the same time.

Due to the deposits the clay would leave in the mould, the average mould's life would not last for more than 100 figures without severe loss of quality. This may be observed by looking at individual figures; the cleaner and crisper the details on a figure, the earlier it was produced in the mould's life. The more often the mould was used, the less the quality of the figure produced.

Slip Moulds

The process of constructing a slip mould is very similar to that of a press mould, the only difference being that instead of pressing the clay in to the mould, the mould was put together and a liquid clay known as 'slip' was poured into it. This was then left for up to half an hour and the residue was then poured out. The remainder was left to dry. When dry it was taken from the mould and the base was applied in the same manner as the press mould, although it was not always common practice to apply a base.

The use of slip moulds was not popular, not because of the process, which if anything was less time consuming, but because a slip mould would deteriorate much quicker, the mould having to be replaced after as little as twenty figures, whereas a press mould could easily produce five times as many. **In practice virtually NONE of the Victorian Staffordshire figures were made by the slip mould method.**

The Use of Colour in Staffordshire Figures

The use of colour in Staffordshire figures was at its height from the 1840s to 1860s. After this period the use of colour gradually declined until little if any was used.

The most vibrant colours on Staffordshire figures were underglaze blue and black. These colours as the name suggests were under the glaze, so even now they are as stunning as the day when they came out of the factory. The other colours that were used were enamels, which were on top of the glaze (even though they had been re-fired in the kiln), so are prone to flaking and discolouring over a period of time. Over glaze black, which is the darkest of all the colours, is the most likely to flake. The darker the enamel colour the more flaking is likely to occur.

Both coloured and white versions of the same figure were made at the same time, as there was a market for both types of figure.

The Use of Gold in Decoration and Titling

During the production of Victorian Staffordshire figures, two types of gilding have been used, and this has now become another useful tool for dating figures. Up until about 1875 'Best gold' was used. This was a mixture of real gold and mercury, applied to the figures before the final firing. This application of 'Best gold' was a time consuming process as when it came out of the kiln the gold was flat and required burnishing.

The other type of gilding used from circa 1875 onwards was 'Bright gold'. Bright gold was painted on and did not need firing or burnishing afterwards. Although a quicker process, it has a brassy harsh appearance when compared to 'Best gold', which was more subdued, more gold than brass. Bright gold was not as permanent as 'Best gold' and has not withstood the test of time. Often figures, which were decorated with 'Bright gold', are now found with most of it missing.

The use of titling on figures varies. It is interesting to note that there are different methods of titling. It is not known whether different potters preferred different titling, it is also unknown why the same figure can be found titled or untitled; the only logical explanation can be cost, as the application of gold required extra work. It is not uncommon to find a figure decorated in gold, but the title has been omitted; no reason for this has been found. One theory is that they might have been intended to sell not as a portrait, but as a decorative figure.

The different types of titling that can be found are listed below:

- **RAISED BLACK CAPITALS** – These seem to appear rarely on figures, but when they do, they are normally complemented by use of best gold, thus confirming they were not used for cheapness, as they would have required burnishing afterwards.
- **BLACK TRANSFERS** – These are also rarely used, but do tend to be used when a lot of script is involved, i.e., quoting large amounts of text, see Portrait Section, Burns Figure 64 for an example.
- **RAISED GILT CAPITALS** – One of the more common methods of titling. In the Victorian era illiteracy was common, particularly amongst the working class, so this method needed little skill to apply, and mistakes could be avoided.
- **GILT SCRIPT** – A form of titling that would require a degree of literacy, although it is possible that the artist was able to copy the name of a famous person but not write his or her own.
- **INDENTED CAPITALS** – This type of titling was used by a small number of potteries. One such firm is the Parr factory, which used black indents in titling its figures. Another pottery using gilt indents of which less is known, is referred to as the 'Alpha' factory', but this pottery was probably a modeller and not a factory. This process would not have been done in the mould, but would have to have been applied quite quickly after it had been removed and prior to its first firing.

Types of Nineteenth Century Staffordshire Figures

By 1875 most of the figures that were being produced had little or no colour at all, and the gold decoration was painted on, giving the figures a harsh, brassy look. Little care seems to have been taken in the original model, and consequently the figures themselves were of little quality. There were exceptions to this, and the Parr factory continued to maintain a standard, although not up to the quality of their earlier work.

Perhaps with hindsight it would have been best for the potters to stop production at this point, but they did not, carrying on producing figures of ever decreasing quality for the next thirty years.

PLATES 20 -23 illustrate the typical pre-, during, and post-Staffordshire figure.

BEFORE: Pre-Victorian figures **PLATE 20**
Illustrated here is a pair of pre-Victorian figures of a boy and a girl playing with a sheep and a goat. These figures are typical of pre-Victorian figures, the arms, legs, heads, and animals all required a number of separate handmade moulds; on this pair there are ten separate flowers on the base alone. They are very well modelled, but all of these moulds were time consuming to produce and therefore expensive to make.
HEIGHT: 6.75 inches

DURING: The Victorian Flatback
PLATE 21
Illustrated is a typical Victorian flatback figure. Made around 1850, this was the time when some of the finest examples were produced. Whilst not a three piece moulded figure, an extra mould would have been required for the sheep's head. This figure has all the spontaneity, detail, charm, and skill associated with Victorian Staffordshire.
HEIGHT: 9.25 inches

AFTER: The Decline
PLATE 22
A typical late nineteenth century, early twentieth century Staffordshire figure of a lion. Sprayed a dull brown, it lacks all but basic decoration, and has late bright gold applied to it, most of which has rubbed off.
This lion is fairly well modelled, but most of this period is not up to this standard. An 'improvement' introduced at the turn of the twentieth century was the introduction of glass eyes, which has now become a good way of dating the figures.

PLATE 23
An early twentieth and mid-nineteenth century version of Burns and Mary, the two figures together show the decline of quality over a fifty-year period. The late version has been made in a slip mould, losing most of its detail and even the dog has been omitted. The only attempt at colouring has been to spray green paint onto the arbour and apply 'bright gold', which has all but worn off.

As with all china, there are usually seconds. Even if at the time Staffordshire figures were the poor man's choice of decoration, it is interesting to see that if a particular figure did not come up to scratch, rather than throw it away, it was still sold.

We have seen many examples of figures like this. The use of gold was expensive, so if the figure was not good enough, rather than use gold, it was cheaper to use black. This can be seen not only on titled figures, but also on figures that have a black lined base instead of a gilded one.

What Was Potted?

The subjects chosen by the potters were as varied as the times in which they lived, but the sole overriding reason for their production was for profit. Each and every pottery, no matter how small, had to be profitable to survive. Artistic merit was hardy contemplated. Above and beyond every other consideration, the figure had to sell. A number of the figures produced did not sell. Today that fact would make them rare, if they are of quality. As well as being rare, they are now highly regarded and consequently will be expensive.

PLATE 25
A figure of Delacy Evans.

PLATE 24
A figure of Christmas Evans, who never had his leg. This leg may have fallen off in the kiln, but rather than waste the figure, or go to the expense of colouring and gilding it, the potter used over glaze black paint to highlight his jacket and titling, and no doubt sold it cheaply as a second.

Normally this figure has the jacket and breeches decorated in underglaze black and the titling is picked out in gold.

There are exceptions to the rule. It would not be correct to suggest that every figure with black instead of gold applied is a second. One notable example is that of a very rare figure of James Braidwood, the superintendent of the London Fire-engine Establishment (Fig. 48), who was killed at a fire he was attending. Of the three examples seen, his name is in raised capitals; but, instead of these being picked out in gold script, a black line runs across them, which suggests that the figure may have been made as a memorial figure.

An example of this rarity is the standing figure of Delacy Evans, (Figure 123), a British General who commanded the 2nd Division in the Crimean War and was invalided home. He was only in the public eye for a short time, but Parliament, looking for a hero, granted him their thanks. The potters, looking for commercial success, produced figures of him, but the public, whose admiration was less than enduring, did not purchase them, and so the potters stopped making them.

In the last thirty years or so, since the publication of P. D. Gordon Pugh's book 'Portrait Figures of the Victorian Era', many other versions of a particular person have been discovered, but only two new personalitys have been recorded, Ibrahim Pasha (Fig. No. 247 Book One) and Pierre Joseph Francois Bosquet (Fig. No. 47 Book One). The figure of Bosquet is a relatively recent discovery and is the only known example in existence, the figure having spent many years in Canada before being sold in London. This example highlights the lack of interest at the time for this figure. He was quite an obscure general of the Crimean War, so it is understandable why not many figures of him were produced, and it is only by chance that one example survived.

How many other lesser-known portraits like Bosquet were produced of which none have survived? We will never know. It is also certain that there are other figures that were made in small numbers, of which no examples have survived the last 150 years.

These three figures were not commercial, and as a result are now very rare. It can be argued that commercial pressures made the figures simple. Three part moulds meant more could be produced for less. As the figure was to be viewed from the front there was no need to decorate the back. All this did lead to a simplicity of design that makes the figures what they are, a naïve folk art.

There are some surprising absentees from the portrait gallery, not one figure of Dickens, who was extremely popular and very famous, was made, although a few of Dickensian characters were. A portrait of the eminently forgettable poetess, Eliza Cook, was made, but not one figure of the Poet Laureate, Alfred Lord Tennyson. A non-portrait figure of 'The Lion Slayer' was made, but none of David Livingstone, the explorer of Africa. Figures of cricketers were made but none were titled and of those made none bear any resemblance to Dr. Grace, arguably the most famous cricketer of all time. The potters did not make figures of the inventor of 'The Rocket', Britain's first train, George Stephenson, or of the architect of the railways, I. Kingdom Brunel. The reasoning why portraits of little known people were made, and not ones of some of the very famous, is obscure. Perhaps there was a reason. If so, it remains unexplained.

Staffordshire figures are a form of folk art, and there are many supreme examples of the potter's art in the non-portrait chapters. Wonderful examples which, when freed from the constraints of portraying a particular person, the modeller could allow his artistry and imagination free rein.

There are many of these figures which we have only seen the once, and perhaps they are the only examples left. These figures, at the time, must have been more expensive and directed at a more discerning market, or perhaps such figures were made as a demonstration of their skills to other potters. Whatever the reason, it is fortunate that such fine examples of the potter's art have survived through the generations.

It is to be remembered that these figures were produced by the working class and sold to a mass market. They were handmade; yet they were part of the industrial revolution, using production line methods. These figures were not only displayed in the cottages and houses of the many cities, towns, and villages of Great Britain, but were exported to America and the Colonies, bringing life and colour to many a Victorian mantelpiece.

This was an age before radio and television, before photography was widely available. It was an age when illiteracy was common; there were many people who could not read about their heroes, they could only hear of their deeds through word of mouth, and heroes were necessary, as was romance and nostalgia. The working class had few pleasure hours and what moments there were would be spent at the circus, fair or theatre, and on Sundays at Church or Chapel. Staffordshire figures were made and bought as a reminder of these happier moments.

Royalty

The Victorians were intensely patriotic. The Royal Family was held in high esteem. During the early part of her reign, many different figures of Queen Victoria and Prince Albert were produced, ranging from figures of them seated, standing, and on horseback. Following the birth of Victoria, Princess Royal, in 1840 and the birth of Albert, Prince of Wales, in 1841, both named after their parents, potters also made figures of them at each stage of their development through childhood to maturity and marriage.

In their relatively short marriage Victoria bore nine children, five daughters and four sons. It is probable that figures were reissued to commemorate the later births. There are no named figures of 'The Royal children' as children, other than The Prince of Wales and Princess Royal. Other figures are titled 'Prince' and 'Princess' and could be of any of the later Princes and Princesses.

Interest continued in the two eldest Princes and figures commemorating their induction into the army and navy were made. With the exception of The Prince of Wales, who continued to be popular with the potters, it was not until the marriages of the Queen's children, Victoria in 1858, Alice in 1862, Albert in 1863, Helena in 1866, Louise in 1871, and Alfred in 1874, that the potters had a demand from the public to continue making figures.

The last two children to marry were Beatrice and Arthur, Duke of Connaught, who married Louise of Prussia in 1879. By this time, interest had waned and there were no figures made to commemorate the marriages of Victoria and Albert's youngest son or daughter.

Politicians

The potters were not prolific in producing figures of politicians. The reason behind this might lie in the fact that the average working class person did not have any interests in the workings of the country, with many of them not being able to vote. It would not be surprising if at the time most of them thought that the monarchy still ran the country.

Of the figures they did produce of politicians, the choice of persons was limited. Potters produced many versions of Arthur Wellesley, the first Duke of Wellington. Although an elder statesman, it is more than probable that people bought figures of Wellesley because he was a war hero. Other politicians produced included Sir Robert Peel, Prime Minister and founder of the police force, Richard Cobden, Thomas Slingsby Duncombe (whose greatest contribution seems to be that he was voted the 'best dressed man in the Houses of Parliament'), and the Earl of Shaftsbury, although even this figure is in doubt as no titled figure or reliable source has been discovered.

Of the figures of foreign politicians made, Louis Kossuth, the Hungarian patriot was very popular. Four different versions of him were made, probably at the time of his visit to England in 1851.

American politicians also proved popular with the potters, making a number of figures of Benjamin Franklin, Thomas Jefferson, and George Washington. However Mr. Washington suffered the ignominy of most of his 'portraits' being figures of Franklin with his name on the bottom!

Whether these figures were made principally for export is in doubt; recently a ship destined to America, but which foundered on the Goodwin Sands off the coast of Kent in the 1850s, was found by divers to contain a number of cases of Staffordshire figures. These figures had been submersed in the sea for over 145 years and were in good condition apart from the colouring, which had been leached away by the salt water. Though there were a great variety of figures found, but there were no portraits of American politicians. The cargo was a mixture of decorative, of animals, and of dogs.

But by far the greatest interest was in the Italian Garibaldi. Whilst a statesman, Garibaldi, like The Duke of Wellington, was also a war leader. Over twenty figures were made of him, some in three sizes, and he figures amongst the strangest of all pairings. His visit to England in 1864 coincided with the tri-centenary of Shakespeare's birth and two differing pairs of these very diverse men were made.

Naval and Military

Wars and violence were seemingly part of the Victorians' daily lives, and the men who led them in these conquests of Empire became household names. Generals, Admirals, and even lowly Colonels were potted, no doubt to be arranged in battle order on many a Victorian mantelpiece.

Sentimentality sold figures. Our brave soldiers and sailors either going off to or returning from war was a constant theme, often with their wives or girlfriends in attendance.

On returning many of these soldiers and sailors were missing limbs, and had to resort to begging to stay alive. Having returned home injured with no job or pension they would be fortunate to be confined to a home, either as a Chelsea Pensioner or a Greenwich Hospital Pensioner, the former for soldiers, the latter being a Royal charity for seamen. They were given 5 pence a week, out of which they had to contribute to the hospitals upkeep. The regime was strict and they were subject to punishment for a variety of offences, including thieving, drinking, smoking, being unclean, and begging outside the hospital grounds. As part of their punishment for these crimes, the old sailors had to wear their coats inside out.

A home fit for heroes, it is unlikely that they would have had either the inclination or wherewithal to buy these figures of themselves. Possibly they were bought by the relations who visited them.

War, or its likelihood, was constant during this period in British history, and many other figures were made on this theme. French and English soldiers clasping hands in eternal friendship, a wounded soldier being assisted by a sailor. Further appeals to patriotism were made with figures titled 'England', 'Scotland', 'Britain's Glory', 'Scotland's Pride' or even 'Ready and Willing'. Sentimentality played its part, and figures of 'The Sailors Farewell' and 'The Soldiers Return' with either a grieving or welcoming wife, or girlfriend, were common.

The Crimean War of 1854-1856, the Indian Mutiny of 1857, the American Civil War of 1861-1865, The Abyssinian Expedition of 1867, and the Franco-Prussian War of 1870 gave the potters whole new fields of figures to produce. This was a time when uniforms turned farmhands into heroes, and there was a romance associated with our brave soldiers and sailors leaving to fight in other parts of the world.

The Alliance of England with France and Turkey during the Crimean War against the Russians produced figures of Royalty with the Allied Heads of States, Queen Victoria, Albert, Napoleon III, and Omar Pasha all being modelled. Also produced were titled figures of both English and French Naval and Military commanders of the time, as well as figures of the Russian fortresses that were under siege and even battlefield scenes. This period also produced the figures of Florence Nightingale, which are now eagerly sought after.

The Indian Mutiny of 1857 led to figures of Sir Henry Havelock, Sir Colin Campbell, and Highland Jessie being produced.

The American Civil War of 1861-65, with the British leaning towards the North, resulted in the production of figures of Abraham Lincoln and John Brown, the abolitionist, whose failed attack on Harper's Ferry lead to his execution.

The Abyssinian Expedition of 1867 produced a figure of Lord Napier of Magdala, with the potters using a mirror image of Garibaldi, with modifications. These figures are paired together today, but it is unlikely that they were ever sold as a pair, as the figure of Garibaldi was produced around 1861 from a print that appeared in 'The Illustrated London News'.

The Franco-Prussian War of 1870 produced figures of both Prussian and French Royalty and Prussian and French Generals. The popularity of both sides is accounted for by the fact that when the war commenced, the English had pro-German feelings, but this waned and the sympathy in this country moved to the French.

Religion

Religion played a major part in the lives of the Victorians, with a number of portrait and allegorical figures being made. Figures of both dead and live preachers were made, many of them leading members of the Methodist and Temperance movement. Both movements were sweeping the country at the time. The American evangelists Moody and Sankey toured England in 1873 and pairs of figures of them were made in no less than four sizes. They must have been popular for they returned in 1881 and 1882.

The potters produced an array of figures of biblical characters and scenes, a number of them titled. Some of the untitled figures have in the past been mistaken for theatrical groups.

Theatre, Opera, Ballet, and Circus

People wanted to be entertained, and this was an age before cinema, television or radio. The masses looked to others to entertain them, this entertainment taking many forms. On high days and holidays the circus came to town, arriving with its sideshows, catchpenny booths, tightrope artist, and lion tamer. The circus would capture the visitor's imagination; they were able to escape for a brief time from the poor living and working conditions they faced. Attendant upon the fairs and circuses were the travelling people, the gypsies, who—adroit at turning a few words into a few coins—would tell the fortunes of the impressionable visitors to these glamorous places.

Fairs were held regularly. They were the hypermarkets of their day, and no doubt Staffordshire figures were sold in quantity there.

The Theatre, like the circus, produced heroes and villains, and the potters were more than willing to produce figures of them. Many such figures were probably sold at the beginning and end of the event.

Astley's Circus, a cross between theatre and circus, enjoyed enormous popularity in its day. This was melodrama at its height; all was either black or white. There was no one to explain away the villain's evil ways with tales of a deprived childhood. It was kept simple, fast, and furious, with horses galloping, wild animals escaping, and guns firing, all to the edification of the audience. The villains were booed and the heroes cheered by the crowd and damsels had their distress relieved.

The potters made figures of many of the famous artists of the time, not usually in their own right, but more often as a character from the productions in which they were appearing. The potters sources and inspiration at times came from prints of various form, but more often from their own imaginations. The itinerant musicians and dancers were features of Victorian street life and the potters captured these too in clay.

Decorative Figures

Many people had left the land to work in the ever-increasing factories of the towns and cities, exchanging the poverty of the countryside for the drudgery of the town. But what better to remind them of what they had left behind than a figure of rural life.

No aspect of country life escaped the attention of the potters: farmers, farmhands, milkmaids, milkmen, poachers, gamekeepers, hunters, shepherds, goat herders, fishermen and women, travellers, and of course the animals they used to tend—sheep, cows, goats, and rabbits. No pastime, recreation, pursuit, craft or occupation was forgotten.

It is here, amongst these decorative figures, that the potters were able to indulge their whims and fancies, producing some of the finest examples of their art. Surprisingly, very few sporting figures were made. A few figures of cricketers and a few jockeys and one group of a pair of wrestlers (though the source for this was a statue and not any particular wrestlers) were made. There are two versions of a boxing group and four extremely rare figures of named boxers; however, no figures of golfers exist, although there is a figure of a man sitting with a rifle which has been passed off as a 'golfer'.

Crime

Criminals, murderers, and their trials always aroused public interest, and the more morbid the news the better. If you could not be at the public hanging, what better than a figure of the murderer to place on the mantelpiece to frighten the children!

The potters not only produced figures of the murderers, but also the buildings involved in them. In the murder of Mr. Issac Jermy, perpetrated by James Rush, figures were made of Rush and his mistress, Emily Sandford, his home, Potash Farm, and the home of his victim, Stanfield Hall. To take the events further, the potters even made a figure of Norwich Castle, inside the grounds of which Rush was hung. They did, however, neglect to make a figure of the victim.

The potters also made a figure of William Palmer, the Rugeley poisoner, and his home, titled 'Palmers House'.

The exceptions were the murderers Fredrick and Maria Manning. The potters made figures of them, but the house where they murdered Patrick O'Connor and buried him under the kitchen floor has never been recorded.

Humour

The potters also had a fine sense of humour with figures like 'Courting under difficulties' and 'Jealous wife', where the errant husband sits cuddling the barmaid who is serving him a mug of beer. What makes the figure so appealing is the expression on the wife's face as she looks down upon the scene from her bedroom window. If looks cannot kill, they at least stand a good chance of souring the beer.

Two new additions to this addendum are the discovery of both the 'naughty lady' and 'naughty man' which turned upside-down reveal...

Hunters

Hunting with horses was a pastime for the rich. Other forms of hunting did however proliferate, particularly hunting with guns, although there are figures of hunters with bows. By far the largest proportion of these figures are clad in highland attire, and none the worse for that. Most of these figures of standing or seated hunters also feature their faithful dog, either seated at their master's feet or jumping up at his side. The animals hunted are also included; dead deer, stags, otters, boars, and pheasants can be found. The hunting of birds with falcons was also popular. Once again the potters, ever commercial, made figures of mounted and standing falconers. The working class pastime of poaching was not forgotten. Although sometimes carried out by netting, most often successful poaching was achieved with the use of whippets, which could be let loose on the master's land, whereas the poacher, if he ventured there, could well be caught in a man trap or even shot.

Dogs

Queen Victoria kept King Charles spaniels as pets and they were the inspiration for the thousand upon thousand of Comforter dogs that were made. These dogs were certainly popular, coming in many shapes and sizes, usually in pairs. Today these figures are recognised as typical Staffordshire. Not only were King Charles spaniels potted but also a whole range of breeds, from Whippets to Bull Mastiff's, Poodles to St. Bernard's.

Amongst the rarities made were pairs of gun dogs and today these are amongst the most sought after figures, and consequently the most expensive. Combining children with dogs was to ensure a wider market for the figures; sentimentality improved sales.

Animals

The potters would have had little firsthand knowledge of the wild animals they made figures of, perhaps seeing them for the first time at the travelling menageries or circuses, where they would have been in particularly confined conditions. The results are, however, startlingly quite fantastic. The life and realism that they managed to portray is quite outstanding. The lions and leopards in particular are now recognised as supreme examples of the potter's art and are priced accordingly. The range of animals made would do justice to a small zoo—not just wild animals, but also domestic fowl, rabbits, cats, donkeys, mules, horses, and sheep.

Pastille Burners

There had been a history of making pastille burners for the more affluent and discerning. These burners were made in the shape of houses and cottages. A small pastille was placed in the figure and lit to give off a perfume that escaped in the form of smoke through the house or cottage chimney. At that time, the smell in the towns and cities was dreadful, and it was still believed that smells carried diseases. Despite the first Public Health Act of 1848, it was to be another twenty years or so before better sanitary conditions prevailed. The potters continued and adapted the pastille burner to become more decorative than utilitarian. They added a range of mainly make believe castles and cottages to their range. By the end of the period most of the cottages, houses, and castles served only decorative purposes.

Pen-Holders/Watch-Holders/Spill Vases

In Victorian times the figures were produced mainly as ornaments, although figures with secondary uses, such as pen-holders, spill vases, watch-holders, and even candlesticks were introduced, no doubt to increase the sales and markets for the figures. All these secondary uses are today obsolete, as even the poorest amongst us use biros, wristwatches, can afford matches, and are equipped for electricity.

Lamps

There has been a trend back to secondary uses. Many figures have and are being turned into lamps. When these conversions are carried out with skill, it allows another way of sympathetically displaying figures. Converted correctly, no damage need be caused to the figure.

There have been, however, some terrible examples where holes have been drilled and bottoms removed, causing avoidable damage, substantially reducing the value, and in no way enhancing the figure. This sort of treatment is little more than vandalism and should be avoided.

Portraits

This Chapter is divided alphabetically into two sections:

1. Portrait figures produced between 1835-1875.
2. Portrait figures of British and Foreign Royalty.

Pairs of figures are cross-referenced against each other, giving the name of the pair and its figure number. Where there is a group figure, we have taken the first titled and catalogued it under that letter in the alphabet. Where figures are allied with Royalty, these have been illustrated in the British and Foreign Royalty section, with a cross-reference to the Portrait section.

Finally, when a source to the figure is illustrated, it keeps the same figure number, but has the letters **SO** by it

P = The figure has a pair
S = The figure is part of a series
SO = The source of the figure

There are certain Staffordshire figures that, although titled, do not appear in this chapter. This is because:

1. The figure is not a true portrait: it is not portraying a particular person but a production of the time (i.e. tam O'Shanter and Souter Johnnie, a titled figure, but only a reference to a Burns poem). Figures such as these will be found in their appropriate chapters.
2. There are figures that have titles but describe an event rather than a person, (i.e. St. Patrick's Day, First Ride, Jealous Wife, the Rival, etc.). These figures will also be found illustrated in their appropriate chapter.

With the diversity of Staffordshire Figures produced in the potteries, the task of categorising figures into particular chapters is not a simple one. Many of the figures could have been included in more than one chapter. We have taken what we believe to be an objective, rather than a subjective, view in allocating them.

Alphabetical List of Persons Portrayed in Volumes One to Four

Listings highlighted in bold type contain additions and alterations which will be found in this addendum, all other Portraits will be found in *Books One and Three, Victorian Staffordshire Figures 1835-1875.*

A
1. **Abd-ul-Medjid, The Sultan of Turkey**
2. Arnaud, Jacques Leroy De Saint

B
3. Bazaine, Francois Achille
4. **Bismark, Otto Edward Leopold**
5. Blake, Robert
6. **Bonaparte I, Napoleon**
7. Bosquet, Pierre Joseph Francois
8. **Braidwood, James**
9. Bright, Ellen
10. Brown, George
11. Brown, John

11A. **Browning, Robert & Elizabeth Barrett**
12. **Burns, Robert (Also Armour, Jean; Campbell, Mary; & Fleming, Agnes)**
13. Bryan, John
14. **Byron, George Gordon (Also Macri, Theresa)**

C
15. **Campbell, Sir Colin**
16. Canrobert, Francois Certain
17. Cathcart, Sir George
18. Clarke, Adam
19. Cobden, Richard
20. Codrington, Sir William John
21. Cook, Eliza
22. Cook, James
23. **Cooke, Henry**
24. Cranmer, Thomas
24A. Cribb, Tom

D
25. Darling, Grace Horsley
26. De Lacy Evans, Sir George
26A. De Sales, St. Francois
27. Duncombe, Thomas Slingsby
28. Dundas, Sir James Whitley Deans
29. Dundas, Sir Richard Saunders

E
30. Elias, John
31. Evans, Christmas
32. Evans, Robert Trogwy

F
33. Fletcher, John William
34. Fletcher, Joseph
35. Franklin, Sir George & Lady Jane
36. Franklin, Benjamin

G
37. Garibaldi, Guiseppe
38. Goulburn, Edward Meyrick
39. Gurney, Joseph John

H
40. Havelock, Sir Henry
41. Heenan, John Carmel & Sayers, Tom
42. Hill, Rowland
43. Hudson, George
44. Huntington, William

J
45. Jefferson, Thomas
46. Jullien, Louis Antoine

K
47. Kossuth, Louis

L
47A. Lane, Tom
48. Latimer, Hugh (See Ridley, Nicholas)
49. Lincoln, Abraham
50. Lind, Johanna Maria (Jenny Lind) (Also Danizetti, Mario)

M
51. MacMahon, Marie Edme Patrice Maurice
52. Macri, Theresa (See Byron, George Gordon)
53. Malibran, Maria Felicita
54. Manning, Frederick George & Maria
55. Manning, Cardinal Henry Edward
56. Matthew, Theobald
57. Milton, John 57A. Molineaux, Tom
58. Molkte, Helmut Count Von
59. Moody, Dwight Lyman
60. Mozart, Wolfgang Amadeus

N
61. Napier, Sir Charles
62. Napier, Robert Cornelis
63. Nelson, Lord Horatio
64. Nightingale, Florence

O
65. O'Brien, William Smith & Lucy
66. O'Connell, Daniel
67. Orton, Arthur (Sir Roger Tichbourne)

P
68. Palmer, William
69. Pasha, Ibrahim
70. Pasha, Omar (Latas, Michael)
71. Peard, John Whitehead
72. Peel, Sir Robert
73. Pelissier, Aimable Jean Jacques
74. Penn, William
75. Pestal, Pavel Ivanovich
76. Pius IX

R
77. Raffles, Thomas
78. Raglan, Fitzroy James Henry Somerset
79. Ridley, Nicholas
80. Rousseau, Jean Jacques
81. Rush, James Bloomfield

S
82. Sale, Sir Robert & Lady Florentia
83. Sandford, Emily
84. Sankey, Ira David
85. Scott, Sir Walter
86. Shaftsbury, Earl of & Elizabeth Fry
87. Shakespeare, William
88. Simpson, Sir James
89. Singh, Gholab
90. Singh, Ranbir
91. Spurgeon, Charles Hadden

T
92. Tann, Baron Von der

V
93. Van Amburgh, Isaac
94. Vincent, De Paul Saint
95. Voltaire, Francois Marie Arouet De

W
95A. Walker (Badman), Johnnie
96. Washington, George
97. Webb, Matthew
98. Wellington, Duke of (Wellesley, Arthur)
99. Wesley, John
100. Williams, Sir William Fenwick
101. Windham, Sir Charles Ash
102. Wood, Jemmy

1. Abd-ul-Medjid,
Sultan of Turkey (1823-1861)

Succeeded to the throne in 1839 from his father Mahud II, and played an active part in the Crimean War of 1854-1856.

See Figures 01–05 Book One

The following figures of Abd-ul-Medjid are included in the Albert alliance section under Royalty in Book One:

Figs. 779/790
Albert and Abd-ul-Medjid on horseback; ALBERT–SULTAN

The following figures of Abd-ul-Medjid are included in the Victoria alliance section under Royalty in Book One:

Fig. 782
Napoleon III, Victoria, Abd-ul-Medjid, FRANCE-ENGLAND-TURKEY
Fig. 783
Abd-ul-Medjid, Victoria, Napoleon III, TURKEY-ENGLAND-FRANCE
Figs. 784/785/786
Napoleon III, Victoria, Abd-ul-Medjid, NAPOLEONVICTORIA-SULTAN
Figs. 787/788/789
Napoleon III, Victoria, Abd-ul-Medjid, FRANCE-ENGLAND-TURKEY

Fig. 2A P
A figure of Abd-ul-Medjid on horseback facing right. He wears a plumed hat, long belted jacket, and trousers. He holds a sword in his right hand and a long cloak is over his arm.
An extremely rare and previously unrecorded figure that is very similar to Figs. 2 and 3 in Book One but facing the other way, this figure Pairs with Omer Pasha Fig. 251A.
TITLE: SULTAN
HEIGHT: 7.5 Inches
PRICE: E.

2. Arnaud, Marshal Leroy De Saint (1796-1854)

See Figures 07 – 10 Book One

3. Bazaine, Francois Achille (1811-1888)
See Figure 11 Book One

4. Bismark, Otto Edward Leopold, Prince Bismark, Duke of Lauenburg (1815-1898)

Born at Schonhausen, was appointed Prussian ambassador to St. Petersburg in 1858, and in 1862 minister in Paris. In 1862 he was recalled and appointed Minister-President of Prussia, a post he kept until 1890, when after a power struggle he was replaced by William II. Known as 'The Iron Chancellor', he was regarded as the chief architect of the German Empire.

See Figure 12 Book One

Fig. 01S
A figure of Abd-ul-Medjid standing on a square base; his right hand resting on his hip, his left resting on a pillar holding a sword, wearing a fez, long tunic, and trousers.
This figure is identical to a figure of Omar Pasha apart from titling.
This figure is in the same series as Lord Raglan, Canrobert, Omar Pasha. See Figures, 256, 297, 102 Book One.
This figure can be found in two sizes, both illustrated.
TITLE: SULTAN
HEIGHT: 12 Inches & 13 Inches
PRICE: E

The Alliance of England, Russia, and Austria invaded Paris, causing him to abdicate. He was then exiled to Elba. A year later he escaped, regrouping his armies, and sailed to meet the English Army at Waterloo on the 18th June 1815. Defeated he returned to Paris and again abdicated, surrendering to the British on the 15th July 1815. He was then banished to St. Helena, where he died in 1840. The French brought his body back to France and laid it to rest in Paris.

See Figures 14 - 44 Book One and Figures 18 - 36 Book Three

Fig. 12
A figure of Prince Bismark on horseback on a titled base with raised gilt capitals, dressed in full military uniform with a plumed helmet.
The figure illustrated is 10.75 inches high; 14.5 and 13 inch versions have previously been recorded and they are in a series with Von Molke, Von der Tann, and Prince Frederick Charles of Prussia, see Figs. 208/335/757 Book One, which means that there are no doubt unrecorded 10.75 inch versions of these figures as well.
TITLE: G. BISMARK
HEIGHT: 10.75 Inches
PRICE: F.

Fig. 17A.P
A figure of Napoleon Bonaparte on horseback; he wears a cocked hat, cloak, and military uniform of tunic, sash around his waist, breeches, and boots, his right hand is pointing and his left holds the reins. This figure was previously unrecorded and is probably the pair to Figure 347 Book One, the Duke of Wellington.
HEIGHT: 9 Inches
PRICE: F.

5. Blake, Admiral Robert (1599-1657)

See Figure 13 Book One

6. Bonaparte I, Napoleon (1769-1821)

Born in Corsica, in 1769, he was appointed Commander-in-Chief of the French army in 1795 and after many victories in Austria and North Africa returned to France in 1799, proclaiming himself 'First Consul'. In 1800, he crossed the Alps, gaining victories in Italy and Austria. In 1804, he was proclaimed Emperor, and after many successful battles with neighbouring countries became dictator of Europe. The success though did not continue, culminating in a disastrous campaign in Russia.

Fig. 27A
A figure of Napoleon standing by a pillar with his arms folded, wearing a cocked hat, jacket with epaulettes, waistcoat, trousers, and knee boots. There is no doubt a pair to this figure, probably of The Duke of Wellington, as yet unrecorded.
HEIGHT: 7 Inches
PRICE: G.

Fig. 28A
A figure of Napoleon standing, wearing a cocked hat, shirt, waistcoat, greatcoat, trousers, and knee boots, his left hand is tucked into his waistcoat and his right holds a scroll. There is no doubt a pair to this figure, probably of The Duke of Wellington, as yet unrecorded.
HEIGHT: 5 Inches
PRICE: F.

Fig. 36A
A figure of Napoleon Bonaparte standing with his arms folded, wearing a cocked hat, tunic with epaulettes, waistcoat, breeches, and knee boots, to his left is a draped pillar and by his right foot a cannon. This figure is on a plinth base.
TITLE: N.B. in capitals surrounded by a palm device.
HEIGHT: 13.5 inches
PRICE: E.

Fig. 29A
A figure of Napoleon standing with arms crossed; he wears a cocked hat, jacket with epaulettes, waistcoat, and breeches with knee boots, to his left side is a large pillar with a cloak draped on it.
HEIGHT: 6 Inches
PRICE: F.

Fig. 43A
A figure of Napoleon Bonaparte standing with his arms crossed on a round stepped base wearing a tricorn hat, military tunic with epaulettes, waistcoat, breeches, and knee boots.
HEIGHT: 21 Inches
PRICE: E.

7. Bosquet, Pierre Joseph Francois (1810-1861)

See Figure 47 Book One.

8. Braidwood, James (1800-1861)

Born in Edinburgh, he spent time in the building trade before being appointed Superintendent of the Fire Engines in Edinburgh in 1830. Two years later, he was appointed to the same position in London, and became a popular figure. During the Great Fire of Tooley Street in 1866, the greatest fire since the Great Fire of London in 1666, he met his death after a wall fell on him. At this time the fire services were paid for by the insurance companies, but after his death renewed pressure caused the government in 1866 to take control of the fire service and established The Metropolitan Fire Brigade.

Fig. 48
A figure of James Braidwood standing on a titled base with a black line running through the title; his right hand resting on a pillar, his left resting on his hip, wearing a helmet, long tunic, and trousers. This figure was probably issued to commemorate his death, as known figures have a black line running through his name
TITLE: BRAIDWOOD
HEIGHT: 15 Inches
PRICE: C.

9. Bright, Ellen (1832-1850)

See Figures 49 - 50 Book One.

10. Brown, Sir George (1790-1865)

See Figures 51 - 53 Book One

11. Brown, John (1800-1859)

See Figures 54 - 55 Book One

11A. Browning, Robert (1812-1889)

An English poet, the author of numerous philosophical and dramatic lyrics, and of several dramas, Robert Browning was born in Camberwell, South London. He became an admirer of Elizabeth Barrett's poetry and corresponded by letter. This was the start of one of the world's most famous romances. They married in 1846, moved to Italy, and had a son named Pen. Robert was buried in Westminster Abbey in Poet's Corner.

Browning, Elizabeth Barrett (1806-1861)

His wife, Elizabeth Barrett, had her first poem published in 1819. She was thirteen at the time. In 1821 she injured her spine as a result of a fall. When her brother died in 1838, she seemingly became a permanent invalid and spent most of her time in her room writing poems. She was attended by her faithful dog 'Flush'. The dog was given her by her friend Miss Mitford and she wrote a twenty verse poem about him titled 'To Flush, My Dog'.

Fig. 55A
A figure of Elizabeth Barrett Browning laying supine on an ornate sofa, wearing a long coat and long skirt, her faithful dog 'Flush' on her lap, all on a gilt lined oblong base.
It is not known if there is a pair to this extremely rare and previously unrecorded figure.
HEIGHT: 5.75 Inches
PRICE: E.

Figs. 55C/55D
A pair of figures of Elizabeth Barrett Browning and Robert Browning seated on chaise longues; she wears an off the shoulder dress with puff sleeves, her right arm rests on the head of the chaise longue, a dog sits on a cushion at the foot, and her right foot rests on a footstool. He wears a shirt, tie, waistcoat, jacket, and trousers, his left hand rests on the head of the chaise longue holding notes, and his right on the head of a dog that sits at the foot, his left foot rests on a footstool.
HEIGHT: 5.5 Inches
PRICE: Pair: D, Singles: E.

12. Burns, Robert (1759-1796)

Scotland's most famous poet, born at Alloway, was educated by his father, a cotter. He first had a small collection of his poems published in 1772. This led to widespread acclaim, and with the money he received he bought a farm. In 1786 he wrote a declaration of marriage to Jean Armour. Meanwhile he had met Mary Campbell (also known as Highland Mary) and was trying to take her to Jamaica as his wife, even though a year later he reacquainted himself with Jean Armour.

See Figures 56 -76 Book One and Figures 65 - 76A Book Three

Fig. 63A
A spill vase figure of a man and woman seated on a bank; he wears a cap, jacket, shirt, tunic, and knee breeches, a scarf is over his shoulder. He holds the woman's hand and his right arm is around her; she is bareheaded and wears a blouse and long skirt, a dog is seated on the base looking up at them. Two figures are illustrated, one with a spill vase and one without; the one without has never had a spill and the figure was made in both forms. The authors are reasonably certain that these figures portray Burns and Mary.
HEIGHT: 8.5 Inches with spill vase, 6 Inches without.
PRICE: F.

Fig. 61
A group of Robert Burns and Highland Mary, standing on a titled, shaped base with raised gilt capitals; Burns holds Mary's hand and he wears a plumed hat, cloak, jacket, and kilt with sporran. Mary wears a hat, cloak, bodice, and long skirt.
This figure is similar to a figure of Burns and Agnes Fleming, see Figure 68 Book One.
The figure illustrated is in the white, although coloured examples can be found.
TITLE: BURNS & HIS HIGHLAND MARY
HEIGHT: 10.5 Inches
PRICE: F.

Fig. 68
A group figure of Robert Burns and Agnes Fleming standing, holding hands, he wearing a plumed hat, scarf, tunic, kilt with sporran, she with her right hand on his shoulder, wearing a neckerchief, bodice, and long skirt. Two figures are illustrated, almost of the same size, but one is far better modelled than the other; the sporran is more delineated, the scarves are differently modelled, and the faces sharper. It is not known for certain why this occurs. It is possible that the figure was popular, but for some reason the master mould was damaged and they had to return to the modeller for another original that was better than the one that went before or after.
TITLE: O NANNY GANG WEE ME
HEIGHT: 8.5 Inches
PRICE: F.

36

Fig. 68B
A group figure of Robert Burns and Agnes Fleming, standing, he with his left arm around her shoulders; he wears a plumed hat, long scarf over his left shoulder, tunic, kilt, and shoes with stockings, she is bareheaded and wears a scarf over both shoulders, blouse, and long skirt.
This figure is a smaller version of Fig. 68 Book One.
HEIGHT: 7 Inches
PRICE: G.

CORRECTION
Fig. 69
The authors are now of the opinion that this is not a figure of Burns. It has been relocated in the unidentified theatrical chapter with its pair. **See Fig. 1439B Book Three.**

Fig. 70
A spill vase group of Robert Burns and Highland Mary standing, he with his right hand resting on his hip, his left arm around Mary's waist, wearing a bonnet, jacket scarf, and breeches with stockings. Mary has her left arm raised to his chest, wearing a bodice and dress. The figure illustrated is in the white although coloured examples can be found.
TITLE: Mony a vow and lock'd embrace our parting was fu' tender. And pledging aft to meet again we tore ourselves asunder.
HEIGHT: 13 Inches
PRICE: F.

Figs. 74/75
A pair of standing figures of Highland Mary and Robert Burns, Mary holding her dress with her right hand, her left holding a book, wearing a headscarf, scarf, bodice, and dress. Burns with his left hand resting on a book, a pillar below, his right resting on his hip, wearing a cap, scarf, jacket, waistcoat, breeches, and stockings.
TITLE: Mary - Burns
HEIGHT: 16 Inches
PRICE: Pair: E, Singles: F.

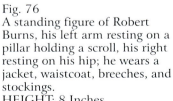

Fig. 76
A standing figure of Robert Burns, his left arm resting on a pillar holding a scroll, his right resting on his hip; he wears a jacket, waistcoat, breeches, and stockings.
HEIGHT: 8 Inches
PRICE: F.

Armour, Jean (1767-1843)

In 1786, Burns wrote a declaration of marriage to her, which her father destroyed, fearing that the loss of her reputation was better than a marriage to Burns.

Campbell, Mary (1768-1786)

Known as Highland Mary, Burns tried to persuade her to go to Jamaica as his wife, but she died later that year of malignant fever. Burns never got over her death, and wrote some of his finest poems in her memory.

Fleming, Agnes (Dates unknown)

A servant at Catlcothill, Lochlea, she was the inspiration for Burns poem 'My Nannie, O!'.

13. Bryan, Rev. John (1770-1856)

See Figure 77 Book One

14. Byron, George Gordon, (Lord Byron) (1788-1824)

Born lame and in poor conditions after his father had wasted his wife's fortune, George inherited his title on the death of his great uncle, the fifth Baron. Educated at Harrow and then at Trinity College, Cambridge, it was here that he produced his first volume of poems. In 1809 he set out on a grand tour of Europe and it was in Athens that he met Theresa Macri, the daughter of a British vice-consul. She inspired him to write The Maid of Athens. He returned to London where he became a popular figure in society. In 1815 he married Anne Isabella, who bore him a daughter. Suspected of having an incestuous affair with his half-sister, Augusta Leigh, he sold up and left for Europe again. It was in Venice that he met the Countess Teresa Guiccioli, who soon became his mistress. He supported the Italian revolution and was active against the Turks. He died of marsh fever at Missolonghi and his body was brought back to England and buried at Hucknall-Torkard.

See Figures 78 - 87 Book One

Fig. 81 A figure of Lord Byron standing on a titled scrolled base with raised gilt capitals; wearing a short jacket, cummerbund, scarf over one shoulder, open necked shirt, skirt, and boots.
This figure has an identical height and design of base as a figure of Falstaff. See Figure 1062 Book One. This figure can be found in two sizes, 17 and 12 inches, 17 inch figure illustrated.
TITLE: BYRON
HEIGHT: 17 Inches, 12 Inches
PRICE: F.

Fig. 79
A figure of Lord Byron seated; he is bareheaded and dressed in a shirt, cravat, and a buttoned long coat with a cloak over both shoulders, one foot is raised onto a cushion and he holds a book in his left hand and a scroll in his right.
This is a larger and more refined version of Fig. 80 Book One and is extremely rare and previously unrecorded.
HEIGHT: 11 Inches
PRICE: D.

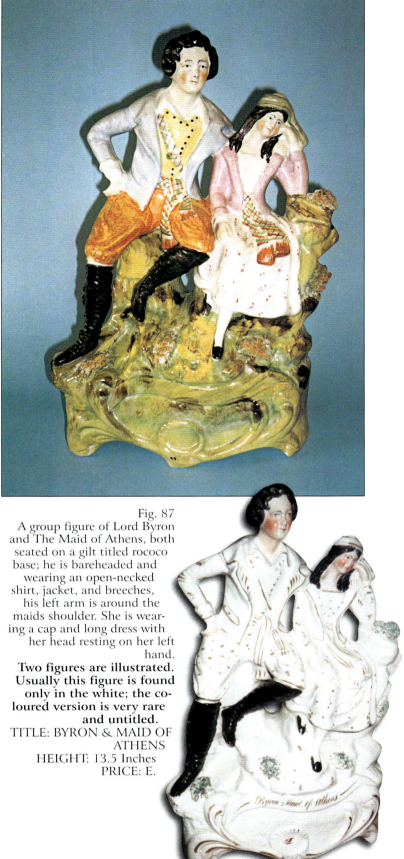

Figs. 82/83 A pair of figures of Lord Byron and The Maid of Athens; he is seated, holding a book in his left hand, his right elbow rests on a pillar on which is a book, his hand is held to his head, his right foot rests on a cushion, he wears a jacket, belted dress, and boots. The Maid of Athens is kneeling on a cushion with her left arm resting on a book, a pillar below, her right hand holds a handkerchief, and she wears a mop cap, cloak, bodice, and dress. **An alternative attribution for Fig. 83 is that it is a portrait of Eliza Cook; the figure has never been found titled, and her headdress is not similar to the known portraits of The Maid of Athens. It is also similar in many respects to the titled figure of Cook. See Fig. 114 Book One. All three of these figures were made by 'The Alpha factory'. This pottery used similar heads for a number of different persons.**
HEIGHT: 6.75 Inches
PRICE: Pair: E, Singles: F.

Fig. 87
A group figure of Lord Byron and The Maid of Athens, both seated on a gilt titled rococo base; he is bareheaded and wearing an open-necked shirt, jacket, and breeches, his left arm is around the maids shoulder. She is wearing a cap and long dress with her head resting on her left hand.
Two figures are illustrated. Usually this figure is found only in the white; the coloured version is very rare and untitled.
TITLE: BYRON & MAID OF ATHENS
HEIGHT: 13.5 Inches
PRICE: E.

Figs. 85A/85B
A pair of figures of Lord Byron and The Maid of Athens, both seated on oval gilt lined bases, he wears a round headdress, jacket, open necked shirt, breeches, and boots. He holds a basket of flowers on his lap. She has a garland in her hair and wears a bodice and long skirt, a long scarf is over her left shoulder, and one end is on her lap, in which are flowers.
These are a very rare pair of figures, and whilst never found titled they are very similar to other known figures of Byron and The Maid of Athens. They were made by the 'Alpha' pottery. This pottery did however adapt existing figures and it is possible that whilst they resemble Byron and The Maid of Athens they were made merely as a decorative pair of gardeners.
HEIGHT: 7.25 Inches
PRICE: Pair: E, Singles: F.

15. Campbell, Sir Colin (Baron Clyde) (1792-1863)

A Field Marshal, he was wounded twice in the Peninsular War; he was awarded a knighthood for his services in the Second Sikh War of 1848-1849. On the outbreak of the Crimean War of 1854-1856, he was appointed to the command of the Highland Brigade and is credited with the victories at Balaclava and Alma. In 1857, Palmerston offered him the post of Commander-in-Chief of the forces in India on the outbreak of the Indian Mutiny. He was created a Baron in 1857.

See Figures 88 -100 Book One and Figure 97 Book Three

Fig. 92SO
A music front titled 'The Highlanders', a Quadrille on Scotch Airs by Giuseppe T. Pietra is the newly discovered source to Fig. 92. It is however strange as Fig. 92 pairs with Havelock, Fig. 164, and these are Indian Mutiny figures dating from 1870, whereas the music cover almost certainly dates from the Crimean War of 1854/6 when Campbell commanded the Highland Brigade. By 1870 he was commander of the whole Indian Army although there was at least one Highland regiment at the Relief of Lucknow. The music front does not mention Campbell by name but it is clearly a portrait of him.

Fig. 91P
A figure of Sir Colin Campbell standing, his right hand raised to his head holding a plumed hat, his left hand rests on his hip, a pair of flags are to his right and a cannon and brickwork to his left; he wears a tunic and trousers, with a sash across his chest.
This figure is similar to Figure 90 Book One, except that the cannon and flags are reversed.
This very rare figure pairs with Sir Henry Havelock, see Figure 163A Book Three.
HEIGHT: 9.75 Inches
PRICE: E.

Fig. 93P
A figure of Sir Colin Campbell mounted, on titled gilt lined base with raised gilt capitals, his right hand raised to his head holding a plumed hat, his left hand holding the reins, wearing a tunic with epaulettes and trousers, with a sash across his chest.
This figure pairs with General Canrobert, see Figure 105 Book One.
TITLE: C. CAMPBELL
HEIGHT: 11 Inches
PRICE: F.

Fig. 100P
A figure of Sir Colin Campbell on horseback on a titled base with gilt capitals, both hands are holding the reins, and he wears a plumed hat, long military jacket, and trousers. There is a sash across his chest.
This figure pairs with Sir Henry Havelock, see Fig. 168 Book One.
TITLE: SIR C. CAMPBELL
HEIGHT: 11.75 Inches
PRICE: E.

16. Canrobert, Francois Certain (1809-1895)

See Figures 102 - 105 Book One

17. Cathcart, Sir George (1794-1854)

See Figure 106 Book One

18. Clarke, Adam LL.D. (1762-1832)

See Figure 107 Book One

19. Cobden, Richard (1804-1865)

See Figures 108 - 110 Book One.

20. Codrington, Sir William John (1804-1884)

See Figures 111 - 112 Book One

21. Cook, Eliza (1818-1889)

See Figure 114 Book One

22. Cook, James (1728-1779)

See Figure 115 Book One

23. Cooke, Rev. Henry (1788-1868)

An Irish Presbyterian who opposed the disestablishment of the Irish Episcopal Church. He was regarded as one of Ireland's most accomplished preachers, publishing many sermons and hymns.
See Figure 116 Book One

Fig. 116/116A
A figure of the Rev. Henry Cooke standing in a pulpit which is flanked by an angel on either side, on a gilt lined rococo base with raised gilt capitals above a clock face, holding a bible in his left hand, his right outstretched pointing.
Two versions are illustrated. In Figure 116 the figure is longhaired and wearing a cassock. This is not a true portrait of Cooke; this is in fact a portrait of Wesley. In Figure 116A, Cooke is wearing a shirt, waistcoat, trousers, and long overcoat. This is a true portrait. As an Irish Presbyterian, this dress was allowed him.
TITLE: H. COOKE. DD (for Doctor of Divinity)
HEIGHT: 10.5 & 11.5 Inches
PRICE: E (For Cooke), F (For Wesley).

24. Cranmer, Archbishop Thomas (1489-1556)

24A. Cribb, Tom (1781-1848) 'The Black Diamond'

25. Darling, Grace Horsley (1815-1842)

26. De Lacy Evans, Sir George (1787-1870)

26A De Sales, St Francois (1567-1622)

27. Duncombe, Thomas Slingsby (1796-1861)

28. Dundas, Sir James Whitley Deans (1785-1862)

29. Dundas, Sir Richard Saunders (1802-1861)

30. Elias, Rev. John (1774-1841)

31. Evans, Rev. Christmas (1766-1838)

32. Evans, Robert Trogwy (1824-1901)

33. Fletcher, Rev. John William (1729-1785)

34. Fletcher, Joseph (1784-1843)

Fletcher, Joseph (1816-1876)

35. Franklin, Sir John (1786-1847)

Franklin, Lady Jane (1792-1875)

36. Franklin, Benjamin (1706-1790)

Born in Boston, Massachusetts, the son of an immigrant from Banbury, England, he published *Poor Richard's Almanac* in 1732 and continued a series of scientific experiments which included the invention of the lightning conductor. Franklin returned to Britain as a representative for his State, staying for eighteen years. On his return, he played a major part in drafting The Constitution of the United States that led to the Declaration of Independence in 1776.

Fig. 137
A figure of Benjamin Franklin standing on a gilt lined circular base; his right hand is holding a scroll, his left a hat, wearing a long jacket, neckerchief, waistcoat, breeches, and stockings. **Figures can be found titled 'Old English Gentleman', a case of the potters changing the title to suit a different market. An example is illustrated.**
HEIGHT: 15 Inches & 10 Inches
PRICE: D.

37. Garibaldi, Giuseppe (1807-1882)

38. Goulburn, Edward Meyrick (1818-1897)

39. Gurney, Joseph John, (1788-1847)

40. Havelock, Sir Henry (1795-1857)

In 1841, Sir Henry Havelock assisted Sir Robert Sale in holding Jellalabad; further campaigns included serving in The Sikh Wars of 1845-1846 and his involvement in The Indian Mutiny of 1857. He had been unsuccessful because of illness in the ranks and was awaiting fresh reserves. These came and they were able to advance only to be besieged again. Meanwhile, Sir Colin Campbell forced his way to their rescue, and a week later Havelock died of dysentery. He was created a Baron for his services.
See Figures 160 - 171 Book One

Fig. 163A P
A standing figure of Sir Henry Havelock, he wears a high collar with neck tie, tunic with a sash around his waist, and trousers. He holds his plumed hat to his head with his left hand and his right is on his hip; behind him and to his left is a small brick wall with cannon balls at the base, above which there are two flags, and behind and to his right is a cannon.
This figure is previously unrecorded and may well be unique, it pairs with Sir Colin Campbell (See figure 91 Book One).
HEIGHT: 9 Inches
PRICE: D.

41. Heenan, John Carmel (1835-1873) & Sayers, Tom (1826-1865)

See Figures 172 - 173 Book One

42. Hill, Rev. Roland (1744-1833)

See Figure 174 Book One

43. Hudson, George (1800-1871)

See Figure 175 Book One

44. Huntington, William (1745-1813)

See Figure 176 Book One

45. Jefferson, Thomas (1743-1826)

See Figure 177 Book One

46. Jullien, Louis Antoine (1812-1860)

See Figure 178 Book One

47. Kossuth, Louis Ferencz Akos (1802-1894)

See Figures 179 - 182 Book One

47A. Lane, Tom (Dates Unknown)

See Figure 182A Book Three

49. Lincoln, Abraham (1809-1865)

See Figure 183 Book One

50. Lind, Johanna Maria (Jenny Lind) (1820-1887)

See Figures 184 -191 and 1330 -1335 Book One

51. MacMahon, Marie Edme Patrice Maurice (1808-1893)

See Figure 192 Book One

53. Malibran, Maria Felcita (1808-1836)

See Figure 193 Book One

54. Manning, Frederick George (1800-1849)

Manning, Maria (1821-1849)

See Figures 194 - 197 Book One

55. Manning, Cardinal Henry Edward (1808-1892)

See Figure 198 Book One

56. Mathew, Theobald (1790-1856)

See Figures 199 - 200 Book One

57. Milton, John (1608-1674)

See Figures 201 -207 Book One and 202A -206A Book Three

57A. Molineaux, Tom (1784-1818)

See Figure 207A Book Three

58. Moltke, Helmut, Count von (1800-1891)

See Figure 208 Book One

59. Moody, Dwight Lyman (1837-1899)

See Figure 209 Book One

60. Mozart, Wolfgang Amadeus (1756-1791)

See Figure 210 Book One

61. Napier, Admiral Sir Charles (1786-1860)

See Figures 211 - 215 Book One

62. Napier, Robert Cornelis (first Baron Napier of Magdala) (1810-1890)

See Figure 216 Book One

63. Nelson, Horatio, (Viscount Nelson, Duke of Bronte) (1758-1803)

He was born at Burnham Thorpe, Norfolk, on the 29th September, his father being rector of the parish. Not much is known of his early childhood apart from his schooling at Norwich. He entered the Royal Navy on the 1st January 1771 as a midshipman, soon joining his uncle on the *Triumph* as a 'captain's servant'. In 1773, at his request, he was transferred to the *Carcass* for a voyage of discovery in the Artic. On returning, he joined *Seahorse*, a frigate, and extensively toured the East Indies, but due to the climate his health failed. He was relieved and returned to England. A few weeks after his return, he was appointed a lieutenant on the *Worcester* under the command of Captain Mark Robinson. In 1777, Nelson was again promoted to lieutenant of the *Worcester* under the command of Captain Mark Robinson. In 1777, Nelson was again promoted to lieutenant of the *Lowestoft* under the command of William Locker, learning many valuable lessons from him. In 1778 he was appointed captain of a captured French ship, renamed *Hinchinbroke*, and led an expedition against Grenada; but, infected with malaria he returned to Jamaica and then to England. In 1783, after various duties, he was appointed to the *Boreas* where he sailed to the West Indies and captured five American ships engaged in illegal trading. Proceedings for illegal detention were served on Nelson and he was made a prisoner on his own ship. Eventually an order came through and the Crown agreed to defend their captain at any cost. In March of 1783, he sailed to St. Kitts. On his arrival he met and fell in love with the young widow Frances Nisbet and in 1787 he married her and returned home. In 1793, with the outbreak of war against France imminent, Nelson was given command of the *Agamemnon* in which he sailed to Naples where he met Emma Hamilton, the wife of Sir William Hamilton the English minister, and began an affair that would continue until his death. In 1796 he was appointed rear-admiral and in 1797, after an unsuccessful landing at Santa Cruz, he was injured and had to have his right arm amputated. In 1798 he attacked the French fleet in Aboukir Bay, during which he lost the sight of one eye. For his services in that year he was created Baron Nelson of the Nile.

Returning to England in 1801 in the company of the Hamiltons, he separated from his wife and lived with the Hamiltons in London. William Hamilton died in 1803 and he and Emma lived together until his death, during which time Emma bore him two daughters.

In May 1803 he was appointed commander-in-chief of the Mediterranean fleet and made the *Victory* his flagship. He set off to do battle with the French fleet and, after chasing Villeneuve, the French commander-in-chief to the West Indies and back, they met at Cape Trafalgar. The English victory was complete and decisive and the outcome decided when Nelson was shot on his quarterdeck from the *Redoubtable* at a range of fifteen yards and within the hour he died. His body was brought back to England where, after laying in state at Greenwich, he was publicly buried at St. Paul's Cathedral on the 6th January 1806.

Of all the monuments erected to his memory, the most famous is the column in Trafalgar Square, London.
See Figures 217 - 232 Book One

Fig. 221A
A group of Horatio Nelson standing, being supported by a sailor; Nelson wears a naval uniform of tricorn hat, jacket with epaulettes, and knee breeches, a barrel of a cannon is at his feet, and to his side a sailor who wears a striped jumper with tie and white trousers has one arm around him. **This figure has never before been recorded and is probably unique. The authors have not examined the figure but from the photograph it would appear that the sailors arm has been badly restored as it is out of proportion with the rest of his body.**
TITLE: Death of Nelson, in gilt script
HEIGHT: Not known
PRICE: C.

64. Nightingale, Florence (1820-1910)

See Figures 233 - 236 Book One

65. O'Brien, William Smith (1803-1864)

O'Brien Lucy (Dates unknown)
See Figures 237 - 239 Book One

66. O'Connell, Daniel (1775-1847)

An Irish patriot, he was born at Carhan, near Cahirciveen, County Kerry. In 1798 he was called to the Irish Bar. In 1829 he was returned as a Member of Parliament for Clare, but could not take his seat as he was a Catholic. He was re-elected in 1830 after the passing of the Catholic Emancipation Act of 1829, a reform that would not have come as soon if it had not been for his efforts. In 1841 he began his greatest agitation for repeal of the Union. He fought against Peel, the Conservative Prime Minister, and the activities of the Catholic Association were revived. Huge meetings were organised and in 1844 O'Connell was imprisoned for sedition, but was released a few months later. His ill-health and the great famine in Ireland combined to defeat his cause. He died in 1847 at Genoa on his way to Rome.
See Figures 240 - 244 Book One

Fig. 244A (Not illustrated)
A standing figure of O'Connell, he is bareheaded and wearing a cravat, frock coat, and trousers. He holds a scroll in his left hand and his right points to it. There is a small tree stump by his right foot.
This figure is extremely rare and has only been recorded in the white.
HEIGHT: 13.5 Inches
PRICE: D.

67. Orton, Arthur (Sir Roger Tichbourne) (1834-1898)

See Figure 245 Book One

68. Palmer, William (1824-1856)

See Figure 246 Book One

69. Pasha, Ibrahim (1798-1848)

See Figure 247 Book One

70. Pasha, Omar (Michael Latas) (1806-1871)

Born in Plasky, Croatia, Omar Pasha served in the Austrian army. In 1828 he deserted to Bosnia and whilst there became a Muslim. He became the writing master for Abd-ul-Medjid. On Abd-ul-Medjid's accession to the throne in 1839 he was appointed colonel. In 1842 he was promoted to Governor of Lebanon. In 1853 he crossed the Danube with 60,000 men and defeated the Russians. He arrived in the Crimea in 1855 and helped defeat 40,000 Russians at Eupatoria.

See Figures 248 - 256 Book One and 248A Book Three

Fig. 249
A pair of figures of Omar Pasha on horseback facing left and right, on a titled base with black transfer capitals, his left hand holds the reins, wearing a turban, tunic, and trousers, with a sash around his waist. Each is a mirror image of the other.
These figures are decorated in the manner of The Parr factory. This figure can be found in two sizes, the 11.25 Inch version pairs with Lord Raglan (See Figure 295 Book One) and the smaller version pairs with a mirror image of itself.
Two large figures illustrated are identical apart from decoration and a pair of smaller figures.
TITLE: OMAR PASHA SUCCESS TO TURKEY
HEIGHT: 11.25 Inches and 6.5 Inches
PRICE: 11.25 Inches: E, Pair 6.5 Inches: F, Singles: G.

Fig. 251A. P
A figure of Omer Pasha mounted on horseback, he wears a turban, long coat buttoned at the neck, he holds the reins in his left hand, and a sword hangs from the saddle.
An extremely rare and previously unrecorded figure which pairs with The Sultan Figure 2A. It is similar to Figures 251 and 252 Book One, but is facing the other way.
TITLE: OMER PASHA
HEIGHT: 7 Inches
PRICE: E.

71. Peard, Colonel John Whitehead (1811-1889)

He joined Garibaldi's forces in 1859, helping Victor Emmanuel in liberating Italy; he fought in 1860 at the battle of Melazzo and was appointed to command the English Legion during the advance on Naples. For his services, Victor Emmanuel awarded him the Cross of the Order of Valour. He became known due to his resemblance to him as 'Garibaldi's Englishman'.

See Figures 257 - 262 Book One and 261 Book Three

For another figure of Peard with Giuseppe Garibaldi see Figure 151 Book One

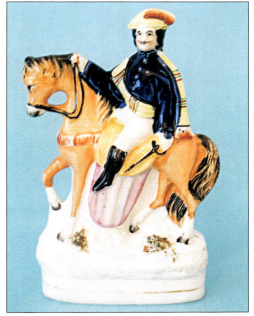

Fig. 257P
An equestrian figure of Colonel Peard facing left; he wears a plumed hat, scarf over his shoulder and across his chest, military tunic, trousers, and boots. He holds a sword in his left hand and the horse's reins in his right.
This is a very rare figure and there must have been made a pair of Garibaldi as yet unrecorded. Figure 155A has been reserved for it.
HEIGHT: 7.5 Inches
PRICE: F.

72. Peel, Sir Robert (Second Baronet) (1788-1850)

Born near Bury, Lancashire and educated at Harrow and Christchurch, Oxford, he obtaining a double first. He entered Parliament in 1809, and the following year was appointed under-secretary for war and the colonies. In 1812 he was appointed Chief Secretary for Ireland, during which time he fought the growing movement for self-rule and established the Royal Irish Constabulary. In 1818 he retired from office, only to be appointed to the office of Home Secretary in 1822. His reforms included the foundation of the Metropolitan Police, hence the name 'Bobbies' and 'Peelers'. In 1829 he backed Wellington on the Catholic Emancipation Act, convinced that it would bring peace to Ireland.

In 1834 he became Prime Minister and Chancellor of the Exchequer, but only held office for a few months. On the opposition benches he reorganised the Conservative Party and in 1841 he became Prime Minister again. During this time he opposed the repeal of the Corn Laws, but due to the failure of the harvest in 1845, he became convinced that he would have to reverse his opinion. He then brought in the Corn Law Bill. A few months later he was defeated on the Irish Bill and retired from office. In 1850 he was thrown from his mare whilst riding at Constitution Hill and died from his injuries three days later.

See Figures 263 - 278 Book One and 271 - 276A Book Three

Fig. 277A
A small figure of a man standing with his legs crossed; he is bareheaded and wearing a long jacket, shirt, tie, waistcoat, and trousers. His left arm rests on a pillar and his right holds a scroll.
This figure, as with Figures 277 and 278, see Book One, have been attributed to Sir Robert Peel. It is possible that one or either of them could be of Richard Cobden.
HEIGHT: 6 Inches
PRICE: G.

73. Pellissier, Aimable Jean Jaques (Duc de Malakoff) (1794-1864)

He was born at Maromme, near Rouen. In 1830 he joined the first expedition to Algiers and in 1839 he was appointed lieutenant-colonel and returned in 1844 to take part in the battle of Isly. In 1850 he was promoted to general and during the Crimean War of (1854-1856) he was commander-in-chief before the battle of Sebastopol. His most notable achievement was the storming of Malakoff. For this he received a marshal's baton and was created Duc de Malakoff. He also received an award of 100,000 Francs. From 1858-1859 he was the French Ambassador in England and from 1860 until his death was the Governor of Algeria.

See Figures 279 - 285 Book One

Fig. 268
A figure of Sir Robert Peel seated in a chair his right hand holds a scroll, his left leans on a pillar, he wears a long jacket, neckerchief, waistcoat, and trousers, all on a shaped gilt lined base.
A very rare figure.
HEIGHT: 9.5 Inches
PRICE: D.

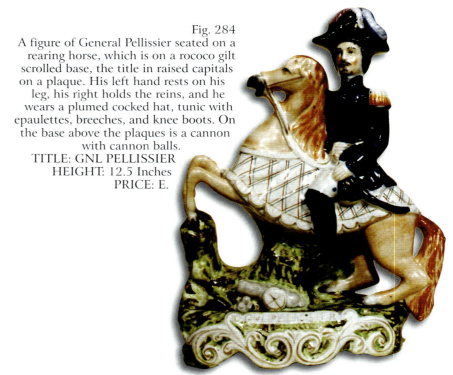

Fig. 284
A figure of General Pellissier seated on a rearing horse, which is on a rococo gilt scrolled base, the title in raised capitals on a plaque. His left hand rests on his leg, his right holds the reins, and he wears a plumed cocked hat, tunic with epaulettes, breeches, and knee boots. On the base above the plaques is a cannon with cannon balls.
TITLE: GNL PELLISSIER
HEIGHT: 12.5 Inches
PRICE: E.

74. Penn, William (1644-1718)

See Figure 286 Book One

75. Pestal, Pavel Ivanovich (1794-1826)

See Figure 287 Book One

76. Pius IX, Pope (1792-1878)

See Figure 288 Book One

77. Raffles, Thomas (1788-1863)

See Figure 289 Book One

78. Raglan, Lord Fitzroy James Henry Somerset (First Baron) (1788-1855)

Born at Badminton, the youngest son of the 5th Duke of Somerset, he entered the army in 1804, and in 1808 was appointed as aide-de-camp to Wellington. He was present at the battle of Waterloo, where he was wounded, losing his right arm. He was returned as a Member of Parliament for Truro and was military secretary at the Horse Guards from 1827-1852. In 1852 he was raised to the peerage. In 1854 he was appointed field-marshal and headed the expeditionary force to the Crimea on the eve of the war.

On the 24th September 1854 he defeated the Russians at Alma, but after the embarrassment of losing the Light Brigade in the infamous charge at Balaclava in October, he ordered Lord Lucan's recall. After many months of siege warfare, the terrible winter conditions, the abortive attacks on Malakoff and The Redan, Raglan was very ill and depressed, culminating in his death on the 28th June 1855 of dysentery.

See Figures 290 - 298 Book One

79. Ridley, Nicholas (Bishop of London) (1500-1555)

48. Latimer, Hugh (Bishop of Worcester) 1486-1555

See Figure 299 Book One

80. Rousseau, Jean Jacques (1712-1778)

See Figure 300 Book One

81. Rush, James Bloomfield (1800-1849)

See Figure 301 Book One

82. Sale, Sir Robert Henry (1782-1845)

Sale, Lady Florentia (1790-1853)

See Figures 302 - 303 Book One

83. Sandford, Emily (Dates unknown)

See Figures 304 - 306 Book One

84. Sankey, Ira David (1840-1908)

See Figure 307 Book One

85. Scott, Sir Walter (1771-1832)

See Figures 308 - 309 Book One

Fig. 294 S
A mounted figure of Lord Raglan, on an oval titled base with raised capitals, his right sleeve across his chest, his left holding the reins, he wears a plumed hat, tunic with epaulettes, and trousers.
This figure pairs with Marshall Arnaud. See Figure 10 Book One or Omar Pasha (See Figure 252 Book One). There is another figure in this series, which pair with either of the above two; this is Abd-ul-Medjid (See Figure 03 Book One).
TITLE: LORD RAGLAN
HEIGHT: 8.5 Inches
PRICE: E.

86. Shaftsbury, Anthony Ashley Cooper (7th Earl) (1801-1885)

Fry, Elizabeth (1780-1845)
See Figures 310 -311 Book One and 312A -313A Book Three

87. Shakespeare, William (1564-1616)

Born at Stratford-upon-Avon, his father was a leading citizen of the town, his mother, Mary Arden, belonged to the landed gentry of Warwickshire. There is little known of his early life or schooling. He was probably educated at the local grammar school. In 1582, at the age of eighteen, he married Anne Hathaway, a farmer's daughter eight years his senior. Six months later she gave birth to their first child, Susanna, three years later she gave birth to twins, Hamnet and Judith. The next seven years of his life are somewhat sketchy, but one theory is that after being caught poaching deer on the estate of Sir Thomas Lucy, to avoid prosecution he left for London to seek his fortune. By 1592 he was established as a playwright and it is in this period that his greatest works were written. In 1599 The Globe Theatre was built in Southwark and in 1603 King James took the company under his patronage as the King's Men coming under the Royal Household. In 1613 The Globe burnt down during a performance of Henry VIII.
See Figures 314 - 326 Book One and 316 - 316A Book Three

There is another figure depicting Shakespeare, which is listed under Milton. John Milton and William Shakespeare standing beside a clock face/watchholder (See John Milton Figure 207 Book One)

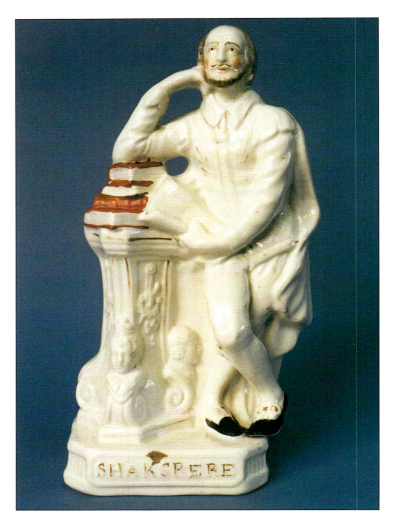

Fig. 320A.P
A figure of Shakespeare standing with crossed legs leaning on a pillar and holding a scroll in his left hand and pointing to it with his right. He wears a cloak, shirt, waistcoat, and knee breeches.
This figure pairs with John Milton (See Figure 202A Book Three).
HEIGHT: 7 Inches
PRICE: F.

Fig. 322.P
A figure of William Shakespeare standing cross-legged, his left hand across his waist pointing at a scroll that rests on a pillar, his right elbow leans on a pile of books that are on top of the pillar, he wears a cloak, doublet, knee breeches, and stockings. The base of the pillar is decorated with the heads of the monarchs Elizabeth I, Henry V, and Richard III. **This figure's source is the monument designed by William Kent, together with the statue by Peter Scheemaker that was erected in The Poets Corner in Westminster Abbey.**

There are illustrated a superb 18.5 inch version and a much debased 10.75 inch version, the smaller version is titled while the large version is not.
It is known that The Parr Factory made the large version; it is unlikely that they made the smaller version. Earlier versions may also be found that are very similar, differing only in decoration. These were made by Enoch Wood in the early 1800s. It is possible that Thomas Parr obtained the moulds from The Wood factory to make his figures.
This figure pairs with John Milton (See Figure 204 Book One).
TITLE: SHAKESPEARE (Small version only)
HEIGHT: 18.5 Inches, 10.75 Inches
PRICE: Large version: C, Small Version: G.

88. Simpson, Sir James (1792-1868)

See Figures 328 - 329 Book One

89. Singh, Gholab (1792-1857)

See Figure 331 Book One

90. Singh, Ranbir (1820-1885)

See Figure 330 Book One

91. Spurgeon, Charles Hadden (1834-1892)

See Figures 332 - 334 Book One

92. Tann, Baron von der (1815-1881)

See Figure 335 Book One

93. Van Amburgh, Isaac (1811-1187)

See Figure 336 Book One

94. Vincent de Paul, Saint (1576-1660)

See Figure 337 Book One

95. Voltaire, Jean Francois Maria Arouet de (1694-1778)

See Figures 338 - 339 Book One

95A. Walker (Badman), Johnnie (Dates Unknown)

See Figure 339A Book Three

96. Washington, George (1732-1799)

See Figures 340 - 344 Book One

97. Webb, Matthew (1848-1883)

See Figure 345 Book One

98. Wellington, Duke of (Arthur Wellesley) (1769-1852)

He was born at Upper Merrion Street, Dublin and was the third son of the Earl of Mornington. He was educated at Eton and Pignerol's Military Academy, Angers. He entered the army in 1787 as an ensign for the 73rd Regiment. His first military command came in 1794 and this was soon followed as a colonel in the Tippoo War in India. In 1803 he was appointed chief political and military agent in the Decccan and South Mahratta States, and after successfully dealing with a number of outbreaks of violence was knighted for his services.

In 1806 he returned to England and resigned his command and was returned as a Member of Parliament for Rye in Kent. In 1807 he was appointed the Chief Secretary for Ireland. With the threat of a French invasion he returned to the military and led a series of victories over the French. In 1814 he was appointed Ambassador to Paris and in 1815 he celebrated his historic victory over Napoleon Bonaparte at Waterloo.

He resumed his political career and from 1828-1830 became Prime Minister, resigning after disagreeing with electoral reform. From 1834-1835 he was Foreign Secretary under Peel, and supported Peel's reform of the Corn Laws. He died sitting in his chair at his home of Walmer Castle in Kent, and was buried at St. Paul's Cathedral next to Nelson.

See Figures 346 - 375 Book One and 351A Book Three

For other figures of the Duke of Wellington see Napoleon Bonaparte 1.

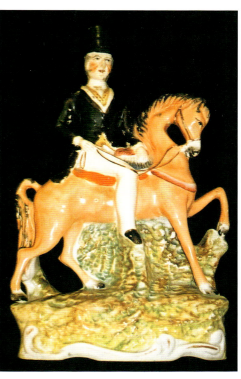

Fig. 351A
A figure of The Duke of Wellington mounted facing right; he wears a top hat, shirt, tie, jacket, and trousers and holds the reins in both hands, all on a rococo style base. **This is a very rare figure, only two are known.**
HEIGHT: 11.5 Inches
PRICE: D

Fig. 374A
A standing figure of The Duke of Wellington; he wears a military tunic, trousers, and knee boots. A large cloak is over his right shoulder and through his left arm. He holds a baton or scroll in his left hand. **The figure illustrated is unfinished; it has been fired with underglaze blue but no finishing enamel colours have been applied. It is also unique. This figure has never before been recorded.**
HEIGHT: 10.75 Inches
PRICE: For a unique unfinished figure, whatever a collector is prepared to pay.

99. Wesley, John (1703-1791)

See Figures 376 - 402 Book One and 379 - 402A Book Three

100. Williams, Sir William Fenwick (1800-1883)

See Figure 404 Book One

101. Windham, Sir Charles Ash (1810-1870)

See Figures 405 - 406 Book One

102. Wood, Jemmy (1756-1836)

See Figures 407 - 410 Book One

Chapter 1: Section 2
Portraits
British & Foreign Royalty

Listings highlighted in bold type contain additions and alterations which will be found in this addendum, all other Portraits will be found in *Books One and Three, Victorian Staffordshire Figures 1835-1875*.

1. Queen Victoria and Prince Albert

i. Victoria and Albert standing
ii. Victoria and Albert seated
iii. Victoria and Albert on horseback
iv. Victoria and Albert with the Royal Children

2. The Royal Children

3. The Royal Children on
Betrothal of Marriage

i. Victoria The Princess Royal, and Frederick William III of Prussia (1858)
ii. Albert Prince of Wales and Princess Alexandra of Denmark (1863)
iii. Princess Alice and Louis Duke of Hesse (1862)
iv. Princess Helena and Prince Christian of Schleswig-Holstein (1866)
v. Princess Louise and The Marquess of Lorne (1871)
vi. Alfred Duke of Edinburgh, and Marie of Russia (1874)

There are no examples of figures having being made for the marriages of Victoria's three youngest children, Arthur in 1879, Leopold in 1882, and Beatrice in 1885.

4. Other British Royalty

i. The Duke and Duchess of Cambridge
ii. King William III and Queen Mary II

5. Foreign Royalty

i. Bonaparte, Napoleon Joseph Charles Paul (Prince Napoleon)

ii. Napoleon Bonaparte III, Charles Louis, and Eugenie Empress of France
iii. Victor Emmanuel II, King of Sardinia and King of Italy
iv. Prince Frederick Charles of Prussia
v. Leopold I and Louise-Marie, King and Queen of The Belgian's
vi. William I, King of Prussia, and Queen Augusta

6. Alliance Groups

The following two categories are figures that include either Victoria or Albert allied with other prominent people.

i. Victoria Alliance
ii. Albert Alliance

1. Queen Victoria and Prince Albert

Victoria (Alexandrina Victoria) (1818-1901)

Born on May 24th 1818 at Kensington Palace, London to Edward and Victoria, the Duke and Duchess of Kent; the Duke was the fourth son of George III. She succeeded William IV. on June 20th 1837, marrying her first cousin, Prince Albert of Saxe-Coburg-Gotha, in 1840. In the first sixteen years of her marriage she bore nine children, being:

1. Victoria, The Princess Royal (1840-1901), who married Prince Frederick William in 1858.
2. Albert, Prince of Wales, later Edward VII (18411910), who married Princess Alexandra of Denmark in 1863
3. Alice (1843-1878), who married Prince Louis, Duke of Hesse, in 1862.
4. Alfred, Duke of Edinburgh (1844-1900), who married Marie of Russia in 1874.
5. Helena (1846-1923), who married Prince Christian of Schleswig-Holstein in 1866.
6. Louise (1847-1939), who married The Marquis of Lorne in 1871.
7. Arthur, Duke of Connaught (1850-1942), who married Louise of Prussia in 1879.
8. Leopold (1853-1884), who married Helen of Waldeck-Pyrmont in 1882.
9. Beatrice (1857-1947), who married Prince Henry of Battenberg in 1885.

Victoria reigned until her death in 1901; she became Empress of India in 1876 and celebrated both a golden and diamond jubilee.

As William IV had left no successor the remaining brothers who at the time were all childless had to provide an heir. Victoria's father, The Duke of Kent, at the age of fifty-two, against all expectations, sired Victoria. He died two years later.

As an interesting side note, there had been no history of Haemophilia in either The Duke of Kent's or his wife's families. This hereditary disease appeared in two of Victoria's children. The incidence of this disease in women is extremely rare; they are usually the carriers. Alice, the third child, carried the disease and, through her, spread it to many of the Royal Houses of Europe. Leopold, the eighth child, was born with and died of it.

There are three explanations as to how any of Victoria's children could have contracted the disease. One is unlikely and that was that it was a spontaneous outbreak in Victoria. The second even more unlikely is that Albert was not the father of either Alice or Leopold. The third is that The Duke of Kent was not Victoria's father, in which case Victoria was not the rightful heir to the throne, and history would have changed dramatically.

Had Victoria not succeeded, there would have been no Princess Royal, therefore no son of the Princess Royal, who became the Kaiser; without the Kaiser it is unlikely that the First World War would have taken place, in which case the Second World War would not have happened, and the world would now be a very different place.

Albert Francis Charles Augustus Emmanuel (1818-1861)

His father was Ernest, Duke of Saxe-Coburg-Gotha. Albert married Victoria, his first cousin, in 1840. Throughout their short marriage he helped Victoria in many of her duties, especially with advice during the Crimean War of 1854-1856. He also helped avoid war with the United States of America during the Trent affair. He died prematurely of Typhoid fever in 1861, aged only forty-two years. Victoria, who was devoted to Albert, stayed in mourning for him for the last forty years of her life.

i. Victoria and Albert Standing

See Figures 421 - 478 Book One and 433 - 480B Book Three

Figs. 411/412
A pair of figures of Albert and Victoria standing, he wearing a top hat, waistcoat, shirt with tie, long jacket, and trousers, and holding a biscuit in his right hand. To his left there is a pillar on which a basket of flowers stand. Victoria wears a bonnet, blouse, and long skirt, she holds a flower in her left hand, and her right arm is around a basket of flowers that stand on a pillar to her right. **This pair of figures was made by The Alpha factory in the late 1840s. They are very similar to other figures of Victoria and Albert also made by this factory (see Figs. 442 and 444, in Book One), a figure of Albert holding a biscuit was also made (see Fig. 542, in Book One). Usually but not invariably Albert is depicted with a moustache. Why the Royal couple should be portrayed with flower baskets is unknown, it is possible that they were not made as portrait figures as they have never been found titled, but merely decorative; but, what is certain is that they are far too expensively dressed to portray flower sellers.**
HEIGHT: 7 Inches
PRICE: Pair: E, Singles: F.

Figs. 413/414
A pair of figures of Albert and Victoria standing; he is bareheaded and wears a three quarter length coat, waistcoat, shirt, and trousers. His left hand is at his waist and his right holds a scroll. Victoria wears a long, low cut dress and holds a scroll in her right hand.
HEIGHT: 6 Inches
PRICE: Pair: F, Singles: G.

Figs. 415/416
A pair of figures of Albert and Victoria standing; he is bareheaded and wears a three-quarter length coat buttoned twice and trousers, his left hand is on his hip and his right rests on rockwork to his side. Victoria is also bareheaded and wears a dress with puff sleeves and cloak. She holds a book in her left hand and her right is held to her breast.
HEIGHT: 5.5 Inches
PRICE: Pair: E, Singles: F.

Figs. 417/418
A pair of figures of Albert and Victoria standing; he wears a military uniform of high-necked jacket with epaulettes, a sash over his shoulder, and another at his waist, and a large cloak and trousers. His left hand holds a sword and his right is on his hip. Victoria is crowned and wears a necklace, ermine edged cloak, bodice with sash, and long dress.
HEIGHT: 8.5 Inches
PRICE: Pair: E, Singles: F.

Fig. 419
A figure of Victoria standing, wearing a bonnet, short cloak, coat, and long dress. She holds an umbrella in her right hand.
A very rare and previously unrecorded figure; a pair would have at one time existed. Fig. 420 has been reserved for it.
HEIGHT: 8.5 Inches
PRICE: E.

Fig. 418A
A figure of Albert standing; he is bareheaded and wears a military uniform of cloak, jacket with epaulettes, and a sash across his chest. His right hand is held at his waist and his left rests on the hilt of a sword.
There is a pair to this figure of Victoria. Fig. 418B has been reserved for it.
HEIGHT: 7.5 Inches
PRICE: Pair: F, Singles: G.

Figs. 477/477A/477B
A pair of figures of Albert and Victoria standing; he is bareheaded and wears a shirt, waistcoat, jacket, and trousers.
His left hand is held to his chest and his right holds a book. Victoria wears a low-fronted dress and a shawl is across her shoulders. She holds a small handbag in her left hand.
There are illustrated two pairs of figures. Albert is the same in both sizes; the model of Victoria has been substantially changed, and it is possible that when the larger size was made they were meant to portray another couple.
HEIGHT: 7.75 & 9 Inches
PRICE: Pairs E, Singles: F.

Fig. 480B
A group figure of Victoria and Albert standing on either side of a clock face; Victoria with her right hand holding a scroll, her left raised to her chest, she wears a crown, and long split dress. Albert's right arm rests on the clock face, his left is on his hip; he wears a shirt with tie, jacket, waistcoat, and trousers.
HEIGHT: 7.5 Inches
PRICE: E.

ii. Victoria and Albert Seated

See Figures 481 - 495 Book One and 487 - 497 Book Three

Figs. 498/499
A pair of figures of Victoria and Albert seated on chairs; she is crowned and wears a large ermine edged cloak, blouse, and long dress. He wears a jacket, waistcoat, large ermine edged cloak, and trousers.
HEIGHT: 5 Inches
PRICE: Pair: F, Singles: G.

iii. Victoria and Albert on Horseback

See also Figures 501 - 517 Book One and 502B - 519 Book Three

Figs. 503A/503B
A pair of figures of Albert and Victoria on horseback; he wears a plumed hat, military jacket, and breeches with boots. His left hand rests on the horse's mane and his right on his leg. Victoria wears a hat with a feather, jacket, and long skirt. Her right hand rests on the horse's mane and her left holds the reins.
HEIGHT: 7.25 Inches
PRICE: Pair: G, Singles: H.

Figs. 511/512
A pair of figures of Victoria and Albert on horseback, Victoria with her left hand resting on the horse's mane, her right holding the reins. She wears a top hat with scarf and long dress. Albert with his right arm outstretched, his left holding the reins. He wears a top hat, long jacket, neckerchief, waistcoat, and trousers. **These figures can be found in two sizes, 9 Inches and 8 Inches. There are illustrated an eight inch pair with horse's legs raised and a 9 inch single with the horse's leg straight down.**
HEIGHT: 9 Inches, 8 Inches
PRICE: Pair: F, Singles: G.

Figs. 520/520A
A pair of figures of Albert and Victoria mounted on horseback; he wears a plumed helmet, jacket with epaulettes, trousers, and knee boots. His right hand is on his knee and his left holds the reins. Victoria wears a plumed hat and long dress. Her right hand is on the horse's head and her left holds the reins. Both horses have large multi-coloured saddlecloths.
As with a number of theses figures that have never been found titled, they may have been made to portray Sir Robert and Lady Sale.
HEIGHT: 7.5 Inches
PRICE: Pair: F, Singles: G.

iv. Victoria and Albert with the Royal Children

In this section there is compiled a comprehensive account of all the figures produced of Victoria and Albert with the Royal children. In many cases they are described as with 'a child'. This is because there is no definite proof as to which of the Royal children they were. As the Princess Royal and the Prince of Wales were born less than a two years apart, it seems reasonable to assume that the figures were used for both births.

Only where there is definite proof have we identified a particular Royal child, i.e. in some cases the Prince of Wales is wearing a hat with three feathers.

See Figures 521 - 552 Book One and 534 - 545 Book Three

Fig. 521
A group figure of Queen Victoria seated in a chair, her hands in her lap, her foot on a cushion. She wears a mop cap, bodice, and long skirt. Standing behind and to her left is The Prince of Wales, his right hand resting on the back of Victoria's chair, his left on his hip, wearing a buttoned jacket and trousers. Kneeling in front of him is Princess Alexandria, wearing a sleeved jacket and long skirt, holding in her lap the baby Duke of Clarence.
This figure is very rare, only three examples are known. Because of its subject matter, it has become known as 'The Three Generations'. It was made by The Parr Factory in 1864.
HEIGHT: 9 Inches
PRICE: C.

Figs. 520B/520C
A pair of figures of Prince Albert and Queen Victoria, each standing with one of their children, Albert stands bareheaded wearing a shirt with cravat, waistcoat, long jacket, and trousers. His left hand is placed on the head of a small boy who stands beside him. Victoria wears a poke bonnet, long dress with a shawl collar, and holds a baby in her arms.
This pair of figures was previously misidentified as Lord Shaftsbury and Elizabeth Fry. The authors are now certain that they portray Albert and Victoria with two of their children
HEIGHT: 7.5 Inches
PRICE: Pair: E, Singles: F.

Figs. 526/527
A pair of figures of Victoria with a child on her lap and Albert seated on chairs, he with both hands in his lap, his right hand holding a book, his left foot resting on a cushion. He wears an ermine edged cloak, jacket, neckerchief, waistcoat, and trousers. She wears a crown, ermine edged cloak, and a long dress. Her left foot rests on a cushion.
This pair of figures is impressed on the reverse Lloyd Shelton and are the earliest known figures with a maker's mark.
HEIGHT: 6.75
PRICE: Pair: E, Singles: F.

Fig. 550
The authors are now of the opinion that this is not a figure of Queen Victoria. It has been relocated with its pair as Fig. 1439C.

Fig. 552
The title of this figure is Queen of England not Queen Victoria.

2. The Royal Children

See Figures 561 - 642 Book One and 553 - 635A Book Three

Figs. 565/566
A pair of figures of the Prince of Wales and the Princess Royal standing by cushioned tables, the prince with his right hand to his side holding a hat, his left resting on the top of a toy boat. He wears a jacket, neckerchief, waistcoat, and trousers. The Princess has her left hand to her side holding a hat, her right holds a bird, she wears a blouse, skirt, and pantaloons.
This pair can be found either titled or untitled on round and stepped bases and in two sizes, all illustrated.
TITLE: PRINCE - PRINCESS
HEIGHT: 6 Inches., 3.5 Inches
PRICE: Pair 6 Inches: F, Singles: G, Pair 3.5 Inches: G, Singles: H.

Figs. 554/553
A pair of figures of The Princess Royal and The Prince of Wales, both standing by Thrones, she with her left hand holding a whirligig, wearing a long tunic, skirt, and knickers, he holding a flag in his right hand, a sailing boat is on the throne, his left hand to his head, wearing a boater, jacket, shirt, neckerchief, waistcoat, and trousers. An anchor is to his left.
HEIGHT: 7.75 Inches
PRICE: Pair: F, Singles: G.

Fig. 574
A group figure of The Princess Royal and The Prince of Wales asleep in a dual sofa with crowns above, a large blanket covers them. Above an angel stands with arms and wings outstretched. This figure can be found in two sizes, the 8.5 inch version is illustrated.
HEIGHT: 9.5 Inches & 8.5 Inches
PRICE: F.

Figs. 583A/583B
A pair of The Royal Children on pony back of The Prince of Wales and The Princess Royal. He wears a plumed hat, shirt, jacket, and trousers. She wears a riding hat and long dress.
Many figures of children have been attributed as being of The Royal Children; with this pair the authors are certain that this is who they portray. They are by the same modeller/factory as produced Figs. 505/506 Book One and form a quartet with them.
HEIGHT: 6 Inches
PRICE: Pair: E, Singles: F.

Fig. 575
A spill vase group previously attributed as being of The Princess Royal and The Prince of Wales asleep under a tree. Both are similarly dressed in a skirt and blouse. An angel with wings closed and hands clasped stands behind the pair and a bird is in the tree.
The authors having examined this figure in detail and are now of the opinion that this does not portray the Royal Children. It is similar in most respects to Fig. 1139A Book Three and 1139B and is probably a melodramatic portrayal of 'Babes in the Wood'.
HEIGHT: 8.5
PRICE: G.

Figs. 584/585
A pair of figures of The Princess Royal and The Prince of Wales on pony back, the Princess with her left hand across her chest, her right to her side, wearing a plumed hat, dress, and pantaloons, the Prince with his left hand to his side, his right across his chest, wearing a plumed hat, tunic, and trousers.
Two versions of these figures can be found, the main difference being that the children both have a separately moulded arm.
HEIGHT: 5.5. Inches
PRICE: Pair: F, Singles: G.

Figs. 613/614
A pair of figures of The Prince of Wales and The Princess Royal seated holding their younger brother and sister; he is bareheaded and wears a shirt, cravat, long coat, and trousers and his younger brother sits in his lap. She is also bareheaded and wears a blouse and long skirt with knickers; her younger sister sits in her lap.
These figures can be found in two sizes, both illustrated. These figures were previously misidentified as being of Lord Shaftsbury and Elizabeth Fry. The authors are now certain that they portray The Prince of Wales and The Princess Royal with their younger siblings.
HEIGHT: 6 Inches, 7.5 Inches
PRICE: Pair: D, Singles: E.

Fig. 634A
A figure of The Prince of Wales standing, his right hand raised holding a staff, his left arm leaning on a trunk, his hand rests on his chin, wearing highland attire of a bonnet, jacket, scarf, kilt with sporran, and shoes with stockings.
Both sizes of figures are illustrated. The smaller figure can be found without a separately moulded right arm. It would have been more expensive to produce a figure with separate moulds and it is probable that the figure with an extra mould was produced first; the moulds would then have subsequently been simplified to reduce production costs. The authors are aware of a number of figures where this simplification has occurred.
HEIGHT: 13.5 & 15.75 Inches
PRICE: F.

Figs. 628/628A
A pair of figures of The Prince of Wales and The Princess Royal standing; he wears a frilled shirt, tunic, knee breeches with boots, a large scarf is over his shoulders, and he holds a plumed hat in his right hand while his left leans on a pillar to his side. At his feet, seated on a cushion, is a spaniel. She wears a tunic, long dress, a scarf is around her waist, she holds her right hand up to two birds, which are perched on a pillar to her side. Both figures are on rococo bases.
These figures can be found in two sizes. There is another figure (See Figure 627 Book One), which can pair with Figure 628 or it is possible they were made as a triptych. They are all finely modelled and quite rare.
HEIGHT: 9.75 & 10.5 Inches
PRICE: Pair: D, Singles: E.

3. The Royal Children on Betrothal of Marriage

See Figures 641 - 714 Book One and 663 - 699 Book Three

i. Victoria, Princess Royal, and Prince Frederick III of Prussia

Victoria Adelaide Mary Louise (Princess Royal of Great Britain and German Empress) (1840-1901)
Prince Frederick III of Prussia (second German Emperor and King of Prussia) (1831-1888)

ii. Albert, Prince of Wales, and Princess Alexandra of Denmark

Albert Edward, Prince of Wales, (18411910)
Edward VII (1901-1910)

Princess Alexandra of Denmark (1844-1925)

The eldest daughter of King Christian IX of Denmark, she married Albert Prince of Wales in 1863.

Louis of Hesse (Grand-Duke of Hesse-Darmstadt) (1837-1892)

Married Princess Alice in 1862 became Grand-Duke on the death of his uncle in 1877.

Fig. 677

A spill vase figure of Princess Alice and Louis of Hesse. They stand on either side of a tree trunk, which forms the spill vase. She wears a plumed hat, short coat, and layered skirt, and holds an ermine edged muff in her right hand, and her left holds Louis' hand. He wears a hat, shirt with tie, waistcoat, jacket, and trousers; his left hand is in his trouser pocket.

A previously unrecorded figure where there are only the figures and an absence of any items; this usually indicates a portrait figure, and both her dress and facial features are similar to known portraits of the pair.
HEIGHT: 11 Inches
PRICE: F.

Fig. 669

A group figure of Princess Alexandra of Denmark and the Prince of Wales standing on a titled base with raised gilt capitals, she with her left arm through his right, her bonnet is over her right arm; she wears a jacket and long dress, he with his right arm across his waist holding a pair of gloves and holding a top hat in his left hand. He wears a tie, waistcoat, jacket, and trousers.

This figure can be found in at least five sizes, two versions illustrated with different titles. The figure can also be found without a title.
TITLE: PRINCE AND PRINCESS
HEIGHT: 5, 8, 10, 12, and 15.5 Inches.
PRICE: F.

iii. Princess Alice and Prince Louis of Hesse

Alice Maud Mary (Grand-Duchess of Hesse) (1843-1878)

The second daughter of Victoria and Prince Albert, she married Prince Louis of Hesse in 1862 and became Grand-Duchess on the death of Louis' uncle in 1877.

Fig. 678

A group figure of Princess Alice and Prince Louis of Hesse standing; she is bareheaded and wears a jacket and long skirt with an apron, her hands are clasped in front, and over her arm is suspended a hat with flowers. Prince Louis has his arm around her and wears a shirt with tie, jacket, short trousers, and ankle boots.

A very rare and previously unrecorded figure.
HEIGHT: 8 Inches
PRICE: F.

Figs. 690/690A/690B
A group figure of Princess Alice and Louis of Hess together with a pair, they both stand, she with both hands across her waist holding a muff and wearing a bonnet, jacket, and double fronted skirt. He wears a hat, shirt with tie, waistcoat, jacket, and trousers. His left hand is tucked into his waistcoat and his right leans on a pillar and holds a walking stick.
The group figure is very similar, other than there is no pillar and they are arm in arm.
HEIGHT: 9.5 Inches
PRICE: Pair: E, Singles: F, Group: E.

Fig. 700
A group figure of Princess Alice and Louis of Hesse; they stand on a cushion decorated with swags and tassels, a filled cornucopia is at her feet with he holding her hand. She wears a hat, short jacket, and skirt with an apron, and her right hand is to her chest. He wears a long jacket, shirt with tie, and knee breeches.
A rare and previously unrecorded figure.
HEIGHT: 9 Inches
PRICE: F.

iv. Princess Helena and Prince Christian of Schlewig-Holstein

Helena Augusta Victoria (1846-1923)

Prince Christian of Schlewig-Holstein (1831-1917)

v. Princess Louise and The Marquess of Lorne

Louise Caroline Alberta, Duchess of Argyll (1848-1939)

John Douglass Sutherland Campbell, Marquess of Lorne, 9th Duke of Argyll (1845-1914)

vi. Alfred, The Duke of Edinburgh and Marie of Russia

Alfred Ernest Albert, Duke of Edinburgh (1844-1900)

Marie-Alexandrovna, Duchess of Edinburgh (1853-1920)

4. Other British Royalty

See Figures 721 - 728 Book One and 699A - 705 Book Three

i. The Duke and Duchess of Cambridge

Cambridge, Duke of, George William Frederick Charles (1819-1904)

Farebrother, Louise (1816-1890)

ii. King William III and Queen Mary II

King William III (1650-1702)

The son of William II, Prince of Orange, and Mary, daughter of Charles I of England. In 1677 he married his cousin Mary, daughter of James II of England. By 1688 the people of England could not accept a Catholic Sovereign; they looked to William, a Protestant, to take the throne. William arrived at Torbay and after Parliament had declared the throne vacant, he and Mary were invested as King and Queen. James II fled to France, where a year later with the help of French troops he attempted to invade Ireland. Defeated at the Battle of the Boyne in 1689 he returned to France and stayed there until his death in 1701. William established the Bank of England and helped mould the British constitution. He died childless, passing the throne to Mary's sister Anne.

Queen Mary II (1662-1694)

The daughter of James I and Anne Hyde, she was brought up a Protestant. She married William III in 1677, arriving in England in 1689 to take the throne with her husband. She died prematurely at the age of thirty-two of smallpox.

Figs. 727/728
A pair of figures of Queen Mary and King William III on horseback, she with her left arm across her chest, her right holding the reins, wearing a hat with headscarf, bodice, and long skirt. He has his right hand resting on the horses mane holding a scroll, his left to his side, a sword is attached to the saddlecloth, he wears a plumed hat, ermine sleeved jacket, breeches, and knee boots.
This pair can be found in two sizes on the smaller version. The saddle cloth is shorter and it is not usually titled. A titled large pair and a smaller single are illustrated.
TITLE: QUEEN MARY - KING WILLIAM III
HEIGHT: 10.5 Inches and 9 Inches
PRICE: Pair: E, Singles: F.

5. Foreign Royalty

See Figures 731 - 765 Book One and 737 - 755 Book Three

i. Bonaparte, Napoleon Joseph Charles Paul (Prince Napoleon) (1822-1891)

Commanded the French troops in the Crimean War of 1854-1856. In 1859 he married the daughter of Victor Emmanuel II of Italy, princess Clotilde. After the Second Empire crumbled in 1870 he left for England but returned in 1872. After the death of the Prince Imperial during the Zulu campaign of 1879, he became heir to the Bonaparte dynasty along with his father, but in 1866 they were both exiled to Italy.

Fig. 731
A figure of Prince Napoleon on horseback on a titled gilt lined base with raised gilt capitals, his hands hold the reins and he wears a cocked hat, tunic with epaulettes, breeches, and knee boots.
An extremely rare figure that pairs with The Duke of Cambridge, Figure 725 Book One.
TITLE: PRINCE NAPOLEON
HEIGHT: 8 Inches
PRICE: F.

ii. Bonaparte III, Charles Louis Napoleon (Napoleon III) (1808-1873)

Eugenie, Empress of France (1826-1920)

Eugene, Louis Jean Joseph (Prince Imperial) (1856-1879)

The third son of the King of Holland, spent many of his early years imprisoned after unsuccessful attempts at securing the French throne. Following the overthrow of Louis-Philippe in 1848 he was able to return to France and with a coup d'etat in 1851, he took the throne and was proclaimed Emperor. He married Eugenie d'Montijo in 1853 who gave him a son, Eugene Louis Jean Joseph (Prince Imperial), who fought alongside his father in the Franco-Prussian War of 1870. He came to England but later died in the Zulu Campaign of 1879.

He became allied to the English and Turks during the Crimean War (1854-1856) and supported them in campaigns in Austria and China. After his surrender at Sedan during the Franco-Prussian War of 1870, the second Empire crumbled and once again France became a republic. In 1871 he fled to England and spent the remainder of his life in Chislehurst Kent.

Eugene Louis Jean Joseph (Prince Imperial) (1856-1879). He fought alongside his father in the Franco-Prussian War of 1870, he came to England but later died in the Zulu Campaign of 1879.

The following Figures of Napoleon Bonaparte III are included in the Albert alliance section in Book One.
Figs. 771, 772, 773, 774, 775, all of Napoleon Bonaparte III and Prince Albert, and Figs. 776/777 Napoleon III and Prince Albert mounted.

The following Figures of Napoleon Bonaparte III are included in the Victoria alliance section in Book One.
Fig. 781 Napoleon Bonaparte III, Victoria and Victor Emmanuel II – THE ALLIED POWERS
Figs. 782, 783 Napoleon Bonaparte III, Victoria, and Abd-ul-Medjid – FRANCE – ENGLAND – TURKEY
Figs. 784, 785, 786 Napoleon Bonaparte III, Victoria, and Abd-ul-Medjid – NAPOLEON – VICTORIA – SULTAN
Figs. 787, 788, 789 Napoleon Bonaparte III, Victoria, and Abd-ul-Medjid –FRANCE – ENGLAND – TURKEY
Fig. 790 Napoleon Bonaparte III and Victoria – **QUEEN – EMPEROR**

Fig. 732
A bust of Eugene Louis Jean Joseph, The Prince Imperial.
This figure was previously misidentified as Lord Byron.
HEIGHT: 6. 75 Inches
PRICE: E.

Figs. 740/741
A pair of figures of Napoleon III and Empress Eugenie seated on thrones on square titled bases with raised black capitals, Napoleon III seated cross-legged with his right hand to his side holding a plumed hat, his left resting on his leg, wearing a tunic, breeches, knee boots, and a sash across his chest. The Empress holds the Prince Imperial. She wears a long dress and her right foot rests on a cushion.
TITLE: EMPEROR - EMPRESS OF FRANCE
HEIGHT: 8.5 Inches
PRICE: Pair: E, Singles: F.

Fig. 750S
A figure of Napoleon III on horseback on a titled base with raised gilt capitals, his left hand rests on the horse's mane, holding the reins, his right resting on his leg, he wears a plumed hat, tunic with epaulettes, breeches, knee boots, and a sash across his waist.
This figure is in the same series as Prince Bismark, VonMolke, and Marshall Bazaine, Figs. 12, 208, 11 Book One.
TITLE: NAPOLEON
HEIGHT: 13 Inches
PRICE: G.

iii. Victor Emmanuel II (1820-1878) (King of Sardinia 1849-1861 and King of Italy 1861-1878)

The following Figures of Victor Emmanuel II are included in the Victoria Alliance section under Royalty.
Victor Emmanuel II, Victoria and Napoleon Bonaparte III - THE ALLIED POWERS.
Victor Emmanuel II, Victoria - QUEEN & KING OF SARDINIA
Victor Emmanuel II, Victoria (See Figs. 791, 791, and 792 Book One)

iv. Frederick Charles, Prince of Prussia
(1828-1925)

Figs. 778/778A
A pair of figures of Napoleon Bonaparte III and Empress Eugenie on horseback, his right hand raised to his head saluting, his left holding the reins, he wears a plumed hat, tunic with epaulettes, breeches, and knee boots. She wears a hat with feather and scarf, blouse, and long dress, one hand holds the reins, and the other is in her lap. **Now that the pair has come to light it can now be said with certainty that this pair is a smaller, untitled version of Figures 743/744 in Book One.**
HEIGHT: 8.5 Inches
PRICE: Pair: F, Singles: G.

v. Leopold I and Louise-Marie, King and Queen of the Belgians

Leopold I, King of the Belgians (1790-1865)

Louise-Marie, Queen of the Belgians (1812-1850)

vi. William I, Seventh King of Prussia and First German Emperor (1797-1888)

The son of Frederick-William II, in 1829 he married princess Augusta of Saxe-Weimar. In 1861 he succeeded his brother Frederick-William IV to the throne. In 1870 he defeated the French during the Franco-Prussian War and was proclaimed the first Emperor of Germany. His son Prince Frederick William married the Princess Royal the eldest daughter of Queen Victoria and Prince Albert in 1858.

Augusta, Queen of Prussia (1811-1890)

Daughter of the Grand-Duke of Saxe-Weimar, married William in 1829.

Figs. 764/765
A pair of figures of William I, King of Prussia and Queen Augusta standing on titled bases with gilt script, he with his right hand resting on his hip, his left leaning on an ermine edged cloak which is covering a pillar, he wears a tunic with epaulettes and trousers, and a sash is across his chest and another around his waist. She has her left hand to her side holding a handkerchief and wears an ermine edged cloak, bodice, and long tiered dress.
A smaller 15 inch version of these figures can be found, the main difference being that the titles are in raised capitals as opposed to gilt script. They are also invariably in the white with little or no decoration. Sampson Smith made all of these figures.
TITLE: KING OF PRUSSIA - QUEEN OF PRUSSIA
HEIGHT: 15.75 & 15 Inches
PRICE: Pair: F, Singles: G.

4. Alliance Groups

i. Albert Alliance

With the outbreak of the war in the Crimea (1854-1856) against the Russians, the Alliance of Britain, France, and Turkey proved a very popular source of inspiration for the potters.

Figs. 776/777
A pair of figures of Napoleon Bonaparte III and Albert on horseback, Napoleon with his right hand raised to his head, his left holding the reins, wearing a plumed hat, tunic with epaulettes, breeches, and knee boots, with a sash around his waist. Albert with his right hand holding the reins, his left to his side, wearing a cocked hat, tunic with epaulettes, breeches, and knee boots, with a sash across his chest.
The figure of Napoleon is a smaller version of Figure 743 Book One titled EMPEROR which pairs with a mounted figure of Eugenie titled EMPRESS.
HEIGHT: 8 Inches
PRICE: Pair: E, Singles: F.

ii. Victoria Alliance

Fig. 796
A figure of Albert with both hands to his side, his left foot resting on a cushion, wearing a tunic, with epaulettes, trousers, and a sash across his chest. Below and at his feet are a lion and a unicorn.
HEIGHT: 7 Inches
PRICE: G.

Chapter 2:
Naval and Military

With the advent of war with the Russians in the Crimea (1854-1856), a new market opened up for the potters. With this major event constantly in the news, the demand and interest in naval and military figures abounded. The British were allied with the French and Turkish forces and figures were made of commanding officers as well as the foot soldiers and sailors of all three armies.

The majority of the figures in this chapter are of that period, but having established a market, figures were than made relating to the Indian Mutiny of 1857, the Anglo-French War scare of 1860 and the Franco-Prussian War of 1870.

Figures continued to be made commemorating later conflicts including the Boer War, but by that time the quality of the figures had diminished and the figures were often badly modelled, undecorated, usually in the white with applied harsh bright gold colouring details of these figures will be found in our book *Victorian Staffordshire Figures 1875 - 1962*.

Listings highlighted in bold type contain additions and alterations which will be found in this addendum. All other Portraits will be found in *Books One and Three, Victorian Staffordshire Figures 1835-1875*.

This Chapter has been divided into the following sections:
i. Naval and Military
ii. Naval
iii. Military
iv. Other Allied Figures

i. Naval and Military

See Figures 801 - 830 Book One and 814A - 820 Book Three

Figs. 808A/808B
A pair of figures of a soldier and sailor standing, the soldier wears a helmet, tunic, and trousers, with a sword to his side. To his right, on a brick emplacement, is a cannon above which are two flags; below at his feet is a drum. The sailor wears a hat, open neck shirt, and trousers; his left arm rests on a cannon mounted on wheels and above the cannon are two flags.
A very rare pair, previously unrecorded, probably unique.
HEIGHT: 7.5 Inches
PRICE: Pair: D, Singles: F.

Fig. 813
A reversible figure of an English sailor and a French soldier, standing with flags on either side, the sailor with his right arm raised holding the flag, his left hand resting on his hip, wearing a hat, shirt with tie, jacket, and trousers. The French soldier with his right arm raised holding the flag, his left resting on his hip, wearing a helmet, tunic with epaulettes, and trousers.
This figure can be found in two sizes, both illustrated.
HEIGHT: 9 Inches, 4.5 Inches
PRICE: 9 Inch: E, 4.5 Inch: F.

ii. Naval
See Figures 836 - 874 Book One and 835 - 873A Book Three

Fig. 831
A group figure of a sailor seated on rockwork asleep wearing a jacket, shirt with tie, and trousers. He is barefooted and holds a flag under his right arm, his head rests on his hand that rests on his raised knee. To his right there is an arch under which a stream flows and, kneeling on rockwork, a woman is praying.
This figure portrays the sailor dreaming of home and his wife praying for his safe return.
HEIGHT: 8.5 Inches
PRICE: F.

Fig. 832A
A group figure of a sailor and his girl, both standing. She is wearing a hat with feather, blouse, jacket, and skirt with an apron; he wears a sailor's suit of hat, shirt, and trousers, his right hand is on her shoulder and between them is a flag.
As both are standing in a dancing pose with their legs crossed, this figure may be of theatrical inspiration.
HEIGHT: 7.5 Inches
PRICE: G.

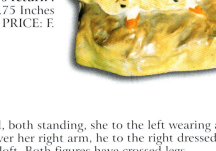

Fig. 832B
A group of a sailor and his girl, both seated. She wears a hat with feathers, jacket tied with a scarf, and a long skirt. She holds a cup in her right hand and her left is around the sailor who wears a hat, open neck shirt with tie, jacket, and trousers; a flag is through his left arm and he holds a bottle in his left hand while his right arm is around his girl.
A portrayal of 'The Sailor's return'.
HEIGHT: 8.75 Inches
PRICE: F.

Fig. 832
A group figure of a sailor and his girl, both standing, she to the left wearing a hat, blouse, and skirt, with a scarf over her right arm, he to the right dressed in a sailor's uniform holding a flag aloft. Both figures have crossed legs.
These figures are probably of theatrical inspiration.
HEIGHT: 6 Inches
PRICE: G.

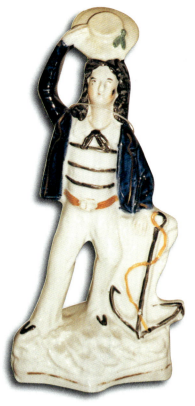

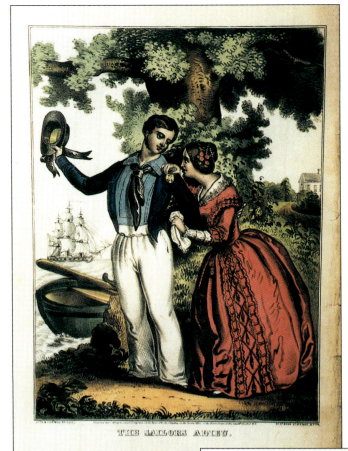

Fig. 833
A figure of a sailor standing, wearing a jacket, shirt with tie, and belted trousers. He holds his hat in the air and a large anchor rests to his left.
This figure is similar in construction to a number of naval figures and it no doubt has a pair that could be a girl, another sailor or a soldier; it is, however, at present unrecorded. Fig. 833A has been reserved for it.
HEIGHT: 8.5 Inches
PRICE: E.

Fig. 836. SO
There are illustrated a pair of newly discovered prints, one titled 'The Sailor's Return' and the other 'The Sailor's Adieu'. Whilst not the actual sources, these images could well be the inspiration for figures 836 and 890 Book One. The clothes of the sailor in one and the girl in the other are remarkably similar to these figures.

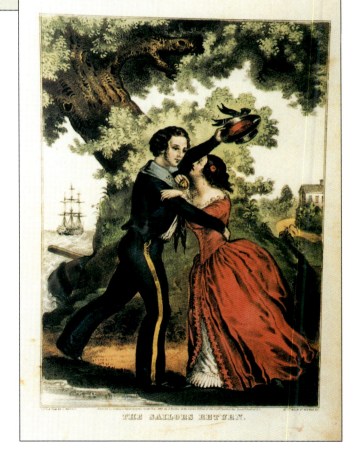

Fig. 834
A figure of a sailor seated, dressed in a hat, shirt, tie, and trousers. His jacket is under his leg. He forms the handle of a pot, the top of which appears to be a coiled rope and the base of which is adorned with an anchor.
HEIGHT: 4 Inches
PRICE: F.

Fig. 840A
A group figure of a sailor and his girl, both seated, she wears a brimmed hat, blouse, and long skirt, and holds a cup in her right hand. He wears a sailor's suit of hat, jacket, open neck shirt, and flared trousers. He holds a bottle in his left hand. HEIGHT: 8 Inches
PRICE: F.

Fig. 844A
A group figure of a sailor and his wife, both standing; he wears a hat, jacket, shirt, and trousers. His right elbow rests on an oar that is by his side. She wears a hat, blouse, jacket, and long dress with an apron, and a basket is over her left arm. On the floor between them is another basket filled with what appears to be shellfish.
It is possible that he portrays a fisherman rather than a sailor.
HEIGHT: 10.5 Inches
PRICE: F.

Fig. 841A
A group figure of a sailor and his girl, both standing with their legs crossed. He rests his head on hers and wears a sailor's uniform. His hat is held in his left hand. She wears a bodice and skirt and carries a basket of fruit in her right hand. HEIGHT: 8.5 Inches
PRICE: F.

Fig. 846A
A group figure of a sailor and his lass; she stands wearing a brimmed hat, ermine edged cloak, bodice, and short skirt with an apron. He is cuddling her with his right arm around her; he wears a sailor's outfit of jacket, shirt with tie, and long trousers, and he holds his hat against his leg in his left hand. **A very rare and previously unrecorded figure portraying 'The Sailor's Return'.** HEIGHT: 9.5 Inches
PRICE: E.

Fig. 846B
A group figure of a sailor and his lass; he stands with his left arm around her shoulders wearing a hat, shirt with tie, jacket, and long trousers. He holds his pack in his right hand. She wears a brimmed hat, bodice, and long skirt, and holds a basket of fish in her left hand. Her right arm is around his shoulders.
HEIGHT: 8 Inches
PRICE: F.

Fig. 852A
A group figure of a sailor seated wearing brimmed hat, open necked shirt, and trousers. His left hand rests on his knee and in his right he holds a drinking vessel on the ground. Between his legs a bottle rests. On his left side a small boy stands who wears an open neck shirt and trousers. The boy's jacket is draped over his left shoulder. There is an object in his left hand and another at his waist.
Exactly what this figure portrays is not clear; it is improbable that he is a begging sailor as he would be unlikely to receive alms if he was seated drinking alcohol. This figure is extremely rare; the figure illustrated is the only one known.
HEIGHT: 6.25 Inches
PRICE: E.

Fig. 848A
A figure of a sailor standing with both hands on his hips wearing a sailor's suit of hat, open neck shirt with tie, and belted trousers. **This figure is similar to Fig. 848 Book One other than he is quite slim as opposed to the others being quite fat.**
HEIGHT: 10 Inches
PRICE: F.

Fig. 868A
A group figure of a girl and a sailor standing on either side of a gravestone. She wears a hat with a feather, blouse with a sash across her chest, and a long skirt and holds flowers in her apron. He wears a short jacket, open neck shirt with tie, waistcoat, and trousers, with a scarf hanging down at his side. His left hand holds his lapel and in his right is a handkerchief. There is an unidentified object at the base of the gravestone.
A very rare figure; the markings on the gravestone are illegible and are probably the result of the decorator being illiterate.
HEIGHT: 8.25 Inches
PRICE: F.

Fig. 875
A double arbour figure of a standing sailor and his girl, both beneath one arbour, he dressed in typical sailor's attire holding a spade in his right hand, she wearing a blouse and skirt with an apron, and a basket of fruit over her right arm. Beside them under another arbour are steps leading up to a small gate.
This is another version of 'The Sailor's Return'.
HEIGHT: 9.75 Inches
PRICE: E.

Figs. 873B/873C
A pair of standing figures of a sailor and girl, she wears a hat, bodice, blouse with puff sleeves, and a skirt. He wears a typical sailor's uniform of hat, shirt with tie, waistcoat, short jacket, and trousers. He holds a moneybag in his left hand and his right is on his hip.
These figures are modelled and decorated in the round and date to about 1840.
HEIGHT: 6 Inches
PRICE: Pair: F, Singles: G.

Fig. 876
A figure of a sailor standing cross-legged wearing a boater, shirt with cravat, jacket, and trousers. His left hand rests on a large anchor and his right on his hip.
This figure has a pair of a woman standing with a basket of oysters at her feet and one in her hand. Fig. 876A has been reserved for it.
HEIGHT: 7.25 Inches
PRICE: F.

iii. Military

See Figures 880 - 925 Book One and 878 - 930A Book Three

Fig. 877
A group figure of a soldier and his girl both standing arm in arm, she to the left wearing a blouse and long skirt with a very large scarf draped over her shoulders, he to the right wearing a military uniform of cap, tunic, and trousers, with a sword at his side and a sash across his chest. He has one leg in front and one behind a small fence.
This figure is another very rare version of the 'Soldier's Return'.
HEIGHT: 8.75 Inches
PRICE: E.

Fig. 877A
A standing group figure of a soldier and his girl, he dressed in full highland attire of plumed hat, red jacket with a sash over his shoulder, sporran, and kilt, she wears a bodice, jacket with a sash over her shoulder, and long skirt. She holds both hands to her waist while he has his right arm around her waist and his left on his hip. **This figure is a previously unrecorded and very rare depiction of the 'Soldier's Return'.**
HEIGHT: 8.5 Inches
PRICE: E.

Fig. 896A
A spill vase figure of a soldier and his girl seated; he is bareheaded and wears a military type jacket, shirt, breeches, and knee boots. His left arm is around the girl and his right holds her wrist. She is also bareheaded and wears a bodice and long dress. A basket is at her feet and a fence is behind him. A tree trunk to her left forms the spill. This group is probably a portrayal of 'The Soldier's Return'.
The figure illustrated has been over painted, at a later date, and the man given a blue jacket. It is possible that the man portrayed is wearing a naval uniform, in which case the figure probably portrays The Sailor's Return. A copy of this figure was made into a fake portrait; the man was given a naval hat and the base was titled 'NELSON & EMMA' in black capitals (See Plate 6).
HEIGHT: 10 Inches
PRICE: F.

Fig. 930A
A figure of a standing soldier holding a rifle by its barrel with its butt on the floor; he is wearing a cap, military tunic, and trousers.
This is an unusual figure and there may be a pair. He appears to be wearing the uniform of a Confederate States soldier but is in fact a British soldier wearing the uniform of the Volunteer movement that was formed in the 1850s in response to an invasion threat. The Volunteer Corps were part of the forces of the Crown and in May 1859 18,000 of them were reviewed by Queen Victoria in Hyde Park.
HEIGHT: 5 Inches
PRICE: G.

iv. Other Allied Figures

See Figures 931 - 939 Book One

Fig. 933A
A group figure of a boy and girl standing on either side of a clock face that is surmounted by two crossed flags. A bugle rests on the top of the clock face and the bottom is decorated with grapes and leaves. The boy wears a shirt, tunic, and kilt with socks. He is playing a drum that is suspended from his shoulders. The girl wears a blouse, short skirt, and knickers. She holds a tambourine in both hands.
This figure was probably made to celebrate the ending of the Crimean War.
HEIGHT: 10 Inches
PRICE: F.

Figs. 940/939
A pair of seated figures of a woman holding a baby on her lap, her right arm resting on a pair of flags, and a wheeled cannon is below. She wears a plumed hat, blouse, and skirt, with a sash over one shoulder and around her waist. He wears highland attire of a plumed hat, cloak, tunic, with a sash across his chest and kilt with sporran. His left elbow rests on a drum and there is a pair of flags to the side and a wheeled cannon below. By the cannon on both figures is a spray of leaves and fruit.
The male figure is another version of 'The Soldier's Dream', see Figures 903, 904, 904B, and 906 Books One and Three and very similar to Figure 905, but the pair to that figure is almost a mirror image.
A very rare pair and very desirable, he is previously unrecorded.
HEIGHT: 8.5 Inches
PRICE: Pair: E, Singles: F.

Chapter 3:
Theatrical and Literary Characters (Including Opera, Ballet, and Circus)

Compiled in this chapter are a listing of theatrical and literary characters, including opera, ballet, and circus. Where figures have been identified, we have included the name of the probable actor or actress who portrayed the role.

Listings highlighted in bold type contain additions and alterations which will be found in this addendum, all other Portraits will be found in *Books One and Three, Victorian Staffordshire Figures 1835-1875*.

This Chapter is divided into four sections:
1. Theatrical and Literary.
2. Opera, Ballet, and Polkas.
3. Circus.
4. Unidentified Characters.

Section 1:
Theatrical and Literary

Section 1 is divided into four parts:

1. A listing of known actors and actresses.
2. Characters portrayed and dramatised by known authors, poets, and publications.
3. Performers who appeared on stage in their own right or performing their own works.
4. A listing of productions by name, including characters, and where known, the actors and actresses portraying the various roles.

1. A listing of known actors and actresses.

Cerrito, Fanny (1817-1909)
See Figure 1797 Book One

Cooper, Thomas Abthorpe (1776-1849)
See Figures 1080/1082 Book One

Cushman, Charlotte Saunders (1816-1876)
See Figures 1071/1072/1073 Book One.

Cushman, Susan (1822-1859)
See Figures 1071/1072/1073 Book One

Egerton. Sarah (1782-1847)
See Figure 1034 Book One

Elssler, Fanny (1810-1884)
See Figures 1522/1797 Book One

Falconer, Edmund (O'Rourke, Edmund) (1814-1879)
See Figure 1144 Book One

Fitzwilliam, Fanny Elizabeth (1801-1854)
See Figure 1066 Book One

Garrick, David (1717-1779)
See Figures 1079/1155 Book One

Glover, Mary (? - 1860)
See Figures 1160/1161 Book One

Glyn, Isbella Dallas (1823-1889)
See Figure 1050 Book One

Hackett, James Henry (1800-1871)
See Figure 1061 Book One

Kean, Charles John (1811-1868)
See Figures 1197/1198 Book One

Kean, Edmund (1787-1833)
See Figures 1057A/1081/1083 Book One

Kemble, John Philip (1757-1823)
See Figures 1044/1045/1053/1054/1055 Book One

Liston, John (1776-1846)
See Figures 1132/1134/1137/1173 Book One

Macready, William Charles (1793-1873)
See Figures 1033/1049/1156/1157 Book One

Marston, Jenny (1827-1861)
See Figure 1086 Book One

Matthews, Charles James (1803-1878)
See Figures 1151/1153/1154 Book One

Quin, James (1693-1766)
See Figure 1062 Book One

Robertson, Agnes Kelly (1833-1916)
See Figure 1144 Book One

Robinson, Frederick (1830-1912)
See Figure 1086 Book One

Siddons, Sarah (Kemble, Sarah) (1755-1831)
See Figures 1051/1054/1056 Book One

Sothern, Edward Askew (1826-1881)
See Figure 1180 Book One

Taglioni, Marie (1804-1884)
See Figure 1797 Book One

Vandenhoff, Charlotte Elizabeth (1818-1860)
See Figure 1069 Book One

Vestris, Lucia Elizabeth (1797-1856)
See Figures 1184/1185/1186/1187/1188 Book One

2. Characters portrayed and dramatised by known authors, poets, and publications

1. Harrison Ainsworth
   i. Rookwood, or the exploits of Turpin and Black Bess.

2. Robert Burns
   i. Auld Lang Syne
   ii. John Anderson, my Jo
   iii. Tam O'Shanter and Souter Johnny

3. Lord Byron
   i. Mazeppa (See Circus section, Mazeppa)
   ii. The Bride of Abydos

4. Cervantes
   i. Don Quixote

5. William Cowper
   i. John Gilpin

6. Daniel Defoe
   i. The life and strange surprising adventures of Robinson Crusoe.

7. Charles Dickens
   i. David Copperfield
   ii. Martin Chuzzlewit
   iii. Nicholas Nickleby
   iv. Pickwick Papers, The
   v. Old Curiosity Shop, The

8. Punch
   i. Punch
   ii. Mr. and Mrs. Caudle

9. Sir Walter Scott
   i. Rob Roy Macgregor
   ii. Marmion
   iii. Bride of Lammermoor, The (See Opera section, Lucia di Lammermoor)

10. William Shakespeare
    i. A Midsummer Night's Dream
    ii. As You Like It
    iii. Hamlet, Prince of Denmark
    iv. Life and Death of King John, The
    v. Macbeth
    vi. Merchant of Venice, The
    vii. Merry Wives of Windsor, The
    viii. Othello, the Moor of Venice
    ix. Romeo and Juliet
    x. Second part of King Henry IV, The
    xi. Tragedy of King Richard III, The
    xii. Winters Tale, The

11. Harriet Elizabeth Beecher Stowe
    i. Uncle Tom's Cabin

1. Harrison Ainsworth

i. Rookwood, or the exploits of Turpin and Black Bess.

A novel by Harrison Ainsworth published in 1834, based on the lives of the notorious highwaymen, Dick Turpin and Tom King. This novel led to many theatrical productions at the time, appearing at the Theatre Royal in 1841.

These figures all appear to be of a theatrical nature, and not portraying the actual people on which the novel was based.

Dick Turpin (1706-1739)

The son of an innkeeper in Hempstead, Essex, he joined a gang of robbers and outlaws, finally entering a partnership with Tom King. In 1735, whilst stealing a horse in Epping, Essex, the owner was about to arrest King for the crime. Turpin rose up to them and fired; he missed the owner and hit King, fatally wounding him. He escaped to Yorkshire where in 1739, he was caught in the act of horse stealing and was tried and hanged at York.

It will be noted that there are a few figures of Dick Turpin titled 'Frank Gardiner'. These are later figures. Frank Gardiner was released in 1874, ten years into a thirty-two year sentence for gold robbery. There was a public outcry at the time due to his early release.

Tom King (? - 1735)

A highwayman and partner of Dick Turpin, who was accidentally shot and killed by Turpin in Epping Forest.
   See Figures 941 - 967 Book One

Figs. 948A/948B
A pair of figures of Dick Turpin and Tom King on horseback, both hold a pistol in their right hand and their left holds the reins, they wear a tricorn hat, neckerchief, waistcoat, jacket, and trousers with knee boots.
These figures are similar to Figures 947 and 948 Book One, apart from the size and shape of the saddlecloth and other minor differences.
HEIGHT: 8.5 Inches
PRICE: Pair: F, Singles: G.

Figs. 956A/956B
A pair of figures of Dick Turpin and Tom King on horseback; both hold a pistol in their right hand and their left holds the reins, they wear a tri-corn plumed hat, waistcoat, ermine edged jacket, and trousers with knee boots.
TITLE: DICK TURPIN - TOM KING in black capitals.
HEIGHT: 7.5 Inches
PRICE: Pair: F, Singles: G.

Burns Characters
For figures of Robert Burns and his lovers see Figures 56 - 76 Book One

i. 'Auld Lang Syne'
See Figures 969 - 972 Book One

A song sung many years before Burn's birth, he kept the name but changed both the words and the melody, now remembered and sung to celebrate the beginning of the New Year.
Should auld acquaintance be forgot,
And never bought to min'?
Should auld acquaintance be forgot,
And days o' lang syne?
CHORUS
For auld lang syne, my dear,
For auld lang syne
We'll tak' a cup o' kindness yet.
For auld lang syne

Fig. 965
A figure of Dick Turpin on horseback on a titled base, his right hand holds a pistol and his left the reins, he wears a tricorn hat, waistcoat, coat breeches, and knee boots. One front leg of the horse is raised.
The figure is on a high-waisted base and is very well modelled and decorated. The title is inset above the base. The figure illustrated is the only one known, it would have had a pair but is unrecorded. Figure 966 has been reserved for it.
TITLE: DICK TURPIN
HEIGHT: 13.5 Inches
PRICE: E.

Fig. 971A
A group figure of three men seated on a cloth covered bench, all are holding mugs and there is a bottle on the bench. The two figures at either end are shaking hands and all are wearing Tam O' Shanters. All three figures have jackets and shirts and ties. One figure wears a kilt, another wears trousers.
This is a 'Green Factory' version of Auld Lang Syne.
HEIGHT: 8 Inches
PRICE: F.

ii. John Anderson, my Jo
See Figures 973 - 974A Book One - Book Three

iii. Tam O'Shanter and Souter Johnnie
See Figures 975 - 979C Book One - Book Three

A Poem by Robert Burns, it tells the story of a farmer, Tam O'Shanter, who returning home after a night of drinking with his friend Souter Johnnie, pass the Kirk of Alloway. He stopped and in the clearing he saw the witches and warlocks dancing to the bagpipe playing of the devil. In his excitement he called to one of the witches and with that the lights went out and the witches chased after him. Tam jumped onto his horse and fled, but not in time, as he had to cross the bridge, which was beyond their powers. As Tam crossed the bridge a witch grabbed the tail of his mare Meg and pulled it off.

These figures are based on the sculptures by James Thom, which were used on the Burns monument at Ayr.

Figs. 978D/978E
A pair of figures of Tam O Shanter and Souter Johnnie, both seated holding jugs.
These figures are modelled and decorated in the round. They were made for a considerable period. These are early versions made in the 1830s. The author's have seen many variations, some dating to the eighteenth century.
HEIGHT: 5.5 Inches
PRICE: Pair: F, Singles: G.

Fig. 975A/975B
A pair of figures of Tam O Shanter and Souter Johnnie seated in chairs, Tam with his legs apart wearing a hat, shirt with cravat, waistcoat, coat, trousers, and riding boots. He holds a whip in his left hand. Johnnie is seated sideways wearing a cap, shirt, large apron, knee breeches, and boots. His left hand rests on the back of the chair and he is holding a cup in his right. There are shoes on the floor by the chair.
Both figures have been damaged; in Tam's right hand he should be holding a mug or bottle. The restorer has not restored the figure correctly, due no doubt to not having a perfect figure or photograph from which to work. Johnnie's right hand is missing.
HEIGHT: 9 Inches
PRICE: Pair: F, Singles: G.

Fig. 979P
A figure of Tam O' Shanter on his horse Meg on a rococo scrolled base with indented capitals. His right hand is raised to his head and he is wearing a brimmed hat, shirt with tie, waistcoat, jacket, and breeches with a scarf over his shoulder and across his chest. **The authors believe that the pair to this figure is John Gilpin, Figure 991, and have seen them sold together as such.**
TITLE: TAM O' SHANTER
HEIGHT: 8 Inches
PRICE: F.

The poem was based on the real life character of John Gilpin, a citizen of London. It tells the story of his twentieth wedding anniversary celebrations. They decided upon travelling to The Bell at Edmonton. His wife, her sister, and children were in a carriage and he was on a borrowed horse, which he lost control of as it began to trot, and rode past Edmonton and ten miles beyond to Ware and back again, he losing his hat and wig along the way.

Fig. 991
A figure of John Gilpin on horseback jumping over a fence on a titled rococo scrolled base with indented capitals. He has lost his hat, which is on the base and is desperately holding onto the horse. He wears a cloak, jacket, breeches, and boots. **The authors believe that the pair to this figure is Tam O' Shanter, Figure 979 and have seen them sold together as such.**
TITLE: JOHN GILPIN
HEIGHT: 8 Inches
PRICE: E.

3. Byron Characters

For figures of Lord Byron and his lovers see Figures 78 - 87 Book One

i. Mazeppa (See Circus section, Mazeppa)

ii. The Bride of Abydos
See Figures 980 - 986 Book One

4. Cervantes

i. Don Quixote
See Figures 987 - 988 Book One

5. William Cowper

i. John Gilpin
See Figures 989 - 994 Book One

A poem by William Cowper, published in 1785, turned into a production at the Astley's Theatre in 1844 as *Harlequin and Johnny Gilpin's Ride*.

6. Daniel Defoe

i. The life and strange surprising adventures of Robinson Crusoe.

See Figures 995 - 999 Book One and Three

A novel by Daniel Defoe published in 1719 based on the real life adventures of Alexander Selkirk (1679 – 1721), the son of a shoemaker, who ran off for a life at sea. In 1704, after a disagreement with the captain of his ship, at his request he asked to be marooned on the uninhabited Pacific island of Juan Ferandez. Whilst on the island the book details how he built a cabin, domesticated animals, and built himself a boat. During his time there, he was visited by cannibals from a neighbouring island, saving one of the savages, who he named 'Man Friday', from death and who then became his companion. In 1709 an English ship in a state of mutiny rescued him.

Even though this story was dramatised on many occasions during the Victorian era and earlier, no source or reference to a production or actor in the part has been discovered.

7. Dickens Characters

i. David Copperfield
See Figures 1001 - 1003 Book One

A novel by Charles Dickens published in 1849 and dramatised in 1850. The characters included David Copperfield, Dora Spencer, Mr. Micawber, Uriah Heap, Clara & Ham Peggotty, and Mrs. Copperfield, who married Mr. Barkis after her husband's death.

Fig. 1000
A standing figure of 'Man Friday' dressed in ragged clothes and holding a gun in his right hand; there is an axe in his waistband.
The authors believe this to be a small version of the pair to Fig. 999 Book One.
HEIGHT: 5 Inches
PRICE: Pair: E, Singles: F.

Figs. 1001/1002
A pair of group figures of a young boy and elderly woman standing, the boy holds a basket in his right arm. He wears a hat, jacket, waistcoat, neckerchief, and trousers; the woman has her right arm around the boy's shoulder. She holds a cane in her left hand, and wears a bonnet, shawl, and long dress. The second group figure is of an elderly blind man standing. He holds a violin in his right hand, dressed in hat, waistcoat, jacket, and knee breeches; his left hand rests on the shoulder of a young girl who stands at his side holding a hat with coppers in it.
The first group has for many years been accepted as being of David Copperfield and Clara Peggotty. As there is now a pair, it begs the question as to which characters the second group portrays. The figure of the man and girl has now been recorded in a larger size and it follows that there must have existed its pair in a larger size as well, although it is at present unrecorded.
HEIGHT: 9 Inches, 7.75 Inches.
PRICE: Pair: E, Singles: F.

ii. Martin Chuzzlewit
See Figures 1004 - 1006A Books One and Three

iii. Nicholas Nickleby
See Figures 1007 - 1010A Books One and Three

A novel by Charles Dickens published in 1838-1839. It tells the story of Nicholas, his sister Kate, and his mother, who are left penniless on the death of their father. With the help of their uncle Ralph, Nicholas, aged nineteen, is sent to work at Dotheboys Hall, where Wackford Squeers mistreats the children under his charge.

The six figures in this series are unusual in that they are modelled in the round and were not made in The Parr factory, the back of each figure is titled 'Published June 15th 1839 by Ridgeway & Robey Hanley', which dated them accurately and to a known pottery. They are extremely rare figures.

Five of these figures are illustrated in Book Three, the figure of Mrs. Nickleby is not illustrated, and Figure 1010B has been reserved for it. If these figures were sold in pairs, the probable pairing would be as follows:

1. Wackford Squeers - Smike
2. Nicholas Nickleby - Kate Nickleby
3. Mrs. Nickleby - Ralph Nickleby

iv. The Pickwick Papers
See Figures 1011 - 1012 Book One

v. The Old Curiosity Shop
See Figures 1013 - 1014 Book One

8. Punch

i. Punch
See Figures 1015 - 1029 Book One

i. Mr. and Mrs. Caudle

'Mrs. Caudle's Curtain Lectures' by Douglas Jerrold first appeared in Punch in 1845, and they proved an immediate success. They were satirical episodes in the life of Mr. Caudle, a toy and doll salesman. His wife, whenever he was about to fall off to sleep, would castigate him about his habits or whatever he had done during the past few days.

Fig. 1032
A group figure of Mr. and Mrs. Caudle seated in a sofa. He is crossed legged and wears a large brimmed hat, shirt with tie, waistcoat, jacket, and trousers. His right arm rests on the arm of the sofa and his left on his chest. Mrs. Caudle is wearing a snood, blouse, and long dress. She is touching the brim of his hat with her right hand.
TITLE: Mr. & Mrs. Caudle
HEIGHT: 6 Inches
PRICE: E.

Fig. 1031
A group figure of Mr. and Mrs. Caudle, both seated, Mrs. Caudle with her left hand on her husband's hat, her right by her waist, wearing a blouse, sleeveless jacket, and dress. Mr. Caudle is positioned with his head resting to the side as if trousers.
TITLE: Mr. & Mrs. Caudle (in gilt script)
HEIGHT: 7 Inches
PRICE: F.

9. Sir Walter Scott

The Bride of Lammermoor (See Opera section, Lucia di Lammermoor Figs. 1308/1309 Book One)
For figures of Sir Walter Scott See Book One, Figures 308/309

i. Rob Roy Macgrego
See Figures 1033 - 1040 Book One

ii. Marmion
See Figure 1041 Book One

10. William Shakespeare

For figures of William Shakespeare See Figures 314-327 Book One

i. A Midsummer Night's Dream

A comedy of plots and sub-plots, the plot relating to the figure concerns Oberon and Titania, the King and Queen of the fairies. Both have argued over Titania's insistence in keeping a little changeling boy as a page. Wanting to get the better of her, Oberon orders Puck to pick a magic flower and press the juice into Titania's eyes while she is asleep, so that she will fall in love with the first thing she sees when she opens them. When she awakes she sees Bottom, a weaver (dressed for a play), wearing an ass's head on his shoulders and she immediately falls in love with him. Oberon finds her toying with his 'amiable cheeks' and 'fair large ears' and demands the changeling boy. In her confusion she relents and gives him up.

ii. As You Like It

The wicked Duke Frederick takes the title belonging to his brother and sends him into exile. Rosalind, the true Duke's daughter, remains with Celia who is Frederick's daughter. They go to a wrestling match and meet Orlando who has also been denied his inheritance. They fall in love, but Frederick now banishes Rosalind because Orlando's father is an old friend of Frederick's brother. Celia goes with Rosalind to the forest and Orlando also goes to the forest and carves her name on trees and leaves sonnets hanging on bushes. After many trials and tribulations Rosalind and Orlando marry. The Duke, shown the wickedness of his ways, gives back the Dukedom to his brother. Orlando saves his wicked brother from a lioness and they all live happily ever after.

Fig. 1042A/1042B
A standing figure of Rosalind wearing a wide brimmed hat, green cloak, blue jacket, and knee breeches, her right hand outstretched as if to carry a crook. The pair, probably Orlando, stands wearing a hat, tunic, skirt, and boots. There is a short sword at his belt that he holds in both hands.
Two figures are illustrated, each slightly different but clearly taken from the same print. A pair are also illustrated, previously unrecorded, it is therefore more than probable that Figure 1042B portrays Orlando. This figure has been identified by the print which is illustrated with the figure; the print is titled 'Mrs. Abington as Rosalind'.
HEIGHT: 9.25 Inches
PRICE: Pair: E, Singles: F.

Fig. 1043
A figure of Titania, Queen of the Fairies, seated holding a wand in her right hand and in her left a posy of flowers. She wears a floral headband and a full length dress decorated with flowers.
This figure was made by The Parr pottery; two figures are illustrated, one in the white and one coloured.
HEIGHT: 9 Inches
PRICE: E.

iii. Hamlet, Prince of Denmark
See Figures 1044 - 1046 Book One

iv. Life and Death of King John, The
See Figure 1048 Book One

v. Macbeth
See Figures 1049 - 1058 Book One

Macbeth and Banquo, the two generals of Duncan, the King of Scotland, stumble across three witches on a remote heath when returning from a victorious battle. They prophesied that Macbeth will become Thane of Cawdor and then king. Later Duncan makes Macbeth Thane of Cawdor. With this, and Lady Macbeth spurring him to complete the prophecy, Macbeth murders Duncan whilst he is visiting his castle and takes the crown. Duncan's two sons, Donalbain and Malcolm, manage to escape. Macbeth then orders the death of Banquo and his son Fleance, but Fleance escapes death.

Macbeth, haunted by the ghost of Banquo, returns to see the witches. They tell him to beware of Macduff, the Thane of Fife. Learning that Malcolm and Macduff are amassing an army in England, he takes the castle of Macduff and kills Lady Macduff and her children. With this the army of Macduff and Malcolm march on Duninane and kill Macbeth, and Malcolm is proclaimed King.

Fig. 1057A
A standing figure of Macbeth, he is bareheaded and wears a cloak, breastplate, and kilt with sporran. He holds a knife in either hand. The figure stands on a scrolled gilt lined base.
A very rare figure, the one illustrated is the only one recorded.
HEIGHT: 8 Inches
PRICE: E.

Fig. 1054B
A standing figure of Lady Macbeth wearing a beige ermine edged cloak, yellow flowered skirt, and purple blouse with a feathered crown on her head. Her right hand is held to her breast and her left holds a bag, all on a shaped gilt decorated base.
There is no doubt a pair to this figure of Hamlet; Fig. 1054A has been reserved for it.
HEIGHT: 9.5 Inches
PRICE: F.

Figs. 1057A.SO
Illustrated is a contemporary print of Mr. Edmund Kean as Macbeth. This is a newly discovered source for Figure 1057A.

vi. Merchant of Venice, The
See Figures 1059 - 1061 Book One

vii. Merry Wives of Windsor, The
See Figures 1062 - 1066 Book One

viii. Othello, The Moor of Venice
See Figure 1067 Book One

ix. Romeo and Juliet
See Figures 1068 - 1077 Book One

A romantic tragedy, it tells the story of the Montague's and the Capulets, the two main families of Verona, who are bitter enemies. At a feast given by Capulet, Romeo meets and falls in love with Juliet. They agree to a secret marriage and wed the next day with the help of Friar Laurence. After a disagreement between one of Romeo's friends and a member of the Capulet family named Tybalt, Romeo enters the scene and after his friend falls, he draws his sword and kills Tybalt. Romeo caught in the act is sentenced to banishment, and after spending one last night with Juliet leaves for Mantua.

Juliet is now alone and her family unaware of her marriage to Romeo arrange a marriage for her to Count Paris. She consults the Friar, who tells her that he will give her a potion which will make her appear lifeless for forty-two hours, and that he will warn Romeo who will come to the vault and rescue her and take her to Mantua. But the message to Romeo is misread and he believes that she is dead, he returns with poison to see her and meets Count Paris outside the vault and after a struggle he kills the Count. He then enters the vault and kisses Juliet for the last time and takes the poison. Juliet then awakes and seeing Romeo dead beside her, stabs herself and dies.

Fig. 1076A
An arbour group figure of Romeo and Juliet on a gilt lined base, both are seated, he with his right arm around Juliet's shoulders and holding her right hand with his left. He wears a cap, waistcoat, short jacket, and knee breeches. A cape is on the ground. She is bareheaded and wears a short jacket and long dress.
HEIGHT: 6 Inches
PRICE: F.

Figs. 1072SO/1073SO
Illustrated is an engraving from The Tallis Shakespeare Gallery of Charlotte and Susan Cushman as Romeo and Juliet, the source for Figures 1072/1073.

Fig. 1076B
An arbour group figure of Romeo and Juliet, both seated, she with her left arm around Romeo. She is bareheaded and wears a long double-skirted dress with a scarf that is over her shoulder and hangs from her waist; her right hand rests on his chest. He wears a hat with a plume, tunic with a sash, and boots. His left hand rests in his lap and there is a scarf on the floor between his legs.
HEIGHT: 10 Inches
PRICE: E.

x. Second Part of King Henry IV, The

xi. Tragedy of King Richard III, The

xii. Winters Tale, The

11. Harriet Elizabeth Beecher Stowe

Uncle Toms Cabin

A novel by Harriet Elizabeth Beecher Stowe published in serial form between 1851 and 1852 in 'The National Era' and in book form in 1852.

The novel was dramatised many times on the English stage, making its debut in E. Fitzball's adaptation in three acts, entitled 'Uncle Toms Cabin, or The Horrors of Slavery' at the Theatre Drury Lane in 1852. It told stories and incidents that happened to the slaves and their masters. Included in the cast of characters were Mr. and Mrs. Shelby, Mr. and Mrs. St. Clare, Simon Legree, Uncle Tom and his wife Chloe, his daughter Topsy, and George and Eliza Harris, and their daughter Eva and son Harry. George was a 'mulatto', half white and half black, and Eliza was a quadroon, a quarter black and three quarters white.

The story was set on the Shelby Plantation in Kentucky before the Civil War. Uncle Tom is one of Mr. Shelby's hardest working slaves, but Shelby encounters financial difficulties and is forced to sell Tom and a young boy, Harry. Harry's mother Eliza overhears this and decides to run away with her son, rather than be parted from him. Her disappearance is soon discovered and Mr. Haley, her new master, is soon searching for her. At one point Mr. Haley was so close to catching her that to escape she runs across blocks of ice on the Ohio River clutching her son. Successful in escaping, she is finally reunited with her husband George in Canada.

Uncle Tom is less fortunate and is sold to a man called Simon Legree, who beats him to within an inch of his life. Whilst Tom is recovering from this beating, he is befriended by another slave named Casey. Casey and another slave named Emmeline also decide to run away. Tom refuses to tell Legree where they might be and is beaten again with no hope of recovery. Just before his death Tom is rescued by Mr. Shelby and given a decent funeral.

This book had a very anti-slavery theme and was popular amongst abolitionists throughout the world. The tale told the truth about how badly the slaves were treated by their masters, with children being parted from their parents.

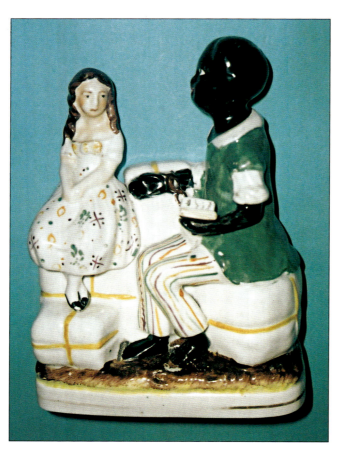

Fig. 1094A
A group figure of Uncle Tom and Little Eva, Eva is seated on a bale of cotton with her feet resting on another. Her feet are crossed and her hands rest in her lap. She wears a long dress with a bow. Uncle Tom sits on a bale of cotton to her left; he wears a jacket and trousers. His right arm is shackled and in his left he holds an open book.
The figure illustrated is the only example the author's have seen. The book has been restored, but having never seen one before, we cannot be certain as to how accurate the restoration is.
HEIGHT: 7 Inches
PRICE: E.

Right:
Figs. 1113/1112
A pair of figures of Ben Backstay and companion, both standing cross-legged on coloured bases, each hold a moneybag aloft, he in his right hand and she in her left. She is bare-headed and wears an open necked blouse, jacket, and long skirt with a large scarf around her waist; her right hand is on her hip holding her hat. He wears a sailor's apparel and a net is draped on the rockwork behind him.
The figures illustrated are extremely well modelled and decorated.
HEIGHT: 10.5 Inches
PRICE: Pair: D, Singles: E.

3. Performers who appeared on stage in their own right or performing their own works

1. Cooke, Thomas Potter
2. Foster, Stephen Collins
3. Rice, Thomas Dartmouth as 'Jim Crow'
4. Waters, Billy
5. Williams, Barney

1. Cooke, Thomas Potter (1786-1864)

For other figures of T. P. Cooke, see The Pilot Figures 1195/1196 Book One, see also Figures 1105 -1117 Book One

The son of a London surgeon, he served in The Royal Navy as a boy, seeing active service in the battle of Cape St. Vincent in 1797 when he would only have been eleven years old. He made his first stage appearance in 1804. His performances included William in *Black Eyed Susan or All in the Downs* in 1829, Long Tom Coffin in *The Pilot*, and Dick Fid in *Red Rover*. Cooke appeared in numerous nautical productions, always playing a sailor, and no titled figures of him have been recorded. It is therefore difficult to attribute some of the figures to a particular production. There are a couple of sources that portray him in a particular role and these are given by the figure.

Fig. 1114B
A figure of a girl standing, she is bareheaded and wears a tight jacket and long skirt with an apron. In her left hand she holds her hat to her side and her right arm is held aloft holding moneybags.
This figure is so similar to other figures in which the pair is Ben Backstay that there is no doubt a figure of him that pairs this; Fig. 1114C has been reserved for it.
HEIGHT: 10.75
PRICE: Pair: E, Singles: F.

Figs. 1114D/1114E
A pair of figures of a man and woman standing in a dancing pose, he is dressed as a sailor wearing a hat, open neck shirt with a tie, waistcoat, short jacket, and long trousers. He holds a moneybag to his head with his left hand and his right is on his hip. A small barrel is on rockwork to his side. She wears a hat, long sleeved blouse, and skirt tied with a scarf. A small barrel is under her left arm and her right is held to her head.
HEIGHT: 9.25 Inches
PRICE: Pair: F, Singles: G.

Figs. 1118/1118A
A pair of figures of a girl and man standing, both have a moneybag held to their head, he wears a sailor's uniform and she wears a jacket, bodice, and short skirt. Her hat is held in her left hand.
These figures are so similar to Figs. 1107/1108 and 1109/1110 it can safely be assumed that they portray the same subjects.
HEIGHT: 8 Inches
PRICE: Pair: F, Singles: G.

2. Foster, Stephen Collins (1826-1864)
See Figures 1119 - 1122 Book One

Born in Pittsburgh, Pennsylvania, he was a song writer who wrote over 120 melodies, including *Oh, Susanna, Old Dog Tray*, and *Old Kentucky Home*. Even though he was an immense success at the time, he died in poverty.

Fig. 1122A
A spill vase figure of a man seated to the side of a tree, wearing a top hat, shirt with tie, waistcoat, long jacket, and knee breeches. One hand is on his knee and the other holds a handkerchief bundle.
To the other side of the tree a spaniel sits on its haunches.
This figure is very similar to Fig. 1122 Book One and although it has never been found titled, it can be considered a smaller version of 'Dog Tray'.
HEIGHT: 8. Inches
PRICE: E.

3. Rice, Thomas Dartmouth as 'Jim Crow' (1806-1860)
See Figures 1123 - 1125 Book One

An American performer and entertainer, he started his career in 1828 performing in-between the acts of plays, impersonating an old black American named 'Jim Crow', singing and shuffling his feet whilst grooming a horse, his face blacked up with burnt cork and wearing ragged clothes. An instant success, Rice travelled the United States performing his act. In 1833, whilst performing in Washington, he teamed up with a young performer by the name of Joseph Jefferson, who was kept in a bag whilst Rice sang his song and released at the end to sing his own. In 1833 Rice visited England and performed at The Royal Surrey Theatre in London.

Fig. 1126
A standing figure of Jim Crow, wearing a straw hat, jacket, shirt with tie, and trousers with patches. He stands in a dancing pose.
This is an extremely rare, previously unrecorded figure. The source for this figure is an illustrated music front that is shown with Fig. 1123, it is almost a mirror image of the print and it is possible that a mirror image figure exists that would pair this figure.
TITLE: Jim Crow, in gilt script
HEIGHT: 7 Inches
PRICE: E.

4. Waters, William, also known as 'Billy Waters' and 'Black Billy' (?-1823)
See Figure 1127 Book One

5. Williams, Barney (1823-1876)

An American actor and entertainer, he travelled the United States with his wife, in a show that portrayed him as a drinking Irishman and her as a 'Yankee gal'. He visited England from 1855 - 1859 performing in 1856 in the production of *'Born to Good Luck'* playing the role of Paddy O'Rafferty at The Adelphi Theatre in London. He retired from the stage in 1875.

Figs. 1128/1129
A pair of figures of Mr. and Mrs. Barney Williams standing cross-legged, he with his right hand on his chest and his left in his jacket pocket, wearing a top hat with a pipe tucked under the band, long jacket, neckerchief, shirt, waistcoat, and breeches, she with her right arm resting on a pillar, her left on her hip. She wears a bonnet, blouse, and a skirt with a sash at the waist.
HEIGHT: 8 Inches
PRICE: Pair: E, Singles: F.

Fig. 1129A
A group figure of Mr. and Mrs. Barney Williams standing side by side; he wears a top hat, shirt with tie, waistcoat, jacket, and knee breeches, his right hand is on his chest and his left in his jacket pocket. She is bareheaded and wears a blouse and skirt with an apron, her left hand is on her hip and her right elbow leans on a covered structure between them.
HEIGHT: 8 Inches
PRICE: F.

4. A listing of productions by name, including characters, and where known the actors and actresses portraying them

Listings highlighted in bold type contain additions and alterations which will be found in this addendum. All other Portraits will be found in *Books One and Three, Victorian Staffordshire Figures 1835-1875.*

1. Adventures of Flick and Fluck, The
2. Ali Baba and the Forty Thieves
3. Babes in the Wood
4. Blue Beard or Female Curiosity
5. Bruce and Wallace
6. Colleen Bawn (The Brides of Garryowen)
6A. Cromwell
7. Dick Whittington
8. Elephant of Siam, or The Fire Fiend
9. Fortune Teller, The
10. He would be an Actor
11. Jealous Wife
12. King of The Commons, The
12A. Lady Godiva
13. Life and Adventures of Peter Wilkins, The
14. Little Pickle
15. Little Red Riding Hood
16. Lord of The Manor
17. Love Chase, The
18. Mother Goose
19. Mother Hubbard
20. Our American Cousin
21. Paul and Virginia
22. Pilot, The
23. Pizarro
24. Rescue, The
25. Rival, The
26. Robin Hood
27. Saint George
28. Saint Patrick's Day
29. Smugglers Quarrel
30. Will Watch

1. Adventures of Flick and Fluck, The
See Figure 1130 Book One

2. Ali Baba and the Forty Thieves
See Figures 1132 - 1137 Books One and Three

3. Babes in the Wood
See Figures 1138 -1140A Books One and Three

Originally a ballad from the mid-seventeenth century, it was part of Thomas Percy's *Reliques of Ancient Poetry*, a collection of old English poetry and lyrics. It was dramatised on many occasions during the Victorian Era. It tells the story of a young brother and sister who, on the death of their father, are left his estate and put into their uncle's charge. The uncle is interested in the estate rather than the children and hires two ruffians to kill them, thus allowing him to acquire the children's inheritance.

On the way to kill the children, one of the ruffian's changes his mind and kills his associate and hides the children in the woods. The children however perish there and a robin comes along and covers them with leaves.

This production was revived as a melodrama in Victorian times, and also became a popular pantomime.

4. Blue Beard; or Female Curiosity
See Figure 1141 Book One

5. Bruce and Wallace
See Figures 1142 - 1143 Book One

Bruce, Robert (1274-1329)
The King of Scotland defeated Edward II at Bannockburn in 1314, making peace in 1328. He was the subject of an opera by Rossini that was performed in 1846. Also a theatrical production was staged entitled Wallace and Bruce, at the Coabridge Adelphi in 1869.

Wallace, Sir William (1272-1305)
A Scottish patriot, devoted to resisting the English, elected to Governor of Scotland. Arrested in 1305 by the English, he was taken to London and condemned to be hung, drawn, and quartered. He was the subject of a poem by Henry the Minstrel (?1440-1492?), which was adapted through the centuries.

The figures 1142 and 1143 in Book One are titled figures, and so far no real evidence has come to light to confirm whether these figures are theatrical, operatic, or from literature.

6. Colleen Bawn (The Brides of Garryowen)
See Figure 1144 Book One

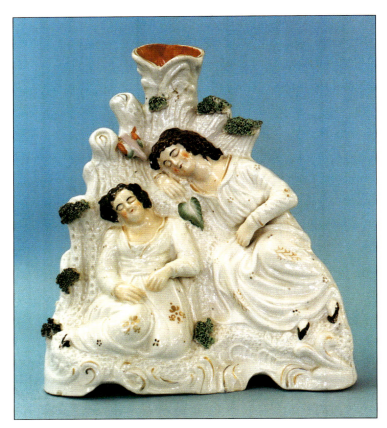

Fig. 1138A
A spill vase figure of two children asleep, both wear flowing garments; she has both hands in her lap and he rests his head on his right arm. A bird is in a tree above his head, all on a rococo base. **The figure illustrated is in the white, but the authors have seen a full colour version that would fetch a comparatively higher price.**
HEIGHT: 10.25 Inches
PRICE: G.

Fig. 1139B
A group figure of two children asleep, she wearing a jacket and long dress, he an open necked shirt, jacket, and trousers. To her right a bird sits on a rocky outcrop and above an angel kneels with folded wings and hands.
HEIGHT: 7 Inches
PRICE: G.

6A. Cromwell
See Figure 1144A Book Three

He was the subject of many satires and odes. John Milton appealed to him in his sonnet, *'Cromwell our chief of men'*; Thomas Carlyle wrote about him in *'On Heroes, Hero-worship and the heroic in History'* in 1840, attracting huge audiences. Also another two volumes were published in 1845 with *'Oliver Cromwell's letters and speeches'*; it is probable that these figures were inspired by a production of this time.

7. Dick Whittington (1359-1423)
See Figure 1145 Book One

8. Elephant of Siam, or The Fire Fiend
See Figure 1146 Book One

9. Fortune Teller, The
See Figures 1147 - 1149 Book One

10. He Would be an Actor
See Figures 1151 - 1154 Book One

11. Jealous Wife
See Figure 1155 Book One

12. King of the Commons, The
See Figures 1157 - 1158 Book One

12A. Lady Godiva
See Figure 1158A Book Three

13. Life and Adventures of Peter Wilkins, The
See Figures 1159 - 1161 Book One

14. Little Pickle
See Figure 1162 Book One

15. Little Red Riding Hood
See Figures 1163 - 1172 Book One

A popular tale from a French collection of fairy tales compiled by Charles Perrault and translated by Robert Samber in 1729. *Little Red Riding Hood* was dramatised many times during the Victorian era.

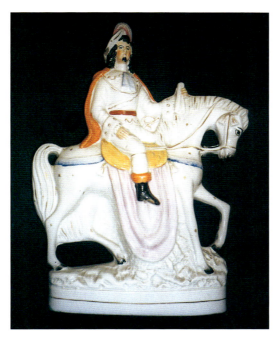

Figs. 1144B/1144C
A pair of equestrian figures of Charles I and Oliver Cromwell, both seated astride their horses, both wearing either traditional Carolean or Puritan dress. Charles holds the reins in his right hand and a scroll in his left. Cromwell holds the reins in his right hand and his left is on the horse's flank. **Whilst these figures have never been found titled, the authors are certain that they portray Charles and Cromwell; during Victorian times there were many plays featuring them, and whilst it is possible that they were made as portraits, it is more likely that they were theatrical in inspiration.**
HEIGHT: 13.5 Inches
PRICE: Pair: E, Singles: F.

It tells the story of Little Red Riding Hood, who was sent on an errand by her mother to take a cake and a pot of butter to her sick grandmother. On the way she stops and speaks to a wolf. On learning of her errand, the wolf runs ahead and eats the grandmother, taking her place in bed disguised as her. Red Riding Hood arrives at her grandmother's cottage and is eaten as well.

Fig. 1168A Correction, it is not Little Red Riding Hood and can now be found under Ref. Fig. 1940D.

16. Lord of the Manor
See Figure 1173 Book One

17. Love Chase, The
See Figure 1174 Book One

A play by James Sheridan Knowles, which when first performed had Louisa Cranstoun Nesbit performing the role of Constance.

Fig. 1174A
A figure of Constance standing, she leans her left arm on a pillar and her right holds an umbrella. She wears a plumed hat, jacket, and long two-tiered skirt; a very long scarf is draped over her right shoulder and tied at the waist. **The identification of this figure is taken from its close resemblance to Fig. 1174.**
HEIGHT: 7.5 Inches
PRICE: F.

18. Mother Goose
See Figures 1175 - 1177 Book One

A popular tale from the French collection of fairy tales compiled by Charles Perrault and translated by Robert Samber in 1729. This tale was dramatised many timed during the Victorian era, and also became a popular pantomime.

Figs. 1178/1178A
A pair of standing figures of Mother Goose and The Jewish Landlord; she wears a steeple hat, cloak, and long dress, and a goose stands by her feet. He is bearded and wears a top hat, shirt, long two buttoned coat, and trousers, holding a round object under his left arm and his right is to his shoulder. HEIGHT: 7 Inches
PRICE: Pair: E, Singles: F.

19. Mother Hubbard
See Figure 1179 Book One

20. Our American Cousin
See Figure 1180 Book One

21. Paul and Virginia
See Figures 1181 - 1194D Books One and Three

A novel by Bernardin de St. Pierre, it was first published in 1787, and was the origin of many lyrical dramas and operas. It was performed at Covent Garden in 1800, and revised on many occasions, the most notable being the 1822 production at Drury Lane with Lucia Elizabeth Vestris in the role of Paul.

The story tells the tale of Paul and Virginia, the children of two mothers who move to Mauritius to escape civilisation. They fall deeply in love but Virginia is sent back to France and the young lovers spend the next few years apart. Paul waits for her return but the ship carrying her back is wrecked by a hurricane in sight of the Island. Paul tries to save her without success. Helplessly, he watches her standing on the poop. A sailor, trying to save her, tells her to take of her clothes and swim to safety. She refuses and drowns. Paul watches her drown and subsequently dies of grief.

The stage adaptation by James Cobb followed the original but changed the ending, with Virginia surviving and the couple happily reunited.

Figs. 1183/1182
A pair of figures of Virginia and Paul standing on coloured rococo style bases, she wears a knee length dress with open sleeves, a scarf is over her shoulders and tied at the waist; he wears a shirt with tie, jacket, and trousers tied at the waist with a scarf. He holds a straw boater in his right hand.
These figures were made by The Parr Factory, one of whose idiosyncrasies was to paint woman's shoes red.
HEIGHT: 8.5 Inches
PRICE: Pair: F, Singles: G.

Fig. 1190A
A spill vase figure of Paul and Virginia seated side by side above rockwork from which water flows; they are both barefooted and she is touching the birds nest that he is holding. She wears a bodice and long dress, he wears a hat, shirt with tie, waistcoat jacket, and trousers rolled up to the knees. **This figure is an adaptation of Figure 1190 and was made in the Parr Factory.**
HEIGHT: 12 Inches
PRICE: G.

Fig. 1192
A group figure of Paul and Virginia seated on rockwork, both are bareheaded, she is bareheaded and wears a blouse and long skirt, one arm is across her chest and the other in her lap. Paul wears a brimmed hat, open necked shirt, jacket, and short trousers, one arm is around Virginia and the other holds a bird's nest. A stream runs on the base below. HEIGHT: 6.75 Inches
PRICE: G.

22. Pilot, The
See Figures 1195 - 1196 Book One For other figures of T. P. Cooke see Figures 1105, 1108, 1109, 1111 to 1117 Book One

23. Pizarro
See Figures 1197 - 1198 Book One

24. Rescue, The
See Figure 1199 Book One

25. Rival, The
See Figures 1200 - 1204B Books One and Three

A comedy by R. B. Sheridan first produced in 1775. The play was set in the town of Bath, and tells the story of Captain Absolute who is in love with Lydia Languish, the niece of Mrs. Malaprop. She however prefers a poor lieutenant to a son of a baronet. He therefore assumes the character of a lowly Ensign named Beverly. Unknown to him, Lydia would lose half her fortune if she marries someone her aunt disapproves of. Sir Anthony Absolute arrives in Bath to see Mrs. Malaprop and proposes a match between his son and Lydia, which she welcomes.

Now the Captain is afraid of revealing his identity, for fear of losing his girl and his rival Bob Acres finds out about the match and challenges him to a duel. On the day of the duel, Bob Acres discovers that his rival, Captain Absolute, is his friend Ensign Beverly and drops the challenge and any claim to Lydia.

Until the discovery of Figure 1204, the figures did not appear to have any relation to the published work. Other than this figure, all the others are probably from a melodramatic version of the play.

Fig. 1201A
A spill vase and arbour group figure of a couple seated in front of a tree, the man with his arm around the woman. He wears a plumed hat, shirt with frilled collar, jacket, and knee breeches with boots; she wears a bodice and long dress and holds a stringed instrument in her right hand. Another man is on and behind the tree holding a knife in his right hand; he wears a plumed hat, shirt with collar, cloak, and knee breeches.
This figure is very similar to Fig. 1201.
TITLE: THE RIVAL
HEIGHT: 12 Inches
PRICE: F.

Fig. 1201B
A group figure of a woman seated wearing a bodice and an aproned dress, her hands are in her lap holding a hat. To her left a man is kneeling, presenting her with a rose. He clasps her hand with his and wears a long cloak and long tunic with boots. Behind an arbour, which is covered with a grapevine, a man stands holding a knife. He wears a plumed hat, cloak, tunic, and knee breeches holding his cloak together with his left hand.
HEIGHT: 12 Inches
PRICE: F.

26. Robin Hood
See Figure 1207 Book One

27. St. George
See Figures 1209 - 1216 Book One

St. George is the patron Saint of England and the figures could be classed as a religious figure, but it is more likely that the figures had their inspiration from theatrical productions of the time.

Fig. 1217
A figure of Saint George on horseback, his horse is rearing and the dragon lies supine below. He wears a plumed helmet, flowing cloak and high-necked buttoned tunic, holding the reins in his left hand and a short sword in his right.
This is a very rare figure and previously unrecorded. Two figures are illustrated, one in full colour and one in white, both are contemporary and date to circa 1850.
HEIGHT: 9 Inches
PRICE: F.

28. St. Patrick's Day
See Figure 1218 Book One

29. Smugglers Quarrel
See Figure 1220 Book One

30. Will Watch
See Figures 1221 - 1223 Book One

Section 2:
Opera, Ballet, and Polkas

Section 2 is divided into two parts:

    1. A listing of known performers.
    2. A listing of productions by name, including characters, and where known the actors and actresses portraying them.

1. A listing of known performers

Listed are actors and actresses with a cross-reference to Figure number. Only when there is a definite source to an identification has a cross-reference been given.

Alboni, Marrietta (1823-1894)
See Figure 1239 Book One

Foote, Maria (4th Countess of Harrington) (1797-1867)

    See Figures 1310, 1311 Book One

Grisi, Carlotta (1821-1899)
See Figures 1279, 1282 Book One

Grisi, Giulia (1811-1869)
See Figure 1312 Book One

Grahn, Lucille (Dates unknown)
See Figures 1234, 1236, 1237 Book One

Isaacs, Rebecca (1829-1877)
See Figure 1318 Book One

Kemble, Adelaide (1814-1879)
See Figure 1338 Book One

Kemble, Fanny (1809-1893)
See Figures 1254/1256 Book One

Lablache, Luigi (1794-1858)
See Figures 1292/1302 Book One

Lind, Johanna Maria (Jenny Lind) (1820-1887)

    For other figures of Jenny Lind see the Portrait Chapter, Figures 184/191
    See Figures 1300/1303, 1330, 1335 Book One

Mario, Guiseppe (1810-1883)
See Figures 1270 Book Three and 1312 Book One

Patti, Adelinna (1843-1919)
See Figure 1270 Book Three

Perrot, Jules Joseph (1800-1892)
See Figures 1234/1235, 1237/1238, 1278, and 1283 Book One

Reeves, John Sims (1818-1900)
See Figure 1308 Book One

Shaw, Mary (1814- ?)
See Figure 1338 Book One

Wood, William Burke (1779-1861)
See Figure 1277 Book One

2. A listing of productions by name, including characters, and where known the actors and actresses portraying them

1. Anna Bolena
2. **Artaxerxes**
3. **Caterina ou La Fille du Brigand**
4. Cinderella
4A. Faust
5. Fra Diavolo
6. **Giselle ou Les Wilis**
7. L'elisir D'amore
8. **La Esmeralda**
9. La Figlia del Reggimento
10. La Muette de Portici
11. Little Jockey
12. Lucia di Lammermoor
13. Lucrezia Borgia
14. **Polkas (including Bloomers & Torquay Polkas)**
15. **Robert Le Diable**
16. Semiramide
17. **William Tell**

1. Anna Bolena
See Figures 1224 - 1225 Book One and 1224A Book Three

2. Artaxerxes
See Figures 1226 - 1233 Book One

This is an opera by Thomas Augustine Arne (1710-1778) that made its debut in 1762 at Covent Garden with Charlotte Brent in the role of Mandane and John Beard as Artabanes. The opera tells the story of Artaxerxes, the son of Xerxes, The King of Persia: Artabanes, his general and Mandane, the sister of Artaxerxes, who is in love with Arbaces, the son of Artabanes.

Mandane and Arbaces must part as her father has banished him from the kingdom, as her father does not agree with the liaison. Meanwhile Artabanes has killed Xerxes and exchanged his sword with Arbaces and tells him to escape. Artaxerxes asks Artabanes to find his father's murderer and he kills Darius in a bid to shift the blame, but Arbaces is found with the murder weapon.

Artabanes then makes it known that he wants Arbaces to take the throne, and wants to help him escape. Arbaces refuses, knowing that escape would confirm his guilt. Artabanes then offers the hand of Semira to Rimenes if he assists in the plot to kill Artaxerxes.

Arbaces is in his prison cell and Artaxerxes, convinced of his innocence, allows him to escape. Artabanes finds his son Arbaces gone and, with Rimenes, plots to poison Artaxerxes at the coronation ceremony. Just as Artaxerxes is about to drink the poison, Semira enters and tells him that the palace is surrounded by troops led by Rimenes. He is ready to defend himself when Mandane arrives to tell him that Arbaces had killed Rimenes and quashed the rebellion. Artaxerxes then offers the poisoned cup to Arbaces, but Artabanes strikes it from his son's lips, admitting his guilt. Artaxerxes spares his life but banishes him from the kingdom.

Figs. 1228/1229
A pair of standing figures of Mandane and Artabanes; she holds a stringed instrument in her left hand, her right is across her waist, wearing a turban, ermine edged cloak, long dress, and pantaloons, with a sash tied around her waist. He holds a dagger in his right hand and wears a turban, ermine edged cloak, long dress tied at the waist with a sash, pantaloons, and pointed toed shoes. The blade of the dagger was a separate metal piece, which – as in the figure illustrated – is usually missing.
These very rare figures can be found with either a round gilt lined base, or an uneven rockwork base; they are modelled in the round and usually extremely well decorated. In the figures illustrated Artabanes has a gilt lined base and Mandane, a rockwork one. They are very similar to Figures 1226 and 1227 in Book One other than they have a more elaborate headdress and an even more elaborate base.
HEIGHT: 11.75 Inches
PRICE: Pair: D, Singles: E.

Figs. 1228A/1229A
A pair of figures of Mandane and Artabanes standing, she holding a stringed instrument in her left hand, her right across her waist, wearing a turban, ermine edged cloak, long dress, and pantaloons. He is similarly dressed with his left hand on his hip and his right held to his chest.
There is illustrated a small 5 inch pair that are porcelaineous and a larger 8 inch pottery version of Mandane of which there must have existed a pair. These figures are smaller versions of Figures 1228 and 1229 Book One.
HEIGHT: 5 Inches 8.5 Inches
PRICE: Pair: E, Singles: F.

Figs. 1233A/1233B
A pair of figures of Artabanes and Mandane dressed in Eastern attire of turban, long coat, dress, and trousers, he holding his hands in front with a pipe on his lap, and she holding a stringed instrument in her left hand and playing it with her right.
These figures are in so many respects similar to Figures 1232/1233 and 1230/1231 in Book One that they must be considered another version.
HEIGHT: 8 Inches
PRICE: Pair: E, Singles: F.

3. Caterina ou La Fille du Brigand
See Figures 1234 -1247 in Books One and Three

A ballet written and performed by Jules Perrot, the music composed by Signor Pugni it was staged at Her Majesty's Theatre in 1846.

It tells the story of Caterina, who on the death of her father becomes the leader of a group of bandits, her lieutenant, a man named Diavolino, and the escapades and tribulations they encountered.

Figs. 1229B/1229C
A pair of figures of Artabanes and Mandane reclining on elaborate six legged couches; both wear turbans and Eastern attire. He has one leg raised and beside the other is a Hubble-Bubble pipe. She holds a stringed instrument in both hands. HEIGHT: 5 Inches
PRICE: Pair: E, Singles: F.

Fig. 1244A
A figure of Diavolino standing holding a rifle by its barrel in his left hand and a cup in his right, wearing a steeple hat with ribbons, frilled shirt, jacket, knee breeches, and long socks. To his right on rockwork rests two barrels, one on top of the other and a small jug.
There are now six figures of Diavolino recorded for which no pair of Catarina has been found; we have however reserved Fig. 1244B in the event that one does come to light, although it is now more than probable that these were all made as single figures.
HEIGHT: 14.5 Inches
PRICE: E.

4. Cinderella (La Cenerentola)
See Figures 1249 -1258 in Books One and Three

Based on the fairy tale by Charles Perrault, it was the inspiration for many operas, the most famous being Rossini's adaptation 'La Cenerentola', performed at Covent Garden in 1848 with Marietta Alboni in the title role. It tells the story of Cinderella, who is forced to do all the household chores by her wicked stepmother and two stepsisters. She is made to stay at home whilst they go to a ball; her fairy godmother appears and grants her wish to go to the ball. Using her wand she turns Cinderella's dowdy clothes into a ball dress, a pumpkin into a carriage, and six mice into horses to pull it. The only condition is that she must return by midnight, when all would return to its original self. Cinderella goes to the ball and meets Prince Charming who falls in love with her, but before he can tell her, she rushes off before the stroke of midnight, leaving a glass slipper behind.

The Prince picks up the slipper and declares that whoever the slipper fits he will wed. Everyone tries on the slipper, even the stepsisters, but to no avail, until Cinderella comes forward and slips it on.

In Book Three two prints of Fanny Kemble are illustrated. There is no evidence that she was ever in a production of Cinderella, but the dress and facial features are similar to Figures 1254 and 1256.

The print, Figure 1257, is of Kemble in the role of Juliet and whilst Figure 1255 does not resemble Romeo, it is possible that a production of Romeo and Juliet may have been staged in contemporary Victorian dress.

4A Faust
See Figure 1270 Book Three

5. Fra Diavolo
See Figure 1277 Book One

6. Giselle ou Les Willis
See Figures 1278 - 1289 Books One and Three

A two act ballet by Vernoy de Saint-Georges, Gautier, and Coralli. It was first performed in Paris in 1841 and in 1842 at Her Majesty's Theatre, with Jules Perrot playing the role of Albrecht and his wife Carlotta Grisi in the role of Giselle.

It tells the storey of Giselle, a young peasant girl who lives by the Rhine. She meets and falls in love with a handsome young man by the name of Loys; but he is in reality Albrecht, The Duke of Silesia. To express their affection for each other, they spend their time dancing. The gamekeeper, Hilarion, who also has feelings for Giselle, tells her that Loys isn't who he pretends to be, and reveals his identity. With this knowledge, she tries to kill herself with her lover's sword. Unsuccessful, she starts a frenzied dance, at the end of which she drops dead. In the second act she returns from the dead as a ghost. Albrecht pursues her only to find out that she is a ghost. She returns to her grave, leaving Albrecht inconsolable with grief.

Figs. 1282/1283
A pair of figures of Giselle and Albrecht standing cross-legged in dancing pose on gilt lined bases, both with one hand raised to their heads and the other at their waist, she wearing a hat, open necked blouse, and skirt with knickers showing, he wearing a headband, tunic, and pantaloons with a sash around his waist.
This pair is a variation on Figures 1278/1279; whilst similar, there are differences: the base and supporting pillars have been changed, as has his sash, and these are in pottery whilst 1278/1279 are porcelaneous. These figures can be found in two sizes.
HEIGHT: 9.5 Inches, 10.5 Inches
PRICE: Pair: E, Singles: F.

7. L'elisir D'amore (The elixir of love)
See Figures 1292 - 1293 Book One

8. La Esmeralda
See Figures 1294 - 1299 Books One and Three

Victor Hugo's novel *Notre Dame de Paris*, about Paris during the reign of Louis XI, was published in 1831. It was the inspiration for La Esmeralda, Jules Perrot's ballet in three acts and five scenes. Not only did Perrot write the ballet, he also took the role of Gringoire, appearing at Her Majesty's Theatre on 9th March 1844.

Fig. 1296
A group figure of Esmeralda and Gringoire standing cross-legged, she with a tambourine in her left hand, her right at her waist, wearing a blouse and knee length skirt, he holding a triangle on his left shoulder, wearing a scarf, jacket, waistcoat, and knee breeches.
HEIGHT: 6 Inches
PRICE: G.

9. La Figlia del Reggimento

For further figures of Jenny Lind see Robert Le Diable (Robert the Devil) Figures 1330-1335 Book One and Jenny Lind Book One Figures 184-191

See Figures 1300 - 1303 Book One

10. La Muette de Portici
(The Dumb Girl of Portici)

See Figures 1305 - 1306 Books One and Three

11. Lucia di Lammermoor

See Figures 1308 - 1309 Book One

12. Little Jockey

See Figures 1310 - 1311 Book One

13. Lucrezia Borgia

See Figure 1312 Book One

14. Polkas

See Figures 1313 - 1325 Books One and Three

Bloomers

Bloomer, Amelia (1818-1894)

Born in Homer, New York, in 1840, she married Dexter C. Bloomer and became the first woman to publish a paper solely for women, entitled *The Lily: A monthly journal devoted to Temperance and Literature*. In the May edition of 1851 she told readers that they should adopt the dress of Mrs. Elizabeth Smith Miller, the daughter of the famous abolitionist Gerrit Smith. Letters poured into the paper by women asking how to make the dress and Bloomer-ism was born. She never visited England and the figures were either inspired by the dress itself or the theatrical productions and music sheets which followed.

The invention of Bloomers caused a storm across the world in ladies fashion in the early 1850s. The figures that the potteries produced did not portray her but were inspired by the many musicals and waltzes produced as 'Bloomer mania' spread across the country.

Amongst the productions were 'The Bloomer Costume' performed at The Strand Theatre in 1851, 'Bloomerism: or The Follies of the day' performed at The Adelphi Theatre in the same year and music sheets of 'I want to be a Bloomer, The new Bloomer Polka, The English Bloomer and The Bloomer Polka.

La Polka

15. Robert Le Diable

See Figures 1330 - 1336 Book One

An opera in four parts by Meyerbeer, it was first performed in Paris in 1831 and performed at Drury Lane Theatre in 1833. Jenny Lind made her debut in the role of Alice in 1847 at Her Majesty's Theatre.

The story is set in Palermo where Robert the sixth Duke of Normandy falls in love with the beautiful Princess Isabella, the daughter of The Duke of Messina. A story of intrigue, Robert is influenced by the evil Bertram and sung about by Raimbaud, a Norman minstrel who is betrothed to be married to Alice, the foster-sister of Robert. Alice, seeing that Bertram has a hold over Robert, sets out to free him from his influence. She is successful, with the opera finishing with Alice accompanying him up the aisle to his bride Princess Isabella.

For further figures of Jenny Lind see La Figlia Del Reggimento and Jenny Lind in Book One

Figs. 1321/1320
A pair of figures of a boy and girl, she wearing The Bloomer costume and holding a flower in her right hand and a basket of flowers in her left. He is bareheaded and wears a frilled shirt, waistcoat, three quarter length jacket tied at the waist with a sash, and knee breeches, holding a bird in his right hand and a basket of fruit in his left.
The brimmed hat was an integral part of The Bloomer Costume and the girl in Fig. 1320 is neither wearing nor holding one. In view of this and the dress of the man, it is possible that she was not made to portray a Bloomer girl.
HEIGHT: 8 Inches
PRICE: Pair: F, Singles: G.

Fig. 1332
A figure of a woman seated with her hands holding the base of a pillar on which is a cross; she wears a blouse and long skirt with a sash over her right shoulder and across her chest. She gazes up. She is in the role of 'Alice' from Meyerbeer's opera.
Three figures are illustrated, varying in size from 8 inches to 9.5 inches; while they are very similar, the main difference is the decoration to the pillar.
TITLE: Jenny Lind in gilt script
HEIGHT: 9.5 Inches titled,
9.25 Inches, & 8 Inches
PRICE: E.

16. Semiramide
See Figure 1338 Book One

17. William Tell
See Figures 1341 - 1347 Books One and Three

An opera by Rossini, from Schiller's 1804 dramatic version, which was in turn taken from a ballad dating before 1474. It made its debut in Paris in 1829.

The story is set in Switzerland in 1307 and tells of the adventures of William Tell, a patriot and skilful archer. He is the leader of the resistance to the tyranny of the Austrian Gessler; supported by the elderly Melcthal, whose son Arnold loves the Austrian Princess Mathide. When they declare their love, Tell arrives to inform them of the death of Melcthal. Arnold agrees to join Tell and overthrow Gessler.

In the main square of Altdorf, Gessler demands that Tell bows to his hat. Tell refuses and is condemned to shoot an arrow from the head of his son Jemmy. He is successful and he reveals that if he had failed the second bolt would have killed Gessler. On learning of this Gessler has him arrested and he is taken to the Castle of Kussnacht in the middle of Lake Lucerne.

Hearing of this, Arnold leads an uprising and after Tell's boat is driven ashore, he shoots Gessler and victory is gained.

Whilst all figures of Tell have been placed in the opera section, there were many theatrical productions, and it may be that some of these are theatrical rather than operatic.

Fig. 1344A
A figure of William Tell standing on a gilt lined rococo style base; he wears a hat with feather, long tunic and a cloak, both arms are raised to his waist, and a long bow is drawn on his tunic.
A larger superior version of Figure 1344 Book One.
HEIGHT: 10.25 Inches
PRICE: F.

Fig. 1340P
A figure of William Tell standing on a titled base with raised gilt capitals; he wears highland dress and holds a long bow in his right hand, his left on his hip, a scarf over his shoulder which touches a quiver full of arrows that are on the ground by his left foot.
This figure pairs with Rob Roy Macgregor, See Figure 1037 Book One.
TITLE: W. TELL
HEIGHT: 19.5 Inches
PRICE: F.

Section 3: Circus.

Section 3 is divided into two parts:

1. A listing of known performers with a short biography of their life and career.
2. Performers and productions portrayed and dramatised.

1. A listing of known performers

Astley, Philip (1742-1814)

On leaving the cavalry in 1768, he opened a riding school and combined this with clowns and tumblers, making it probably the first true circus. In 1788 he built his first Amphitheatre, but because he had no license he was forced to close. He then went to Paris and opened there, but due to the revolution he returned home and in 1804 built another Amphitheatre which at a cost of £800 housed 2,500 spectators.

Hippodrama

In Hippodrama the trained horses are considered the actors, with their own parts to play. It caught on and made its first real impact at Astley's Amphitheatre at the beginning of the nineteenth century, with productions such as *The Blood Red Knight* in 1810 and *Blue Beard* in 1811. The most popular production however was *Mazeppa*, which was revived many times.

Ducrow, Andrew (1793-1848)

The son of a Flemish strong man, he was an accomplished mime act, acrobat, and horse rider. He made his debut at Astley's in 1814, returning in 1824 to become the chief attraction, and performing a re-enactment of The Battle of Waterloo. In 1827 his piece de resistance was riding six horses at the same time. In 1830 he took on the lease of the Amphitheatre and introduced the spectacle of Mazeppa. In 1842 the Amphitheatre was destroyed by fire for the third time.

Rarey, John Solomon (1827-1866)
See Figures 1367/1368 Book One

Stratton, Charles Sherwood (Tom Thumb) (1832-1883)

See Figure 1373 Book One

2. Performers and productions portrayed and dramatised

1. Amazon
2. **Mazeppa**
3. **Horse Acts**
4. Rarey, John Solomon
5. **Tightrope Walkers**
6. Tom Thumb
7. Clowns

1. Amazon
See Figure 1351 Book One

2. Mazeppa
See Figures 1352 - 1356 Books One and Three

In 1819 Byron published a poem based on a description of the ride Mazeppa took in Voltaire's novel Charles XII, which in turn was based on the real life adventures of Ivan Stapanovich Mazeppa (1644-1709). He was caught having an illicit love affair with a nobleman's wife and as a punishment he was bound naked to the back of a wild horse. The horse was beaten until it was mad and it galloped through the forest reaching the Ukraine where it dropped dead. Mazeppa was rescued by peasants and joined the Cossacks rising quickly through the ranks to become a commander in 1687. He was made Prince of the Ukraine by Peter the Great but changed his loyalties and fought for Charles XII of Sweden. In 1709 at the battle of Pultowa he was defeated and fled to Bender.

It was adapted for the stage by H. M. Milner and performed at The Old Vic in 1823 and later at Astley's Amphitheatre in 1831 where it continued to be performed late into the 1870s.

The part of Mazeppa was played over the years by a number of performers, playbills of the time name Mr. West Jnr. circa 1838 and Miss Adah Isaacs Menken circa 1864.

Fig. 1352
A mirror image pair to this figure can be found Fig. 1352A has been reserved for it.

3. Horse Acts
See Figures 1357 - 1365 Books One and Three

Figs. 1357/1357A
A pair of figures of a boy and girl standing on the backs of rearing horses that have their front feet on the top of a gate. Both children have one hand raised to their head holding a hat; he wears a long tunic with a scarf around his waist, she wears a bodice, short skirt with knickers, and a scarf is draped around her. The horses have saddles and decorated saddlecloths.
These figures portray a circus act, probably Astley's.
HEIGHT: 10 Inches
PRICE: Pair: D, Singles: E.

Fig. 1366
A figure of a boy seated on the back of a rearing horse; he wears a hat, open necked shirt, jacket, and breeches. The horse's saddlecloth is multi-coloured as are the reins.
This figure is similar to Fig. 1360A for which there is a pair and it is probable that a pair exists for this figure. Fig. 1366A has been reserved for it.
HEIGHT: 7 Inches
PRICE: Pair: E, Singles: F.

4. Rarey, John Solomon
See Figures 1367 - 1368 Book One

5. Tightrope Walkers
See Figures 1369 - 1372 Book One

The notable female tightrope walker of the early part of the Victorian era was Louisa Woolford. She was the second wife of Andrew Ducrow, however no source identifying her with any figure has ever been recorded.

Fig. 1368
Illustrated is a figure of a man standing wearing shorts and shoes, holding a balancing pole, and standing beside a coiled rope.
Jean Francois Gravelet became famous in 1859 when using the name Blondini he crossed Niagara Falls on a tightrope. The figure is not well modelled and no gilding has been used. It would have been produced quite cheaply, and as it is titled, it was probably made to have been either given away or sold at his performances.
TITLE: BLONDINI in raised capitals
HEIGHT: 5 Inches
PRICE: F.

6. Tom Thumb
See Figures 1373 - 1373A Books One and Three

7. Clowns
See Figures 1374 - 1376A Books One and Three

Section 4:
Unidentified Characters

In this section actors, actresses, musicians, and dancers who have yet to be identified and for which sources have yet to be found are illustrated.

Section 4 is divided in four parts:

1. Unidentified Actors and Actresses
2. Unidentified Characters in Boats
3. Unidentified Dancers
4. Unidentified Musicians

1. Unidentified Actors and Actresses

Figs. 1385C/1385D
A pair of figures in Tyrolean costume standing, he with his legs crossed, she wears a hat necklace, bodice, and long skirt. She holds an object in her left hand. He wear as steeple hat, short sleeved jacket, waistcoat, and knee breeches. He holds a pistol in his right hand and a knife in his left.
This pair was made by the Parr Factory; they are unidentified but, with all the items they are holding, it is more than likely that they portray a particular scene for a theatrical production.
HEIGHT: 8.75 Inches
PRICE: Pair: E., Singles: F.

Fig. 1386D
A figure of a beaded man dressed in Eastern attire, his left hand is on his hip and his right holds a 'Hookah pipe', the tube of which is in his mouth.
There is probably a pair to this figure. Fig. 1386E has been reserved for it.
HEIGHT: 6.5
PRICE: G.

Figs. 1386F/1386G
A pair of figures of a man and woman standing, leaning against rockwork, wearing plumed hats, he with a jacket, shirt with a tie, and trousers, she a blouse and long skirt with bloomers. She has her right hand on her hip. He has his left hand on his hip. They both hold what appears to be a posy. HEIGHT: 8.5 Inches
PRICE: Pair: E, Singles: F.
CORRECTION
Fig. 1392A is now Figure 2105 as this is the pair to Fig. 2104.

Fig. 1396A
A figure of a man standing wearing a top hat adorned with a feather and a cross, a tunic with a breastplate of armour, and a skirt. The breastplate also has a cross on it. He is bearded and has a moustache. His right hand is on his hip, holding an object to his chest in his left hand.
This is a very large and imposing figure, and has so far defied identification. He is invariably in the white; the authors have never seen a coloured example. He always has a ferocious expression and no one has been able to discern what the object is he is holding in his hand. Various attributions have been suggested, none in the author's opinion acceptable. Sir Francis Drake and a Conquistador are the two most suggested. The author's favourite, though even less likely, is that he is holding a seventeenth century mobile telephone and his expression is due to the fact that he is in an area of poor reception.
HEIGHT: 19 Inches
PRICE: F.

Figs. 1398A/1398B
A pair of figures of men standing on circular, gilt lined bases; both men are dressed similarly in a Cavalier style costume, both wear hats with brims, shirts, and jackets buttoned at the waist, knee breeches with boots, and a belt across their chests. The left hand figure has his right arm to his side resting on a cloaked pillar, his left raised to his face holding a letter. The right hand side figure holds an empty basket in his left hand and one full of grapes in his right.
HEIGHT: 11 Inches
PRICE: Pair: F, Singles: G.

Fig. 1403B
A figure of a man standing on a round gilt lined base, wearing a plumed hat, shirt, tunic, sash across his chest, and knee breeches with boots. A large cloak is across his shoulders and rests on the ground; he holds a sword in his right hand.
This figure is similar to Figure 1403 Book One and may be portraying the same individual.
HEIGHT: 13.75
PRICE: F.

Figs. 1404C/1404D
A pair of figures of men, both standing wearing plumed hats, large cloaks, tunics with a belt that holds knives, and knee boots. The man on the left has an open necked tunic with a frilled shirt collar and is holding a box shaped object in his right hand. The tunic of the man on the right is buttoned to the neck, he holds a rifle in his left hand, and his cloak is ermine edged. Both men have shoulder length hair. **In Book One the figure on the left was included in 'unidentified musicians'. With the discovery of the pair, it is now certain that they portray actors, but until the object the man is holding is identified precisely, who they portray remains a mystery.**
HEIGHT: 11 Inches
PRICE: Pair: E, Singles: F.

Figs. 1405/1406
A pair of figures of a man and woman standing; he wears a plumed hat, frilled shirt, coat, knee breeches, and boots. A long cloak is over his right shoulder. He holds a sword against a shield. She wears a plumed hat, bodice, and long skirt with an apron. An open book is held in her right hand and by her left on rockwork a bird is perched.
HEIGHT: 10.5 Inches
PRICE: Pair: E, Singles: F.

Fig. 1406E
A figure of a man and woman standing; he wears a shirt, jacket, waistcoat, and knee breeches. His right hand is in his trouser pocket and his left is around the shoulders of a woman who wears a blouse and long skirt. She holds a handbag in her right hand; a man's head emerges from behind the man's leg.
This is a rare figure and the man's face and head at the bottom has defied explanation, it is possibly theatre – crime. At one time an attribution of 'The Brothers Grimm' was given but we know of no evidence to support this.
HEIGHT: 7.5 Inches
PRICE: E.

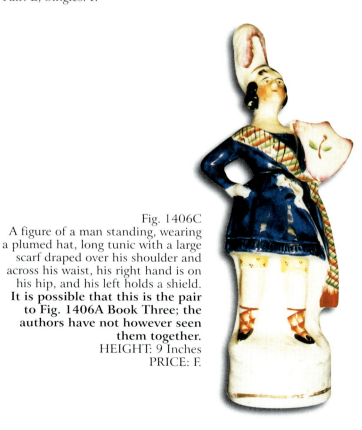

Fig. 1406C
A figure of a man standing, wearing a plumed hat, long tunic with a large scarf draped over his shoulder and across his waist, his right hand is on his hip, and his left holds a shield.
It is possible that this is the pair to Fig. 1406A Book Three; the authors have not however seen them together.
HEIGHT: 9 Inches
PRICE: F.

Fig. 1407A
A figure of a man standing, legs astride, wearing a hat with two feathers, shirt with neckerchief, jacket, and kilt with boots. He holds a pistol in his right hand and a knife in his left; at his feet there are two barrels.
This figure is identical to Figure 1407 Book One other than the head has been changed. The original head must have broken and the restorer has found a head from another figure. In fact it is a head from Figure 1411 Book One. It has been done very well, but as a marriage it is really a fake.
HEIGHT: 11.75 Inches
PRICE: H.

Figs. 1412/1413
A pair of figures of standing shepherds, both on rococo bases,
he with his right hand leaning on rock-work, his left on his
hip. He wears a cap, tasselled jacket, skirt, and pantaloons.
His dog sits below. She wears a scarf on her head, bodice, and
long skirt with trousers; she rests her left arm on rockwork.
Below her is a sheep.
The discovery of the pair has confirmed that these figures portray shepherds; it is possible in view of their attire that they are theatrical but more likely that they are not.
The sheep's head in Fig. 1413 has been very badly restored.
HEIGHT: 12.5 Inches
PRICE: Pair: F, Singles: G.

Fig. 1413A
A group figure of a man standing with his right arm across the shoulders of a small boy who sits on rockwork to his side; he wears a plumed hat, shirt, and tunic, with a scarf across his shoulder and tied at the waist with a sash. He holds a drinking horn in his left hand and a dog is drinking from it. The boy wears a long tunic and has one hand on the dog's head.
In view of the attire, it can be assumed that this figure portrays a scene from an as yet unidentified play.
HEIGHT: 8 Inches
PRICE: F.

Fig. 1414
A figure of a man standing on rockwork holding a scroll in his right hand, his left resting on his leg or in the 9 inch version aloft. He wears a plumed hat, cloak, tunic, short trousers with tights, and short boots.
This figure can be found in four sizes, all illustrated. Two attributions have been given to these figures, firstly as Conrad a pirate chief from Byron's poem 'The Corsair' and secondly as Edmund Kean as Richard III. No source or evidence as yet supports either attribution, and with the discovery of a pair to the smallest size (See Fig. 1414A) both these suggestions seem unlikely.
HEIGHT: 9, 8, 7.25, and 6.25 Inches
PRICE: 9 Inch: E, 8 and 7.25 Inch: F, 6.25 Inch: G.

Figs. 1416/1417
A pair of figures of a man and woman standing; he has his right hand across his chest, his left resting on his hip and wears a plumed hat, tunic with sporran, and long scarf over his shoulders, she wears a turban with a feather, shawl over her shoulders, bodice, and long two-tiered skirt.
This pair has a marked resemblance to Fig. 1393/1394 Book One and it is probable that they are portraying the same characters.
HEIGHT: 9.5 Inches
PRICE: Pair: E, Singles: G.

Fig. 1414A
A figure of a man standing on rockwork, holding a pistol in his left hand, his right holding his jacket; he is wearing a plumed hat, jacket, tunic, skirt, and boots.
This figure is almost a mirror image of Fig. 1414 and is its pair. It possibly portrays the same character.
They are reminiscent of Figs. 1925/1926 Book One and it may be that all these figures, together with Figs. 1414/1414A and 1927, portray the same characters.
HEIGHT: 6.25 Inches
PRICE: F.

Fig. 1415B
A figure of a man sitting on rockwork; to his right are two casks. He holds a mug in his right hand and the barrel of a rifle in his left. The rifle is between his legs with the butt on the ground. He wears a steeple hat with a long ribbon, shirt, jacket, breeches, stockings, and shoes.
This very rare figure has been found titled 'Brigand'. It is possible that it portrays Perrot in the role of 'Diavolino'. There were many melodramatic productions in Victorian times of plays containing 'Brigands' and in particular a production that was revived at the Surrey Theatre in 1867 of that title with a character of 'Massaroni' in the title role.
HEIGHT: 14.25 Inches
PRICE: E.

Fig. 1420
A standing figure of a man wearing a short jacket, skirt, shoes, and long socks. His left hand is on his hip and his right holds a very large hat with plumes.
This figure appears very theatrical in his dress and stance, and there is probably a pair to it. Fig. 1420A has been reserved for it.
HEIGHT: 4.5 Inches
PRICE: G.

Fig. 1428C
A figure of a woman standing wearing a hat, low cut blouse, and long skirt with an apron; she holds a posy in her right hand and is lifting her apron with her left. **There is a pair to this figure. Fig. 1428D has been reserved for it.** HEIGHT: 7 Inches PRICE: F.

Figs. 1424A/1424
A pair of figures of a man and woman standing on circular, orange lined bases; he wears a hat, long jacket, shirt, and breeches. She wears a loose sleeve coat, blouse, and long skirt. She holds a stringed instrument in both hands.
HEIGHT: 6 Inches
PRICE: Pair: G, Singles: H.

Figs. 1425/1425A
A pair of figures of a man and woman standing, he bearded with his right arm raised to his waist, his left to his side holding a sword, wearing a turban, long jacket, shirt, and Eastern trousers, she with both hands to her side, wearing a turban, long jacket, waistcoat, shirt, and eastern trousers.
Two pairs of figures are illustrated, one delicately coloured and the other mainly white. These figures are again similar to Figures 1386B, 1386C, and 1424B Book Three; a popular pair but the roles and play are still unidentified.
These figures can be found in two sizes, the larger size having a rococo base. The larger version of the man is also illustrated.
HEIGHT: 10.25 Inches, 8.25 Inches
PRICE: Pair: E, Singles: F.

Figs. 1430/1429
A pair of figures of a man and woman seated; he wears an open necked shirt, jacket, belted tunic, and loose trousers, holding a scroll in his right hand. She is similarly dressed and holds a book in her left hand.
The discovery of the male figure probably provides identification of the pair; he is similar in many respects to a figure of Byron (see Figure 80 Book One). The head is identical. This would usually be enough to confirm the identification, but these figures are the product of The 'Alpha' factory and the heads on many of their figures are similar. Her features are very similar to Fig. 1427 Book One. Taking all this into account, the authors are of the opinion that this pair of figures does portray Byron and The Maid of Athens.
HEIGHT: 6.5 Inches
PRICE: Pair: E, Singles: F.

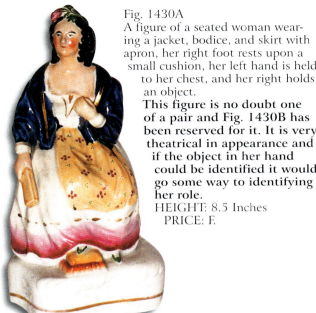

Fig. 1430A
A figure of a seated woman wearing a jacket, bodice, and skirt with apron, her right foot rests upon a small cushion, her left hand is held to her chest, and her right holds an object.
This figure is no doubt one of a pair and Fig. 1430B has been reserved for it. It is very theatrical in appearance and if the object in her hand could be identified it would go some way to identifying her role.
HEIGHT: 8.5 Inches
PRICE: F.

Fig. 1430E
A group figure of a man standing and a woman seated. He wears a long tunic and boots, he holds a flower in his right hand and his left is around the shoulders of the woman who wears a long coat and skirt. She holds a bowl of flowers in her lap.
The dress of this couple is very theatrical but is as yet unidentified.
HEIGHT: 8.5 Inches
PRICE: F.

Fig. 1430C
A figure of a man with long hair standing hunched over, wearing a top hat, long jacket, and knee length trousers.
This figure is very theatrical but has not been identified. There is probably a pair. Figure 1430D has been reserved for it. One possible attribution is 'Smike' from Dickens's *Nicholas Nickleby*.
HEIGHT: 9 Inches
PRICE: F.

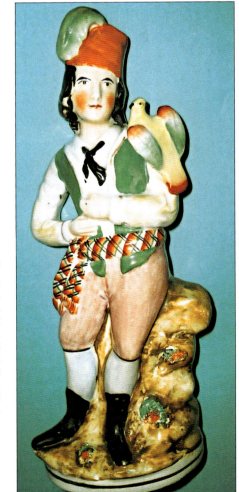

Fig. 1430F
A figure of a man standing, wearing a fez, shirt with tie, waistcoat, sash around his waist, knee breeches, and boots, with both hands clasping his waistcoat. A bird is perched on his shoulder.
This figure has a pair as yet unrecorded; he has been included in this chapter due to his attire. It is possible that he is not theatrical and portrays a falconer, or is purely decorative. Discovery of the pair may be enlightening.
HEIGHT: 9.75 Inches
PRICE: F.

Figs. 1433A/1433B

A pair of standing figures of a sailor or brigand and his girl; he wears a cap, jacket, open necked shirt, and knee length trousers with boots. He has a sash around his waist in which two pistols are tucked. His right hand holds an object and rests upon two stringed parcels by his side; a barrel is at his feet. She wears a headdress, jacket, blouse with sash, and a skirt with an apron. She holds a bag in her right hand and her left rests on the top of three stringed parcels. Both figures are on rococo bases.
HEIGHT: 8 Inches
PRICE: Pair: E, Singles: F.

Fig. 1437E
A figure of a bearded man standing, wearing a plumed hat, tunic, kilt, and boots with a scarf over his shoulder and around his waist, holding what appears to be a knife in his right hand. **There is probably a pair to this figure. Fig. 1437F has been reserved for it.**
HEIGHT: 8.5 Inches
PRICE: F.

Fig. 1437C
A figure of a man standing, wearing a hat, cravat, shirt, long jacket, and trousers, and holding a walking stick in his right hand. **There is probably a pair to this figure. Fig. 1437D has been reserved for it.**
HEIGHT: 7 Inches
PRICE: F.

Fig. 1439A
A group figure of a man and woman seated on an elaborately framed couch; he wears a flat cap, ermine edged cloak, tunic, and knee breeches, and holds the hand of the woman who wears a hat, blouse, jacket, and long dress.
HEIGHT: 7 Inches
PRICE: F.

Figs. 1439B/1439C
A pair of figures with a man seated in a chair, wearing a tie, full-length waistcoat, long jacket, and knee breeches; he appears to be taking snuff from a box held in his right hand. The woman is also seated in a chair with one foot on a footstool; she wears an open sleeve blouse and long dress. A girl child stands on the chair with both arms around the woman's neck.
These two figures were not before recognised as a pair. She appeared as Fig. 550 Book One Victoria and The Princess Royal, he appeared as Fig. 69 Book One Robert Burns. The authors believe that both these attributions can now be discounted. It is possible that they are portraits but more likely that they are either theatrical or from literature.
HEIGHT: 7.5 Inches
PRICE: Pair: E, Singles: F.

Fig. 1444A
A group figure of a boy standing and a girl seated; he wears a shirt with tie, jacket, and long trousers tied with a belt. His left hand is on his hip and his right rests on the back of the girl. She wears a short sleeve blouse and long skirt. They are both barefooted, and there is a large plant to his side.
It is possible that this group portrays 'Paul & Virginia' but no titled figure has been recorded to confirm this attribution.
HEIGHT: 10.5 Inches
PRICE: G.

Figs. 1441A/1441B
A pair of figures of a man and woman standing; he wears a long coat, waistcoat, and knee breeches. He holds a tricorn hat in his right hand and his left is on his hip; a small pillar is to his left. She wears a headdress, jacket, and long dress decorated with flowers; a small pillar is to her right.
With figures of this size, there is usually a larger version, but none have been recorded.
HEIGHT: 4 Inches
PRICE: Pair: F, Singles: G.

Fig. 1445A
A group figure of a boy and girl standing in front of a brick wall and holding a child aloft between them. The girl has long hair and wears a blouse and long skirt with knickers showing. The boy stands with one foot on steps and wears an open necked shirt, jacket, and skirt with trousers. The child sits on their shoulders and wears a blouse and skirt. The base is oddly shaped.
There has been much speculation as to what this group portrays. It is probably a scene from a play, but it is possible that it is a portrayal of the Royal Children. It is very well modelled and coloured.
HEIGHT: 9.5 Inches
PRICE: F.

Fig. 1448A
A standing figure of a woman who wears
a plumed hat, bodice, and a two-tiered
skirt with pantaloons. She holds a bird in
her right hand and a nest in her left.
**There is no doubt a pair to this figure.
Fig. 1448B has been reserved for it.
The pair is not known to the authors,
and it is possible that this figure is
not theatrical.**
HEIGHT: 9 Inches
PRICE: G.

Fig. 1448C
A figure of a man standing, wearing a
plumed hat, cloak, open neck jerkin, and
knee length breeches tied with a sash.
His left arm is across his waist and his right
arm rests on a small harp.
**From his dress and posture this is
clearly a theatrical figure and it may
well be the pair to Fig. 1448A.**
HEIGHT: 9 Inches
PRICE: F.

Fig. 1449A
A figure of a seated woman with long hair,
wearing a helmet, bodice, and skirt with
socks. She holds a letter in her right hand
and her left rests on a shield. A long sword
lies on the ground in front of her.
**There is a pair to this figure, a mirror
image, and Fig. 1449B has been reserved for it. A number of attributions
have been made for these figures, both
'Joan of Arc' and 'France' has been suggested but no evidence or source has yet
been found.**
HEIGHT: 7 Inches
PRICE: Pair: F, Singles: G.

Figs. 1450/1450A
A pair of figures of a man and woman standing dressed in Eastern attire; he wears a turban, ermine edged cloak, tunic tied at the waist with a sash, and breeches. His left hand is around a large pot that rests on rockwork. She wears a headscarf, long jacket, long skirt, and pantaloons. Her right hand rests on a large pot that rests on rockwork.
The dress of this pair of figures is of a very theatrical nature and no doubt depicts characters from an as yet unidentified play.
HEIGHT: 8.5 Inches
PRICE: Pair: F, Singles: G.

Fig. 1452A
A spill vase group of a man sitting and a woman kneeling in front of a tree, both wear plumed hats. She wears a bodice and long skirt, holds a basket of fruit in her right hand, and her left is held in his right. His other arm is around her. He wears an ermine edged jacket, loose shirt, and a skirt over striped trousers.
HEIGHT: 8.5 Inches
PRICE: G.

Fig. 1450B
A standing figure of a woman who wears a large hat, bodice, cloak, and two-tiered skirt with pantaloons. A necklace is around her neck, her left hand holds her cloak, and a basket is held in her right hand.
There is no doubt a pair to this figure. Fig. 1450C has been reserved for it.
HEIGHT: 9 Inches
PRICE: G.

Fig. 1455A
A standing figure of a man dressed in Eastern attire of plumed hat, long coat over a dress with trousers, and holding what appears to be a bunch of grapes in his right hand. At his side a cockerel and a chicken are perched, one above the other.
A very attractive and well-modelled figure. There is very likely a pair for which Fig. 1455B has been reserved. It is very theatrical in appearance and with all the 'clues' it should be possible to ascertain which production was its source.
HEIGHT: 9 Inches
PRICE: F.

Fig. 1458D
A spill vase group figure of a woman seated in the branch of a tree clad in Eastern attire of turban, jacket, and long skirt tied at the waist with a scarf. Standing below and to her right, a man stands wearing a turban, jacket, shirt, and Eastern trousers tied at the waist with a sash. He is holding a basket of grapes in his right hand and he peers into the distance holding his left hand to his forehead. A basket of grapes is on the ground beneath a fence.
There are a number of figures portraying this man and woman; it was clearly a popular subject, but the characters and the play are all still unidentified.
HEIGHT: 11 Inches
PRICE: E.

Figs. 1458/1459
A pair of groups of figures of a woman seated upon a camel with a man standing below. She is taking a cup from him and is wearing a turban, blouse, and dress with a sash around her waist; he is holding a bottle in his right hand, wearing a turban, jacket, and pantaloons. There is a small pond on the base.
This figure can be found in two sizes, a 10.75. Inch pair and an 8-inch single illustrated.
The large left hand side figure has a potter's error; the man who is a separate mould is missing altogether. It has been suggested that these groups portray Lady Hester Stanhope, but there is no evidence to support this and the author's opinion is that this is unlikely.
HEIGHT: 10.75 Inches, 8 Inches
PRICE: Pair: D, Singles: E.

Fig. 1458E
A spill vase group figure of a standing man and seated woman, both dressed in Eastern attire, he with a turban, shirt, ermine edged jacket, and pantaloons, she with a turban, blouse, jacket, and long skirt.
HEIGHT: 8 Inches
PRICE: F.

Fig. 1467

A group figure of a standing boy and girl, she leaning on his shoulder, he with his left hand raised to his head gazing into the distance. A basket rests on his hip, a fishing net over his right arm. He wears a cap, jacket, shirt, and trousers; she wears a coat and a long dress.

It has been suggested that this figure is of operatic inspiration. If so it probably depicts Fenella and Masaniello from the opera 'The Dumb Girl of Portici'.

Three figures are illustrated, identical apart from decoration.
HEIGHT: 14 Inches
PRICE: F.

Fig. 1473A

A group figure of a woman standing, leaning on a brick pillar wearing a plumed hat, long jacket, and long dress. A man sits to her right, also wearing a plumed hat, shirt, jacket with short sleeves, and kilt, holding an object in his lap. There is a large flowering plant adorning the base.
HEIGHT: 11 Inches
PRICE: F.

Figs. 1459E/1459F

A pair of figures of a man and woman seated on standing camels, he with his right hand holding the reins, wearing a cap, scarf, jacket, and kilt; she has her right arm across her chest, her left to her side holding the reins, wearing a head dress, bodice, and skirt.

It is possible that these and figures 1459B/1459C in Book Three are portraits of Florence and Sam Baker. He was an adventurer and explorer who left England after his wife died. He saw Florence in a slave market, her real name was Barbara Maria Szasz, and she had been born in Transylvania in about 1845. Her parents had died in the Hungarian revolt against Austria and slave traders had captured her as a child. He tried to buy her but was bidding against The Pasha, the Ottoman ruler of the region. Unsuccessful, he then persuaded her attendant slave by means of a bribe to hand her over to him and they fled to the Romanian border. They went to Egypt and explored the Nile; part of their journey past the Sudan was accomplished on camelback. After many adventures, including the discovery of the Murchison falls, they arrived back in England after four years and married in Piccadilly. Sam received a hero's welcome from the Royal Geographical Society, and its President, Murchison, who Sam had tactfully named the falls after, contacted *The Times,* which published a glowing report as did *The Illustrated London News.* Their fame spread and Sam received a knighthood. An engraving appeared in *The Illustrated London News* showing both Sam and Florence on camelback and could be the source or inspiration of these figures.
HEIGHT: 9 Inches
PRICE: Pair: E, Singles: F.

111

Fig. 1473B
A group figure of a man and woman standing; he wears a plumed hat, decorated shirt tunic, and leggings. A knife is suspended from his belt. She wears a hat, blouse, and a skirt with an apron. Each figure rests their chin on their hand.
This figure is very theatrical in appearance and the authors are in no doubt that it portrays a scene from a play, but which play is not known. This is a very rare figure and the one illustrated is the only one known to the authors.
HEIGHT: 8.75 Inches
PRICE: E.

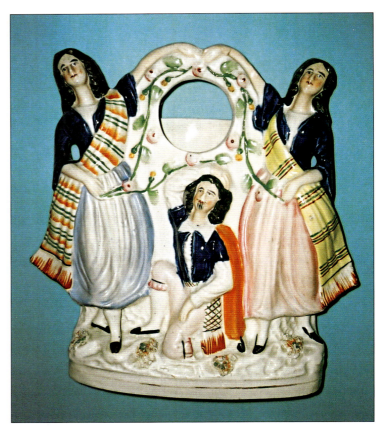

Fig. 1473D
A watch holder group figure of two women and a man, the women are on either side of the watch holder, both similarly dressed in jacket, blouse, and long skirt. A large scarf is over one shoulder and across their chest, one arm is on top of the watch holder and the other hand holds a garland, which is draped around. The man kneels on one knee with his right arm across his head. He wears a frilled shirt, short-sleeved jacket, cloak, and breeches; all the figures are in a dancing pose.
HEIGHT: 10.25 Inches
PRICE: E.

Fig. 1473C
A group figure of a man standing and a woman seated, both dressed in Turkish style garb of turban, shirt, jacket, and skirt with trousers. He holds a bird on his right shoulder and she holds a dog that is half on her lap.
This figure is similar to Figures 1472/1473 in Book Three and probably depicts the same scene from an as yet unidentified play.
HEIGHT: 9.5 Inches
PRICE: G.

Figs. 1474/1475
A pair of figures of a woman and man, both seated and wearing a theatrical costume of plumed hats and ermine edged coats, she with an apron and pantaloons, he with a long tunic. Both figures hold a bird aloft with their arm resting on a birdcage, which in turn rests on a dog kennel. At their feet a dog is recumbent. Each is a mirror image of the other.
HEIGHT: 8.5 Inches
PRICE: Pair: E, Singles: F.

Fig. 1475A
A figure of a woman standing, dressed in a plumed hat, bodice, skirt with knickers, and a tartan sash over her right shoulder; she holds a handkerchief in her right hand.

There is no doubt a pair to this figure; Fig. 1475B has been reserved for it. From the expression on her face, the woman appears to be either regretting or mourning the loss or departure of a loved one. Should the pair come to light perhaps the reason for her grief might become apparent.
HEIGHT: 9 Inches
PRICE: F.

Figs. 1477A/1477B
A pair of figures of a Chinese man and woman both seated, both wearing similar attire of coolie hat, long jacket, and skirt with pantaloons. He is holding a spade in his right hand and a flower in his left; she holds a flower in her right hand and there are more flowers in her lap.
It is not known for certain what this pair portrays. They could be theatrical or they might be Chinese gardeners.
HEIGHT: 6.5 Inches
PRICE: Pair: G.,
Singles: H.

Fig. 1476
There is a pair to this figure. It is of a woman standing, wearing a large hat, long coat tied with a scarf, skirt, and trousers. She holds a flag in her left hand and a shield in her right. Fig. 1477 has been reserved for it.

Fig. 1477C
A figure of a standing woman dressed in Chinese attire with a headband and loose-sleeved blouse, skirt with an apron, and pantaloons. She holds an object in her left hand and a fan in her right. **There is probably a pair to this figure. Fig. 1477D has been reserved for it. This is a very theatrical figure, which awaits the discovery of its source—possibly Choo-Chin Chou.**
HEIGHT: 8 Inches
PRICE: F.

Fig. 1480A
A group figure of two men and a woman standing in a boat which floats on a sea. The man in the middle is dressed in full highland attire of plumed hat, shirt, tunic, long scarf, and kilt, holding and playing a set of bagpipes. His left foot is raised and rests on a barrel. He is flanked on his right by a man dressed as a sailor who holds a flag to his side and aloft and on his left by a woman who also holds a flag in a similar position and wears a jacket and short skirt. Both the man and woman's legs are crossed in a dancing pose.
This figure is in the author's opinion the finest of all the boat figures, very rare, and like many of the boat figures probably has its origins in Astley's circus.
HEIGHT: 13.5 Inches
PRICE: D.

Fig. 1479C
A figure of a woman seated in a throne-like chair that has a wheel at the top and a large leaf on either side. She wears a bodice, jacket, and hoop skirt with knickers. **A strange figure that has so far defied identification. St. Catherine has been suggested. It is possible that it depicts a circus act, and it is probable that a pair exists. Fig. 1479D has been reserved for it.**
HEIGHT: 7 Inches
PRICE: F.

Fig. 1481A
A group figure of a man and woman, both standing in dancing poses in a boat. He is dressed as a sailor and she wears a plumed hat, bodice skirt with a sash over her shoulder and across her chest. They both hold flags.
HEIGHT: 7.5 Inches
PRICE: F.

Fig. 1481B
A group figure of a man and woman standing side by side in a boat; both wear plumed hats and both have scarves over their shoulders. She wears a blouse and short skirt with apron, he a smock with a sporran. Her apron is filled with an unidentified object, there are more on the base, and he also holds some. **If these objects could be identified it would go some way to identifying the figure, and possibly the theatrical production involved.**
HEIGHT: 6 Inches
PRICE: G.

Fig. 1485A
An arbour group figure of a man and woman seated in a boat with a swan figurehead; he wears a plumed hat, cape, jacket, and breeches with boots. She is bareheaded and wears a jacket and long dress. His right arm is around her and his left hand holds her right arm by the wrist aloft. **This figure depicts a scene from an Astley's production though which one is still not known, a very rare figure.**
HEIGHT: 10 Inches
PRICE: E.

Fig. 1482A
A group figure of a man and woman standing on rockwork. He is dressed as a sailor and she wears a bodice and long skirt with a sash around. She holds a small flag in her right hand and he a larger one in his left; below them is an unturned boat.
HEIGHT: 8 Inches
PRICE: F.

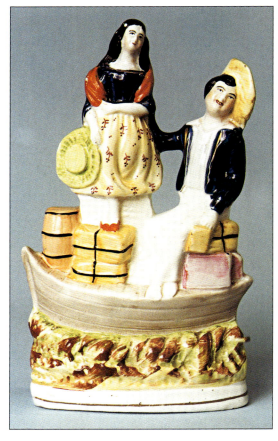

Fig. 1488A
A group figure of a man and woman in a boat surrounded by strung bales and a barrel. He, dressed as a sailor, sits on a bale and rests his arm on the woman who stands on two other bales. She is bareheaded and wears a bodice and long dress, a scarf is over her shoulders and she holds her hat in her right hand.
HEIGHT: 8 Inches
PRICE: F.

Fig. 1488B
A group figure of a man and woman standing in a houseboat; he is dressed as a sailor and leans against one end of the house resting his hand on the top. She wears a hat, bodice, and skirt with apron and rests her hand on the roof at the other end.
HEIGHT: 7.5 Inches
PRICE: F.

Fig. 1489A
A group figure of a man and woman standing in a boat that rides on waves, he wears a plumed hat, shirt, tunic, and kilt with a scarf across his shoulder, holding the hand of the woman who wears a hat, blouse, and skirt with an apron. A large cushion is at her feet.
HEIGHT: 8.75 Inches
PRICE: F.

Fig. 1489B
A group figure of a sailor and his girl in a boat; he stands to the right dressed in sailor attire holding a flag in his left hand. An anchor wound with rope is at his feet. She sits to the left wearing a hat, blouse, and skirt with an apron; a scarf is over her arm.
HEIGHT: 7.5 Inches
PRICE: G.

Fig. 1488C
A group figure of two sailors in a boat, one seated on a barrel, the other standing holding an oar. There is a small flag to either side of them.
HEIGHT: 7.5 Inches
PRICE: G.

Figs. 1489C/1489D
A pair of figures of a woman and sailor standing in small boats, she wearing an ornate headdress, cloak, jacket, blouse, and a skirt with apron. She holds a handkerchief in her left hand and a rose in her right. He wears a hat, open necked shirt with tie, waistcoat, jacket, and trousers, and holds an object in his right hand. There are anchors overhanging the boats.
On his own he could have been identified as just a sailor; in view of the woman's headdress, the authors are certain that these figures are of theatrical inspiration.
HEIGHT: 9.5 Inches
PRICE: Pair: E, Singles: F.

Fig. 1491A
A group of a man and woman dancing; he wears a Scottish hat with feather, open neck shirt, jacket, and kilt with sporran. She wears a hat with feather, blouse, and skirt with a sash. He has his right hand on his hip and his left is held aloft, holding a scarf that she also holds with her right hand. The scarf is draped across her shoulders and in her left hand she holds a garland.
HEIGHT: 11 Inches
PRICE: F.

Fig. 1503C
A group of a man and woman standing cross-legged in a dancing pose, one hand on hip and one held aloft. She wears a blouse, tunic, and short skirt; he wears a sailor's outfit of hat, shirt with tie, jacket, and trousers. A large scarf is draped over their head and shoulders.
HEIGHT: 8 Inches
PRICE: G.

Fig. 1503B
A spill vase group figure of two dancers standing side by side, she to the left with her right hand on her hip and her left holding a garland aloft, wearing a blouse and short skirt. He is to the right wearing a hat, shirt with tie, short jacket, and knee breeches. His right arm is around her waist, his left leg is raised and holding a garland upon it. The spill vase is decorated with grapes.
HEIGHT: 17.5 Inches
PRICE: E.

Figs. 1503D/1503E

A pair of figures of a man and woman standing, he in a dancing pose of legs crossed, one hand on hip and the other holding a bird aloft. He wears a plumed hat, open neck shirt, waistcoat, knee breeches, socks, and shoes. She wears a plumed hat, low cut blouse, and skirt with an apron, one hand holds the apron and the other holds a bird aloft. **Whilst holding birds aloft, it is unlikely in view of their dress and pose that these portray falconers.**
HEIGHT: 9.5 Inches
PRICE: Pair: F, Singles: G.

Fig. 1504B

A group figure of a boy and girl, both standing cross-legged, each wearing plumed hats and short skirts, he in a shirt, she a blouse and jacket, both hold garlands aloft and another to their side. A large pot of flowers is behind them.
HEIGHT: 8.5 Inches
PRICE: G.

Figs. 1503F/1503G

A pair of figures of a boy and girl standing in a dancing pose on cushion bases; he wears a hat, shirt, tunic, and kilt with sporran. He holds a garland in his right hand and his left holds a scarf above his head, which is draped onto his shoulder and waist. She is a mirror image and wears a headdress, blouse, and short skirt with boots.
HEIGHT: 9 Inches
PRICE: Pair: F, Singles: G.

Fig. 1504C

A group figure of a girl and young man, both standing with legs crossed in a dancing pose, holding a scarf aloft between them. She wears a hat, bodice, short jacket, and skirt; he wears a sailor's attire and holds his hat in his left hand. **But for the garland, this figure could be taken for a portrayal of the 'Sailor's Return' or a 'Sailor and his lass'. It is probably a depiction of a scene from a play or melodrama with a nautical theme.**
HEIGHT: 8 Inches
PRICE: G.

Fig. 1504F/1504G
A pair of group figures of two girls and a boy and a girl, one standing cross-legged in a dancing pose and the other seated on a cushion holding and playing a lute. The standing girl wears a blouse, jacket, and short skirt, and holds a flag in her right hand. The seated girl wears a blouse and long skirt. There is a scarf over her shoulder. In the other, a boy standing with legs crossed, wearing a shirt, blouse, and kilt with sporran, holds a flag in his left hand and a scarf over his right arm. Next to him, seated on a cushion, a girl sits wearing a blouse and skirt; she holds one hand to her head.
These figures can be found in two sizes, one of each illustrated.
HEIGHT: 7 & 7.75 Inches
PRICE: Pair: F, Singles: G.

Fig. 1504D
A group figure of a boy seated playing pipes, and a girl standing, dancing, holding a round garland aloft; both wear plumed hats, he with a large collared shirt, long jacket, and knee breeches, she with a scarf over her shoulder and through her arm, bodice, and short skirt.
HEIGHT: 9 Inches
PRICE: G.

Fig. 1504E
A group figure of a boy and girl standing on a bridge above a stream, she is bareheaded and wears a bodice and short skirt with an apron. She holds a flag aloft in both hands. He wears a plumed hat, shirt with a collar, jacket, and kilt, holding a basket of fruit in both hands. She is clearly dancing and it may be that this figure represents the conclusion of a successful harvest.
HEIGHT: 8 Inches
PRICE: G.

Fig. 1504H
A group figure of a man and woman standing in dancing poses on either side of a clock face which rests on a pillar; both figures wear hats with feathers, tunic/blouse with a sash, and skirt/kilt with sporran. They hold a garland of flowers on the top of the clock face.
HEIGHT: 8.75 Inches
PRICE: G.

Figs. 1505D/1505E
A pair of figures of a woman standing with her legs crossed in a dancing pose, and a man holding and playing a stringed instrument. She wears a hat, bodice, short jacket, and long skirt with an apron. Her left hand is on her hip and her right holds her apron out, all on a shaped base. He wears a tricorn hat, cravat, shirt, waistcoat, jacket, and knee breeches.
This pair probably portrays itinerant Irish musicians.
HEIGHT: 7.5 Inches
PRICE: Pair: F, Singles: G.

Fig. 1505B
A figure of a woman standing with her legs crossed in a dancing pose by a pillar that has a plant growing up it. She wears a plumed hat, ermine edged cloak, bodice, short skirt, and stockings. She holds a flower-covered scarf in both hands.
There is no doubt a pair to this figure. Fig. 1505C has been reserved for it.
HEIGHT: 10 Inches
PRICE: G.

Fig. 1508A
A figure of a girl standing with legs crossed in a dancing pose, wearing a plumed hat, bodice, and short skirt with boots. She holds a garland in each hand and a bird is perched on her shoulder. To her left, perched on rockwork, is a birdcage.
There is no doubt a pair to this figure that would be a mirror image with a boy replacing the girl. Fig. 1508B has been reserved for it. This pair portrays a performing act at the circus or theatre.
HEIGHT: 7.5 Inches
PRICE: Pair: F, Singles: G.

Fig. 1513B
An arbour group figure of a girl seated holding pipes, wearing a brimmed hat, bodice, and long skirt. Below, a man and woman are dancing. Both stand, she wearing a hat, short jacket, and skirt. One hand is on her hip and the other in the air. He stands behind, wearing a hat, jacket, and kilt. HEIGHT: 8 Inches
PRICE: G.

Fig. 1513A
A spill vase group figure of a boy and girl standing, dancing, holding each others' hand; both figures wear three cornered hats, he a tunic and kilt, she a long jacket, dress, and knickers, a scarf is wrapped around them.
HEIGHT: 8 Inches
PRICE: G.

Fig. 1517A
A group figure of a man and woman dancing; she is bareheaded and wears a blouse, scarf over her left shoulder and through her arm, and a skirt with apron. One of her hands is clasped to her breast and the other holds a posy of flowers. He wears highland attire of plumed hat, tunic with sash, and kilt with sporran.
HEIGHT: 7 Inches
PRICE: G.

121

Fig. 1531B
A figure of a woman standing in a dancing pose; she wears a bodice and long skirt with an apron. A scarf is over her shoulder and around her waist. She holds a flower garland above her head and a dog is on her dress. She has her left hand around it; a basket of fruit is on the base. **There is a pair to this figure; Fig. 1531C has been reserved for it.**
HEIGHT: 10 Inches
PRICE: G.

Figs. 1520A/1520B
A pair of figures of a man and woman in dancing pose with legs crossed, both have one hand to their hat and the other on their hip. He wears a plumed hat, tie, shirt, waistcoat, and trousers. A large scarf is over his left shoulder and across his chest. She wears a plumed hat, short jacket, skirt, and knickerbockers. A large scarf is over her right shoulder and across her waist. To her right and his left are tall pillars.
HEIGHT: 9 Inches
PRICE: Pair: E, Singles: F.

Figs. 1531/1531A
A pair of figures of a man and woman dancing; they both hold garlands of flowers in one hand and a dog in the other. She wears a headdress, bodice, blouse, and skirt with an apron. A scarf is around her waist. He wears a shirt with a large collar over a jacket, knee breeches, and socks with tassels.
HEIGHT: 9.75 Inches
PRICE: Pair: E, Singles: F.

Figs. 1532/1533
A pair of figures of Harlequin and Columbine, both standing, dancing on circular bases. Harlequin has his left hand raised to his head, his right resting on his hip holding a sword, wearing a close fitting suit decorated with diamonds. Columbine has her right hand to her head and her left at her waist, wearing a bodice and short skirt.
Harlequin was a character in English pantomime; he was mute and carried a wooden sword as a magic wand. Columbine was his mistress.
The figures were made by the Parr/Kent factory. There is illustrated a rare Parr figure of Harlequin and a later Kent figure of Columbine.
HEIGHT: 6.75 Inches
PRICE: Parr versions Pair E, Singles: F.

Figs. 1545/1546
A pair of figures of a boy and girl dancing with flags, both stand with their legs crossed and their arms crossed holding flags in each hand; he wears a hat, long jacket, and tights with boots, she wears a hat, blouse, and short skirt.
HEIGHT: 10 Inches
PRICE: Pair: E, Singles: F.

Fig. 1546B
A group figure of a man and woman in a dancing pose and holding a flag in one hand, the other arm is around each others' shoulders. Both the man and woman wear plumed hats; she with a bodice, long skirt, and a scarf over her left shoulder and across her chest. He wears a tunic, shirt with collar, kilt, and a scarf over his left shoulder.
This is the finest of the flag dancing figures and very rare, probably portraying 'The Flag Polka'.
HEIGHT: 10.5 Inches
PRICE: E.

Fig. 1546A
A group figure of a man and woman per-forming the 'Flag'
dance, he to the left wearing a jacket, waistcoat, and short trousers, she to the right wearing a hat, bodice, and skirt with knickers. Both characters hold flags and wear dancing pumps.
There was a dance, 'The Flag Polka', which was popular and it could well be that this and figures 1545/1546 in Book One portray that dance.
HEIGHT: 7 Inches
PRICE: G.

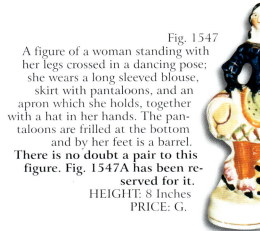

Fig. 1547
A figure of a woman standing with her legs crossed in a dancing pose; she wears a long sleeved blouse, skirt with pantaloons, and an apron which she holds, together with a hat in her hands. The pan-taloons are frilled at the bottom and by her feet is a barrel.
There is no doubt a pair to this figure. Fig. 1547A has been re-served for it.
HEIGHT: 8 Inches
PRICE: G.

Fig. 1547D
A figure of a woman standing in a dancing pose; she wears a hat, blouse, tiered skirt with an apron, and knickers. Her right hand is held to her head and her left holds her apron.
There is a pair to this figure. Fig. 1547E has been reserved for it. It is possible that this is the pair to Figure 1551, but the authors have not seen them together to confirm this.
HEIGHT: 7 Inches
PRICE: G.

Fig. 1547B
A figure of a man standing in a dancing pose; he wears a jacket, open neck shirt, waistcoat, and trousers. His hat is on the ground by his feet, which are bare; he holds his right hand to his head and his left to his hip. He holds an object in each hand.
There is a pair to this figure, which was made by the Parr pottery. Fig. 1547C has been reserved for it.
HEIGHT: 7 Inches
PRICE: G.

Fig. 1548A
A group figure of a man and woman dancing; both wear plumed hats, she a blouse, bodice, and long skirt with a scarf over her arm. She holds a garland in her right hand. He wears an open necked shirt, jacket, and kilt with sporran; a scarf is over his shoulder and through his arm.
HEIGHT: 7 Inches
PRICE: G.

4. Unidentified Musicians

Fig. 1548B
A group figure of a man and woman dancing, both stand with their legs crossed and wear plumed hats, she with a coat with split front and skirt beneath, he with an open necked shirt, long tunic, and jacket. Each dancer has one arm around the other and the other hand on their hips.
HEIGHT: 7.5 Inches
PRICE: G.

Fig. 1554A
A spill vase figure of a man seated, wearing a brimmed hat, scarf, jacket, trousers with frills at the knees, boots, and an ermine edged cape. He is playing a stringed instrument with both hands and to his left his dog is seated. At his feet a goat is recumbent.
This figure, whilst rare, is poorly decorated; the base has been left white and it is late from the mould. An example earlier from the mould and a better-decorated would be a very fine figure.
HEIGHT: 12.5 Inches
PRICE: E.

Fig. 1550B
A figure of a man dressed in Scottish attire of plumed hat, open neck shirt, waistcoat, short jacket, and kilt with sporran, his right hand is on his hip and his legs are crossed in a dancing pose.
In The Laing Art Gallery and Museum, Newcastle upon Tyne, there is a 10 inch titled figure of a Scotsman standing dressed and posed similarly to this figure, the main difference being that it has a peg leg. The figure has been the subject of much discussion and research; it is titled in capital letters 'MR FALAHAA'. It is unique and no other examples have ever been recorded and no reference anywhere can be found to a character of this name. There is possibly a pair to this figure. Fig. 1550C has been reserved for it.
HEIGHT: 6 Inches
PRICE: G.

Fig. 1554B
A watch and candleholder group figure of a Scottish boy and girl dancing, dressed in typical highland garb and holding a flag between them. They stand with a large tulip above that serves as a candleholder and below is the watch holder; seated on the base another boy holds a Celtic harp. The watch holder is flanked on both sides by a large bird.
HEIGHT: 10.5 Inches
PRICE: F.
Figs. 1560/1560A Book Three. The male figure has been paired with two different versions of the female figure. See Figs. 1968D/1968E, where the female figure has been altered, she no longer plays a squeeze box, and a large sheep has been added.

125

Fig. 1562A
A figure of a standing musician, he wears a plumed turban, cloak over a jacket that is tied with a large scarf, long trousers, and short boots holding a stringed instrument in his left hand and plays it with his right.
There is a pair to this figure. Fig. 1562B has been reserved for it.
HEIGHT: 9.5 Inches
PRICE: G.

Figs. 1570A/1570B
A pair of figures of a boy and girl seated on rockwork; he wears a waistcoat, shirt, and knee breeches, and is sitting on his coat. He is holding and playing a stringed instrument with both hands. She wears a blouse, bodice, and long skirt, and is holding and playing a tambourine with both hands.
These figures made at The Parr pottery are very finely decorated and modeled; there is a pair of figures similar and certainly by the same modeller but depicting fruit sellers. See Figs. 2002/2003 Book Two.
HEIGHT: 14 Inches
PRICE: Pair: E, Singles: F.

Fig. 1562C
A spill vase figure of a musician playing a stringed instrument; he wears a plumed hat, jacket with large scarf over his shoulder, and kilt with knee boots.
There is a pair to this figure. Fig. 1562D has been reserved for it.
HEIGHT: 9.25 Inches
PRICE: G.

Fig. 1572B
A group figure of a man standing and woman sitting on rock-work; he wears a plumed hat, frilled shirt with collar, jacket, and knee breeches. A drum is suspended at his side by a strap over his shoulder. She wears a bodice and long skirt with an apron, and holds a stringed instrument in her left hand. Between them a spaniel stands on its hind legs and the man has his left arm around it.
This group probably portrays itinerant musicians with their performing dog.
HEIGHT: 8.5 Inches
PRICE: G.

Figs. 1580A/1580B
A pair of figures of a man and woman seated, wearing turbans, jackets with open sleeves, she with a two tiered skirt and pantaloons and he long trousers. They both hold a stringed instrument in their left hand and are playing it with their right.
Both are dressed in very theatrical attire but a source has yet to be discovered.
HEIGHT: 7 Inches
PRICE: Pair: E, Singles: F.

Fig. 1578B
A figure of a man standing, wearing a cap, shirt, jacket, and trousers; he is holding a stringed instrument in his left hand and is playing it with his right. His legs are crossed in a dancing pose.
There is no doubt a pair to this figure. Fig. 1578C has been reserved for it.
HEIGHT: 6 Inches
PRICE: G.

Fig. 1580H
A figure of a seated woman wearing a headdress, blouse, and skirt with an apron. She holds and plays a stringed instrument in both hands. **There is a pair to this figure. Fig. 1580J has been reserved for it.**
HEIGHT: 11.25
PRICE: G.

Figs. 1580C/1580D
A pair of figures of standing musicians, both holding and playing stringed instruments in both hands, wearing plumed hats, she with a puff sleeved blouse, three-quarter length coat, and long skirt, he wearing a tunic and knee length breeches with slashed vents. Both figures are on rococo bases.
HEIGHT: 7.75 Inches
PRICE: Pair: F, Singles: G.

Fig. 1580E
A figure of a woman who is leaning against rockwork holding a stringed instrument in both hands. She wears a brimmed hat, long scarf, jacket, and long skirt. **There is no doubt a pair to this figure. Fig. 1580F has been reserved for it.**
HEIGHT: 5.5 Inches
PRICE: G.

Figs. 1585/1586
A pair of figures of a woman and man standing cross-legged; she is holding a pair of cymbals and a stringed instrument stands by her feet. She wears a turban, ermine edged cloak, bodice, dress with pantaloons, and a sash is tied around her waist. He is holding and playing a stringed instrument and wears a turban, ermine edged cloak, tunic, trousers, and a sash is around his waist.
These figures can be found in two sizes, 10.25 and 14 Inches. A small pair and a large version of the male musician are illustrated. There is damage to the stringed instrument on the large musician that has not been repaired.
HEIGHT: 14 & 10.25 Inches
PRICE: Pair: 14 Inches: D, 10.25 Inches: E, Singles: F.

Fig. 1586A
A figure of a man standing, wearing
a plumed hat, long tunic, trousers,
ankle boots, and a large ermine
edged cloak is over his shoulders. He
holds a stringed instrument in his
left hand and plays it with his right.
The base of this figure is scrolled
and gilded, which will help identify
its pair should it come to
light. Figure 1586B has been reserved for it.
HEIGHT: 7.5 Inches
PRICE: F.

Figs. 1588C/1588D
A pair of figures of a man and woman seated on rockwork dressed
in highland attire; he wears a plumed hat, tunic, kilt, and shoes
with stockings. A large scarf is over his shoulders, he is holding
and playing bagpipes, and a dog sits at attention at his feet. She
also wears a plumed hat, bodice, long skirt with an apron, and a
scarf is over her right arm. Her left hand holds a stringed instrument and a dog sits at attention at her feet.
HEIGHT: 10.5 Inches
PRICE: Pair: F, Singles: G.

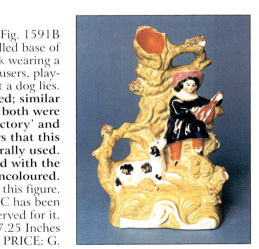

Fig. 1591B
A spill vase figure on a scrolled base of
a boy standing on rockwork wearing a
brimmed hat, smock, and trousers, playing a mandolin, and at his feet a dog lies.
**Two figures are illustrated; similar
apart from decoration, both were
made by the 'Green; factory' and
show the two base colours that this
factory generally used.
Figures can also be found with the
base left uncoloured.**
There is probably a pair to this figure.
Fig. 1591C has been
reserved for it.
HEIGHT: 7.25 Inches
PRICE: G.

Fig. 1588A
A figure of a woman standing
on rockwork dressed in Turkish
attire of turban, blouse, scarf
over her shoulder, long skirt,
pantaloons, and a large sash tied
around her waist. Her right
hand rests on a small harp.
**There is no doubt a pair to
this figure. Fig. 1588B has
been reserved for it.**
HEIGHT: 9 Inches
PRICE: F.

Fig. 1592D
A figure of a male musician standing with his
legs crossed, his right hand on his hip, the
other holding a stringed instrument, wearing a
plumed hat, shirt with tie, jacket, kilt, and
knee boots with a scarf is tied around his waist.
A sheep is recumbent at his feet.
HEIGHT: 9.5 Inches
PRICE: F.

Fig. 1596
A group figure of a seated highlander with crossed legs, wearing a
plumed hat, tunic, kilt and sporran, socks and shoes, playing the
bagpipes. To his left a small child stands on a fence and at his feet
a dog sits with its paws on his leg. HEIGHT: 10 Inches
PRICE: F.

Fig. 1592E
A figure of a woman
seated on rockwork;
she wears a hat with
a plume, blouse,
long skirt with an
apron, and holds a
harp on her lap with
her left hand. Her
right hand rests on
the back of a sheep
that has its forepaws
on her lap.
**This could possibly
be the pair to Fig.
1592D.**
HEIGHT: 9 Inches
PRICE: F.

Figs. 1598B/1598A
A pair of figures of a man and woman standing, playing mandolins; he wears a hat, frilled shirt, jacket,
and knee breeches with boots. She wears a hat, bodice, and short skirt. To his left and her right there is a
cushioned pedestal on which a spaniel reclines.
HEIGHT: 11.5 Inches
PRICE: Pair: E, Singles: F.

Figs. 1601/1602
A pair of figures of a man and woman standing with a peacock perched on rockwork to their side; the man wears a plumed hat, scarf, jacket, shirt, and kilt with sporran. His right arm is across his chest and he is holding a stringed instrument in his left. She wears a plumed hat with scarf attached, short jacket, blouse, and long skirt tied at the waist by a scarf. Her legs are crossed in a dancing pose. Her right arm is across her waist and her left hand rests on the peacock.
A very attractive, rare, and desirable pair.
HEIGHT: 14.5 Inches
PRICE: Pair: D, Singles: E.

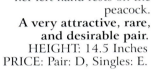

Figs. 1602A/1602B
A pair of figures of a boy and girl seated in a decorated arbour playing stringed instruments; he is crossed-legged and wears a blouse, kilt, and knee boots with a scarf to his side. She wears a blouse and a three-tiered skirt.
HEIGHT: 9 Inches
PRICE: Pair: F, Singles: G.

Figs. 1604/1603
A pair of figures of standing musicians, both playing stringed instruments and both dressed in an extravagant costume, he with plumed hat, frilled shirt, and knee length breeches with frilled cuffs, and a long cloak. She wears a plumed hat, long cloak over a short jacket, pleated blouse, waistcoat, and long skirt. **The extravagance of the costume would denote that these figures portray theatrical or fairground musicians. The bases of these figures are decorated in the manner of The Parr factory.**
HEIGHT: 9.75
PRICE: Pair: E, Singles: F.

Figs. 1604C/1604D
A pair of figures of a man and woman standing, both holding cymbals and wearing very theatrical costumes, he with a steeple hat with sash, waistcoat, jacket, and short decorated trousers tied at the waist with a scarf. She wears a tie in her hair, open sleeved blouse, and skirt. Both the man and woman are on rococo bases. **He is dressed very similarly to a number of figures of Diavolino and it is possible that this pair portrays Diavolino and Catarina, but no titled figures or source have ever been seen for this very rare pair.**
HEIGHT: 9.5 Inches
PRICE: Pair: E, Singles: F.

Figs. 1604A/1604B
A pair of figures of a man and woman standing beside rockwork on which a goat is standing on its hind legs; he wears a plumed hat, open necked shirt, waistcoat, jacket, and knee breeches with boots. A sash is over one of his shoulders and across his chest, while one hand rests on the goat's head and the other is on his hip. A stringed instrument rests against his leg. She wears a plumed hat, bodice, short skirt with a scarf tied loosely around her waist, one hand is on the goats back and the other holds a tambourine.
The figure of the woman has in previous publications been misidentified as 'Esmeralda'.
HEIGHT: 12.25 Inches
PRICE: Pair: D, Singles: E.

Figs. 1605/1606
A pair of figures of standing musicians; she holds a small tambourine and wears a headscarf, blouse, and long skirt. He is holding a stringed instrument in both hands and wears a hat, shirt, jacket, waistcoat, and trousers. **These figures are decorated in the manner of The Parr factory; they were produced for a considerable time and late Kent versions can be found.**
HEIGHT: 8 Inches
PRICE: Pair: E, Singles: F.

Fig. 1605A
A figure of a woman standing, bareheaded, wearing an open sleeved top and long skirt with an apron. She holds a tambourine in her right hand.
This figure is very similar to Fig. 1605 and was also made in The Parr Factory; like all Parr figures the modelling is in the round and very good. The pair for this figure would be Figure 1606 or a variant of it.
HEIGHT: 11 Inches
PRICE: Pair: E, Singles: F.

Fig. 1606C
A spill vase figure of a boy seated wearing an open neck shirt, jacket, and knee breeches with leggings; he is holding and playing pipes with both hands, and his dog sits at his feet begging.
There is a pair to this figure that was made by the 'Alpha' factory; Fig. 1606D has been reserved for it.
HEIGHT: 7 Inches
PRICE: Pair: F, Singles: G.

Fig. 1616A
A figure of a woman seated, wearing a brimmed hat, jacket, and long skirt with petticoat showing, holding and playing a small harp with both hands.
There is a pair to this figure. Fig. 1615B has been reserved for it.
HEIGHT: 7 Inches
PRICE: Pair: F, Singles: G.

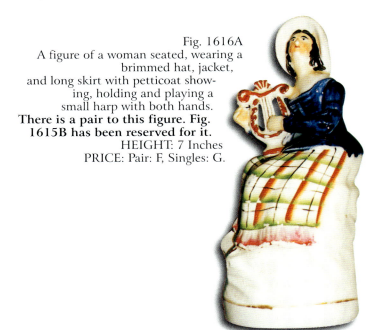

Figs. 1612/1613
A pair of figures of a boy and girl seated; he wears a hat, shirt with tie, jacket, and trousers. By his side on the rockwork is an organ on which a monkey sits. She wears a cap, blouse, and scarf tied around her shoulders, and holds a castanet in her left hand.
HEIGHT: 7 Inches
PRICE: Pair: F, Singles: G.

Figs. 1621/1621A
A pair of figures of a boy and girl seated on rockwork, above a bridge, below which a stream flows. She holds a harp in both hands, her hat is on the rockwork to her right, and she wears a bodice, scarf over her shoulder, and a double-skirted dress. One goat sits to her left and another stands below. Holding a pipe in his right hand, his hat rests on rockwork to his left; he wears a shirt with tie, long jacket with knee breeches, and a scarf is over his shoulder and through his arm. A goat sits to his right and below a dog stands with one paw raised.
This pair of figures depicts shepherds and could just as well have been included in that chapter.
HEIGHT: 10.5 Inches
PRICE: Pair: E, Singles: F.

Fig. 1621B
A standing figure of a woman, dressed in Eastern attire of a turban with a feather, blouse, jacket over one shoulder, long skirt, and pantaloons. A scarf is tied around her waist and she holds a small harp with her right hand.
There is a pair to this figure. Fig. 1621C has been reserved for it.
HEIGHT: 9 Inches
PRICE: G.

Figs. 1623B/1623A
A pair of figures of seated musicians; he is dressed in Scottish attire and holds bagpipes under his arm, she is bareheaded and wears a necklace, low cut blouse, and long dress. She is playing a stringed instrument. At her feet sits a dog and at his a cat, all on raised irregular shaped bases.
These figures are very similar to Figs. 1622/1623.
HEIGHT: 6 Inches
PRICE: Pair: F, Singles: G.

Fig. 1623C
A figure of a seated musician playing the bagpipes, dressed similarly to Figs. 1623A and Fig. 1622. As with Fig. 1623A, his dog is seated at his feet and the base is of a cut out rococo style.
There is no doubt a pair to this figure. Fig. 1623D has been reserved for it.
There are at least three different pairs in various sizes of these figures and all are modelled in the round with a number of subsidiary moulds; it is probable that they are copies of earlier porcelain factory figures.
HEIGHT: 6.25 Inches
PRICE: G.

Figs. 1622/1623
A pair of figures of a boy and girl seated on gilt lined rococo bases. He is holding bagpipes in both hands, wearing a hat, long jacket, waistcoat, and breeches. She holds a stringed instrument in her left hand and plays it with her right; she wears a headscarf, bodice, and long skirt.
These figures can be found in two sizes, both illustrated.
HEIGHT: 11 Inches, 6 Inches
PRICE: Pair: F, Singles: G.

Fig. 1623E
A figure of a man standing with his legs crossed, wearing a plumed hat, shirt, jacket, pantaloons tied at the waist with a scarf, and short boots. His right arm rests on rockwork and his left holds musical pipes. His dog sits at his left side, all on a rococo base. **This figure probably depicts a shepherd. There is a pair for this figure. Fig. 1623F has been reserved for it.**
HEIGHT: 9.5 Inches
PRICE: F.

Fig. 1623G
A spill vase group figure of a couple standing on either side of a tree, dressed in highland attire, both wear plumed hats, she a blouse, coat, and dress with an apron, he a shirt, coat, kilt with sporran, and a cloak over his left shoulder, holding a set of pipes in both hands. She holds a tambourine aloft. Between them a dog sits and below are two sheep, one standing and one recumbent.
HEIGHT: 15 Inches
PRICE: F.

Fig. 1623H
A spill vase group figure of a couple sitting on either side of a tree, both wear hats, she a dress, he a shirt, coat, and kilt, a cloak over his left shoulder. He is holding and playing a stringed instrument. She has an open book on her lap. Between and below them three sheep are recumbent; a waterfall and stream are on the base.
HEIGHT: 11 Inches
PRICE: G.

Figs. 1623J/1623K
A pair of standing figures dressed in Eastern attire, he wearing a turban, shirt, coat, and trousers with an ermine edged long coat holding and playing a stringed instrument with both hands. She wears a hat, long flowing dress, and ermine edged coat. She holds a tambourine aloft in her left hand. Both figures are on oval bases with grape and leaf decoration. HEIGHT: 13.25 Inches
PRICE: Pair: F, Singles: G.

Fig. 1625C
A watch holder group of a boy and girl seated on either side of a large vase of flowers; both children wear a hat with a plume, she a long tunic with skirt, one hand is in her lap and the other holds a tambourine. He wears a shirt, jacket, and kilt, and holds pipes in both hands. Below them and on the base two sheep are lying.
HEIGHT: 9 Inches
PRICE: G.

Fig. 1625B
A spill vase group of a man seated playing a stringed instrument and a girl standing dancing holding a tambourine above her head. He wears a hat, frilled shirt, jacket, kilt, and a scarf over his shoulder. She wears a long sleeved blouse and short skirt with a scarf over her shoulder and across her chest.
HEIGHT: 8.25
PRICE: G.

Fig. 1625D
A clock face group of a girl laying down and playing a stringed instrument; seated next to her is a boy wearing a hat with feathers, frilled shirt, short jacket, and knee breeches. His right hand is clasped to his chest and his left is on his knee. Below on a scrolled base is the clock face.
HEIGHT: 9 Inches
PRICE: G.

Fig. 1625E
An arbour figure of a man and woman standing; she is bareheaded and wears a jacket and skirt with an apron. He stands to her left and wears a cap, open neck shirt, jacket, and pantaloons. He holds and plays a stringed instrument in both hands.
HEIGHT: 8.75 Inches
PRICE: G.

Fig. 1628A
A group figure of a woman standing, dancing, and holding a tambourine over her head; she wears a scarf headdress, bodice, and long skirt. A man is seated cross-legged next to her and wears a plumed hat, ermine edged cape, shirt, jacket, and knee length trousers holding a set of pipes in both hands. **This figure, like many others in this chapter, portray itinerate or strolling street musicians and dancers who earned their living rather precariously wherever a crowd could be gathered and entertained for a few coppers.**
HEIGHT: 10 Inches
PRICE: F.

Fig. 1628B
A group figure of two standing female musicians, both similarly dressed in hats, jackets, and long dress with an apron, one holds a stringed instrument in both hands and the other holds a tambourine aloft. **The figure illustrated is in the white and gilded; coloured versions do exist. At the time of writing and as a general rule white figures fetch about a third the price of coloured ones.**
HEIGHT: 8.5 Inches
PRICE: G. (In the white).

Fig. 1630C
A figure of a woman standing, wearing a large brimmed hat with a feather, blouse, bodice, short skirt, and a sash around her waist and pantaloons. Her left hand is on her hip and her right holds a tambourine that rests on rockwork to her side.
This figure has a pair. Fig. 1630D has been reserved for it.
HEIGHT: 8.5 Inches
PRICE: F.

Fig. 1630A
A figure of a woman standing, wearing a large plumed hat, blouse, skirt with split apron, and a scarf over her shoulder. She holds a tambourine aloft in both hands.
This figure was made by the 'Beta' factory, and there is no doubt a pair, as yet unrecorded. Fig. 1630B has been reserved for it.
HEIGHT: 10.5 Inches
PRICE: F.

Fig. 1632A
A figure of a man seated on rock-work playing the bagpipes; he wears highland dress of Tam O Shanter, tunic, kilt with sporran, socks with shoes, and a scarf is over his shoulder.
Two figures are illustrated, identical apart from minor decoration differences.
HEIGHT: 12.5 Inches
PRICE: F.

Fig. 1635A
A group standing figure of a boy to the left dressed in sailor attire playing a harp and a girl dressed in long blouse and skirt playing a stringed instrument.
HEIGHT: 7 Inches
PRICE: H.

Fig. 1632B
A figure of a Scotsman seated with his legs crossed, playing the bagpipes; he wears highland attire of feathered cap, tunic, kilt with sporran, socks, and shoes. A large scarf is across his chest and shoulders.
HEIGHT: 13.5 Inches
PRICE: F.

Figs. 1635B/1635C
A pair of figures of a boy and girl dressed in highland attire, he with a hat, tunic with sash, kilt, and knee boots. She wears a blouse and long skirt, both hold harps, and behind each is a sheaf of wheat.
HEIGHT: 6.5 Inches
PRICE: Pair: G, Singles: H.

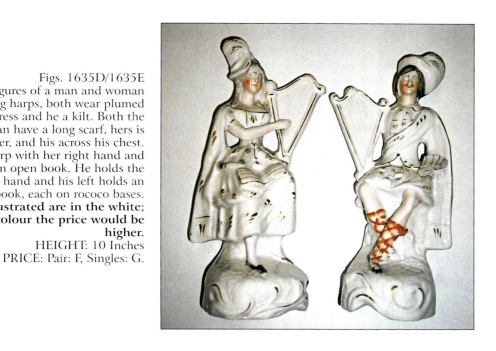

Figs. 1635D/1635E
A pair of figures of a man and woman seated playing harps, both wear plumed hats, she a long dress and he a kilt. Both the man and woman have a long scarf, hers is over her shoulder, and his across his chest. She plays the harp with her right hand and on her lap is an open book. He holds the harp in his right hand and his left holds an open book, each on rococo bases.
The figures illustrated are in the white; were they in colour the price would be higher.
HEIGHT: 10 Inches
PRICE: Pair: F, Singles: G.

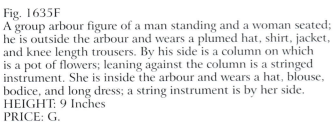

Fig. 1635F
A group arbour figure of a man standing and a woman seated; he is outside the arbour and wears a plumed hat, shirt, jacket, and knee length trousers. By his side is a column on which is a pot of flowers; leaning against the column is a stringed instrument. She is inside the arbour and wears a hat, blouse, bodice, and long dress; a string instrument is by her side.
HEIGHT: 9 Inches
PRICE: G.

Fig. 1635G
A group arbour figure similar to the preceding figure other than the figure of the man has been omitted, his stringed instrument has been hidden under an application of shredded clay, and a figure of a small dog has been added.
This figure is an example of the potter's adaptability; it would appear that they no longer had figures of the man, which was a separate mould (Figure 1635F), so they disguised his stringed instrument with clay and added a dog, and thus produced another figure.
HEIGHT: 9 Inches
PRICE: G.

Fig. 1636A
A group figure of two musicians, man and woman, both reclining; she holds a stringed instrument in her right hand and wears a plumed hat, blouse with bodice, and long skirt. He wears full highland attire of plumed hat, tunic, scarf, kilt with sporran, and his stringed instrument rests on the ground between them.
HEIGHT: 8.5 Inches
PRICE: F.

Fig. 1636C
A group figure of a man and woman standing; both wear plumed hats, she a jacket, blouse, and long dress with a large scarf wrapped over her shoulder and around her. She holds a filled basket over her right arm. He wears a long jacket with a scarf over both shoulders and knee breeches and holds a pipe in both hands.
HEIGHT: 9.5 Inches
PRICE: G.

Fig. 1636B
A group figure of a man standing, wearing a jacket, shirt, and knee breeches; he holds a pipe in both hands. Seated to his right is a woman who wears a long dress with a sash over her right shoulder. In her left hand she holds a tambourine that rests on a small gate to her left.
HEIGHT: 7.5 Inches
PRICE: G.

Fig. 1636D
A figure of a standing man wearing a plumed hat, cloak, frilled shirt, jacket, and knee breeches. His legs are crossed and he holds a set of pipes in both hands.
There is probably a pair to this figure. Fig. 1636E has been reserved for it.
HEIGHT: 14.5 Inches
PRICE: G.

Fig. 1636F
A group figure of a man and woman standing with their legs crossed in a dancing pose, both wear plumed hats, he a tunic, kilt, and stockings with shoes. He holds and plays the bagpipes with both hands. She wears a bodice and long skirt with an apron, and holds a tambourine in her left hand. A large scarf is draped between them and over both their shoulders.
This group portrays itinerate street musicians/dancers.
HEIGHT: 9 Inches
PRICE: G.

Fig. 1636G
A figure of a man wearing highland attire of plumed hat, tunic, kilt with sporran, and a large scarf draped over his shoulders. He is holding a set of bagpipes.
There may well be a pair to this figure. Fig. 1636H has been reserved for it.
HEIGHT: 11 Inches
PRICE: G.

Fig. 1636J
A figure of a Scotsman standing, wearing highland attire of plumed hat, open necked shirt, long coat with sporran, socks, shoes, and a scarf over his shoulder and around his waist. He holds a set of bagpipes in both hands.
There is a pair to this figure. Fig. 1636K has been reserved for it.
HEIGHT: Not available
PRICE: G.

Fig. 1638A
A group figure of two musicians seated above a brick bridge under which a stream flows. She wears a hat, bodice, jacket, and long skirt around which is tied a scarf. Her right hand is in her lap and her left holds a tambourine above her head. He wears a fez, jacket, frilled shirt, and knee breeches around which a scarf is tied; he is holding and playing a stringed instrument with both hands.
HEIGHT: 10 Inches
PRICE: F.

Fig. 1637A
A spill vase figure of a seated man wearing a shirt, ermine edged jacket, and leggings, playing a mandolin and gazing up at a standing woman who leans against a tree with her hands crossed in front with a brimmed hat over one arm and wearing a long dress, all on a rococo base.
The reverse of this figure is also illustrated. Round patches can be seen where the glaze has blown off in the kiln. This is caused by dirt or other imperfections that were attached to the figure. Usually when this occurred the figures were either wasted or sold as seconds.
HEIGHT: 8 Inches
PRICE: G.

Fig. 1640A
A group figure of a boy wearing a plumed hat, blouse, and kilt, stands with one leg raised, holding a set of pipes, a girl to the right seated wearing a plumed hat, blouse, and skirt with knickers playing a stringed instrument. Above them, surrounded by grapes, is a clock face and between them a stream flows.
HEIGHT: 8.5 Inches
PRICE: G.

Fig. 1640B
A clock face group of a woman and man standing on either side with their legs crossed in a dancing pose; both characters wear plumed hats, long jacket, and dress/tunic. She has her right hand on her hip and her left holds a tambourine, which rests on the top of the clock face. He has his left hand on his hip and his right is held to his head.
HEIGHT: 8 Inches
PRICE: F.

Fig. 1644A
A figure of a man standing with his legs crossed. He holds a garland in his left hand and a musical pipe in his right. He wears a hat, open necked shirt, waistcoat, jacket, and pantaloons. A sash is around his waist, seated on rockwork. To his right a dogs sits.
There is no doubt a pair to this figure. Fig. 1644B has been reserved for it.
HEIGHT: 10 Inches
PRICE: F.

Fig. 1651C/1651D
A pair of equestrian figures of a man and woman wearing Eastern dress of turban, long fur edged coat, tunic, and skirt with trousers. They are each seated on a horse and hold a stringed instrument, he in his right hand and she in her left, resting it on the horse's flank, the other hand holds the reins. A flowering plant grows between the horse's legs.
It is possible that these figures portray Mandane and Arta-banes from the opera Artaxerxes. See Figures 1226 - 1233 Book One, he is rare, she is extremely rare.
HEIGHT: 11.5 Inches
PRICE: Pair: D, Singles: E.

Fig. 1649A
A group figure of a man and woman seated above a clock face; he is holding a set of bagpipes in both hands, wearing a plumed hat, scarf, tunic, kilt and sporran, she has both hands in her lap and wears bodice, scarf, and long skirt.
At first sight this appears the same figure as 1649 Book One; it is however a superior version. It is larger and better modelled as instanced by the plume of the man's hat and the decoration around the clock face.
HEIGHT: 14.5 Inches
PRICE: F.

Figs. 1651A/1651B
An equestrian pair of figures of a boy and girl; he wears a plumed hat, shirt, tunic, kilt, and a scarf over his right arm and shoulder. He holds the horse's reins in his right hand and a large drum on his lap. She wears a hat, blouse, a scarf over her shoulder and across her chest, and a skirt with an apron. She holds the horse's reins in her right hand and her left holds a tambourine aloft.
HEIGHT: 7 Inches
PRICE: Pair: E, Singles: F.

Fig. 1652A
A double spill vase group of a man and woman seated under an arbour, she to the left wearing a blouse and long skirt, her right hand held to her head, a stringed instrument lies at her feet. He wears a shirt, waistcoat, and knee breeches. His right arm is around her waist and holding his hat by his feet.
HEIGHT: 7.75 Inches
PRICE: G.

Figs. 1655/1656
A pair of figures of a man and woman musician both seated on rockwork; she wears a plumed hat, jacket, and two tiered skirt with a scarf tied around her waist, and holds a tambourine in her right hand. Her left hand holds a garland on the back of a fawn that stands on rockwork with its front leg extended onto her shoulder. He wears a plumed hat, shirt with tie, jacket, knee breeches, and boots. A stringed instrument rests on the ground beside him and his right hand holds a garland on the back of a sheep that stands with its front leg in his hand.
An extremely well modelled and rare pair of figures, the man and woman's dress is very theatrical; they probably portray fairground or circus performers.
HEIGHT: 10.25 & 11 Inches
PRICE: Pair: E, Singles: F.

Fig. 1652B
An arbour group of two lovers seated side by side, he wearing a plumed hat, shirt, jacket, and kilt. His right arm is around her and his left holds a stringed instrument. She is bareheaded and wears a blouse and long dress with an apron. A scarf is over her arm and both hands rest in her lap. The top of the arbour is decorated with grapes and grape leaves.
HEIGHT: 7.75
PRICE: G.

Fig. 1657A
A clock face group of a man and woman standing on either side in a dancing pose; both wear plumed hats, she with a bodice, cloak, and short skirt with an apron. She holds a tambourine aloft in her left hand. He wears an open necked shirt, long jacket, and knee breeches. He holds and is playing a stringed instrument with both hands. Below the clock face is a pot containing a flowering plant.
HEIGHT: 8 Inches
PRICE: F.

Figs. 1656A/1656B
A pair of figures of a boy and girl kneeling on the back of a recumbent stag; the boy wears a plumed hat, shirt, tunic, skirt, shoes and socks, and a sash over one shoulder and across one arm. In his left hand a large flag is held and in his right a drum. The girl is almost a mirror image, other than she wears a blouse and holds a tambourine in her left hand.
A very fine pair of figures and very rare. The flag on the figures has been inaccurately restored, as presumably the restorer had neither a photograph of nor a perfect figure from which to work.
HEIGHT: 10 Inches
PRICE: Pair: D, Singles: F.

Fig. 1657B
A group of a standing man dressed in Scottish attire of plumed hat, jerkin, and kilt with boots. One hand is on his hip and the other rests on the shoulder of a girl seated. She is bareheaded and wears a long dress and blouse; a large scarf is over her left shoulder and around her waist. She holds a mandolin in her left hand and plays it with her right. On the base is a bundle and stick. **This figure portrays itinerant musicians.**
HEIGHT: 9 Inches
PRICE: F.

Figs. 1659A/1659B
A pair of figures of standing musicians both wear plumed hats, he an ermine edged cape, jacket, trousers with frilled bottoms and boots, holding a stringed instrument in both hands. She wears a top with wide loose sleeves and long skirt and holds a small harp in her left hand.
HEIGHT: 9 Inches
PRICE: Pair: F, Singles: G.

Figs. 1661C/1661D
A pair of figures of musician/dancers both stand in dancing pose with one hand to their head and legs crossed, both with plumed hats, he with a scarf over his right shoulder and through his left arm, wearing a long jacket and short frilled bottom trousers with boots. A stringed instrument is suspended from his left arm. She wears a bodice and short skirt with ankle boots; a garland is held in each hand and a tambourine is suspended from her waist by a band over her shoulder.
HEIGHT: 10 Inches
PRICE: Pair: F, Singles: G.

Figs. 1661E/1661F
A pair of figures of standing musician/dancers; he wears a hat with a feather, jacket, frilled shirt, knee breeches, and ankle boots. His left hand is raised to his hat and his right holds a stringed instrument. She is similarly dressed with hat with feather, frilled blouse, jacket, and short skirt with a sash. Her left hand is on her hip and her right holds a tambourine. By her feet is a barrel-shaped object. Both figures have their feet crossed in a dancing pose.
HEIGHT: 10 Inches
PRICE: Pair: E, Singles: F.

Fig. 1662A
A standing figure of a highlander holding bagpipes dressed in a plumed hat, shirt, jacket, kilt with sporran, shoes and socks, with a scarf over his shoulder. A dog stands at his feet.
HEIGHT: 16.5 Inches
PRICE: F.

Figs. 1662B/1662C
A pair of figures of standing musicians; both wear plumed hats, he a long coat, shirt, waistcoat, and trousers. He holds a stringed instrument in his left hand and a bow that is playing it in his right. She wears a blouse and long skirt and holds a tambourine in both hands, all on a shaped gilt lined base.
HEIGHT: 7.5 Inches
PRICE: Pair: F, Singles: G.

150

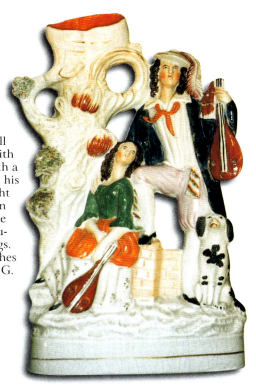

Fig. 1668A
A spill vase group figure of a standing man with one foot raised on a small brick wall wearing a plumed hat, open necked shirt with a loose tie, jacket, and knee breeches tied with a scarf, holding a stringed instrument aloft in his left hand. A dog sits at his feet and his right hand is placed on the shoulder of a woman who is seated on the wall. She wears a bodice and long skirt with an apron, a stringed instrument rests against her legs.
HEIGHT: 12 Inches
PRICE: G.

Fig. 1669B
A figure of a man seated wearing a brimmed hat, open neck shirt, jacket, and knee breeches holding a horn or pipe in his right hand. **Illustrated with the figure is Fig. 1669. The factory that made these figures made a series, many of which could be taken to pair each other. There is a pair to this figure, not yet recorded. Fig. 1669C has been reserved for it.**
HEIGHT: 7.25 Inches
PRICE: F.

Fig. 1668B
A figure of a man standing with legs crossed holding an accordion above his head. He wears a frilled shirt with tie, jacket, and knee breeches secured at the waist with a belt and ankle boots.
A very attractive figure to which there must be a pair. Fig. 1668C has been reserved for it.
HEIGHT: 13.5 Inches
PRICE: F.

151

Figs. 1669D/1669E
A pair of figures of a man and woman standing; she wears a hat, jacket, and long skirt and holds a stringed instrument in both hands. He wears a tricorn hat, cravat, long jacket, waistcoat, and knee breeches, holding a fiddle in his left hand held to his chin and plays it with a bow held in his right.
The man is dancing an Irish jig. This pair was made by the 'Alpha' factory and is of two itinerant Irish street musicians; both are very rare and previously unrecorded.
HEIGHT: 8.25 Inches
PRICE: Pair: E, Singles: F.

Figs. 1670D/1670E
A pair of figures of a boy and girl standing playing an organ which has a bird perched on the top. The girl wears a blouse and skirt with a bow at the back. A dog is recumbent at her feet. The boy wears a blouse, skirt, and trousers. A dog is begging by his side.
HEIGHT: 11 Inches
PRICE: Pair: E, Singles: F.

Figs. 1670F/1670G
A pair of figures of a man and woman standing holding and playing squeeze boxes; to his left and her right a large pot filled with grapes and leaves stand, below which a dog sits. The man wears a plumed hat, shirt, jacket, and knee breeches with boots. She wears a plumed hat, blouse, jacket, and dress with apron.
HEIGHT: 11. Inches
PRICE: Pair: E, Singles: F.

Book 2: Chapter 1:
Religious and Temperance Figures

Figures of Preachers will be found in the Portrait Chapter, in this Chapter the Bible is the inspiration for most of the figures.

During the early part of Queen Victoria's reign *The Illustrated Family Bible* was published. Included therein were a number of prints, some of which were either the source or inspiration for figures. It is also possible that the water stoups seen in churches were copied and adapted by the potters and supplied to Roman Catholics for use in their homes.

The Church and the Temperance Movement were inextricably linked, and it would not be surprising to find that these figures had been commissioned by either or both The Band of Hope and The Independent Order of the Good Templars.

Listings highlighted in bold type contain additions and alterations which will be found in this addendum, all other Portraits will be found in *Books One and Three, Victorian Staffordshire Figures 1835-1875*.

This Chapter has been divided into two sections:

1. Religious
2. Temperance

1. Religious

i. Abraham
ii. Angels
iii. Apostles, The
iv. Balaam
v. Christ, Jesus
vi. Daniel
vii. David
viii. Jacob and Rachel
ix. Lot and his daughters
x. Mary and Joseph
xi. Moses
xii. Popery and Protestantism
xiii. Prodigal Son
xiv. Rebekah
xv. Ruth
xvi. Saints
xvii. Samson
xviii. Samuel
xix. Saul
xx. Other related figures

2. Temperance

i. Band of Hope
ii. Faith, Hope, and Charity
iii. Independent Order of Good Templars

i. Abraham
See Figures 1671 - 1675 Book Two

ii. Angels
See Figures 1677 - 1683 Book Two

iii. Apostles, The
See Figures 1687 - 1690 & 1684A - 1686A Books Two and Three

Fig. 1691S
A standing figure of 'St Jean', bearded and with long hair, dressed in flowing robes and holding a flagpole in his left hand from which a banner is draped over his left shoulder. **A very rare figure and in the same series as Fig. 1766 St. Pierre and Fig. 1765 St. Winifride Book Two, all made for the French market; the discovery of this figure begs the question of how many more were made in this series and are yet to be discovered.**
TITLE: ST JEAN
HEIGHT: 10.75 Inches
PRICE: E.

iv. Balaam
See Figure 1692 Book Two

v. Christ, Jesus
See Figures 1694 - 1719 Book Two

Fig. 1693
A figure of Christ on the Cross with two angels standing with wings outstretched to either side of a Holy water stoup that is decorated with an angel's head.
This is by far the finest of the Christ on the Cross figures. The decoration is particularly good. This a superior and larger version of Fig. 1707 Book Two
HEIGHT: 14.5 Inches
PRICE: E

vi. Daniel
See Figures 1721 - 1723 Book Two

Fig. 1720
A figure of Daniel standing on rockwork wearing a turban and holding a cloak at the neck that is worn over a long coat and skirt and sandals, holding an object in his left hand, and a lion is recumbent at his feet.
This is probably the pair to Fig. 1675 Abraham Book Two or there may be others in a series.
HEIGHT: 9 Inches.
PRICE: E.

vii. David
See Figures 1724 - 1728 Book Two

Fig. 1726A
A figure of two boys standing to either side of a brick pillar, each holding a lamb and dressed in short tunics.
The boys are dressed in a similar manner to David in figures 1725/1728 Book Two, and they are both holding lambs; they appear to be derivations of those figures.
HEIGHT: 6 Inches
PRICE: G.

viii. Jacob
See Figures 1729 - 1730B Books Two and Three

Fig. 1729A
A figure of Jacob standing barefooted, dressed in a robe with a short skirt, holding a crook in his left hand, which rests against a large tree that branches above his head. His right hand rests on the head of a standing sheep and another sheep lies on the ground below.
This is a very rare figure and it is probable that a pair exists. Fig. 1729B has been reserved for it.
HEIGHT: 12 Inches
PRICE: E.

ix. Lot and his Daughters.
See Figure 1731 Book Two

x. Mary and Joseph
See Figures 1733 - 1743 Books Two and Three

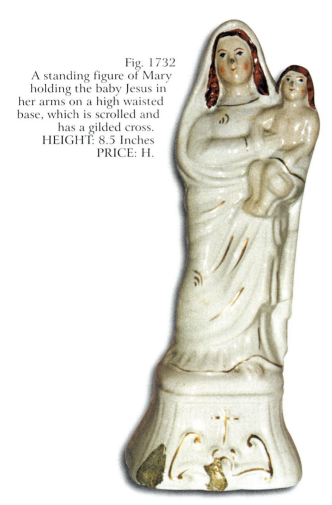

Fig. 1732
A standing figure of Mary holding the baby Jesus in her arms on a high waisted base, which is scrolled and has a gilded cross.
HEIGHT: 8.5 Inches
PRICE: H.

Fig. 1744
A group figure of 'The Flight to Egypt'; Mary is seated on a donkey holding the Christ child in her arms. Joseph stands at the head of the donkey holding a bundle on his shoulder.
This figure is modelled in the round and is a product of The 'Alpha' factory.
HEIGHT: 8 Inches
PRICE: F.

xi. Moses
See Figures 1745 - 1746 Book Two

xii. Popery and Protestantism
See Figures 1748 - 1750 Book Two

xiii. Prodigal Son
See Figures 1751 - 1752 Book Two

xiv. Rebekah
See Figures 1753 - 1759 Book Two

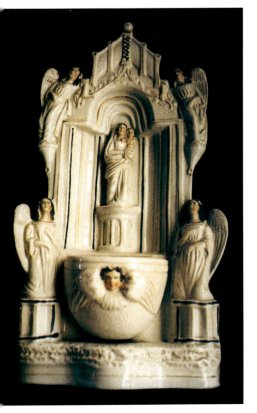

Fig. 1740A
A group figure of Mary holding the baby Jesus in her arms standing on a pedestal in a niche. Below her feet is a holy water stoup with an angel's face and wings on the front. To either side of the niche a winged angel stands on a pedestal, and above, also on either side, two more angels rest. All are dressed in flowing robes.
HEIGHT: 13.5 Inches
PRICE: F.

Fig. 1758A
A spill vase group figure of Rebekah and Abraham's servant at the well, she wearing a head-dress, cloak, and long dress. She holds a jug to the servant, who wears a headdress, cloak, and long dress. There is a well with steps leading from it on the base.
This figure is similar to Fig. 1758 Book Two, but there are significant differences. It would appear that both have as their source the painting by Vernet.
HEIGHT: 12.25
PRICE: E.

Fig. 1759A
A standing figure of Abraham's servant, wearing a turban, shirt, jacket, and pantaloons tied at the waist with a scarf. His right hand is around a jug that rests on rockwork to his side. A stream runs below.
The identification of this figure is taken from Fig. 1759 Book Two, and there is no doubt a pair to it. Fig. 1759B has been reserved for it. If there were a nine-inch version, it would pair with Fig. 1756
HEIGHT: 11.5 Inches
PRICE: F.

Fig. 1760
A group figure of Rebekah and Abraham's servant at the well; she wears a headdress, long dress with a sash tied around, and holds a water jug in both hands, which she offers to the servant. He wears a long cap and gown with a scarf around him and over both arms; a stick is held in his left hand. **This is a rare figure and the only one recorded where Rebekah stands on the right.**
HEIGHT: 12 Inches
PRICE: E.

xv. Ruth
See Figures 1761 - 1762 Book Two

xvi. Saints
See Figures 1765 - 1767 Book Two

St. Patrick

Fig. 1764
A standing figure of St. Patrick wearing vestments and holding a crook in his left hand.
TITLE: St. Patrick
HEIGHT: 11.75 Inches
PRICE: F.

xvii. Samson
See Figure 1768 Book Two

xviii. Samuel
See Figure 1770 Book Two

xix. Saul
See Figure 1773 Book Two

Fig. 1771
It has been reported to the authors that a source for this figure has been seen, and that it does not portray Saul anointing David, but is of St. John the Baptist.

156

xx. Other Related Figures
See Figures 1775 - 1788 Books Two and Three

2. Temperance

i. Band of Hope
See Figures 1790 - 1791 Book Two

ii. Faith, Hope, and Charity
See Figures 1792 - 1797 Book Two

Fig. 1777A
A figure of a sparsely dressed woman who is kneeling on one knee with her hands held together in prayer. She is long haired and bare-chested and the base is a cushion with strings and tassel decoration.
HEIGHT: 10.75 Inches
PRICE: F.

Fig. 1795
A watch holder group of the Three Graces, Hope, Faith, and Charity, represented by three women all in bodice and long skirts and scarves, two standing and one kneeling, all with their hands supporting the watch holder.
This figure can be found in at least two sizes, 10.5 inch figure illustrated.
HEIGHT: 9.5 Inches. 10.5 Inches.
PRICE: F

Fig. 1778A
A holy water stoop of two children dressed in flowing robes and seated on either side of an ornate cross; each child has one hand holding the cross.
A very rare figure previously unrecorded; the figure illustrated is very sharp and therefore very early from the mould.
HEIGHT: 10.5 Inches
PRICE: F.

Fig. 1796A **(Not illustrated)**
A group figure of three women standing side by side, all wearing long flowing dresses and each have garlands on their heads; the woman in the centre has her arms crossed and is holding a hand of the woman on either side. They in turn hold a garland of flowers on the head of the woman in the centre. All have their legs crossed in a dancing pose.
It is probable in view of the finding of the source to Figure 1797 that this figure also depicts a theatrical moment from 'The Three Graces'.
HEIGHT: 9.5 Inches
PRICE: F.

1. Marie Taglioni, Fanny Elssler, and Fanny Cerrito in
THE THREE GRACES

Fig. 1797SO Illustrated is a newly discovered contemporary print of The Three Graces, which is the source for Fig. 1797. What is interesting is that the print is titled 'Marie Taglioni, Fanny Elssler, and Fanny Cerrito in 'THE THREE GRACES'; consequently, this figure must now be considered theatrical and should really have appeared in that chapter. Marie Taglioni (1804-1884) was a prima ballerina and has often received the credit and blame for being the first to dance 'on point'. Fanny Cerrito (1817-1909) was a famous ballet and Court dancer who was on a par with Taglioni; her most celebrated performance was in 'Minuet de la Cour' when she danced as a couple with Fanny Elssler. Fanny Elssler (1810-1884) popularised an earthier, sensuous style and, whilst not of the standing of Taglioni and Cerrito, was a first rank ballerina, and other figures were made depicting parts she had performed. It would appear that these three great ballerinas came together for a performance of 'The Three Graces'.

Fig. 1801
A group figure of three women standing on a titled oval base, all wear long gowns. The woman on the left holds an open book, the one in the middle stands on a pedestal and holds an anchor (the Hope Anchor), and the one on the right holds a child in her arms. The pedestal is inscribed **FAITH HOPE AND CHARITY**. The Independent Order of Good Templars was founded in New York State in 1851 with the aim of the world wide abolition of alcohol; the order came to Britain in 1868. This figure can be found in two sizes, both illustrated.
HEIGHT: 10.5 & 15.5 Inches
PRICE: F.

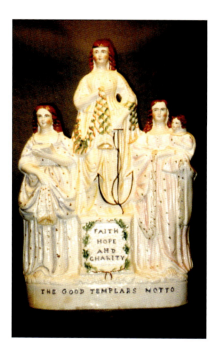

Figs. 1798/1798A
Two figures, the first of a man standing in flowing robes, his left hand on his hip, his right resting on an anchor, the second of a woman also in flowing robes, holding a child in her left arm. Another child stands by her side; the woman's right hand rests on the child's shoulder. **These figures are smaller versions of Figs. 1793/1794. There is another version of FAITH, not illustrated. Fig. 1798B has been reserved for it.** TITLE: HOPE. CHARITY HEIGHT: 10 Inches PRICE: F.

Chapter 2:
Hunters and Huntsmen

The potters were very fond of portraying hunters and huntsmen and women. This chapter illustrates the range of figures that were produced, from hunters with either bows or rifles, to hunters with falcons, on foot and on horseback with and without their dogs. The combinations that were modelled seem endless. Using their imagination, the potters were able to produce some of the finest examples of their art. It has been difficult if not impossible to find sources for any of the figures in this chapter, which would seem to confirm that the figures are imaginative rather than actual.

The popularity of decorative figures has been rising steadily with a corresponding increase in prices, and now many of the finest hunting figures exceed the prices for portrait figures which is a reversal of the situation that held for many years.

Figs. 1809/1809A
A pair of spill vase group figures of huntsmen standing on scrolled gilt lined bases. They are both dressed similarly with plumed hats, short jackets, long cloaks, boots, and pantaloons. One holds a long bow in his right hand and his dog sits at his feet. The other has his legs crossed and holds a deer suspended by its hind legs.
HEIGHT: 13 Inches
PRICE: Pair: E,
Singles: F.

Fig. 1808A
A figure of a bearded, kilted Scotsman standing, wearing a short jacket, plumed hat, frilled shirt, and an ermine edged cloak over his left shoulder. His dog is begging to his left with its paws on the mans leg. To his right his rifle stands against a tree stump. He holds a hare by its hind legs and a rabbit and bird lay on the base.
This is an altogether superior version of Fig. 1808 Book Two; the basic model is the same but additional moulds have been added. A very rare version, the figure illustrated is the only example the authors have seen.
HEIGHT: 14 Inches
PRICE: E.

Figs. 1810A/1810B
A pair of figures of a huntsman and wife standing, both wear plumed hats, she with a blouse and long skirt, and holds a basket of fruit in her left hand. Her right hand is on the head of a dog that stands on her right. He wears a long jacket and a sash over his shoulder supporting a bag. His right hand is held aloft holding a hunting horn and his left holds his rifle by its barrel with the butt on the ground. His dog stands beside him.
These figures are modelled and decorated in the round and a number of separate moulds were needed to complete the figures. They are early, made in the 1830s, whilst the original maker is not known. Sometime late in the century the moulds were acquired by the Kent factory and later figures made.
HEIGHT: 7.5 Inches
PRICE: Pair: E, Singles: F.

Fig. 1811B
A spill vase group of a hunter wearing a plumed hat, ermine edged cloak, shirt, jerkin, and knee length trousers with boots; his right hand is on his hip and his left hand holds a hunting horn aloft. Against the spill his long bow rests. A woman is seated at his side, wearing a plumed hat, loose sleeved blouse, and a long skirt with an apron. Her left hand rests in her lap and her right is around a small stag whose forehooves rest on her.
HEIGHT: 11.5 Inches
PRICE: F.

Fig. 1812A
A figure of a standing hunter with long hair and wearing a cap, belted tunic, breeches, and knee boots. A jumper is tied by its sleeves over his shoulders. A shot bag is suspended from his shoulder and he holds a rifle by its stock and barrel in both hands. His dog stands at his feet.
HEIGHT: 14 Inches
PRICE: G.

Figs. 1811C/1811D
A pair of spill vase figures of a hunter and his wife; he wears a hat with feather, long tunic, shoes and socks, and a quiver is on his back secured by a strap across his chest. He holds a long bow in both hands. A dead deer lies on the base and his dog stands on its hind legs by his side. She wears a hat with feather, blouse, and skirt with an apron. There is a small basket at her feet and a doe stands on its hind legs with its forehooves in her lap. She has one hand on its back and the other to its jaw.
This pair was made by the 'Green Factory'.
HEIGHT: 9.5 Inches
PRICE: Pair: E, Singles: F.

160

Fig. 1812B
A figure of a hunter standing with one foot raised above the other on rockwork; he wears a hat with a plume, ermine edged cloak, jacket, frilled shirt, knee breeches, and boots. His right arm rests on rockwork holding the barrel of his rifle, the butt of which rests on the ground. His dog sits at attention at his side.
HEIGHT: 13 Inches
PRICE: G.

Fig. 1817C
A standing figure of a hunter wearing highland attire; he has a bag on his side suspended by a strap over his left shoulder. His right hand holds a lead to which is attached a dog that sits between his legs. A weapon is held in his right hand. HEIGHT: 12 Inches
PRICE: G.

Fig. 1812C
A figure of a hunter standing; he wears a plumed hat, ermine edged cloak, short belted jacket, knee breeches, and boots. A small deer is held over his right shoulder and his left hand holds the barrel of his gun with its butt on the ground. His dog sits to attention by his feet.
HEIGHT: 10 Inches
PRICE: E.

Fig. 1821A
A figure of a man standing with his legs crossed, wearing a short jacket, shirt, waistcoat with sash, knee breeches, and boots, holding his plumed hat in his right hand and his left rests on rockwork to his side. A dog stands on its hind legs with its forepaws on his leg, on a shaped and scrolled base. **This is a very rare figure and its pair is unrecorded. Fig. 1821B has been reserved for it. It appears to be a hunter but no weapon is in evidence.**
HEIGHT: 10.5 Inches
PRICE: F.

Fig. 1824C
A spill vase figure of a woman standing, wearing a turban with a large feather, bodice, and long skirt with an apron. She holds a bird aloft in her right hand and her left holds her apron in which three dead rabbits lay.
This is probably the pair to Fig. 1824B. See Book Three.
HEIGHT: 8.5 Inches
PRICE: G.

Fig. 1824E
A spill vase figure of a hunter standing, wearing a plumed hat, ermine edged cloak, short jacket, shirt, kilt, and boots with short stockings. His right hand rests on his hip and his left holds his rifle. His dog stands on its hind legs with its forepaws on his knee. A dead bird lies on the base.
HEIGHT: 13.5 Inches
PRICE: E.

Fig. 1824D
A spill vase figure of a hunter seated, wearing a plumed hat, shirt, waistcoat, long jacket, and knee breeches. His left hand is in his jacket pocket and his right arm around his dog, which is to his right and is on its rear legs with its front paws in his lap. A rifle is also in his lap. At his feet a dead bird lies.
Two figures are illustrated, identical apart from decoration.
HEIGHT: 9 Inches
PRICE: F.

Fig. 1825A
A spill vase figure of a standing Scotsman dressed in highland attire, a large tartan scarf is across his shoulder and over his left arm. One hand is on his hip and his right hand rests on the head of a dog, which stands on its hind legs with its front paws on his kilt.
Whilst no weapon is evident, the authors are of the opinion that this portrays a hunter. It is possible that a pair may exist to this figure. Fig. 1825B has been reserved for it.
HEIGHT: 9 Inches
PRICE: F.

Fig. 1825C
A watch holder figure of a standing huntsman, his left arm leans on a closed spill vase in the form of a tree trunk. He wears a plumed hat, shirt, waistcoat, long jacket, and knee breeches. His rifle rests against the tree. Hanging from its branches are a dead bird and rabbit. His dog sits below the tree.
It is rare to find figures that are both a spill vase and a watch holder; it is not known why the spill was sometimes closed.
HEIGHT: 10.5 Inches
PRICE: E.

Fig. 1828F
A figure of a hunts-man standing by a small gate; he wears a cap, jacket, and knee breeches. A bag is suspended from his shoulder. In front of the gate a dog stands. **This figure probably has a pair. Fig. 1828G has been reserved for it.**
HEIGHT: 4 Inches
PRICE: G.

Fig. 1831A
A figure of a hunter kneeling on the back of a stag; his dog stands on its hind legs at his side with its front paws on his waist. His right arm is raised to his head holding a hunting horn and his left is holding the stag's antlers. He wears a plumed hat, tunic, kilt with sporran, and a large scarf over his shoulder and across his chest.
This figure can be found in two sizes, 13.5 inch illustrated.
HEIGHT: 13.5 Inches, 15.5 Inches
PRICE: E.

Fig. 1831B
A spill vase figure of a hunter seated with his right arm leaning against a tree holding a rifle by its barrel. He is wearing highland attire of plumed hat, open necked shirt, jerkin, kilt, and boots. A large scarf is over his left shoulder and across his chest. To his left a spaniel lies recumbent on rockwork. The hunter rests his left hand on the spaniels head. At his feet two birds lay dead.
HEIGHT: 14 Inches
PRICE: E.

Fig. 1831D
A seated figure of a hunter wearing highland attire of cap, jacket with scarf, kilt with sporran, and shoes and socks. He rests his left arm on rockwork and his rifle is by his side with its stock on the ground. By his feet his dog sits.
HEIGHT: 12.5 Inches
PRICE: E.

Fig. 1831C
A seated figure of a hunter wearing a large plumed hat, shirt three-quarter length jacket, knee breeches, and boots. An ermine edged cloak is draped over one shoulder and reaches the ground behind him, holding a hunting horn in his right hand and his left is held aloft and from which is suspended a dead deer. **The figure illustrated is the only example that the authors have seen and is probably unique; it is superbly modelled and decorated.**
HEIGHT: 14 Inches
PRICE: E.

Fig. 1832B
A figure of a seated hunter wearing highland attire of hat, jerkin, kilt with sporran, and a scarf over his right shoulder and across his chest. His left hand is held to his chin and his right rests on a walking stick. His legs are spread and two dead birds lay between.
HEIGHT: 10 Inches
PRICE: E.

Fig. 1833A/1833B
A pair of spill vase groups of a standing Scotsman and woman, both dressed in a plumed hat and blouse, he with a kilt, she with a skirt and knickers, a scarf is over one shoulder and across their arms. His right arm and her left is held at the waist and a bird is perched on it. A stag stands below him and his left arm rests on its antlers. A deer stands below her.
This pair probably portrays falconers.
HEIGHT: 10 Inches
PRICE: Pair: E, Singles: F.

Figs. 1835A/1835B
A pair of spill vase figures of hunters, one seated cross-legged on rockwork, his right arm raised to his chest holding a knife and his left holding a dead deer by its hind legs. He is wearing a plumed hat, shirt, long tunic, and a hunting horn is suspended at his waist. The other hunter is also seated and similarly dressed. He holds a longbow in his right hand and his left rests on his hip. At his feet a dog is recumbent. HEIGHT: 7.75 Inches
PRICE: Pair: F, Singles: G.

Fig. 1834A
A figure of a standing hunter wearing a high crowned plumed hat, shirt, jacket, kilt, boots, and a large ermine edged cloak over his right shoulder, holding a rifle by its barrel in his right hand and a deer suspended by its hind feet in his left.
The authors believe that this is the pair to Fig. 1834 Book Two but have not seen them together.
HEIGHT: 10 Inches
PRICE: F.

Figs. 1835C/1835D
A pair of spill vase figures of standing huntsmen; both huntsmen wear similar clothes of plumed hat, long tunic with a scarf across their chest, and boots. The left hand side figure holds a knife in his right hand and a deer by its hind legs in his left. The right hand side figure holds a longbow in his right hand and his left rests on the head of a dog that sits by his feet.
The left hand side figure is very similar to Fig. 1835A and is probably an adaptation of it.
HEIGHT: 8.5 Inches
PRICE: Pair: E, Singles: F.

Fig. 1840B
A standing spill vase figure of a hunter; he wears a large plumed hat, frilled shirt with neckerchief, waistcoat, long jacket, pantaloons, and knee boots. His legs are crossed and his dog sits behind him. His left hand holds the rear legs of a hare, which is suspended by a small fence on which his rifle rests. On the base is a large dead bird.
A very rare figure.
HEIGHT: 14.75 Inches
PRICE: E.

Fig. 1840A
A standing figure of a hunter who wears a hat with tassel, ermine edged cloak and jacket, short smock belted at the waist, knee breeches, and boots, holding a rifle in his right hand and a horn hangs from his belt. A large deer is suspended from his shoulder.
This is a very large, impressive, and rare figure.
HEIGHT: 18 Inches
PRICE: E.

Fig. 1840C
A spill vase figure of a hunter standing; he wears a plumed hat, coat split at the waist, and leggings. A scarf is around his waist and drapes to the floor. He holds a bird in his left hand and his dog lies at his feet looking up at the bird. 1855A, 1855C
HEIGHT: 14 Inches
PRICE: E.

Figs. 1842C/1842B
A pair of spill vase standing figures of a hunter and his wife; she wears a hat with feather, blouse, and skirt with an apron, and holds a bird which is perched on her right shoulder. Her other hand holds her apron, which is filled with dead rabbits. He wears a plumed hat, shirt, jacket, and kilt. A scarf is over his left arm and he holds a rifle in the crook of his right. His dog stands on its hind legs with its forepaws on his leg. There is a dead bird on the base.
HEIGHT: 9 Inches
PRICE: Pair: F, Singles: G.

Fig. 1843B
A spill vase figure of a standing hunter holding his rifle vertically by the breech. His dog sits at his feet and below a large bird lies dead. He wears a turban with two large feathers, shirt, open jacket, kilt boots, and cape over one shoulder.
A superbly modelled and decorated figure and very rare and similar to Fig. 1843 Book Two other than minor modelling differences.
HEIGHT: 16 Inches
PRICE: E.

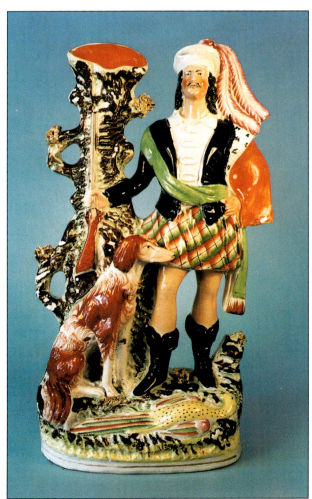

Figs. 1852C/1852B
A pair of spill vase figures of a standing hunter and wife; he wears a cap, waistcoat, jacket, trousers, and boots. His rifle is to his left with its butt on the ground. His left hand rests on his hip and his right on the tree below which his dog sits. She wears a mop cap, scarf across her shoulders, bodice, and dress with an apron. She has a basket over her right arm in which there are dead rabbits. In her right hand she holds a dead bird by its feet. Another basket is at her feet.
These figures are representative of a successful hunt. The wife carrying the animals that her husband has shot.
HEIGHT: 11 Inches
PRICE: Pair: F, Singles: G.

Fig. 1852D
A spill vase figure of a standing hunter; he is long haired and bearded and wears a hat with feather, tunic, ermine edged long cloak belted at the waist, and ankle boots. His left hand rests on his waist and his right holds a long bow. A dog sits at his feet. All these items are mounted on an arched bases with a shell decoration. **There is a pair to this very large figure. Fig. 1852E has been reserved for it.** HEIGHT: 17 Inches PRICE: E.

Fig. 1854C
A figure of a standing hunter who wears a turban, ermine edged jacket, tunic, and breeches with stockings. He rests his head on his right hand and holds his rifle by its barrel, the stock of which rests on a dead animal at his feet. **There is a pair to this figure. Fig. 1854D has been reserved for it.** HEIGHT: 7 Inches PRICE: G.

1855A/1855B/1855C
A pair of figures of a man and woman standing on a circular gilt lined base; he holds a rifle in his right hand and a dead bird in his left. A dog stands on its hind legs with its front paws resting on his coat; the man wears a brimmed hat, long jacket, and breeches. She wears a hat, low cut blouse, and skirt with an apron. She holds a lamb on her lap.
This male figure has a different pair, very similar but instead of a sheep in her lap she has a rabbit, and a dog jumps up by her side. Her dress is also differently modelled.
It is not known why such changes should be made to a pair; one explanation is that the original mould of her was destroyed and another was made. Both pairs are illustrated modelled in the round. These are early figures, circa 1835/40. HEIGHT: 7 Inches
PRICE: Pair: F, Singles: G.

1866A
A pair of spill vase figures of standing hunters; both are dressed in plumed hats, belted tunics with straps, and boots. A hunting horn is at their waists. One leans against the spill vase holding a club in his left hand, his dog sits on the other side of the spill vase. The other hunter has his left hand on his hip, his long bow resting against the spill to the side of which a dead deer hangs.
HEIGHT: 12.25 Inches
PRICE: Pair: E, Singles: F.

Figs. 1866C/1866D
A pair of spill vase figures of standing hunters, both wearing plumed hats, belted tunics with straps across their chests ,and a hunting horn at their belt. One stands beside a tree trunk holding a large club in his left hand and his right hand is on his hip holding a dead deer by its hind legs. His companion has his left hand on his hip and his right holds a long bow. A dog sits at his feet. **These two particular gentlemen do appear, as a pair or in a group quite often (See Figs. 1866, 1867/1868/1869/1870 Book Two). This pair are by far the rarest, largest, and finest. Their source is the crest of The Ancient Order of Foresters, this crest portrays these two men standing to either side of a shield which is quartered with a handshake, three running stags, a decorated chevron, and a hunting horn. The shield is surmounted with a stag's head. The Ancient Order of Foresters began in 1834 but its origins lie in an older society called Royal Foresters that was formed in the eighteenth century, it continues to this day with 'courts' or branches in many countries including America, it is basically a self help society.**
HEIGHT: 16.5 Inches
PRICE: Pair: D, Singles: F.

Fig. 1866C/1866D SO Illustrated in the 1875 version of the crest of The Ancient Order of Foresters which is the source of a number of figures.

Fig. 1866E
A standing figure of a man dressed in highland attire of plumed hat, ermine edged cloak and jerkin, kilt, and ankle boots. He holds a long bow in his right hand and a dog sits by his left leg.
This is a very rare figure. The authors have not seen it before. There is no doubt a pair and Fig. 1866F has been reserved for it. It is by the same modeller who made the figures of William Tell and Rob Roy (See Figs. 1038 & 1341 Book One) and is very similar to the William Tell figure.
HEIGHT: 8.75 Inches
PRICE: F.

Fig. 1870B
A group figure of two men standing on either side of a fruiting plant that is surmounted by a stag's head; both men wear tunics and boots, both carry weapons, one a club, and both have hunting horns suspended from their belt.
HEIGHT: 9.5 Inches
PRICE: H.

Fig. 1870A
A clock face group of two standing hunters dressed in ermine edged Lincoln green tunics and large plumed hats. The man to the left holds a long bow in his right hand and a hunting horn hangs from his belt; the man to the right has one hand on his belt and the other holds a large club. Between them a deer sits.
HEIGHT: 9.5 Inches
PRICE: H.

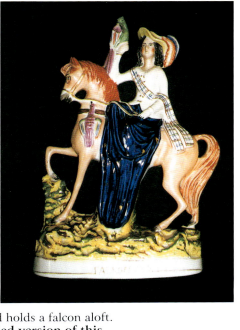

Figs. 1871/1872
A pair of figures of equestrian falconers, he facing to the right and wearing a plumed hat, long jacket, frilled shirt, breeches, and boots. His left hand holds a falcon aloft and a dead bird is tied to the horse's neck. She is facing left and wears a plumed hat, short jacket, and long dress. A scarf is over her shoulder and across her chest. Her right hand holds a falcon aloft.
There is also illustrated a titled figure of Fig. 1872. A titled version of this pair has never before been recorded and is therefore extremely rare. The title has been miss-spelt 'FALKONESS'. A titled figure of Fig. 1871 has also been recorded, titled 'FALCONER'.
HEIGHT: 13.5 Inches
PRICE: Pair: C, Singles: D.

Figs. 1876A/1876B
A pair of figures of a man and woman, both dressed in a Roman type costume, both with plumed hats, she a long robe, he with a long tunic tied at the waist. Each figure holds a bird aloft, she in her left hand, he in his right and a garland is held in the other hand. They are both barefooted and stand on an unusual cubed base.
This pair probably portrays falconers, but their dress and the garland suggest theatrical dancers.
HEIGHT: 10 Inches
PRICE: (In the white) Pair: F, Singles: G.

Fig. 1877A
A watch holder group figure of standing falconers, he to the left wearing a shirt, jacket, tunic, kilt, and cape draped over his right shoulder, she to the right wearing a blouse and long skirt, and a scarf is over her arm. They each hold one hand aloft, holding a bird. Below and between them is a spaniel.
This is very similar in design to Fig. 1877 Book Two and has therefore been included in this chapter; but, a spaniel is an unusual choice of dog to take falconing.
HEIGHT: 8 Inches
PRICE: H.

Figs. 1878/1879
A pair of figures of mounted male and female falconers; he wears a high buttoned jacket, shirt, knee breeches, and boots, and holds a plumed hat in his right hand. His left hand holds a bird on the horse's mane. She wears a plumed hat, jacket, and long skirt, holding a bird on the horse's mane with her right hand. Her left hand is in her lap.
HEIGHT: 9 Inches
PRICE: Pair: E, Singles: F.

Figs. 1879C/1879D
A pair of figures of mounted hunters; he wears a brimmed hat, cloak, jacket, blouse, and trousers with knee boots, while a dead bird is strung over his saddle. She wears a hat with scarf and long dress. She holds a bird in her left hand and the reins in her right.
HEIGHT: 8 Inches
PRICE: Pair: F, Singles: G.

Fig. 1879A
A mounted figure of a hunter, he wears a turban, tunic, kilt with sporran, and a scarf is draped over his shoulder. He holds one hand to his chest and in the other holds the barrel of his rifle. There is an unusual decorative saddlecloth on the horse.
There is a pair to this figure. Fig. 1879B has been reserved for it.
HEIGHT: 7.5 Inches
PRICE: Pair: E, Singles: F.

Figs. 1880/1881
A pair of figures of seated falconers; he wears a plumed hat, cloak, jacket, waistcoat, and knee breeches. He holds a falcon aloft in his left hand and his right rests on his knee. His dog is recumbent at his feet. She wears a plumed hat, wide sleeved blouse, and long dress. She holds the falcon aloft in her left hand. A dog has leaped onto her lap. Each figure is on a shaped base decorated with gold sprays.
HEIGHT: 15 Inches
PRICE: Pair: E, Singles: F.

Figs. 1883A/1883B
A pair of figures of standing falconers, both wear plumed hats and hold a falcon aloft, he with his left hand, she with her right. He wears a jacket with sash, shirt, breeches, and thigh boots. A bow is held in his right hand. She wears a long dress with a sash over her shoulder. Her left hand rests on her longbow. On the base of each figure a dead bird lies.
HEIGHT: 12.25 Inches
PRICE: Pair: E, Singles: F.

Fig. 1893C
A figure of a woman standing on rockwork wearing a plumed hat, blouse with sash over her shoulder and across her chest, and skirt with an apron. She also appears to have a full quiver on her back. To her left side, also resting on rockwork, is a basket filled with dead birds. On the base below her a spaniel stands. **This figure is one of a pair. Fig. 1893D has been reserved for it. An attractive figure that the authors have not seen before, should the pair come to light it probably portrays a hunter responsible for the dead birds.**
HEIGHT: 9.75 Inches
PRICE: F.

Figs. 1893A/1893B
A pair of figures of a standing hunter and his wife; he wears a hat with feathers, shirt with a frilled collar, tunic with belt, short skirt, and a cloak over his shoulder. He is holding a shot bag in his left hand. A shot gun rests against his leg and a dead bird lies on the base. She wears a feathered hat, cape, bodice, and skirt with an apron, and holds a basket under her left arm that has a dead bird in it.
HEIGHT: 10 Inches
PRICE: Pair: F, Singles: G.

Figs. 1893E/1893F
A pair of figures of a man and woman standing; he wears a hat, frilled shirt with tie, jacket, and knee breeches. Over his shoulder is the strap of a bag which he holds at his waist. His right hand holds the barrel of his gun with its butt on the ground. A dead bird is suspended from his right hand and his dog sits to attention at his feet. She wears a hat, bodice, jacket, and long skirt with an apron. There are two dead birds suspended from her left arm and her dog sits to attention at her feet. Both figures are on scrolled bases.
A particularly fine pair of hunters, very rare, and claimed to have been made by the Dudson pottery.
HEIGHT: 10.75 Inches
PRICE: Pair: D, Singles: E.

Figs. 1893J/1893K
A pair of standing figures of a man and woman, both wearing large plumed hats. She wears a very short jacket and a skirt with an apron; she is holding a dead bird in both hands. He wears a shirt with a frilled collar, jacket, and knee breeches with boots. He holds a rifle in both hands and a dog sits at his feet.
The price given is for a pair in the white; should a coloured pair come to light they would be more expensive.
HEIGHT: 9 Inches
PRICE: Pair: F, Singles: G.

Figs. 1893G/1893H
A pair of figures of a man and woman standing; he wears a hat with feathers, open neck shirt with tie, long jacket, knee length breeches, boots, and a sash across his chest. His left hand is in his jacket pocket and his right holds a rifle by its barrel. A dog sits at his feet. She wears a hat with feathers, long jacket, a dress, and a large scarf over her arm.
These figures were made by the Sampson Smith pottery, circa 1860. In 1949 a mould of her was found in a disused part of the factory and a number of figures were then made. Care should be taken as both the 1860 and 1949 figures were very similarly decorated.
HEIGHT: 10.25 Inches
PRICE: Pair: F, Singles: G.

Fig. 1894C
A watch holder group figure of a man and woman standing on either side; he wears a plumed hat, open necked shirt, jacket, kilt, and knee boots. A bag is strapped over his left shoulder and he holds a rifle in his right hand. She wears a plumed hat, bodice, and a long skirt with an apron. Above the watch holder a bird is perched and another swims in a pond on the base.
HEIGHT: 11 Inches
PRICE: F.

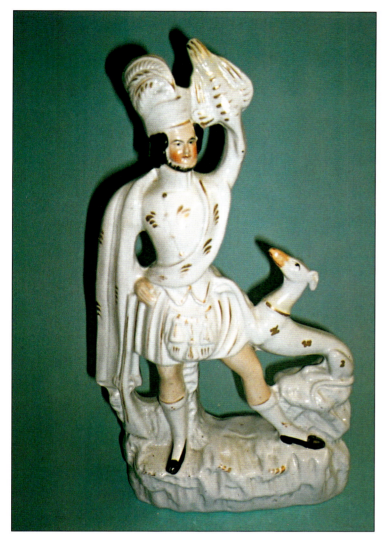

Fig. 1894F
A figure of a man standing, dressed in highland garb of hat with feathers, tunic, kilt with sporran, shoes and socks, and a large scarf tied around his waist. He holds a dead rabbit aloft in his left hand and holds a rifle by its stock in his right. The base is decorated with large leaves. **It is possible that there is a pair to this figure; it would be easily identifiable by the base. Fig. 1894G has been reserved for it.**
HEIGHT: 14.75
PRICE: F.

Fig. 1894D
A figure of a man standing, dressed in highland garb of plumed hat, tunic, large scarf over his shoulder, and kilt with sporran. He holds a dead bird aloft in his left hand and his right is on his hip. His dog stands on rockwork to his left with its forepaws on his kilt. **There is probably a pair to this figure. Fig. 1894E has been reserved for it.**
HEIGHT: 10.5 Inches
PRICE: F.

Fig. 1895B
A figure of a woman falconer seated sidesaddle on a horse; she wears a plumed hat, blouse, and long skirt. She holds the falcon in her right hand and the reins in her left.
There is a pair to this figure. Fig. 1895A has been reserved for it.
HEIGHT: 10 Inches
PRICE: Pair: E, Singles: F.

Figs. 1898/1898A
A pair of figures of standing falconers, both dressed similarly with plumed hats, he with a shirt, jacket, short trousers tied at the waist with a belt, boots, and a large scarf over both shoulders and through his arm. His left hand is on his hip and his right holds a bird. She wears a jacket and long dress with knickers showing, a large scarf is tied to her hat and through her right arm which is on her hip. She holds a bird in her left hand.
HEIGHT: 8.75 Inches
PRICE: Pair: F, Singles: G.

Fig. 1898D
A standing figure of a woman dressed in a plumed hat, blouse, bodice, and long skirt with a scarf over her arm. She holds a dead bird aloft. A dog sits on rockwork to her right with its paws on her skirt.
There is a pair to this figure. Fig. 1898E has been reserved for it.
HEIGHT: 12 Inches
PRICE: Pair: E, Singles: F.

Figs. 1898B/1898C
A pair of figures of standing falconers, both dressed similarly with plumed hats, jackets, dresses with loose trousers, and cloaks over their shoulders. On her left and his right shoulder a bird is perched. They both appear to hold a nest of eggs in their hand; the other hand is on their hips.
An unusual pair, it is possible that they portray falconers but they could be theatrical.
HEIGHT: 11.5 Inches
PRICE: Pair: E, Singles: F.

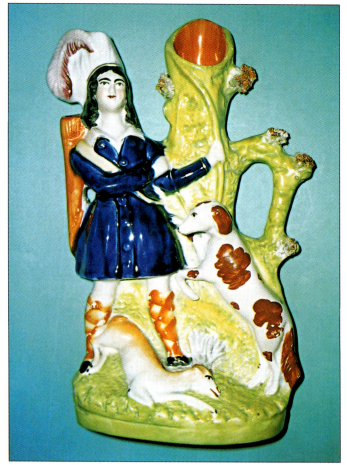

Figs. 1901C
A spill vase figure of a huntsman standing; he wears a plumed hat, open neck shirt, and long tunic with tartan socks and shoes. He holds a longbow in both hands and a quiver is strapped to his back. His dog stands on its hind legs with its forepaw on his tunic. On the base a dead stag lies. **There is a pair to this figure. Fig. 1901D has been reserved for it.**
HEIGHT: 9.5 Inches
PRICE: Pair: E., Singles: F.

Fig. 1899F
A figure of a woman standing, wearing a large hat, jacket with open sleeves, long skirt, and a sash over her right shoulder and tied at the waist in a bow. She holds a rabbit in her right hand and a dead bird in her left, which rests on a tree stump. **There is a pair to this figure. Fig. 1899G has been reserved for it.**
HEIGHT: 10.5
PRICE: Pair: E, Singles: F.

Fig. 1901B
A spill vase figure of a hunter, he wears a hat with feathers, tunic, jacket, ermine edged cloak, and kilt. His right hand is on his hip and his left holds a bow. A dead deer lies at his feet and he stands with one foot on it.
HEIGHT: 10 Inches
PRICE: G.

Fig. 1902B
A group clock face figure of a hunter standing, wearing a plumed hat, frilled shirt, jacket, and knee breeches with boots, holding a rifle by its butt in his right hand, and his left is around a large dog that sits above the clock face. To the right, a woman sits wearing a plumed hat, bodice, long coat, and dress. Her hands are in her lap and at her feet lies a dead bird and rabbit.
HEIGHT: 12.5 Inches
PRICE: E.

Fig. 1914B
A spill vase group figure of a man seated, wearing a brimmed hat, cravat, shirt, jacket, and trousers with leggings, holding a rifle by its barrel between his legs. A dog lies at his feet.
Another figure made by the 'Green' factory.
HEIGHT: 7 Inches
PRICE: F.

Fig. 1913B
A spill vase group figure of a man wearing a plumed hat, cloak, frilled shirt, and kilt with boots, holding a bird aloft with his right hand and his left is at his waist. To his right a child sits in a tree with its hand reaching up to the bird; below a dog sits.
A very large and imposing figure and very rare, the figure illustrated is the only example the authors have seen.
HEIGHT: 16.5 Inches
PRICE: E.

Fig. 1914C
A spill vase group of a kneeling man wearing a hat, jacket, shirt with tie, waistcoat, knee breeches, and boots. One dog is to his left side with its forepaws on his lap, another is by his left hand, and yet another lies below. On the base is his rifle and a dead rabbit.
The 'Green' factory also made this figure, and it is probably a pair with Fig. 1914 or Fig. 1914B
HEIGHT: 7.5 Inches
PRICE: F.

Figs. 1915/1916
A pair of figures of equestrian archers, the left hand figure is seated astride his rearing horse and wears a plumed hat, short jacket, knee breeches with boots, and an ermine edged cloak is around his shoulders. He is holding a longbow in his left hand and there is a quiver at his waist. The right hand side figure is bareheaded and wears a short jacket, cloak with sash across his chest, and short trousers with boots. He is seated side saddle and has been struck by an arrow that he is attempting to remove from his chest as he falls from his horse; his longbow is on the ground below.
These figures are probably depictions of an act at Astleys Circus.
HEIGHT: 9.75
PRICE: Pair: D, Singles: E.

Fig. 1924A
A group spill vase figure of a highland hunter who stands dressed in plumed hat, jacket, shirt, and kilt with sporran. A rifle is held in both his hands. His wife stands beside him, wearing a dress with a shawl over her head. A bird is perched on her left hand.
This is a very well constructed and modelled figure. The authors have only seen the figure illustrated; should it exist in full colour, it would fetch a higher price than the guide price given.
HEIGHT: 14.5 Inches
PRICE: (In the white) F.

Fig. 1924B
A spill vase group of a hunter and his wife; he wears a flat cap, long jacket, flowered waistcoat, and knee breeches with boots. He holds his rifle by its barrel in his right hand and his left is around his wife. His wife is bareheaded and wears a bodice and a long skirt with an apron. Her hat is held in her right hand and a filled basket is over her left arm. A small picket fence is by her feet and a dog sits by his master. The spill is decorated with grapes and vine leaf.
If decorated in full colour this would be a very large and imposing figure. The authors have only seen the example illustrated.
HEIGHT: 16 Inches
PRICE: F.

Fig. 1924C
A group figure of a girl standing on rockwork wearing a hat with feathers, bodice, and short skirt with knickers showing. She holds a bird aloft in her right hand. A boy sits below on the back of a dog and wears a hat with feathers, shirt, tunic, and kilt. A rifle lies on the ground.
An attractive figure, there is probably a pair to this figure. Fig. 1924D has been reserved for it.
HEIGHT: 9.5 Inches
PRICE: F.

Figs. 1935A/1935B
A pair of figures of a man and a shepherdess, both standing, he wearing a cap, jacket, scarf, and breeches with leggings. His gun stands on its butt between his legs and he is filling it with shot from a bag held in his hand. His dog sits to his side. She wears a brimmed hat, bodice, and skirt with an apron. She holds a sheep by its neck and appears to be removing wool from it.
These are early figures, modelled in the round with a number of separate moulds, made in about 1830/35.
HEIGHT: 8 Inches
PRICE: Pair: F, Singles: G.

Fig. 1933A
A figure of a woman who wears a plumed hat with scarf attached, cloak, bodice, and skirt with an apron. She stands above a small stream and holds a dead deer by its hind legs in her left hand.
There is a pair to this figure. Fig. 1933B has been reserved for it.
HEIGHT: 10.75 Inches
PRICE: F.

Fig. 1935E
A standing figure of a man wearing a tricorn hat, long tunic, and shoes and socks. His right hand rests on the head of a dog that stands on its hind legs and his left holds the barrel of his rifle that has its butt on the ground.
There is a pair to this figure. Fig. 1935F has been reserved for it. Modelled in the round, this is an early Victorian figure made in about 1840.
HEIGHT: 9 Inches
PRICE: G.

Figs. 1939/1940
These figures are a smaller debased version of figures 1937/1938, almost the same apart from the size. The shape of the saddlecloth, the treatment of the foreground, and the reduction in size have been synonymous with a reduction in quality. The modelling is not as good and the decoration not to the standard of the larger figures.
In view of the fact that they are only carrying pistols, and there are no dead animals or dogs, it is possible that all four figures portray brigands, not hunters.
HEIGHT: 12 Inches
PRICE: Pair: E, Singles: F.

Figs. 1940C/1940D
An equestrian pair of figures of a hunter seated astride his horse wearing a Scots cap, tunic with scarf over his shoulder and across his chest, and kilt. He holds the reins in his right hand and a small rifle in his left. A brace of dead birds lie across the saddle. She wears a cap, cloak, blouse, and long skirt; she sits side saddle and holds a basket over her arm. HEIGHT: 7 Inches
PRICE: Pair: F, Singles: G.

Fig. 1940A
A figure of a mounted hunter facing right, wearing a plumed hat, cloak, shirt, jacket, kilt, and boots. His right hand is on the reins and his left rests on a dead deer, which is draped over the saddle.
There is a pair to this figure that would be facing the other way. Fig. 1940B has been reserved for it.
HEIGHT: 7 Inches
PRICE: G.

Figs. 1941/1942
A pair of figures of equestrian hunters, each seated astride his horse facing left and right, both similarly dressed in a hat, cloak, jacket tied with a scarf, kilt, and boots. Both horses have a long saddle-cloth. The hunter on the left holds his rifle on the horse's flank with his right hand and the reins with his left. The hunter on the right holds the reins with his right hand and a dead deer across the horse's rump with his left.
An extremely finely modelled, delicately coloured, and rare pair of equestrian figures.
HEIGHT: 13.5 Inches
PRICE: Pair: D, Singles: E.

Figs. 1950C/1950D
A pair of figures of men facing left and right mounted on rearing horses, the front legs of which are resting on a fence. The men are dressed in round hats, shirt, waistcoat, long jacket, and trousers with leggings. They hold the reins in one hand.
Each is a mirror image of the other.
A very rare pair of figures, usually when depicting hunters either a weapon or game are included; as neither are, it is possible that some other pursuit is being portrayed.
HEIGHT: 9 Inches
PRICE: Pair: F, Singles: G.

Fig. 1945
A rare spill vase version of Figures 1943/1944 Book One; the man on the left wears a top hat, neckerchief, long jacket, waistcoat, and trousers with leggings, being clubbed by a pistol held by the man on the right, who is similarly dressed but is bare-headed. A dog attacks the man in the top hat and there are dead birds on the base.
This figure can be found in two sizes; in the smaller size the legs are not separately moulded.
HEIGHT: 8.5 & 9.75 Inches
PRICE: 9.75 Inches: E, 8.5 Inches: F.

Figs. 1951/1952 A pair of figures of equestrian hunters; they are truncated versions of Figures 1949/1950. The huntsmen are identical, but the hunt has gone and has been replaced by a small bridge over a stream.
HEIGHT: 8.5 Inches
PRICE: Pair: E, Singles: F.

Figs. 1955A/1955B
A pair of mounted figures of huntsmen wearing Welsh costume of top hat, cravat, jacket, waistcoat, and trousers. The huntsman on the left has a dead rabbit and dead bird over the horses back. Whilst the huntsman on the right has two dead rabbits, apart from this they are a mirror image of each other.
TITLE: WELCH HUNTERS
HEIGHT: 11 Inches
PRICE: Pair: D, Singles: E.

Fig. 1952D
A spill vase figure of a huntsman who stands to the left of the spill, wearing a hat, shirt with cravat, long coat, and breeches with boots, holding a rifle by its barrel in his right hand. He leans his left arm against a tree, holding the reins of his horse, which stands with one leg raised, rearing its head. On the ground a dead bird lies.
It is probable that a pair exists for this figure. Fig. 1952C has been reserved for it.
HEIGHT: 9 Inches
PRICE: F.

Figs. 1957/1958
A pair of equestrian figures of a huntsman seated astride his horse, both wearing a cap, high necked jacket, and trousers with boots, one hand holding the horse's reins, the other holding a dead rabbit by its tail.
HEIGHT: 8 Inches
PRICE: Pair. F, Singles: G.

Fig. 1952E
A spill vase figure of a hunter seated, wearing a plumed hat, shirt, cloak, and kilt with boots, holding a pail in both hands from which his horse is drinking. Over the saddle of the horse a dead bird and rabbit lay and below a dog is recumbent.
It is probable that a pair exists for this figure. Fig. 1952F has been reserved for it.
HEIGHT: 12 Inches
PRICE: E.

Fig. 1958D
A figure of an equestrian huntsman wearing a cap red jacket and trousers with boots. He holds the reins in his left hand and in his right he holds a rabbit aloft.
This figure is illustrated with a left hand side figure of Fig. 1957, as this has a mirror image pair; it is probable that this figure also has a mirror image pair in which the rabbit is held aloft. Fig. 1958E has been reserved for it.
HEIGHT: 8 Inches
PRICE: Pair: F, Singles: G.

Figs. 1958A/1958B
A pair of figures of huntsmen seated on rearing horses, wearing plumed hats, cloaks, long jackets, knee length breeches, and boots, each with one hand holding the reins. The left hand side figure is holding the hind legs of a stag that lies across the saddle cloth. The right hand side figure is almost a mirror image other than a larger cloak, different breeches, and instead of a stag two rabbits hang from the saddlecloth.
There is a larger version of this pair (see Figures 1959/1960 Book Two).
HEIGHT: 12 Inches
PRICE: Pair: D, Singles: E.

Fig. 1960E
A figure of a hunter seated on rockwork, dressed in highland attire of plumed hat, long tunic, shoes and socks, with a large scarf draped over his left shoulder and holding bagpipes. To his right his horse stands with a dead deer tied over the horse's back.
There is probably a pair to this figure. Fig. 1960F has been reserved for it.
HEIGHT: 11 Inches
PRICE: E.

Chapter 3:
Shepherds, Gardeners, Harvesters, and Pastoral Scenes

Many workers had left the land to find a better living in the rapidly expanding towns and cities; this included workers living around the potteries. Some did improve their lot, though others found that the poverty they had left behind in the countryside was replaced by the drudgery to be found in the towns.

To any number the poverty could be forgotten and an idealised version of what they believed lost in the country could be found in a Staffordshire figure. It was romantic and nostalgic but it was not accurate. The potters capitalised on this nostalgia and produced figures of shepherds, shepherdesses, gatherers, water carriers, harvesters, gardeners, farmers, and many other rural and pastoral scenes and people.

Figs. 1961B/1961C
A pair of figures of a highland shepherd and his wife standing with legs crossed; he wears a plumed hat, shirt, jacket, and kilt with boots, holding a sheep under his right arm. A water bottle and pipe are suspended from his waist. His dog sits at attention to his left side and another sheep lies on the base. She wears a hat with feather, blouse, and skirt with an apron which has grapes in it. She holds a lamb under her left arm and another sheep stands on the base to her left.
HEIGHT: 10.5 Inches
PRICE: Pair: F, Singles: G.

Fig. 1961A
A figure of a standing shepherd, wearing a plumed hat, long jacket, shirt, waistcoat, and knee breeches with a cloak over his shoulder. His right hand is on his hip and his left holds a crook. A sheep lies at his feet and to his side on rockwork a poodle sits with its paw on his shoulder. **A very rare group, it is also unusual to have a poodle as a sheepdog!**
HEIGHT: 13.5 Inches
PRICE: D.

Fig. 1961D
A figure of a girl standing, wearing a plumed hat, bodice, and long skirt with a scarf over her shoulders. She holds a basket of flowers in her right hand and her left is around a sheep that stands on its hind legs with its front feet on her waist.
There is a pair to this figure. Fig. 2100G has been reserved for it.
HEIGHT: 10 Inches
PRICE: Pair: F, Singles: G.

Figs. 1965C/1965D
A pair of figures of standing shepherds, both wear plumed hats, she a blouse, long coat, and long skirt, he a long jacket, shirt with tie, and knee breeches. She holds a lamb in her left arm and another lamb lies on the base. A small fence is to her right. He holds a dog under his right arm and two lambs lay on the base.
HEIGHT: 6.25 Inches
PRICE: Pair: G, Singles: G.

Fig. 1965A
A figure of a man standing on a grassy mound; he wears a plumed hat, smock, short trousers, and long jacket. His left hand is on his hip and his right holds a shepherd's crook. A sheep is laying on the base, which is rococo shaped.
There is no doubt a pair to this figure. Fig. 1965B has been reserved for it.
HEIGHT: 9.5 Inches
PRICE: G.

Figs. 1967A/1967B
A pair of figures of a boy and girl, both standing on rockwork and wearing plumed hats, he with a shirt, jacket, and knee breeches with his right arm around a spaniel that stands on its hind legs beside him, she wearing a bodice and long skirt, holding an apron that is filled with fruit. A lamb stands on rockwork to her side.
HEIGHT: 8.5 Inches
PRICE: Pair: F, Singles: G.

Fig. 1967C
A figure of a man standing, wearing a brimmed hat, open neck shirt, jacket, and trousers. His right arm rests on rockwork and his left hand is on his hip. Below a sheep is recumbent.
There is a pair to this figure. Fig. 1967D has been reserved for it.
HEIGHT: 7 Inches
PRICE: Pair: F, Singles: G.

Fig. 1965G
A figure of a shepherd standing with one foot raised onto a bank; he wears a hat, tie, waistcoat, jacket, and knee breeches. A cloak is over his right shoulder and he holds it with his right hand. His left arm rests on a tree stump. His crook rests against his chest and a sheep lies below his feet. The base of the figure is decorated with large leaves.
Two figures are illustrated; the coloured figure is unusual in so far as the shepherd's left arm is missing, as is the sheep on the base. Neither item has ever been there and the figure left the pottery like this and was probably sold as a second.
HEIGHT: 13 Inches
PRICE: F.

Fig. 1967E
A figure of a woman standing, wearing a hat with veil, bodice, and long skirt with an apron. She holds a full basket in her right hand and her left is around a sheep that stands on its hind legs on a pillar beside her. **This is a porcelaneous figure with a hollow base, decorated and modelled in the round, made about 1835. There is a pair to this figure. Fig. 1967F has been reserved for it.** HEIGHT: 7.5 Inches PRICE: F.

Fig. 1967H
A figure of a woman seated, wearing a hat decorated with flowers, long jacket, and skirt. She has her left arm around a lamb that sits on rockwork; she holds an object in her right hand. **There is a pair to this figure. Fig. 1967G has been reserved for it.** HEIGHT: 6.75 Inches PRICE: G.

Fig. 1967J
A figure of a woman standing, wearing a plumed hat, blouse, and tartan skirt. A large scarf is over her right shoulder and her left hand rests on a lamb that stands on its hind legs by her side. **There is a pair to this figure. Fig. 1967K has been reserved for it.** HEIGHT: 9.25 PRICE: G.

Fig. 1967L
A figure of a woman standing, wearing a mop cap, bodice, blouse, and skirt. a lamb stands on its hind legs with its fore hooves on her skirt.
There is a pair to this figure. Fig. 1967M has been reserved for it.
HEIGHT: 6.5 Inches
PRICE: G.

Fig. 1967N
A figure of a girl standing, wearing a hat, bodice, blouse, and skirt with an apron. She holds a lamb in both hands and at her feet a large jug rests.
There is a pair to this figure. Fig. 1967P has been reserved for it.
HEIGHT: 7.5 Inches
PRICE: G

Figs. 1968D/1968E
A pair of figures of highland shepherds, both standing; he wears a plumed hat, long tunic, tartan socks, shoes, and a large scarf draped over his left shoulder. He holds a set of bagpipes in his left hand. Below him on the base his dog lies. She wears a plumed hat, long sleeved blouse, long skirt, and a large scarf over her right shoulder and across her chest. A sheep stands on its hind legs to her side with its forehooves on her waist. Two lambs lay on the base.
See also Fig. 1560A Book Three for an almost identical figure of him. This is an example of where a figure has two quite different pairs; Fig. 1560A is similar but the shepherdess is playing a squeezebox and there is no sheep to the side.
HEIGHT: 11 Inches
PRICE: Pair: E, Singles: F.

Figs. 1968A/1968
A pair of figures of a shepherd and shepherdess, both wearing highland attire of plumed hat, blouse/tunic with sash, and skirt/kilt, he with boots, she with shoes. He stands and holds a set of pipes in both hands. Below him a dog is recumbent. She sits cross-legged and holds an open book in both hands. At her feet a sheep sits.
The figure of the shepherdess is similar in some respects to a Pre-Victorian figure titled 'The Reading Maid'. Illiteracy being common, it was a source of amazement that a young girl could read. There are a number of shepherdess figures that portray the shepherdess reading.
HEIGHT: 11 Inches
PRICE: Pair: E, Singles: F.

Fig. 1968F
A figure of a woman standing on rockwork wearing a plumed hat, blouse, long skirt, knickers, and a sash over her shoulder and across her chest. Below her feet two sheep lie.
There is a pair to this figure. Fig. 1968G has been reserved for it.
HEIGHT: 12 Inches
PRICE: F.

Figs. 1969D/1969E
A pair of figures of a shepherd and shepherdess; both characters sit on a grassy bank. She wears a hat, blouse with open sleeves, and a long skirt. Her left arm rests on rockwork and her left foot rests on a cushion. A sheep lies at her feet. He wears a hat, shirt, jacket, knee breeches, and a scarf over his shoulder. His dog stands on its hind legs with its paws on his leg; his crook rests on the bank.
HEIGHT: 7 Inches
PRICE: Pair: F, Singles: G.

Figs. 1969F/1969G/ 1969H
A pair of figures of a man and woman standing, he with legs crossed wearing a hat with feather, shirt with tie, jacket, kilt with sporran, and a large scarf over his shoulder and arm. A sheep stands on its hind legs on rockwork beside him with its forehooves on his waist. She wears a hat with feather, bodice, long skirt, and a scarf over her shoulders. She carries a basket of fruit on her right arm and a sheep stands on its hind legs with its forehooves on her waist.

Figs. 1969B/1969C
A pair of spill vase figures of a shepherd and shepherdess standing; she wears a plumed bonnet, bodice, aproned skirt, and a sash across her chest. Her left hand is raised holding a crook and a sheep stands at her side. He wears a plumed hat, shirt, jacket, and knee breeches. A bottle is at his side held by a strap across his chest. He hold a set of pipes in both hands and his dog sits begging at his feet.
He was previously catalogued as Fig. 1614 in the unidentified musician's chapter.
HEIGHT: 9.5 Inches
PRICE: Pair: F, Singles: G.

There is also illustrated another Fig. 1969G, which is a mirror image of the woman together with a further figure of Fig. 1969E. There is probably a mirror image of the man that would pair this figure.
HEIGHT: 10.5 Inches
PRICE: Pair: F, Singles: G.

Fig. 1969J
A spill vase figure of a woman standing, wearing a hat with tassel and long dress with aprons. She holds a musical instrument in her right hand. To her side the spill is decorated with grapes and a sheep is recumbent on rockwork, below which a stream flows from an arch. **There is probably a pair to this figure. Fig. 1969K has been reserved for it.**
HEIGHT: 12.5 Inches
PRICE: F.

Figs. 1970E/1970F
A pair of figures of a boy and girl seated, both asleep with an elbow resting on rockwork to their side. He wears an open neck shirt, waistcoat, jacket, and knee breeches, with one leg crossed under the other. A dog sits on his lap. She wears a blouse and long skirt. Her handbag rests on rockwork by her side and a lamb sits to her left. Her left arm is around it.
The figure of the boy is an adaptation of Fig. 3336, 'The Red Boy'.
HEIGHT: 4.5 Inches
PRICE: Pair: F, Singles: G.

Figs. 1970/1970AA
A pair of spill vase figures of a standing shepherdess and shepherd, both wear plumed hats, she with a blouse, long skirt, and a scarf wrapped across her neck and around her waist. Her right arm leans on a tree trunk and her left hand is on her waist. A dog lies at her feet and her crook rests on the tree. He is almost a mirror image and wears an open neck shirt, cloak, jacket, and trousers tied at the waist with a scarf. His left arm rests on the tree and his right hand is on his hip. His crook rests on the tree and a sheep lies on the base.
HEIGHT: 9.75
PRICE: Pair: E, Singles: F.

Figs. 1970G/1970H
A pair of figures of a boy and girl seated; he wears an open neck shirt, waistcoat, jacket and trousers. His left hand rests on his hip and his right is placed on an object by his side. A spaniel sits below. She wears a bodice, blouse, and long skirt. A sheep sits at her feet.
Usually where a dog and sheep are depicted with the figures, they were made to portray a shepherd and shepherdess; in this instance, both figures appear too well dressed to be so.
HEIGHT: 7 Inches
PRICE: Pair: F, Singles: G.

Fig. 1970C
A figure of a shepherdess standing, wearing a brimmed hat, bodice, full-length skirt, and a long scarf draped over both her shoulders. She has her hands around a lamb which stands on its hind legs at her side, all on a rococo base.
There is a pair to this figure. Fig. 1970D has been reserved for it.
HEIGHT: 9.5
PRICE: Pair: F, Singles: G.

Fig. 1971D
A spill vase figure of a child standing, wearing a loose tunic tied with a sash and holding a garland. To the other side of the spill a sheep stands.
There is a pair to this figure. Fig. 1971C has been reserved for it. It is possible that this figure and its pair are of religious inspiration and may be depicting Rachael and Jacob.
HEIGHT: 6 Inches
PRICE: Pair: G, Singles: H.

Fig. 1971J
A figure of a shepherdess standing, wearing a hat, blouse, and skirt with an apron. She holds a crook in both hands and a sheep lies on the base.
There is a pair to this figure. Fig. 1971K has been reserved for it.
HEIGHT: 12.25
PRICE: F.

Fig. 1971F
A figure of a woman standing, wearing a hat, split bodice, and long skirt with an apron. She holds the apron in both hands and it contains fruit. A sheep sits at her feet.
There is no doubt a pair to this figure. Fig. 1971E has been reserved for it.
HEIGHT: 7.5 Inches
PRICE: G.

Fig. 1971G
A figure of a woman standing, wearing a plumed hat, blouse, and short skirt with pantaloons; both hands are on her hips and her legs are crossed. A sheep lies at her feet.
This woman is very well dressed for a shepherdess and if the sheep had not been included, the authors would have included this figure in the unidentified dancers. There is no doubt a pair to this figure. Fig. 1971H has been reserved for it.
HEIGHT: 9 Inches
PRICE: F.

Fig. 1971L
A standing figure of a woman who wears a cap, blouse, jacket, and long dress with a long apron. Her left arm is around a sheep that lies on rockwork beside her.
There is a pair to this figure. Fig. 1971M has been reserved for it.
HEIGHT: 9.25
PRICE: G.

Figs. 1972E/1972F
A pair of figures of a boy and girl seated on rockwork; he is bare-headed and wears a tunic and kilt. Under his right arm he holds his hat, which is upturned and holds chicks. His dog is recumbent at his feet. She wears a hat with feathers, bodice, and long skirt. She holds a lamb under her arm. HEIGHT: 7 Inches
PRICE: Pair: G, Singles: H.

Figs. 1972J/1972K
A pair of figures of a man and woman standing; he wears a brimmed hat, open necked shirt, jacket, and knee breeches. His left hand is around the neck of a goat that stands on its hind legs and is feeding from a bowl that he holds in his right hand. She wears a plumed hat, bodice, and long skirt. She holds a garland in her right hand and a jug in her left. A lamb sits at her feet.
The 'Alpha' factory made these figures.
HEIGHT: 6.5 Inches
PRICE: Pair: F, Singles: G.

Figs. 1972G/1972H
A pair of figures of a girl and boy standing; she wears a hat, bodice, and long skirt. A scarf is held aloft in her right hand and is draped across her shoulders. She holds a lamb under her left arm. He wears a plumed hat, tunic, kilt, and a scarf draped over his shoulders. He holds a dog in his right arm. HEIGHT: 7 Inches
PRICE: Pair: F, Singles: G.

Fig. 1973 SO
Illustrated is a Pre-Victorian figure of 'Lost Sheep Found', the probable source for Fig. 1973.

193

Fig. 1973A
A spill vase group of a boy and girl with a sheep below; he stands with his right hand resting on his hip and his left around her shoulders. He is wearing a jacket, shirt, and kilt. She is seated and wears a blouse, long skirt, and a scarf over her arm. **This figure can be found in two sizes, both illustrated. There are minor modelling differences. It has been suggested that this group portrays 'Burns and Mary'; it is possible, but we know of no evidence to confirm this and a titled figure has not been recorded.**
HEIGHT: 6.25 & 8 Inches
PRICE: G.

Fig. 1973H
A spill vase group figure of a shepherd and shepherdess, he standing and she seated, both leaning against a tree trunk. He wears a plumed hat, jacket, waistcoat, and knee breeches. His left foot is raised onto a mound and by his feet a dog sits and a sheep lies. She wears a hat, bodice, and long skirt; she rests her head on her right hand.
HEIGHT: 10 Inches
PRICE: F.

Figs. 1973F/1973G
A pair of spill vase figures of a boy and girl seated, each wearing a hat, blouse, and skirt/kilt. A stream runs at their feet and a lamb stands to their side with its forehooves on their lap.
HEIGHT: 6 Inches
PRICE: Pair: G, Singles: H.

Fig. 1973J
A watch holder group of a man and woman standing, both wearing plumed hats, he with a tunic with sash across his chest, she wears a blouse and long skirt. At their feet a dog and sheep sit. Above them is an arbour covered in a fruiting grapevine.
HEIGHT: 9 Inches
PRICE: G.

Fig. 1974B
A spill vase group of a man standing with his legs crossed and a woman seated; he wears a hat, shirt, waistcoat, and trousers. He leans against a tree stump. She wears a blouse and skirt with an apron. Her hands are in her lap. A dog is seated between them and a sheep is by her side.
HEIGHT: 12.5 Inches
PRICE: G.

Figs. 1976C/1976D
A pair of spill vase figures of a sleeping shepherd and shepherdess; both are laying down with their heads resting on the spill. He wears a hat, shirt, jacket, and trousers, she a hat, blouse, and long skirt. Their crooks rest on the spill and there is a dog at his feet and a sheep at hers.
HEIGHT: 5.5 Inches
PRICE: Pair: G, Singles: H.

Fig. 1974C
A group figure of a shepherd and his wife; she is bareheaded and wears a necklace, bodice, and long skirt with an apron. A sheep stands on its hind legs with its fore-hooves on her apron. He wears a hat, shirt, jacket with cape, and knee breeches. The base is covered with large leaves.
HEIGHT: 9.75 Inches
PRICE: H.

Figs. 1976E/1976F
A pair of groups of a shepherd and shepherdess, both seated on a grassy mound; he wears a bonnet, shirt, long jacket, and knee breeches. He holds pipes in both hands. Standing on their hind legs on either side is a dog and a sheep, each of which have their forepaws/front hooves on the man's shoulders. She wears a hat, jacket, blouse, and skirt with an apron. To either side a sheep stands with its forehooves on her shoulder. On the base below each figure a stream flows. HEIGHT: 8 Inches
PRICE: Pair: F, Singles: G.

Figs. 1977/1978

A pair of figures of a shepherd and shepherdess; he wears a hat, waistcoat, shirt with tie, and knee breeches. A sheep feeds from a bowl that is held in his hand. She wears a brimmed hat and long dress. A large dog sits to her side and feeds from a bowl held in her hand.

An almost identical figure of Fig. 1978 was made in Parian by Samuel Alcock & Co., circa 1840/1850. This figure also had a pair, but the pair to the Alcock figure is of another girl feeding a lamb.

HEIGHT: 7 Inches
PRICE: Pair: F, Singles: G.

Figs. 1979F/1979G/1979H

Three figure are illustrated, part of a series of figures depicting country occupations and pursuits. The figure on the left is of a shepherd, standing wearing a hat, open necked shirt, jacket, and short trousers with boots, holding a sheep under his right arm. The figure in the middle is of a woodman and the figure on the right is of a musician who holds bagpipes under his arm.

There are more figures in this series.

The 'Woodman' figure can be found in a larger version that has a standing poodle on the base.

The source for the centre figure is an engraving by Bartolozzi after the painting by Thomas Barker of Bath that was titled 'The Woodman'. All three of these figure were made by John & Rebecca Lloyd.

HEIGHT: 9 Inches
PRICE: E (Each).

Fig. 1978C

A spill vase group figure of a shepherd who stands to the right of a tree trunk wearing a cap, open neck shirt, large scarf, long jacket, and knee breeches with leggings. He holds a crook in his right hand and his left rests on the top. A sheep lies at his feet.
HEIGHT: 13 Inches
PRICE: F.

Figs. 1981C/1981D

A pair of figures of a boy and girl, he seated, she laying, both wearing plumed hats, tunic/blouse, and kilt/skirt. The boy holds a dog on his lap and the girl a sheep. Below another sheep is recumbent.
The small holes on the base are for use as quill holders.
HEIGHT: 4.75 Inches
PRICE: Pair: G, Singles: H.

Figs. 1981E/1981F
A pair of figures of a boy and girl reclining with an elbow resting on rockwork; she is bareheaded and wears a blouse and long skirt. A sheep stands by her side with its forehooves on her lap. Her left arm rests on its back. He wears an open neck shirt, short jacket, kilt, and boots. A dog stands by his side with its forepaws on his lap. His right arm rests on its back.
The 'Alpha' factory made these figures, and the modeller used very similar heads on many of his figures, some of which portrayed The Royal Children.
HEIGHT: 5.5 Inches
PRICE: Pair: F, Singles: G.

Figs. 1982C/1982D/1982E
A pair of spill vase figures and a single of standing figures of a man and woman; the girl holds a cat in her lap, with a goat rearing on its hind legs to her right. She wears a bodice and long dress. The man is a mirror image and he wears a brimmed hat, waistcoat, jacket, and knee breeches.
In Book Three we illustrated a different pair to Fig. 1982C. It can be seen from the figures illustrated that the man and woman with a goat is a pair as the rococo base is the same.
HEIGHT: 7.5 Inches
PRICE: Pair. F, Singles: G.

Figs. 1981G/1981H
A pair of figures of seated shepherds on round coloured bases. She wears a hat, blouse, and long skirt; her hands are in her lap and on the base to either side of her a sheep stands. He wears a hat, frilled shirt with tie, jacket, and knee breeches. At his feet to his left a sheep lies and to his right a goat stands.
HEIGHT: 10 Inches
PRICE: Pair: G, Singles: H.

Fig. 1982F
A spill vase figure of a girl leaning against a tree trunk wearing a hat, blouse, jacket, and a skirt with an apron. She is holding a basket of fruit in both hands. A dog sits at her feet. **The strange hat the girl is wearing appears on a number of figures. The authors have been told that it is of Welsh origin, but know of no evidence to confirm this. There is illustrated above the pair to this figure, Fig. 1982E.**
HEIGHT: 7 Inches
PRICE: G.

Fig. 1982H
A spill vase and arbour group figure of a boy and girl standing to either side of a goat; he wears a plumed hat, shirt, coat, and trousers and is holding a pipe. She wears a plumed hat, blouse, and long skirt. Below them a sheep and a dog are recumbent.
HEIGHT: 10 Inches
PRICE: F.

Fig. 1982G
A spill vase and arbour group figure of a man and woman seated holding hands, he wearing a large cap, shirt, jacket, and kilt with a scarf over his shoulder and draped across his chest, she wearing a short jacket and long skirt. Below them a dog sits and a sheep is recumbent. **The authors have seen a white example of this figure titled 'Swiss Lovers'. With such an unusual title it may be that this figure is of theatrical source or inspiration.**
TITLE: 'Swiss Lovers' in gilt script
HEIGHT: 16 Inches
PRICE: E.

Fig. 1983D
A spill vase group figure of a standing shepherd dressed in highland attire playing his pipes. To either side of him on an outcrop stands a sheep and above the spill is in the form of a large tree.
HEIGHT: 7 Inches
PRICE: G.

Fig. 1983E
A figure of a standing shepherd; he is barefooted and wears a frilled shirt with tie, long coat, and knee length trousers, holding flowers in his right hand and his left hand rests on the back of a sheep that stands on rockwork to his left.
There is no doubt a pair to this figure. Fig. 1983F has been reserved for it.
HEIGHT: 11.5 Inches
PRICE: F.

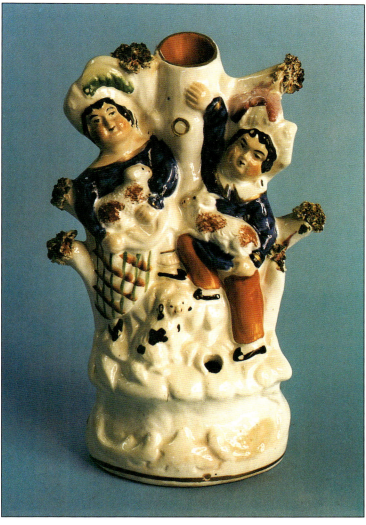

Fig. 1983H
A spill vase group depicting a boy and girl, either seated in or climbing a tree; both wear plumed hats, she also wears a blouse and long skirt, he wears a smock and trousers. Both children are holding lambs in their laps.
HEIGHT: 7 Inches
PRICE: H.

Fig. 1983G
A spill vase group of a girl standing and a boy seated; both wear large brimmed hats, she with a bodice, jacket, and long skirt, he with a short jacket, open necked shirt, and knee breeches. She has her left arm outstretched and he has one hand to a goat's mouth, which lies below.
HEIGHT: 8 Inches
PRICE: H.

Fig. 1983J
A spill vase group of a boy standing in a tree holding a large brimmed hat in his hand and wearing a shirt, jacket, and knee breeches. Below sits a girl wearing a blouse and long skirt. A goat sits at her feet with its head in her lap.
HEIGHT: 9.5 Inches
PRICE: G.

Figs. 1984G/1984H
A pair of figures of a shepherd and shepherdess, both seated and wearing plumed hats, he with a jacket and kilt. His left hand is in his lap and his right around the neck of a poodle which stands with its hind legs on rockwork and its forepaws in his lap. She wears a long dress and both arms are around a lamb that has its hind legs on rockwork and its fore-hooves in her lap.
Whilst these figures are not coloured they are gilded with best gold, modelled in the round, and are early,
c. 1840. The main colouring has been applied to the vegetation on the rockwork and base; this vegetation is a common feature on Victorian Staffordshire and was made by forcing wet clay through a sieve and then applying whilst still wet.
HEIGHT: 6 Inches
PRICE: Pair: F, Singles: G.

Figs. 1983K/1983L
A pair of figures of a woman and man seated; she wears a hat, blouse, and skirt with an apron. Her right hand is on the head of a small deer that sits beside her. He wears a hat, shirt, waistcoat, and knee breeches. His left hand is on the back of a spaniel that sits beside him.
HEIGHT: 6.5 Inches
PRICE: Pair: F, Singles: G.

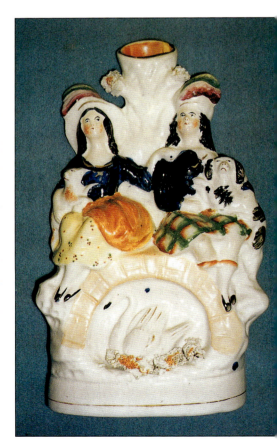

Fig. 1984J
A spill vase group figure of a boy and girl seated on a brick arch below which a swan swims; both children wear plumed hats, she with a bodice and skirt with an apron. She holds a lamb on her lap. He wears a tunic and kilt and holds a dog on his lap.
HEIGHT: 9 Inches
PRICE: G.

Figs. 1984M/1984N
A pair of Parr figures of sleeping shepherds both rest with one arm on a tree stump with crooks on the ground. His dog is recumbent on the base; a sheep and a lamb rest on the base of her figure. He wears a shirt with tie, jacket, and knee breeches; she wears a jacket and skirt with an apron.
HEIGHT: 6.75
PRICE: Pair: E, Singles: F.

Fig. 1984K
A group figure of a girl and man seated on rockwork; she wears a blouse and long skirt with an apron and holds a basket of fruit on her lap. He has his right arm around her and wears a frilled shirt, jacket, and short trousers. His hat is suspended from his waist and he holds a bird in his left hand. Below another bird swims in a stream.
This figure may be a portrayal of 'Paul and Virginia'.
HEIGHT: 8.5 Inches
PRICE: H.

Fig. 1984L
An arbour group figure of a boy and girl asleep; he is lying above the girl and is bareheaded and wears a shirt with tie, waistcoat, jacket, knee length trousers, and shoes and socks. Below him, the girl lies wearing a puff sleeved blouse and long skirt with an apron. By her a sheep reclines, the arbour is decorated with grapes and grape leaves.
A very well modelled and decorated figure, it could be theatrical in inspiration. It is not believed to be a 'Babes in the wood' figure as there are no birds and the boy and girl are two old to portray 'Babes' and there was no sheep in that tale; possibly it is another version of 'sleeping shepherds'.
HEIGHT: 11 Inches
PRICE: F.

Fig. 1984P
A spill vase group figure of a man and woman, he standing wearing a hat with feather and a long tunic with a sash. A dog stands with its forepaws on his waist and a sheep lies below. She is seated and wears a hat with feather, blouse, and long dress. She holds flowers on her lap and a small stream runs below.
HEIGHT: 7.75 Inches
PRICE: H.

Figs. 1986C/1986D
A pair of figures of shepherds seated on rockwork; he wears a hat, shirt buttoned, jacket, and trousers. She wears a blouse, short jacket, and skirt with a scarf. Both characters are barefooted, holding a horn. Recumbent below him are a sheep and a goat; below her are two sheep.
These figures were made by The Parr factory.
HEIGHT: 8 Inches
PRICE: Pair: F, Singles: G.

Fig. 1984R
A group figure of a boy and girl seated on a brick built bridge above a stream; he wears a shirt, waistcoat, long jacket, and breeches. He holds a bunch of grapes above his head in his right hand, his left is around the girl who wears a hat, blouse, and long skirt. A dog sits to the side.
HEIGHT: 7.5 Inches
PRICE: H.

Fig. 1984S
An arbour figure of a girl asleep; she wears a bodice and long dress, her right arm rests on the arbour, and she holds her hat. Her left arm is around a sheep which stands on its hind legs with its forehooves in her lap. **There is a pair to this figure. Fig. 1984T has been reserved for it.**
HEIGHT: 8 Inches
PRICE: G.

Figs. 1986E/1986F
A pair of spill vase figures of shepherds, both stand on rockwork holding a crook aloft against the spill, she in her left hand, he in his right. She wears a hat, bodice, jacket, and skirt with an apron; he wears a hat, jacket, open neck shirt, waistcoat, and knee breeches. On each spill, each above the other, three sheep lay.
HEIGHT: 10.5 Inches
PRICE: Pair: F, Singles: G.

Figs. 1990/1991
A pair of group figures of a man and woman wearing Turkish type costumes, both with turbans with plumes. They each hold a basket of fruit, resting on one knee, and he holds an apple in his hand. To her left and his right a small child stands, a boy with the woman and a girl with the man. The girl holds a bird on her left arm and a hat in her right; the boy has a plumed hat and holds a bird aloft in his right hand. HEIGHT: 14 Inches
PRICE: Pair: E, Singles: F.

Fig. 1995C
A spill vase group figure of a woman seated; she is bareheaded and wears a bodice, long skirt, and a scarf over her right arm. To her left a child stands on rockwork wearing a blouse and short skirt; both her hands rest on the branches of a tree.
A large and attractive figure made by 'The Green Factory'. There is probably a pair to this figure. Fig. 1995D has been reserved for it.
HEIGHT: 11 Inches
PRICE: F.

Fig. 1995A
A figure of a woman standing holding a basket of strawberries that rests on a pillar of rockwork to her side; she wears a headdress, buttoned long coat over a skirt and pantaloons. **There is a pair to this figure. Fig. 1995B has been reserved for it.**
HEIGHT: 9.5 Inches
PRICE: F.

Fig. 1997B
A group figure of a girl seated under an arbour decorated with flowers, wearing a plumed hat, bodice, jacket, and shirt with an apron. Her left arm is around a bird which sits on her lap, and her right rests on the head of a dog that has its forepaws on her apron. Below there is a small bridge under which a stream flows. **There is probably a pair to this figure. Fig. 1997C has been reserved for it.**
HEIGHT: 10 Inches
PRICE: G.

Fig. 1997D
A spill vase group of a gardener and his wife, both dressed in highland attire, she wearing a cap, long dress with a scarf over her shoulder. In her left hand she holds a large pot of flowers. He is seated wearing a cap, jacket, shirt with tie, and knee breeches. His right hand is on his leg and left on his hip. A spade rests between his legs and a basket of apples is at his feet.
This group is so similar to the pair of Figures 72/73 Book One that it could be taken for the centerpiece; however, Figs. 72/73 have always been accepted as being portraits of Highland Mary and Robert Burns, so either this group is also of Burns and Mary or Figs. 72/73 are not.
HEIGHT: 12.5 Inches
PRICE: G.

Fig. 2003C
A standing figure of a man wearing a hat, shirt with tie, waist-coat, and trousers; he holds a basket of fruit on his left arm and a spade in his right.
There is a pair to this figure. Fig. 2003D has been reserved for it.
HEIGHT: 11.5 Inches
PRICE: F.

Figs. 2003A/2003B
A pair of figures of standing gardeners, both wearing brimmed hats; he wears a long waistcoat, shirt with tie, and knee breeches with leggings and holds flowers in each hand. She wears a blouse and top, knickers, and a dress with an apron that is held in both hands and contains fruit. To the side of each is a stump covered in greenery.
The Parr Factory made this pair and they were part of a series of pairs made of rural occupations. See Figs. 2127/2128 Book Two for a pair of fisher-folk, Figs. 2015A/2015B for a pair holding birds, and Figs. 2051C/2051D for a pair of harvesters in Book Three.
HEIGHT: 12 Inches.
PRICE: Pair: E, Singles: F.

Figs. 2005A/2005B
A pair of figures of a man and woman standing, both similarly dressed with plumed hats, bodice/tunic, and skirt/kilt. She has her right elbow – and he his left – leaning on a pillar in front of which is a large basket of flowers. They both hold a posy in their hand.
HEIGHT: 6.75 Inches
PRICE: Pair: F, Singles: G.

Figs. 2005C/2005D
A pair of spill vase figures of highland gardeners, each stands wearing plumed hats, she a bodice, cape, short skirt, and knickers, he a long tunic with a scarf over his shoulder and through his arm. They each hold a basket of flowers in one hand and another basket is on the floor by the spill. HEIGHT: 9.5 Inches
PRICE: Pair: F, Singles: G.

Figs. 2005G/2005H
A pair of figures of a man and woman standing; he wears a hat with feather, shirt, waistcoat, jacket, and knee breeches with boots. He holds a basket of flowers in his left hand and his right is around a vase of flowers which stands on a pillar. She wears a hat with feather, blouse, and skirt with knickers showing and her left arm is around a vase of flowers, which stand on a pillar to her left.
HEIGHT: 7 Inches
PRICE: Pair: G, Singles: H.

Figs. 2005E/2005F
A pair of spill vase figures of a man and woman dressed in highland attire, he with a Tam O' Shanter, shirt with cape, and kilt with boots, she with a headscarf, blouse, and long skirt. They each have a basket of fruit under one arm and stand by rockwork from which a stream issues. On the base of each figure a swan swims.
HEIGHT: 9.5 Inches
PRICE: Pair: F, Singles: G.

Fig. 2005J
A figure of a man standing with his legs crossed; he wears highland attire of hat with feather, open neck shirt, jacket, kilt with sporran, and a scarf over his shoulder and across his chest. He holds a vase of fruit and flowers aloft in his left hand and a basket of fruit in his right.
There is a pair to this figure. Fig. 2005K has been reserved for it.
HEIGHT: 10.25 Inches
PRICE: F.

205

Figs. 2007A/2007B
A pair of figures of a man and woman standing beside a large plant, he wearing a hat, shirt with tie, jacket, and trousers. A basket is held in his right hand. She wears a hat, jacket, skirt with an apron, and knickers.
HEIGHT: 7 Inches
PRICE: Pair: F, Singles: G.

Figs. 2008A/2008B
A pair of figures of a boy and girl standing on shaped gilt lined bases; the boy wears a hat, shirt with tie, waistcoat, jacket, and trousers. He holds a basket of fruit on his left hip and an apple in his right hand. She wears a hat, bodice, and long skirt with an apron, which is full of fruit and held in her left hand.
These figures are a variation of Figures 2008/2009 Book Three and can be found in two sizes, both illustrated.
HEIGHT: 7 Inches & 5 Inches
PRICE: Pair: G, Singles: H.

Figs. 2007C/2007D
A pair of figures of a boy and girl seated; she wears a headscarf, bodice, and long skirt, and holds a basket of flowers in her left hand and a posy in her right. He has his legs crossed and wears a shirt with tie, waistcoat, and trousers; there is a quantity of fruit at his feet.
HEIGHT: 7.5 Inches
PRICE: Pair: F, Singles: G.

Fig. 2010B
A group figure of a girl seated wearing a hat, bodice, and dress with an apron. She leans her left arm on a tree stump and gazes at a boy who kneels at her side. He wears a brimmed hat, jacket with tie, and knee breeches, holding one hand to his hat and the other holds a bird that he is presenting to her.
HEIGHT: 5 Inches
PRICE: G.

Fig. 2010D
A spill vase figure of a boy and girl seated, he above her and dressed in a hat, cape, jacket, trousers, and boots. A bag hangs from his belt and his right hand rest on the head of a dog that sits at his feet. The girl is to his side and wears a blouse, long skirt, and a scarf across her chest.
HEIGHT: 8.5 Inches
PRICE: G.

Fig. 2010C
A group figure of a girl standing barefooted with her legs crossed wearing a jacket, bodice, and long skirt. Her hands are held in front and one holds the ribbons of her hat. To her side a boy sits wearing a jacket, shirt with tie, and knee breeches. He rests one arm on his knee and gazes up at the girl.
HEIGHT: 9 Inches
PRICE: G.

Fig. 2010E
A group figure of a boy and girl standing before a tree; they each have one arm around the other and are holding hands. He wears a hat with a feather, a scarf around his neck, shirt, waistcoat, jacket, and knee breeches. She wears a hat, bodice, jacket, and skirt with an apron.
HEIGHT: 8 Inches
PRICE: F.

Fig. 2010F
An arbour group figure of a boy and girl seated beneath the arbour; both are bareheaded, she wears a long dress and cloak, he wears a jacket, waistcoat, and knee breeches. His hat is by his feet. He has his right arm around the girl and his left hand holds hers.
HEIGHT: 6.5 Inches
PRICE: G.

Fig. 2010G
A group figure of a man seated on a bench, holding the hand of a woman who stands beside him. He wears a tricorn hat, long jacket, shirt, waistcoat, and knee breeches. She wears a mop cap, scarf, blouse, and skirt with an apron. **There are many of these group figures, which portray a man beseeching his lover. This particular example is earlier than most, decorated in both underglaze and enamel colours and modelled in the round with a number of secondary moulds. It is early, circa. 1840.**
HEIGHT: 8.5 Inches
PRICE: F.

Fig. 2010H
A spill vase group figure of a woman and man standing on either side of the spill; he has his right arm around her shoulder and wears a hat, tie, shirt, waistcoat, and knee breeches. She is bareheaded and wears a blouse and long skirt. Her hands are clasped together in front. A cat lies on the base.
HEIGHT: 8.25 Inches
PRICE: G.

Fig. 2010J
A group figure of a man and woman standing; he has his right hand on his hip and his left around the woman's waist. He wears a hat with feather, shirt with tie, jacket, and knee breeches tied at the waist with a scarf. She wears a hat with feather, long coat, and skirt; she holds a flower in her left hand.
HEIGHT: 10.75 Inches
PRICE: G.

Fig. 2011A
A spill vase group figure of a woman standing, wearing a plumed hat, blouse, and long skirt, holding a sheaf of wheat under her arm. To her right a boy stands wearing a hat, shirt with tie, coat, and trousers. A sickle is held in his left hand.
HEIGHT: 8 Inches
PRICE: G.

Fig. 2011C
A large group of male and female harvesters, both sitting, he with his right arm around her and his left hand holding her hand. He wears a tie, shirt, waistcoat, jacket, and knee breeches. A sheaf of wheat is at his feet. She wears a bodice and long skirt and holds a sheaf of wheat on her lap.
HEIGHT: 14.5 Inches
PRICE: F.

Fig. 2011B
A group figure of a man and woman standing arm in arm; he is long-haired and wears a hat, shirt with tie, waistcoat, jacket, and knee breeches. She wears a plumed hat, jacket, long skirt, and a scarf around her waist that hangs down the front of her skirt. **This and figures like it are difficult to identify as to what they portray; there are no objects that would give some clue. It could be theatrical or it may just symbolise a man and his girl dressed in their Sunday best.**
HEIGHT: 9 Inches
PRICE: F.

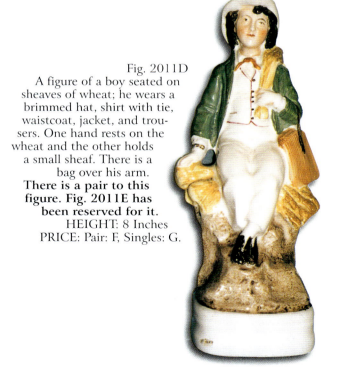

Fig. 2011D
A figure of a boy seated on sheaves of wheat; he wears a brimmed hat, shirt with tie, waistcoat, jacket, and trousers. One hand rests on the wheat and the other holds a small sheaf. There is a bag over his arm. **There is a pair to this figure. Fig. 2011E has been reserved for it.**
HEIGHT: 8 Inches
PRICE: Pair: F, Singles: G.

Fig. 2011G
A spill vase group of a girl and boy standing on either side of a tree trunk; they both hold sheaves of wheat under their arm. She wears a cap, bodice, and skirt with an apron. He wears a hat, jacket, shirt, and short trousers and holds a sickle in his right hand.
HEIGHT: 8 Inches
PRICE: H.

Fig. 2011F
A large standing group figure of male and female harvesters; she wears a hat with feather and long dress with an apron in which she carries sheaves of wheat. He stands with legs crossed by her side with his right arm around her waist. He wears a brimmed hat, shirt with tie, jacket, and knee breeches, holding a sheaf in his left hand.
This figure is particularly well modelled and decorated unusually; the back of the figure has been decorated as well. It was made by the same modeller who made a fisherman group (see Fig. 2124D), probably at The Parr factory.
HEIGHT: 13 Inches
PRICE: E.

Figs. 2014/2015
A pair of figures of a man and woman standing with their legs crossed, each holding birds on their shoulder, a sheaf of wheat under an arm, and a pitcher in a hand. She wears a brimmed hat, bodice, and long dress with an apron; he wears a hat, frilled shirt with tie, waistcoat, and short trousers tied with a sash. There is a small brick built well by his feet from which water pours.
HEIGHT: 10 Inches
PRICE: Pair: E, Singles: G.

Figs. 2015B/2015A
A pair of figures of a boy and girl standing holding a bird aloft, he in his left hand, she in her right. She wears a jacket and dress with an apron. Her left hand rests on a tree stump. He wears a hat, shirt and tie, waistcoat, jacket, and knee length trousers. His right hand is held behind his back.
It is possible that this pair was meant to portray falconers; they were made by The Parr factory.
HEIGHT: 13 Inches
PRICE: Pair: E, Singles: F.

Fig. 2015C
A figure of a man standing, wearing a cap, frilled shirt, jacket, and kilt tied with a scarf; his legs are crossed and he rests his right arm on rockwork. To his side a large plant decorated the rockwork. In his left hand, he holds a bird to his chest.
The bird is too small to be a falcon and it is unlikely that if this figure was portraying a falconer he would be holding the bird so near his face. There is a pair to this figure. Fig. 2015D has been reserved for it.
HEIGHT: 9 Inches
PRICE: G.

Figs. 2015E/2015F
A pair of figures of a boy and girl standing with their legs crossed, both wearing plumed hats, he a shirt, tunic, kilt with sporran, and shoes and socks, she a jacket and skirt with an apron. Under her right arm and his left is a sheaf of wheat and under her left and his right a goat. To her right and his left, resting on rockwork, is a large jug.
HEIGHT: 10 Inches
PRICE: Pair: E, Singles: F.

Fig. 2015G
A standing figure of a man wearing a plumed hat, shirt with collar, jacket, and knee breeches. He has a small barrel attached to him by a strap over his shoulder; his right hand rests on rockwork and his left hand holds a sickle that rests on a large sheaf of wheat.
There is a pair to this figure. Fig. 2015H has been reserved for it.
HEIGHT: 10 Inches
PRICE: F.

Fig. 2015L
A group figure of a man and woman standing, he dressed in Scottish attire of hat with feather, shirt with tie, jacket with scarf over both shoulders, and kilt with sporran. He holds a sheaf of wheat under his right arm and a small barrel over his left. She wears a blouse and a long skirt with a double apron. A sheaf of wheat is under her right arm and a filled basket over her left.
HEIGHT: 11.75 Inches
PRICE: F.

Fig. 2015J
A standing figure of a girl wearing a brimmed hat, blouse, open sleeved jacket, and skirt; she holds a bag of fruit in her right hand and a large sheaf of wheat in her left. A dog sits at her feet.
There is a pair to this figure. Fig. 2015K has been reserved for it. It is possible that this figure pairs with Fig. 2015G, but the authors have not seen them together to confirm this.
HEIGHT: 9 Inches
PRICE: F.

Figs. 2015M/2015N
A pair of spill vase group figures of a man standing, wearing a hat with feather and a long tunic. He rests one hand on the head of a dog which is held in the lap of a boy child seated next to him. She wears a plumed hat, jacket, and long dress. Her hand rests on the head of a dog, which sits on the lap of a girl child who stands next to her.
HEIGHT: 8.75 Inches
PRICE: Pair: F, Singles: G.

Fig. 2016B
A spill vase group figure of a boy seated with a girl standing below; she wears a blouse and skirt and has one arm around the boy and the other on his knee. He wears a brimmed hat, open neck shirt, jacket, and trousers. He is holding a bird in his right hand and his left is around a dog that has its forepaws on his lap.
HEIGHT: 6.5 Inches
PRICE: G.

Fig. 2016D
A spill vase group of a boy kneeling and a girl standing on a bridge above, below which a swan is swimming. The boy wears a plumed hat, cloak, blouse, and kilt. At his feet a dog is reclining watching the swan. The girl wears a bodice and short skirt and rests her arm on the trunk of a tree.
HEIGHT: 8.5 Inches
PRICE: G.

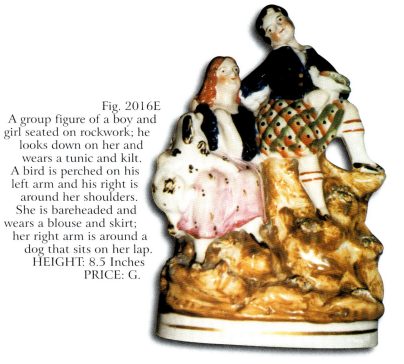

Fig. 2016C
A group figure of a boy standing on rockwork wearing a plumed hat, jacket, and kilt. He holds a garland in his right hand. A girl stands below wearing a hat, bodice, and short skirt. Her right hand is on her hip and her left holds a bird aloft. A dog sits by her feet.
HEIGHT: 8 Inches
PRICE: H.

Fig. 2016E
A group figure of a boy and girl seated on rockwork; he looks down on her and wears a tunic and kilt. A bird is perched on his left arm and his right is around her shoulders. She is bareheaded and wears a blouse and skirt; her right arm is around a dog that sits on her lap.
HEIGHT: 8.5 Inches
PRICE: G.

213

Fig. 2016F
A spill vase group figure of a man and girl standing; he wears a tunic, cloak, kilt, and knee boots. He holds a bird that has a long tail in both arms. She wears a large hat, blouse scarf, and skirt with knickers showing. Her right arm is around a dog that has its forepaws on her waist.
HEIGHT: 8 Inches
PRICE: G.

Fig. 2016H
A spill vase group figure of a boy climbing a tree wearing a shirt, waistcoat, jacket, and trousers. He is handing fruit to a girl who stands below, wearing a hat with feathers, blouse, and tiered skirt with knickers.
HEIGHT: 7 Inches
PRICE: G.

Fig. 2016G
A spill vase group figure of a boy and girl birdnesting; he kneels on rockwork wearing a short jacket, shirt, and trousers. He has one hand in a nest from which a bird flies, with his other he hands an egg to the girl who stands below wearing a blouse and short skirt.
HEIGHT: 11 Inches
PRICE: F.

Fig. 2016J
A group figure of a boy seated on another's shoulders; the boy above wears a jacket, shirt, and trousers while the boy below wears a blouse and skirt with trousers. Both boys are taking fruit from a tree that is to their left. Below a dog plays and on the ground is a hat with fruit in it. **This is another version of children 'scrumping' (see Fig. 2199A Book Three).**
HEIGHT: 9 Inches
PRICE: F.

Figs. 2016K/2016L
A pair of figures of a boy and girl standing in front of a tree stump; he wears an open neck shirt, waistcoat, jacket, and knee breeches. He holds a nest with chicks in his left hand and a bird in his right. She is bareheaded and wears a bodice and aproned skirt and holds a bird in both hands.
HEIGHT: 6 Inches
PRICE: Pair: G, Singles: H.

Fig. 2016N
A spill vase group figure of a girl standing and a boy seated with legs crossed; he wears a brimmed hat, open neck shirt, jacket, and knee breeches. He is playing a pipe, which he holds in both hands. She leans her left elbow on the tree and her right on her hip. She wears a brimmed hat, bodice, long skirt, and a scarf over her shoulders and around her waist. A large basket of fruit is on rockwork between them and a dog lies on the base.
HEIGHT: 9.5 Inches
PRICE: F.

Fig. 2016M
A spill vase group figure of a man standing, wearing a hat with feather, ermine edged cloak tied with a sash, tunic, breeches, and boots. His left hand is on the head of a dog that stands on its hind legs at his feet. His right hand is on the head of a girl who sits holding a basket of flowers. She wears a hat, blouse, and long skirt. Two objects lay on the ground by her feet.
HEIGHT: 9.5 Inches
PRICE: G.

Fig. 2016P
A spill vase group figure of a boy seated on a grassy bank with one hand in his lap wearing a shirt, waistcoat, jacket, and short trousers with shoes and socks. His left hand is held aloft holding a bird and a girl stands on the bank wearing a blouse and long skirt stroking the bird.
HEIGHT: 10 Inches
PRICE: F.

215

Fig. 2019B
A group figure of a man and woman standing on either side of a clock face that is decorated with a grapevine. A deer stands below. She is bareheaded and wears a bodice and dress with an apron in which are bunches of grapes. She holds a flower in her right hand. He wears a shirt with a wide collar, long jacket, and knee breeches. His left hand is on his hip and his right holds a large jug decorated with grapes on top of the clock face.
HEIGHT: 12 Inches
PRICE: G.

Fig. 2019C
A figure of a woman standing, wearing a plumed hat, blouse, long skirt with knickers, and a scarf over her right arm. Her left arm is around a pot filled with fruit on which a bird is perched. The pot rests on a shaped column.
There is a pair to this figure. Fig. 2019D has been reserved for it.
HEIGHT: 8.75 Inches
PRICE: G.

Figs. 2024/2024A
A monumental pair of standing grape sellers; he wears a hat, jacket with scarf over his shoulder, shirt tied at the neck, knee breeches tied at the waist, and thigh boots. He holds a basket of grapes under his right arm and another in his left hand. She wears a hat, bodice, and long skirt with an apron. She also holds a basket of grapes under her left hand and another in her right hand.
A very large and previously unrecorded pair.
HEIGHT: 14 Inches
PRICE: Pair: E, Singles: F.

Figs. 2024B/2024C
A pair of figures of a man and woman standing with their legs crossed; he wears a brimmed hat, shirt, waistcoat, short trousers, and long socks. His left arm is through the handle of a basket of flowers that rest on rockwork to his side. She also wears a brimmed hat, loose-sleeved blouse, and long skirt. Her right arm is through the handle of a basket of flowers that rests on rockwork to her side.
HEIGHT: 9 Inches
PRICE: Pair: E, Singles: F.

Figs. 2024D/2024E
A pair of figures of a man and woman standing; each has a basket of fruit over one arm and a large pot with a flowering plant, which rests on brickwork to his left and her right. Both wear a hat with a feather and have a scarf draped across their shoulders. He wears a shirt with tie, long jacket, knee length trousers, and boots. She wears a bodice and long skirt. HEIGHT: 10 Inches
PRICE: Pair: E, Singles: F.

Figs. 2024H/2024J
A pair of figures of a man and woman standing with pillars to the side; she wears a hat, blouse, and long skirt with an apron and pantaloons. A large basket of fruit and flowers rests by her side and she has her arm around it. Her other hand holds a watering can below which there is a flowering plant. He wears a hat with feather, frilled shirt, ermined edged jacket, and knee breeches. He holds a spade in his right hand and his left arm is around a large basket of flowers that he holds in his left arm.
HEIGHT: 9.75 Inches
PRICE: Pair: F, Singles: G.

Figs. 2024F/2024G
A pair of figures of a man and woman seated on rockwork; she wears a hat, blouse, and long skirt with an apron. A large basket of fruit and flowers rests by her side and she has her arm around it. Her other hand holds her apron, which is filled with fruit. He wears a hat, frilled shirt, jacket, and pantaloons. He holds an apple in his right hand and his left arm is around a large basket of fruit and flowers that rests on rockwork to his side.
HEIGHT: 9.5
PRICE: Pair: F, Singles: G.

Figs. 2024K/2024L
A pair of figures of a man and woman standing with pillars to the side; she wears a hat with feather, blouse, long skirt with an apron, and a scarf over her shoulder and through her arm. A large basket of fruit and flowers rests on the pillar and she has her arm around it. The pillar has a bucket at the bottom and a stream runs beneath. He wears a hat with feather, open neck shirt, jacket, and kilt; his right arm rests on a pillar on which is a large basket of flowers. A bucket is at the bottom of the pillar from which a stream flows.
HEIGHT: 10.75
PRICE: Pair: F, Singles: G.

Fig. 2024M
A figure of a woman standing, wearing a plumed hat, red shawl, and a long dress with an apron. She holds the apron in her left hand and over her right arm is a basket in which is a dead rabbit.
It is possible that this figure portrays 'Red Riding Hood'; if so it is unlikely there is a pair. Should a pair come to light, Fig. 2024N has been reserved for it.
HEIGHT: 13.5 Inches
PRICE: G.

Figs. 2028C/2028D
A pair of figures of a boy and girl standing on rococo style bases, each holding a basket of fruit on their heads. The boy holds an object in his right hand and wears a jacket, shirt, waistcoat, and knee breeches. The girl wears a mop cap, bodice, and long skirt with an apron.
These figures were made by The Parr pottery and can be found in two sizes (8.25 Inch pair and 6 Inch single illustrated).
HEIGHT: 6 Inches, 8.25 Inches
PRICE: Pair: F, Singles: G.

Fig. 2026B
A figure of a woman standing, leaning on rockwork; she wears a hat with feathers, bodice, jacket, long skirt, and a scarf over her shoulders and across her arms. She holds a milk churn in her left hand and a sheep lies at her feet.
There is a pair to this figure. Fig. 2026C has been reserved for it.
HEIGHT: 9.75
PRICE: G.

Fig. 2028E
A figure of a boy standing with legs crossed on rockwork; he is longhaired and bareheaded, wearing a frilled shirt with tie, long jacket, knee breeches tied at the waist with tags hanging, and a large sash over his shoulder and across his chest. He holds his jacket, which is open, with his left hand and his right holds a large basket of fruit on his head.
There is a pair to this figure. Fig. 2028F has been reserved for it. This figure is similar in many respects to the preceding figure.
HEIGHT: 8 Inches
PRICE: Pair: F, Singles: G.

Fig. 2028K
A figure of a man standing with his legs crossed, wearing a plumed hat, shirt with tie, waistcoat, long jacket, and knee breeches. He holds a filled basket to his head with his right hand and his left is on a ewer which rests on rockwork. There is a flower pot with flowers by his feet. All of this is on a gilt lined and scrolled rococo style base. **There is a pair to this figure. Fig. 2028L has been reserved for it.** HEIGHT: 9.75 Inches
PRICE: Pair: E, Singles: F.

Figs. 2028G/2028H
A pair of figures of a boy and girl standing holding baskets of fruit on their heads with their right hand; she wears a bodice and long skirt with an apron, he wears a shirt, waistcoat, jacket, and knee breeches.
HEIGHT: 8.5 Inches
PRICE: Pair: F, Singles: G.

Fig. 2028J
A group figure of a boy and girl standing, she holding a basket of fruit on her head and wearing a blouse and skirt with an apron, which also holds fruit. He holds a basket of fruit on his left shoulder with his right hand and wears a shirt, jacket, and knee breeches.
HEIGHT: 8.5 Inches
PRICE: H.

Fig. 2030C/2030D
A pair of figures of a man and woman, she standing cross-legged; she wears a plumed hat, blouse, jacket, and skirt with an apron. She holds a large scarf aloft and this is across her shoulders and over her arm. On rockwork to her right side is a large vase of flowers. He wears a plumed hat, shirt with tie, jacket, and knee breeches with boots. He holds a scarf aloft, which is draped over his shoulder and around his arm. To his left is a large vase of flowers.
HEIGHT: 10 Inches
PRICE: Pair: F, Singles: G.

Fig. 2030E
A group figure of a man standing and woman seated with a large urn between them that contains a bunch of grapes and grape leaves. He wears a plumed hat, pleated shirt, jacket, kilt, and a scarf over his shoulder. His legs are crossed and holding a basket filled with grapes in both hands. She wears a plumed hat, blouse, jacket, long skirt with an apron, and a scarf around her waist. She holds it with both hands.
HEIGHT: 9.5 Inches
PRICE: F.

Fig. 2033B
A spill vase group of two grape pickers standing before a large vine, she to the left wearing a hat, short jacket, and skirt with an apron, he to the right wearing a hat, shirt with a ruff collar, jacket, and knee breeches. His left hand is on his hip and his right holds a bunch of grapes aloft. There is a basket of grapes on a pillar between them.
HEIGHT: 11 Inches
PRICE: F.

Fig. 2030F
A group figure of a man standing and a woman seated; he is dressed in highland attire of cap with feather, shirt with tie, jacket, kilt with sporran, and a scarf over his shoulder and through his arm. His right arm rests on a pillar on which is a vase filled with grapes and leaves. She wears a blouse with frilled sleeves and a skirt with an apron. Between them a goat sits with its forehooves on her lap.
HEIGHT: 10.5 Inches
PRICE: F.

Figs. 2033C/2033D
A pair of figures of a man and woman standing, she with a scarf over her head and wearing a laced bodice and long skirt with an apron. He wears a headscarf, jacket, blouse, and kilt. Both figures have one hand on their hips and hold a staff or similar object in their other hand; both are also barefooted.
These figures are difficult to identify; it has been suggested that they portray grape pressers and this is possible. They are a very rare and well-modelled group.
HEIGHT: 9.5 Inches
PRICE: Pair: F, Singles: G.

Fig. 2033G
A group figure of a man and woman standing with legs
crossed on either side of a large pot filled with grapes that stands on a brick arch below which a swan swims. The man wears an open necked shirt, long jacket, and knee breeches with leggings. His plumed hat is held over his left arm, which rests on the pot. The woman wears a plumed hat, blouse with open sleeves, and a two-tiered skirt. She holds an open garland in both hands.
HEIGHT: 9 Inches
PRICE: G.

Fig. 2033E
An arbour group figure of a man and woman seated beneath a grapevine; he wears a plumed hat, coat, shirt, knee breeches, and a large scarf draped over his shoulder and around his arm. She is long haired and wears a tasselled cap and long dress with a full skirt between them. On rockwork rests a large basket of grapes that she holds. At his feet is a smaller basket and a small stream runs out of the rockwork. HEIGHT: 14 Inches
PRICE: F.

Fig. 2033F
An arbour figure of a girl seated and a boy standing on either side of a gate. Above the gate is a clock face surrounded by a grapevine in which two birds are perched. The girl wears a jacket and skirt with an apron and her hat is over her arm; the boy wears a shirt with collar, tunic, and knee breeches. A small cloak is over his shoulder holding a basket of fruit in his left hand. Beneath the gate a small dog is recumbent.
HEIGHT: 9.5 Inches
PRICE: G.

Fig. 2033H
A clock face group of a man and woman seated on either side of a small stand on which is a flowering plant pot. Above the pot is the clock face surrounded by grapes and grape leaves. Both wear plumed hats, he a frilled shirt, jacket, and knee breeches. She wears a short jacket and long dress.
HEIGHT: 8 Inches
PRICE: G.

221

Fig. 2033J
A group figure of a man and woman, both standing on rock-work beneath arches; she wears a hat, coat, and long skirt with an apron. He wears a hat, coat, shirt, and short trousers with stockings; they each hold a full basket in one hand. Beneath the rockwork is another arch under which a stream flows. A small boat floats on the stream.
HEIGHT: 7.6 Inches
PRICE: H.

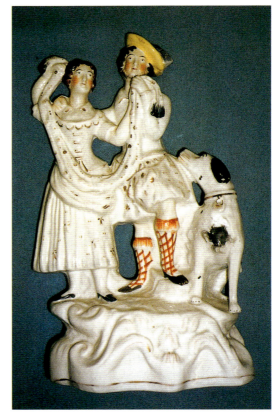

Fig. 2035A
A group figure of a man and woman standing, she wearing a bodice and long skirt, he in highland attire of Tam O' Shanter, tunic, kilt with sporran, shoes and socks. He has his right hand on her shoulder and they hold between them a large scarf. A dog sits to his left, all on a high scrolled base. HEIGHT: 12 Inches
PRICE: F.

Fig. 2033K
A figure of a boy seated on a pony; he wears a plumed hat, tunic, and kilt. A basket of grapes is over his right arm and he holds a bunch of grapes aloft in his left.
There is no doubt a pair to this figure. Fig. 2033L has been reserved for it.
HEIGHT: 7 Inches
PRICE: G.

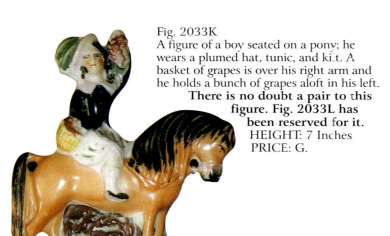

Fig. 2035B
A group figure of a girl seated and a boy standing on rock-work; he is bareheaded and wears a shirt, waistcoat, jacket, and knee breeches. She wears a brimmed hat, blouse, and long skirt. They both hold the end of a large decorated scarf between them.
HEIGHT: 8.5 Inches
PRICE: F.

Fig. 2041
A group of a man and woman standing on either side of a clock face that is decorated with grapes; he wears highland attire of cap, coat, cloak, and kilt with stockings, she a bodice and long skirt with knickers. Both figures hold one hand to the clock, holding grapes. **It has been suggested that this group is a portrayal of 'Burns and Mary'. This is possible but we know of no evidence to support this attribution and a titled version has never been recorded.**
HEIGHT: 12.5 Inches
PRICE: G.

Fig. 2041C
A spill vase group figure of a woman and man seated by a tree trunk; both are bareheaded and he has his right arm around her waist. She wears a blouse and long skirt, he a shirt with tie, waistcoat, and knee breeches. **This figure was made at The 'Alpha' factory; it has been suggested that they are meant to portray Burns and Mary, but we know of no evidence to support this attribution.**
HEIGHT: 5 Inches
PRICE: G.

Figs. 2041A/2041B
A pair of spill vase figures of a man and woman seated on rockwork on either side of the spill; he wears highland attire of cap, coat, and kilt with stockings, she is bareheaded and wears a bodice and long skirt. Both figures are holding garlands. **These figures are very similar to the persons portrayed in Fig. 2041.**
HEIGHT: 6.5 Inches
PRICE: Pair: G, Singles: H.

Fig. 2041D
A group figure of a man standing and a woman seated; she wears a blouse, jacket, and long dress. A handkerchief is held in her right hand and her left holds the man's right hand. He wears a shirt with tie, jacket, and long trousers. He holds a book in his left hand. **This figure, like the preceding one, was made at The 'Alpha' factory, it is possible that they also were meant to portray Burns and Mary. The modeller of many of the 'Alpha' factory figures was limited in his ability to model heads and they all look very alike.**
HEIGHT: 7.5 Inches
PRICE: G.

Fig. 2042B
A group figure of a man seated astride a barrel holding a pipe wearing a hat, shirt with tie, long coat, and trousers. Below and to either side of him a man and woman are dancing; she wears a dress with skirt and he a coat, shirt with tie, and knee breeches. Both dancers hold one hand to their hats and have sheaves of wheat under one arm. Below the barrel is a jug and below that more sheaves of wheat.
This figure depicts harvest thanksgiving; the harvest is home and is being celebrated.
HEIGHT: 8.5 Inches
PRICE: F.

Fig. 2045D
A spill vase figure of a man and woman standing side by side; he wears a hat, shirt, jacket, knee breeches tied at the waist with a sash, and a cloak over his shoulder. She wears a hat, blouse, jacket, and a skirt with an apron. A dog sits on the base between them. The spill is decorated with grapes and grape leaves.
HEIGHT: 9 Inches
PRICE: H.

Fig. 2045C
A group figure of a boy and girl seated on a grassy bank; both children wear a blouse and kilt/skirt. She holds a sheaf of corn above her head and another is in her lap. He rests his right arm on her knee and behind him is a large sheaf of corn.
HEIGHT: 7 Inches
PRICE: H.

Fig. 2046A
A spill vase group of gardeners; he stands to the left wearing a hat, jacket, blouse, and knee breeches holding a pot of flowers in his left hand and a spade in his right. She sits wearing a plumed hat, jacket, blouse, and long skirt with an apron with her hands in her lap.
HEIGHT: 7.5 Inches
PRICE: G.

Fig. 2046B
A spill vase group of gardeners; she stands wearing a large hat, blouse, jacket, and long skirt with an apron. A basket of fruit is held in her right hand and her left is in her apron, which is also filled with fruit. He stands wearing a hat, open neck shirt, jacket, knee breeches tied with a scarf, and leggings. A pot of flowers is held under his left arm, resting on his knee, and an object is held in his right hand.
HEIGHT: 9 Inches
PRICE: G.

Fig. 2046E
He wears a frilled shirt with tie, jacket, and knee breeches. One hand is in his lap and the other is around the girl, who wears a blouse and long dress with an apron. The arbour is covered with a climbing, flowering plant.
HEIGHT: 7.25
PRICE: H.

Fig. 2046C
A figure of a woman standing on rockwork, wearing a hat, blouse, and long skirt with an apron. Over her left arm is a basket filled with fruit. Her right arm stretches out over the head of a dog that stands on its hind legs with its forepaws on her waist.
The figure illustrated has had her right arm restored. There is no doubt a pair to this figure. Fig. 2046D has been reserved for it.
HEIGHT: 10.5 Inches
PRICE: F.

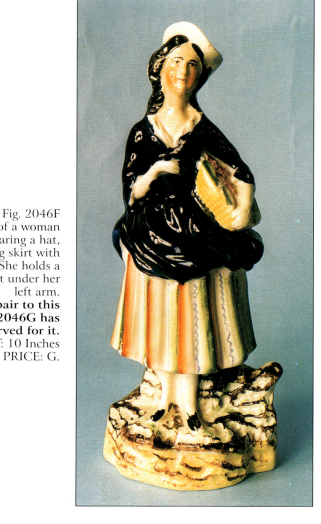

Fig. 2046F
A figure of a woman standing, wearing a hat, blouse, and long skirt with an apron. She holds a basket of fruit under her left arm.
There is a pair to this figure. Fig. 2046G has been reserved for it.
HEIGHT: 10 Inches
PRICE: G.

Fig. 2047D
A figure of a boy standing to the side of a truncated fruit tree; he is picking fruit from the tree and other fruit is in his hat held in his left hand. He wears an open necked shirt, waistcoat, jacket, and short trousers with long socks.
There is a pair to this figure. Fig. 2047C has been reserved for it.
HEIGHT: 9.25
PRICE: G.

Fig. 2048C
An arbour figure of a man standing, wearing a hat, shirt with tie, waistcoat, and knee breeches. He holds a fruit aloft in his right hand and a basket of fruit is held in his left.
There is probably a pair to this figure. Fig. 2048D has been reserved for it.
HEIGHT: 6 Inches
PRICE: G.

Fig. 2047F
A spill vase figure of a boy leaning against a tree trunk, holding a bunch of fruit aloft in his right hand and a basket of fruit in his left. He wears a jacket, shirt, and long trousers.
There is a pair to this figure. Fig. 2047E has been reserved for it.
HEIGHT: 7 Inches
PRICE: G.

Figs. 2051E/2051F
A pair of figures of a man and woman standing on either side of a series of arches that are decorated with grapes. Beneath the lower arch a stream flows. Both figures wear plumed hats, she with a blouse, jacket, and long skirt with an apron, he a shirt with wide collar, jacket, and knee breeches with boots. Each figure has a hand placed on the top arch.
In the figure illustrated part of the arch on the figure of the woman is missing.
HEIGHT: 9 Inches
PRICE: Pair: F, Singles: G.

Fig. 2048A
A figure of a man standing, wearing a hat, shirt, coat, and knee breeches. There is a pillar to his right, a spade leans against it, and a basket of fruit rests on top. His right hand rests on the basket and he holds another basket in his left hand.
Figures of this size usually are of little quality; a considerable amount of flaking has occurred and, at present, the cost of repairing the figure is more than it is worth. There is probably a pair to this figure. Fig. 2048B has been reserved for it.
HEIGHT: 4.5 Inches
PRICE: H.

226

Figs. 2051G/2051H
A pair of figures of a man and woman standing, he wearing a plumed hat, scarf, long jacket, waistcoat, shirt, and knee breeches. His dog sits between his feet and he has one hand on his hip and the other holds the top of a fruiting grapevine. Below the vine on a stand is a beehive. She wears a hat with feather bodice, open sleeved jacket, and a skirt with an apron. There are grapes in the apron and her left hand rests on the top of a fruiting grapevine. Below the vine on a stand is a beehive. Her dog sits at her feet.
A very well modelled and rare pair of figures.
HEIGHT: 10.75 Inches
PRICE: Pair: E, Singles: F.

Fig. 2051L
A figure of a boy standing, wearing a shirt and short trousers. His right hand holds a sheaf of wheat on his head while his left rests on his hip. By his side a small deer stands. **There is a pair to this figure. Fig. 2051M has been reserved for it.**
HEIGHT: 9.5 Inches
PRICE: F.

Fig. 2051J
A figure of a woman standing beside a fruiting grapevine at the base of which is a basket filled with grapes. She is bareheaded and wears a blouse, short jacket, and long skirt with an apron. Her hat is suspended from her waist. Her left hand rests on the vine and her right holds a bunch of grapes. **There is a pair to this figure. Fig. 2051K has been reserved for it. Modelled in the round, they were made by The Parr Pottery.**
HEIGHT: 8.75 Inches
PRICE: Pair: E, Singles: F.

Fig. 2053C
A group figure of a man and woman standing on either side of, and holding, two large sheaves of corn. He wears a hat, open necked shirt, knee breeches tied with a scarf, and holds a sickle in his right hand; she wears a hat, bodice, jacket, and long skirt. She holds a handbag in her left hand.
HEIGHT: 11 Inches
PRICE: F.

Fig. 2053D
A standing figure of a man wearing a hat, waistcoat, open neck shirt, and leggings. He holds what appears to be a sheaf of wheat under his left arm and a sickle in his right hand. **There is no doubt a pair to this figure. Fig. 2053E has been reserved for it.**
HEIGHT: 8 Inches
PRICE: G.

Fig. 2053H
A spill vase group figure of a boy and girl standing on either side of an enormous sheaf of wheat that serves as a spill. She wears a bodice, short skirt, and trousers and has her left arm around the sheaf and her right on her hip; he wears an open neck shirt and knee breeches. His right arm is around the sheaf and his left on his hip.
HEIGHT: 7 Inches
PRICE: H.

Figs. 2053F/2053G
A pair of figures of standing harvesters; he wears a hat, open necked shirt, jacket, and knee breeches. He carry's a sheaf of wheat under his left arm and a sickle is held in his right hand. She wears a bodice and long skirt with an apron. Her hat is tied around her waist. She holds a sheaf of wheat on her head with her right hand and carries another under her left arm.
HEIGHT: 7.5 Inches
PRICE: Pair: F, Singles: G.

Fig. 2053J
A spill vase group figure of a woman and man standing in front of a tree trunk; she wears a hat with feathers, blouse, jacket, and long skirt. A sheaf of wheat is under her right arm. He wears a hat, shirt with tie, waistcoat, jacket, and trousers. He holds a sheaf of wheat under his left arm.
HEIGHT: 9.75
PRICE: H.

Fig. 2055E
A group figure of harvesters, a man standing and woman seated; he wears a hat, open necked shirt, and kilt, and holds a sickle in his right hand and a sheaf of wheat in his left. She wears a hat with ribbon, blouse, jacket, and long skirt, and hold a sheaf of wheat in both hands.
HEIGHT: 8.5 Inches
PRICE: G.

Fig. 2056C
A standing figure of a woman wearing a blouse and long skirt. Her left arm is around a large sheaf of corn and she holds a sickle in her right hand. **There is a pair to this figure. Fig. 2056D has been reserved for it.**
HEIGHT: 9 Inches
PRICE: Pair: F, Singles: G.

Figs. 2055C/2055D
A pair of spill vase figures of a boy and girl harvester asleep on sheaves of corn; she wears a brimmed hat, blouse, and a long skirt. He wears a hat, blouse, and knee breeches. There is a sickle at his feet and both figures have sheaves of corn to either side.
HEIGHT: 7 Inches
PRICE: Pair: F, Singles: G.

Fig. 2056E
A figure of a boy seated, wearing a blouse and knee breeches with long socks. He holds a basket in his right hand and a sickle in his left. **There is a pair to this figure. Fig. 2056F has been reserved for it.**
HEIGHT: 6.25 Inches
PRICE: Pair: G, Singles: H.

Figs. 2057E/2057F
A pair of figures of a man and woman standing on circular coloured bases; both figures wear hats, he a jacket, shirt, and knee breeches, she a bodice and long dress with an apron. He is holding a basket of fruit on rockwork to his side; she has her arm through the handle of a basket that also sits on rockwork.
HEIGHT: 9.25 Inches
PRICE: Pair: G, Singles: H.

Fig. 2057G
A figure of a man standing, wearing a brimmed hat, tie, waistcoat, jacket, and trousers with an apron, holding a bunch of grapes in his right hand and a basket of fruit under his left. **There is a pair to this figure. Fig. 2057H has been reserved for it.**
HEIGHT: 7 Inches
PRICE: Pair: G, Singles: H.

Figs. 2057C/2057D
A pair of figures of a man and woman standing, she wearing a bonnet tied with a ribbon, a laced bodice, jacket, and long skirt with an apron. Her right hand is at her waist and her left holds a basket of flowers, which rests on rockwork. Another basket is at her feet. He wears a hat, jacket, blouse, and skirt with socks. His left hand is to his chest and his right holds a basket of flowers, with another at his feet. A flowering plant grows on the rockwork on both figures.
HEIGHT: 8.5 Inches
PRICE: Pair: F, Singles: G.

Figs. 2058C/2058D
A pair of spill vase figures of a man and woman seated on rock-work; he wears a short jacket with a sash over his shoulder and a kilt and holds a bird aloft with his right hand to his side. Beneath the spill is a beehive. The woman is a mirror image and she is similarly dressed.
HEIGHT: 8 Inches
PRICE: Pair: G, Singles: H.

Fig. 2058E
A spill vase group figure of a girl standing, wearing a turban, blouse, and skirt. She holds a full basket in both hands. Below her, a man sits with his legs crossed, wearing a plumed hat, jacket, and trousers. On the base a bird is swimming.
HEIGHT: 7.25 Inches
PRICE: H.

Figs. 2059A/2059B
A pair of figures of a man and woman standing beside beehives that are on stands to their side; both figures wear plumed hats, she with a bodice, blouse, and skirt with an apron. Her right arm rests on a branch. He wears highland attire of belted tunic, cloak, and kilt with sporran and his left arm rests on a branch.
Two pairs of figures are illustrated, one coloured and one in the white. At the time of writing, white figures are not so well regarded, often fetching one third the price of the coloured equivalent. The price guide given is for coloured versions.
HEIGHT: 9.25 Inches
PRICE: Pair: E, Singles: F.

231

Figs. 2059C/2059D
A pair of figures of children standing beside flowered arches below which beehives rest on a brick wall; both children are similarly dressed in plumed hat, blouse/shirt, and skirt/kilt. Both children have their hands clasped in front of them with a shopping basket is over one arm.
A charming pair of figures well modelled and coloured.
HEIGHT: 7.5 Inches
PRICE: Pair: E, Singles: F.

Figs. 2059G/2059H
A pair of figures of a girl and boy standing by a small fence; she wears a hat with a feather, bodice, blouse, and long skirt with a double apron. She holds a watering can in her right hand and her left rests on a pot of flowers that is on the fence. He wears a hat, frilled shirt, jacket, and a scarf tied at the waist of his knee breeches. He holds a spade in his right hand and there is an arrangement of flowers on the fence. On the base of both figures there is a beehive.
HEIGHT: 8.5 Inches
PRICE: Pair: F, Singles: G.

Figs. 2059E/2059F
A pair of spill vase figures of a boy and girl seated, both holding a flower in their hands and with a beehive to her left and to his right a bird sits in a tree to the side of the spill. A cat sits at her feet and a dog at his. She wears a plumed hat and long dress; he wears a plumed hat, coat, and a dress with trousers.
HEIGHT: 6.75 Inches
PRICE: Pair: F, Singles: G.

Figs. 2059J/2059K
A pair of figures of a man and woman standing, both holding garlands aloft. To her left and his right is a small arbour covered in flowers and leaves, below which a bee hive stands on a brick wall that in turn stands on a rock arch beneath which a stream flows. She wears a frilled blouse, coat around which is tied a scarf, and a skirt. Her brimmed hat is suspended from her waist. He wears a frilled shirt, coat across which is a sash, and knee length trousers. A hat is by his side.
These are by far the best of the beehive groups that the authors have seen and are very rare.
HEIGHT: 11.75
PRICE: Pair: E, Singles: F.

Fig. 2060A
A group figure of a girl seated and a boy standing by her side; she wears a blouse, bodice, and skirt with an apron and holds in her apron a quantity of fruit. At her feet is a basket filled with fruit. He has one arm around the girl and the other on his hip holding his hat; he wears a shirt with tie, waistcoat, and trousers.
HEIGHT: 8 Inches
PRICE: G.

Fig. 2060C
A standing figure of a man dressed in Scottish attire of Tam O' Shanter, long tunic with a scarf over both shoulders, and tartan socks with shoes. He holds a pot of flowers in his right hand. **There is a pair to this figure. Fig. 2060D has been reserved for it.**
HEIGHT: 7 Inches
PRICE: Pair: F, Singles: G.

Fig. 2060B
A double spill vase figure of a man and woman seated; he wears a brimmed hat, jacket, and knee breeches and has one hand on her shoulder. She wears a jacket and long skirt and has a basket of fruit over her left arm.
This figure is badly modelled and poorly coloured; it lacks charm and is crude rather than naïve.
HEIGHT: 7 Inches
PRICE: H.

Fig. 2061B
A figure of a woman standing, wearing a plumed hat, bodice, long jacket, skirt with an apron, and a scarf across her shoulders. There are flowers in the apron and on rockwork to her side. Her left arm rests on a basket. Below the rockwork a stream flows from a brick arch.
There is a pair to this figure. Fig. 2061C has been reserved for it.
HEIGHT: 10 Inches
PRICE: Pair: F, Singles: G.

233

Fig. 2061D
A figure of a woman standing, wearing a plumed hat, bodice, dress with an apron, and a scarf over her right arm. Her left arm rests on a large pot of fruit and flowers that is on a pillar. **There is a pair to this figure. Fig. 2061B has bee reserved for it.**
HEIGHT: 9.5 Inches
PRICE: Pair: F,
Singles: G.

Figs. 2069/2069A
A pair of spill vase group figures of woman and man seated on rockwork; she wears a hat, bodice, coat, and a long dress with a sash. In her right hand she holds a mandolin. Below her a goat stands, a doe which reclines on the base, and a stream runs between them. He wears a hat, shirt with tie, waistcoat, jacket, and knee breeches. By his side is a pipe. Below a goat stands and a stag reclines on the base while a stream runs between them.
HEIGHT: 9.25 Inches
PRICE: Pair: E, Singles: F.

Fig. 2068C
A group figure of two girls, one standing and one sitting on rockwork. Both girls wear plumed hats, blouses, short coats, and long skirts with knickers. The girl sitting has one hand on a large jug that rests on rockwork; the girl standing holds a sheaf of corn under her arm.
HEIGHT: 7.75 Inches
PRICE: F.

Figs. 2069C/2069D
A pair of figures of a man and woman standing; she wears a large hat, bodice, blouse with puff sleeves, and dress with an apron. She holds a shopping basket in her right hand and a rake in her left. He wears a hat and long tunic with a sash over his shoulder. He holds a set of musical pipes in his hands.
HEIGHT: 8 Inches
PRICE: Pair: F, Singles: G.

Fig. 2073B
A group figure of a girl seated and a boy standing on rock-work; she wears a bodice, short coat, and dress with an apron. She rests one arm on a large sheaf of corn. He wears a hat, shirt with collar, jacket, and kilt and has one arm around a large pot of flowers that rests on a ledge underneath which a stream flows.
HEIGHT: 8.5 Inches
PRICE: G.

Figs. 2071A/2071B
A pair of figures of a man and woman mounted, he astride, she sidesaddle, on a standing horse, which has one foreleg resting on a fence. He wears a plumed hat, short jacket, and kilt with a large scarf over his left shoulder. He holds the reins in his left hand and a basket on the horse's rump in his right. She wears a plumed hat, blouse, long skirt, and a sash over her right shoulder and across her chest. She holds the reins in her right hand and a full basket in her left.
This figure and its pair are probably a version of 'Going to market and Returning home' and there is illustrated a pair in the white and a single in full colour.
HEIGHT: 9.5 Inches
PRICE: Pair: E, Singles: F.

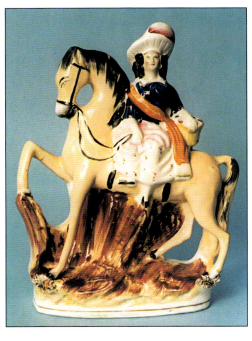

Fig. 2073C
A group figure of a man and woman standing; she wears a hat, blouse, jacket, and long skirt with an apron. She holds a basket of fruit in her right hand. He wears a hat with feather, shirt with tie, long jacket, and knee breeches with boots. His right arm is around her and his left rests on her arm. A large sheaf of wheat stands by his side.
HEIGHT: 9.5 Inches
PRICE: F.

Fig. 2074B
A figure of a girl seated on rockwork wearing a blouse and long skirt with a scarf over her shoulder and in her lap. To her right is a tall brick built lighthouse. At the base of the building is an arch and to either side are two more arches. Under each arch a swan swims. **If the building is a lighthouse it is clearly out of proportion with the girl. It is possible that the figure is meant to depict Grace Darling. It is also possible that there is a pair to this very rare figure. Fig. 2074C has been reserved for it.**
HEIGHT: 7.5 Inches
PRICE: F.

Fig. 2077A
A spill vase group figure of a man and woman seated above a brick arch under which a stream flows. She wears a plumed hat, cloak, jacket, and long skirt. She holds a basket of fruit in her right hand. He wears a plumed hat, shirt with collar, and long tunic with boots. His right arm is around the woman and holding her hand with his. To their left is a tree
in which a bird is perched.
HEIGHT: 12 Inches
PRICE: G.

Fig. 2076A
A spill vase and arbour group of a man and woman seated on either side of a tree trunk attached to which is a large fruiting grapevine. She is bareheaded and wears a long dress. To her side is a basket filled with grapes. He wears a tunic and long coat. At his feet a dog lies.
HEIGHT: 12.75
PRICE: H.

Fig. 2077C
A spill vase group of a boy and girl wearing brimmed hats, she with a bodice and long skirt, he a jacket, shirt, and kilt. They are seated before a tree. Below them a large bird swims.
HEIGHT: 7.5 Inches
PRICE: H.

Fig. 2078A
A double spill vase figure of girl and boy standing on either side of a picket fence. She wears a blouse and long skirt and looks down at a sheep which is seated by her feet. He wears a shirt, jacket, and kilt and leans against a tree.
HEIGHT: 6.5 Inches
PRICE: H.

Fig. 2079A
A group figure of a man and woman standing on rockwork above two swans; she wears a plumed hat, long coat, and skirt, holding an object above her head with her left hand. Her right hand holds a full basket. He wears a hat, jacket, short coat, and skirt with trousers and holds a bird aloft.
HEIGHT: 6 Inches
PRICE: G.

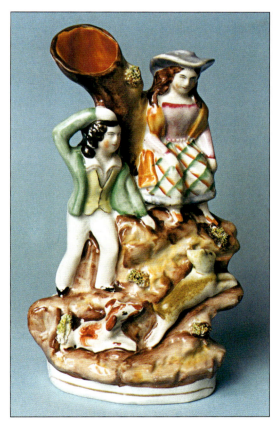

Fig. 2078B
A spill vase group figure of a boy and girl standing on rock-work; he wears an open necked shirt, waistcoat, jacket, and trousers and has one hand raised to his head. She wears a hat, bodice, long skirt, and a scarf over her shoulders. Both children are watching below where a dog is chasing a cat.
HEIGHT: 9 Inches
PRICE: G.

Figs. 2079B/2079C
A pair of figures of a man and woman seated on high rock-work, both holding a bird in their hand. They are similarly dressed in plumed hats, blouse/tunic, skirt/kilt, and each leans one arm on the rockwork. To the side of each a stream flows and on the bottom a bird swims.
HEIGHT: 6.5 Inches
PRICE: Pair: F, Singles: G.

Fig. 2079D
A spill vase group of a man and woman standing in a boat; both adults are dressed in plumed hats, blouses, and skirts. Between them they hold a bird aloft. To the bow of the boat two swans swim.
This figure is similar in content to 2079A and it is possible that they are both theatrical in inspiration.
HEIGHT: 9.5 Inches
PRICE: G.

Figs. 2080A/2080B
A pair of spill vase group figures of a man and woman, she standing wearing a long coat and dress, holding her hat in one hand and a basket in the other. He is seated on a fence wearing a hat, long jacket, shirt, and knee breeches. A dog lies on the ground at their feet. One figure is the mirror image of the other.
It is unusual for group figures of this nature to be paired; they are usually singles.
HEIGHT: 6.5 Inches
PRICE: Pair: E, Singles: G.

Fig. 2079E
An arbour group figure of a woman flanked by two men, all are standing. The men are both dressed the same in frilled shirt, jacket, and breeches. The woman wears a large hat, blouse, and long skirt. In front of her is a cushioned stool on which is a filled cornucopia of flowers and fruit.
This figure, like many others, was made to portray a particular event or scene; however, the meaning has been lost. It could be theatrical, it could be a harvest scene, or the men could be twins. The clues are there waiting to be unravelled or for the finding of a source.
HEIGHT: 7 Inches
PRICE: G.

Fig. 2081A
A spill vase figure of a girl and boy standing; she wears a hat, coat, and skirt with knickers showing. She holds a small animal in her right hand. He wears a hat, coat, waistcoat, and trousers. He holds a garland in his left hand. On the ground by his feet a bottle rests.
Whilst decorated in underglaze blue, this is not a very well modelled figure. It is possible, in view of the boy's apparel, that this figure is meant to portray 'The sailors return'.
HEIGHT: 6 Inches
PRICE: H.

Figs. 2084C/2084D
A pair of standing figures of a man and woman; he wears a flat cap, open necked shirt with tie, jacket, and knee breeches tied at the waist with a scarf, holding a large pot of flowers with his left hand that rest upon a rockwork pillar. His right hand is around a goat, which stands on its hind legs at his side with its forehooves resting on his chest. She wears a headdress, bodice, and long skirt with an apron. She holds a pot of flowers in her left hand and her right is around a goat, which stands on its hind legs with its forehooves resting on her waist.

Fig. 2082A
A spill vase figure of a woman seated to the side of a tree, wearing a turban, ermine edged cloak, bodice, jacket, and long skirt with an apron. Both hands are in her lap and a dead bird hangs head down in it. To the other side of the tree a spaniel sits on its haunches. **There is possibly a pair to this figure. Fig. 2082B has been reserved for it.**
HEIGHT: 10 Inches
PRICE: F.

A pair of large and imposing figures, a pair in the white and a single of him in colour are illustrated.
HEIGHT: 13.5 Inches
PRICE: Pair: E, Singles: F.

Fig. 2082C
A figure of a woman standing, wearing a blouse and long skirt with an apron that she holds in her right hand, and in her left she holds a small dog. **There is no doubt a pair to this figure. Fig. 2082D has been reserved for it. Without having seen its pair, it is difficult to ascertain exactly what this figure is portraying and consequently whether we have included it in the correct chapter.**
HEIGHT: 8 Inches
PRICE: G.

Fig. 2086C
A group arbour figure of a boy seated on a tree branch; he wears a shirt, jacket, and knee breeches. He holds a bird in his lap and is offering an object to a girl who stands on rockwork. She wears a hat, jacket, and long dress.
HEIGHT: 8 Inches
PRICE: H.

Fig. 2086A
A spill vase group figure of a man standing above a woman seated, both hold baskets of flowers. He wears a plumed hat, open necked shirt, jacket, and knee breeches. His right hand is upon his hip. She is seated beneath an arbour and wears a blouse and long skirt, all on a rococo base.
HEIGHT: 8 Inches
PRICE: H.

Fig. 2086B
A group figure of a man standing, wearing a steeple hat with scarf attached, shirt, three-quarter length jacket and loose knee breeches. He carries a basket over his right arm and holds a shotgun by its barrel. His left hand is on the head of a woman who sits next to him wearing a headscarf, blouse, and long dress. Her hand rests on a jug below which a dog is begging. **This figure bears similarities to Brigand figures and may be theatrical in inspiration.**
HEIGHT: 9.5 Inches
PRICE: F.

Fig. 2086D
A spill vase arbour group of a man standing and a girl seated, she wearing a turban, blouse, and long skirt. She holds a basket of flowers on her knee. He wears a hat with feather, shirt, jacket, and knee breeches and in his right holds a basket of fruit resting on rockwork.
HEIGHT: 7.25 Inches
PRICE: H.

Fig. 2090A
A spill vase group figure of a man and woman seated on
rockwork; she wears a plumed hat, blouse, and long skirt. He wears a plumed hat, shirt, jacket, and short trousers. A bird is perched upon his left arm. **This figure is very similar to Fig. 2090 Book Two. The particular figure illustrated is badly flaked and the base was never coloured. Figures like the one illustrated will fetch relatively low prices due to their condition.**
HEIGHT: 8 Inches
PRICE: (As illustrated) H.

Fig. 2092B
A spill vase group figure of a man and woman seated; she wears a mop cap, blouse, and skirt with an apron. One hand is in her lap and the other around the man who wears a tricorn hat, shirt with tie, jacket, knee breeches, and boots. One hand is on his knee and the other around the woman. There is a small fence by his feet.
HEIGHT: 7.5 Inches
PRICE: G.

Fig. 2092A
A group arbour figure of a man and woman seated; he wears a jacket, shirt with tie, and knee breeches. She wears a jacket with blouse and long skirt. They hold a garland of flowers between them and the arbour is covered with a fruiting grapevine.
HEIGHT: 8 Inches
PRICE: H.

Fig. 2092C
A group figure of a lover and his lass; he wears a plumed hat, open neck shirt, long jacket with a sash over his shoulder and across his waist, and short trousers. His left arm is around her waist. She wears a hat with scarf, bodice, jacket, and long skirt with a decorated apron, and leans into her lover.
HEIGHT: 10.5 Inches
PRICE: F.

Fig. 2093A
A group figure of a boy standing and a girl sitting to the side of a rabbit hutch on top of which is a flowering plant. The boy is wearing a hat, jacket, waistcoat, and trousers, and holds a hoop and stick in his right hand. The girl is wearing a blouse and long skirt. Her right hand is in her lap and her left rests on a rabbit that sits on the roof of the hutch.
HEIGHT: 7 Inches
PRICE: H.

Fig. 2093E
A watch holder group of a boy and girl standing, both similarly attired, both wearing hats, blouse/tunic, and kilt/skirt. Between them is a vase containing flowers; he holds one hand to the vase and she holds a bloom in her right hand. The watch holder is decorated with trailing leaves.
HEIGHT: 9 Inches
PRICE: G.

Fig. 2093B
A spill vase group figure of a boy half kneeling wearing a jacket, shirt, waistcoat, and trousers, holding a rabbit by its ears. Another rabbit sits on the ground at his feet. To his right on rockwork is a hutch on top of which a fox is standing looking down on the rabbits.
HEIGHT: 7 Inches
PRICE: G.

Fig. 2093D
A watch holder group figure of a boy and girl; the girl is seated and the boy is standing on a grassy bank to either side of a rabbit hutch. The girl wears a blouse and long skirt. She holds a baby rabbit in her right hand. Her left hand rests on the head of a dog that sits at her feet. The boy wears a cap, tunic, kilt, and long socks. His right hand rests on the back of a large rabbit that sits on top of the hutch. All of this is above the watch holder that has trailing flowers up both sides.
HEIGHT: 10 Inches
PRICE: F.

Fig. 2096B
An arbour group figure of two lovers; he stands, wearing an open neck shirt, jacket, long waistcoat, and knee breeches. He holds his tricorn hat in his right hand and his left arm is around the shoulders of his girl, who is seated, wearing a low cut jacket and long dress. She holds her hat in her right hand, which is filled with grapes and leaves. The arbour is covered with a grape vine and kneeling at one end is a bare cherub. HEIGHT: 12 Inches
PRICE: F.

242

Figs. 2098B/2098C
A pair of figures of a boy and girl seated, both are bareheaded and he wears a shirt, waistcoat, and trousers. He is holding an object in his left hand and on his lap and a bird in his right that he holds to his face. She wears a blouse and long skirt with an apron in which she has a quantity of fruit her right hand and holds more fruit to her mouth.
The figures illustrated are a matched pair as the bases are decorated differently.
HEIGHT: 7 Inches
PRICE: Pair: F, Singles: G.

Figs. 2099/2100
A pair of figures of a boy and girl seated on tree stumps on co-loured circular bases. He is holding a bird aloft in his left hand and a nest in his right, wearing an open necked shirt, waistcoat, jacket, and rumpled knee breeches. She wears a bodice and skirt with an apron. She holds fruit in her left hand and her right rests on a basket of fruit that is in her lap.
Fig. 2100 was previously erroneously included in Book One as Fig. 1192 Virginia.
HEIGHT: 7.5 Inches
PRICE: Pair: F, Singles: G.

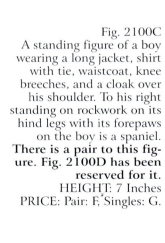

Fig. 2100C
A standing figure of a boy wearing a long jacket, shirt with tie, waistcoat, knee breeches, and a cloak over his shoulder. To his right standing on rockwork on its hind legs with its forepaws on the boy is a spaniel.
There is a pair to this fig-ure. Fig. 2100D has been reserved for it.
HEIGHT: 7 Inches
PRICE: Pair: F, Singles: G.

Figs. 2098D/2098E
A pair of figures of a boy and girl seated by a tree stump; he wears an open necked shirt, waistcoat, jacket, and trousers. He holds a bird in his left hand and a bird's nest filled with eggs in his right. She wears a short jacket, long dress with an apron, and laced boots. In her apron she holds fruit and a bird is perched on her right hand, which she holds to her face.
HEIGHT: 7.25
PRICE: Pair: F Singles. G.

Fig. 2100E
A standing figure of a
man wearing a hat, frilled
shirt, waistcoat, and knee
breeches. One hand is
on his hip and the other
around a spaniel that
stands on its hind legs on a
fence with its forepaws on
the man.
**There is a pair to this
figure. Fig. 2100F has
been reserved for it.**
HEIGHT: 6.5 Inches
PRICE: Pair: F, Singles: G.

Fig. 2101G
An arbour group figure of a girl sitting on a brick
built bridge below which runs a stream. She wears
a blouse, sash, and long skirt. A filled basket is
over her right arm. Standing on either side of
her are two chickens. The arbour is covered in a
grapevine.
**There is probably a pair to this figure. Fig.
2101H has been reserved for it.**
HEIGHT: 8 Inches
PRICE: G.

Figs. 2102C/2102D
A pair of spill vase figures of a boy and girl, both seated on the top
of a flight of steps. He wears a plumed hat, shirt with collar, jacket,
a sash across his chest, kilt with sporran, shoes and socks. To his
right and her left there is perched in a tree a cockerel below which
is a fence and below that are two standing chickens. She wears a
plumed hat, blouse, long skirt with an apron, and a scarf over her
right arm.
HEIGHT: 8.75 Inches
PRICE: Pair: E, Singles: F.

Figs. 2102E/2102F
A pair of figures of a man and woman standing; both adults wear plumed hats, he with a frilled shirt with tie, jacket, and knee breeches. His left arm rests on rockwork. She has a large scarf draped over both shoulders and around her waist and holds one end in her right hand and wears a bodice, short jacket, and long skirt. On the base of both figures on either side is a chicken and a cockerel.
The figures of the chicken and cockerel are identical to those in Fig. 2102C and the same modeller would have made all these figures.
HEIGHT: 10 Inches
PRICE: Pair: F, Singles: G.

Fig. 2105A
A figure of a man seated with legs crossed wearing highland attire of Tam O' Shanter, waistcoat, kilt with sporran, and scarf across his chest. His right arm is around rockwork to his side.
This figure is similar to Fig. 2104 and could be a portrait figure of Burns. Where there are no objects or ancillary items incorporated into the figures, they are often Portraits. It is not known whether there is a pair to this figure. Should one come to light, the identity of the pair may be confirmed. Fig. 2105B has been reserved for the pair.
HEIGHT: 10 Inches
PRICE: F.

Figs. 2104/2105
A pair of figures of a man and woman standing; he wearing a highland garb of Tam O' Shanter, tunic, kilt with sporran and stockings, and a large scarf across his chest and over his shoulder. His right hand is on his hip and his left arm rests on rockwork to his side. She wears a hat and a long dress with an apron. Her hands are clasped together.
It has been suggested that this pair represent 'Burns and Mary', whilst no titled figures have ever been recorded. The authors are of the opinion that this is in all probability a correct attribution.
HEIGHT 12 Inches
PRICE: Pair: E, Singles: F.

Fig. 2105C
A spill vase figure of a man standing leaning against
a tree; he wears a Tam O' Shanter hat, ermine edged
cloak, jacket, waistcoat, and trousers with knee boots.
His right hand is placed inside his coat and his dog lies
on rockwork by his feet.
**This is a common figure but it is not known who it
portrays. He is very well dressed and he could well
be theatrical in inspiration.**
HEIGHT: 13.25 Inches
PRICE: F.

Fig. 2105E
A standing figure of a
man dressed in Scottish
attire of Tam O' Shanter,
blouse, kilt with spor-
ran, and shoes and socks;
his left hand is on his
hip and his right holds a
drinking vessel.
**This figure is a direct
copy of a Portobello
pearlware figure of a
highlander that was
made circa 1820; this
figure was made circa
1845.**
HEIGHT: 11.25 Inches
PRICE: F.

Fig. 2105F
A group figure of a girl and boy standing on either side of a
table; she wears a plumed hat, bodice, jacket, and skirt with
an apron in which she holds flowers. A garland of flowers is
held aloft. He wears a plumed hat, tunic, and kilt, and holds
a spaniel in both hands. The whole figure is upon a shaped
and waisted base.
HEIGHT: 9 Inches
PRICE: G.

Fig. 2108C
A group figure of a man standing, dressed in theatrical attire of a hat with ribbon, frilled shirt with tie, jacket, knee breeches, and boots. His right hand is on the head of a dog that stands on its hind legs with its forepaws on his waist. His other arm is around the shoulders of a woman who stands on a brick arch under which a swan swims. She wears a plumed hat, bodice, and long dress with a scarf over her shoulder and across her waist.
HEIGHT: 11 Inches
PRICE: E.

Fig. 2107B
A standing figure of a woman wearing a plumed hat, blouse, and skirt with an apron. Her left hand rests on rockwork and her right holds a nest of eggs in her apron and there is a quantity of fruit. A dog stands on its hind legs on rockwork to her side with its front paws in her lap.
This figure has a scrolled base, which will help with the identification of its pair. Fig. 2107C has been reserved for it.
HEIGHT: 7.5 Inches
PRICE: F.

Fig. 2107D
A group figure of a boy standing, wearing a plumed hat, shirt with collar, blouse, and kilt with boots. His hands are on his hips and a large bird is perched on his shoulder. A cloak is over his arm. To his right, standing on a chair, is a girl who is bareheaded, wearing a blouse and skirt she holds. Both her hands up are to the boy's neck.
It is possible that a pair exists for this figure. Fig. 2107E has been reserved for it. This group is reminiscent of groups of the Royal children, as the use of birds in figures often denotes that Royalty was being portrayed.
HEIGHT: 8 Inches
PRICE: E.

Fig. 2108D
A figure of a boy standing, wearing a hat with feather, frilled shirt, jacket, skirt, and a scarf over his shoulders. He holds a basket under his right arm and his left rests on a swan, which is seated on a brick built bridge beneath which a stream flows.
There is a pair to this figure. Fig. 2108E has been reserved for it.
HEIGHT: 8.5 Inches
PRICE: G.

Fig. 2109D
A spill vase group of a man and woman standing on either side of a tree trunk; he wears a shirt with tie, jacket, and knee breeches. He holds a horn in his right hands and gazes at the woman who wears a hat, sleeved bodice, and skirt with an apron. She holds her hat in both hands and her foot rests on a fence. **This figure was made by the Parr Factory.**
HEIGHT: 11.5 Inches
PRICE: F.

Fig. 2109B
A group figure of a boy standing cross-legged and a girl seated on either side of a flowering plant. He wears a hat, blouse with shirt, and a skirt. She wears a plumed hat, blouse, and long dress. She holds a garland in her left hand.
HEIGHT: 7 Inches
PRICE: H.

Fig. 2109C
A spill vase figure of a man and woman standing, he wearing a shirt, long jacket, and knee breeches with his arms crossed holding an object and looking at the woman who leans back against a tree, wearing a cap, bodice, short jacket, and skirt with an apron. She holds the man's hat in her hand and there is a bucket on the ground.

Two figures are illustrated, virtually identical in modelling other than one has a rococo base and one does not.
HEIGHT: 8 Inches
PRICE: F.

Fig. 2109E
A group of a woman standing and a man seated on rockwork; she wears a jacket with short sleeves and long skirt. Her left arm is around the shoulders of the man and her right is placed on his hand. He wears a jacket, shirt, waistcoat, and knee breeches. His hat is by his shoulder and on the base is a stick and bag.
The figure depicts a woman comforting a weary traveller on his return; it could be of theatrical inspiration.
HEIGHT: 9.5 Inches
PRICE: G.

Fig. 2109F
A group figure of a man standing and a woman seated; he wears a cap, tunic, kilt, and scarf. She wears a hat with feather, bodice, and long skirt.
HEIGHT: 6.25
PRICE: H.

Fig. 2110C
An arbour group figure of a woman seated, wearing a hat and long dress with an apron, and holding a baby in her arms. A man stands to her side with his legs crossed, wearing a hat, shirt, waistcoat, jacket, and knee breeches. His right hand rests on the woman's shoulder.
HEIGHT: 9 Inches
PRICE: H.

Fig. 2110B
A spill vase group of a boy and girl seated on a mound before a tree, both wear brimmed hats, she with a jacket and skirt, he a jacket, shirt, and kilt. His right leg rests on the top of a kennel and a dog sits outside it. **This figure is a product of 'The Green factory'.**
HEIGHT: 9 Inches
PRICE: F.

Fig. 2110D
An arbour group of a man and woman seated, he with his arm around her; she wears a brimmed hat, bodice, long skirt, and a scarf over her shoulder. By her feet is a milk churn and a crook. He wears a hat, shirt with tie, waistcoat, jacket, and trousers. A dog sits in his lap. **This figure is unusual in so far as the decorator has stopped painting half way up the arbour.**
HEIGHT: 12 Inches
PRICE: G.

Figs. 2111E/2111F
A pair of spill vase figures, the spills in the form of tulips, with a girl and boy seated to the side of the tulips. She wears a hat, shawl, and long dress. A cat stands on its hind legs with its forepaws in her lap. He wears a hat, shirt, jacket, and trousers. A spaniel is recumbent at his feet. To the side of each of them on a stool is a beehive.
HEIGHT: 6.5 Inches
PRICE: Pair: F, Singles: G.

Fig. 2113E
A group figure of a boy and girl standing to either side of a watch holder. A dog is lying on the base between them. Both children are dressed in blouses with sashes across their chests and a kilt/skirt. **This figure can be found as either a watch holder or a clock face group, both illustrated.**
HEIGHT: 9.5 Inches
PRICE: G.

Figs. 2111G/2111H
A pair of spill vase figures of a boy and girl seated; both wear similar dress of brimmed hat, blouse/tunic, and skirt/trousers. They both sit with their hands in their lap and a dog at their feet. In the spill above them is a bird's nest and perched above is a bird.
HEIGHT: 4.5. Inches
PRICE: Pair: G, Singles: H.

Fig. 2113F
A group figure of a girl and boy seated above a clock face; both children are bareheaded and wear blouses with a sash across their chests and skirts. She holds a nest of eggs in her lap and a bird is perched on his left arm.
HEIGHT: 6.25 Inches
PRICE: H.

Figs. 2112A/2112B
A pair of figures of a boy and girl seated on rockwork above a stream; he holds a bird's nest in his lap with both hands and has a bag over his right arm. He wears a brimmed hat, shirt with tie, waistcoat, jacket, and trousers. She wears a long jacket and skirt and holds a small bird in both hands; her hat is by her feet.
HEIGHT: 8 Inches
PRICE: Pair: F, Singles: G.

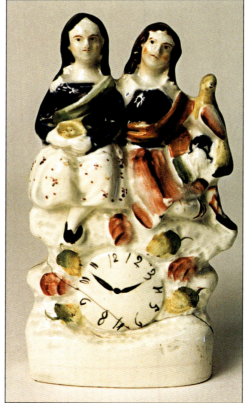

Chapter 4:
Other Pursuits, Pastimes, and Occupations

In this chapter many decorative figures are included which do not sit happily elsewhere. It is rather general in its content. Here will be found fishermen and fish sellers, water and milk fetchers, and all sorts of occupations, pursuits, pastimes, and domestic scenes.

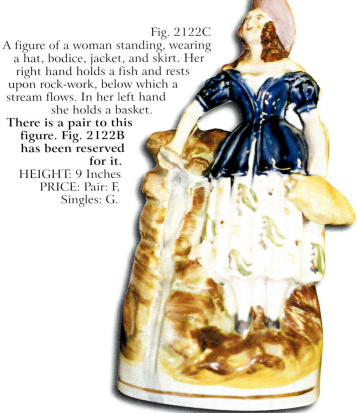

Fig. 2122C
A figure of a woman standing, wearing a hat, bodice, jacket, and skirt. Her right hand holds a fish and rests upon rock-work, below which a stream flows. In her left hand she holds a basket.
There is a pair to this figure. Fig. 2122B has been reserved for it.
HEIGHT: 9 Inches
PRICE: Pair: F,
Singles: G.

Fig. 2122E
A group figure of a fisherman and woman seated on rock-work on either side of a lighthouse; she wears a plumed hat, bodice, long scarf over her shoulders, long skirt, and boots. She holds a basket of fish in her left hand. He wears a hat, jacket, shirt with tie, and trousers. She holds a fishing net in his right hand.
HEIGHT: 9 Inches
PRICE: F.

Fig. 2122F
A group figure of two fisher girls, one seated, one standing; they both wear long flowing robes and each hold a fish in one hand. At the feet of the standing woman is a basket filled with fish. The base is quite unusual as it is square with cut corners on which is set round rock-work and then what appears to be a plank of wood. **An example of this figure was found with a handwritten paper label on the bottom of which read, 'This ornament – 'The Fisher girls' – was bought by my mother in the first Exhibition of 1851; held in Hyde Park'. The Exhibition referred to was The Great Exhibition of 1851.**
HEIGHT: 15 Inches
PRICE: F.

Fig. 2122D
A spill vase group figure of a fisherman and his wife standing on either side of a tree trunk; he wears a fisherman's cap, shirt, jacket, and knee breeches with boots. A fish net is over his right shoulder and he holds the ends with both hands. She is bareheaded and wears a short jacket, blouse, and skirt with an apron; she holds a basket full of fish in both hands.
HEIGHT: 8 Inches
PRICE: H.

Fig. 2123C
A standing figure of a fish-wife wearing a headscarf, blouse, and skirt with an apron. Her arms are folded across her waist and she carries a fish basket filled with fish on her back.
This figure is by the same modeller as Figs. 2123A/2123B Book Three and there is probably a pair. Fig. 2123D has been reserved for it.
HEIGHT: 7.5 Inches
PRICE: F.

Fig. 2124D
A group figure of a man standing, wearing a brimmed hat, shirt with tie, jacket, and belted kilt. His legs are crossed, he holds a fish in his left hand, and a net in his right. The net falls to the floor and he is standing on it. She wears a hat and a long dress with an apron, and holds a basket of fish under her left arm. Her right foot rests on a basket.
HEIGHT: 13 Inches.
PRICE: E.

Fig. 2124C
A standing group of a fisherman and wife; he wears a brimmed hat, loose shirt, and short trousers tied with a scarf. He holds in his right hand a long fishing net that is draped over both shoulders. His left hand is on the shoulder of his wife, who wears a hat, bodice, and long skirt. She holds a basket of fish in both hands.
It has been suggested that this figure, along with others such as Fig. 1467 Book Three, may portray Masaniello and Fenella (see Fig. 1306 Book One); this is possible but no titled figures or source are known that would confirm this attribution.
HEIGHT: 9.5 Inches
PRICE: F.

Fig. 2124E
A group figure of a fish seller and his wife, both seated; she wears a blouse with frilled sleeves and a long skirt with an apron. She holds a basket filled with fish on her lap. He wears a collared shirt with a tie, long jacket, and knee length trousers. His right arm is around his wife and his left rests on her lap. He has a large creel filled with fish on his back secured by a strap across his chest.
HEIGHT: 10.5 Inches
PRICE: E.

Fig. 2124F
A standing figure of a fisherman, he has a moustache and goatee beard and wears a cap, open neck shirt, waistcoat, jacket, and a Greek style kilt. He holds a large net over his shoulder that is draped to the ground behind him. **A large and imposing figure, there is probably a pair to this very rare figure. Fig. 2124G has been reserved for it. It is also possible that it is theatrical in inspiration as it resembles in some respects the figures of Masaniello.**
HEIGHT: 12 Inches
PRICE: E.

Figs. 2126C/2126D
A pair of figures of a fisherman standing with one foot raised on rockwork; his left hand rests on a basket that in turn rests on a small flowered arbour. He wears a stocking cap, open necked shirt, long jacket, and knee breeches with high boots. Over his right shoulder is a large net and in his right hand he holds a fish. Below, under a bridge, a stream runs. His companion wears a hat with scarf attached, bodice, and skirt with an apron. She is similarly posed with her right hand on the arbour and a fish in her left hand. **A very fine pair and very rare to find them decorated with underglaze blue and in full colour. A single of the fisherman and a pair mainly in the white are illustrated.**
HEIGHT: 11.25 Inches
PRICE: Pair: E, Singles: F.

Fig. 2124H
A group figure of a boy and girl standing on rockwork; she wears a hat with feather, blouse, jacket, and long skirt. She holds a basket in her right hand. He wears a cap, shirt, jacket, and long trousers. He holds a large basket with two fish in it in his right hand.
HEIGHT: 8.75 Inches
PRICE: G.

Fig. 2126E
A group figure of a fisherman seated on rockwork with his right hand to his eyes peering into the distance. He wears a brimmed hat, open neck shirt, jacket, and short trousers; a net is over his shoulder. Below him a woman sits bareheaded with a scarf over her shoulders, wearing a bodice, jacket, and long skirt. She holds on her lap a bowl that contains eels. At her feet a dog sits, all on an arched gilded base. **This figure was made by The Parr factory.**
HEIGHT: 11.5 Inches
PRICE: E.

Figs. 2126/2125
A pair of figures of a fisherman and fish seller. He wears a cap, shirt with tie, jacket, and trousers tied at the waist. He is bare footed and holds a large net over his left shoulder. She wears a cap, shawl, jacket, and long dress, holding a basket of fish under her arm. **These figures are decorated in the manner of The Parr factory.**
HEIGHT: 11.25 Inches
PRICE: Pair: E, Singles: F.

Fig. 2126F
A group figure of a boy and girl on a bridge, he seated, she standing, both similarly dressed in a blouse and kilt/skirt. A dog sits on the boys lap with its forepaws on the girl. Beside both of them is a basket filled with fish. A rod rests on the ground with its end in a stream that runs below.
HEIGHT: 8 Inches
PRICE: H.

Figs. 2128B/2128C
A pair of figures of a man and woman standing; he wears a hat, shirt, jacket, and breeches and is holding what appears to be a pumpkin in his left hand and a spade in his right. She wears a brimmed hat, blouse, and skirt with an apron in which she holds a number of fish. There is a large fish basket standing to her side on which she rests her hand.
HEIGHT: 6.5 Inches
PRICE: Pair: F, Singles: G.

Fig. 2126G
A figure of a fisherman standing in his boat with one foot on the prow and casting a net with both hands; he wears a hat, shirt with tie, waistcoat, jacket, and trousers. There is a basket in the back of the boat.
This figure is modelled in the round and was made in the 1830s. There is a pair to this figure, a mirror image. Fig. 2126H has been reserved for it.
HEIGHT: 8.25 Inches
PRICE: F.

Figs. 2128D/2128E
A pair of figures of a man and woman standing on arched gilt lined bases; she wears a hat, bodice, jacket, and skirt with an apron. She holds a bowl of oysters in her right hand and an oyster in her left. He wears a hat, shirt with tie, waistcoat, jacket, and knee breeches. A bag is held at his waist by a strap over his shoulder and two fish protrude from it. He holds a larger fish in his right hand.
HEIGHT: 9.25
PRICE: Pair: F, Singles: G.

Figs. 2130E/2130F
A pair of standing figures of a fisherman and his wife; he has his left hand to his shoulder holding a basket of fish, his right to his side holding a net. He wears a cap, shirt, short-sleeved jacket, and kilt. She wears a bodice, long skirt, and a scarf over her right shoulder and tied to her side. Her left hand holds a basket of fish on her head and her right holds a fishing net.
HEIGHT: 10 Inches
PRICE: Pair: F, Singles: G.

Figs. 2130J/2130K
A pair of standing figures of a man and woman oyster sellers; both sellers have a basket of oysters on their heads and another basket over one arm. He wears an open neck shirt, jacket, and rolled up trousers. She wears a headscarf, jacket, and skirt with an apron.
HEIGHT: 8.75 Inches
PRICE: Pair: F, Singles: G.

Fig. 2130G
A figure of a man standing, holding a basket of shellfish under his left arm and holding a shell in his right hand, wearing a hat, open necked shirt, jacket, and trousers. He is barefooted.
There is a pair to this figure. Fig. 2130H has been reserved for it.
HEIGHT: 12.5 Inches
PRICE: Pair: F, Singles: G.

Figs. 2132F/2132G
A pair of figures of a seated fisherwoman; each figure is a mirror image of the other. Both women wear a headscarf, jacket, blouse, and a skirt with an apron and each has one hand resting on a basket filled with fish.
The source of these figures is a print titled 'Fish woman' that contains only Fig. 3132G. The potters made a mirror image figure to make a pair.
HEIGHT: 7 Inches
PRICE: Pair: E, Singles: F.

Fig. 2132H
A figure of a fishwife standing, wearing a headscarf, scarf, blouse, and long skirt with an apron. She holds both hands in front of her, and at her feet is a large basket that is full of fish.
There exists a companion figure of a woman similarly dressed but the basket is on her back. Fig. 2132J has been reserved for it.
Shards of pottery have been found on the site of The Benfield pottery in Prestopans, Scotland, that suggests that this figure was made there by Watson's. In September 2003 in Edinburgh at auction a similar figure to this and two companion figures were sold at prices ranging between £900 and £1250; the figures were dated to circa 1825, which is unlikely as this would predate all similar Staffordshire figures. In the authors' opinion the figure is more likely to have been made in the late 1830s/1840s.
Both the back and front of the figure is illustrated.
HEIGHT: 8 Inches
PRICE: D.

Fig. 2134A
A clock face group of a man and woman standing on either side; he wears a hat, jacket, shirt with tie, waistcoat, and trousers. She wears a bonnet, jacket, skirt with an apron, and a scarf over her shoulder and held in her left hand. They both rest a hand on a shield that contains various articles, including a beehive, open book, bird, leaf, and two other items.
The shield clearly has significance, although the authors are unaware as to what it is. If it can be determined exactly what the shield represents, then what this figure represents might be known.
HEIGHT: 9 Inches
PRICE: F.

Fig. 2137A
A group figure of a girl seated and a boy standing to the side of a water fountain from which water flows; she is bareheaded and wears a blouse and skirt with an apron. She holds a bucket on her lap. He stands cross-legged, wearing a plumed hat, frilled shirt with tie, jacket, and knee breeches. To his left on rockwork is a large jug.
HEIGHT: 6 Inches
PRICE: G.

Fig. 2137B
A figure of a man standing, wearing a plumed hat, jacket with short sleeves, knee breeches, and boots. His left hand rests on rockwork in which there is a bowl from which water pours. There is a jug below catching the water.
This figure is quite rare and very well modelled. It is probable that there is a pair but it is as yet unrecorded. Fig. 2137C has been reserved for it.
HEIGHT: 11.75 Inches
PRICE: E.

Fig. 2139C
A figure of a boy standing, wearing a hat, frilled shirt, jacket, and knee breeches, holding a spaniel under his right arm. At his feet on rockwork stands a large jug. **There is a pair to this figure. Fig. 2139D has been reserved for it.**
HEIGHT: 8 Inches
PRICE: Pair: F, Singles: G.

Fig. 2139A
A figure of a boy standing, wearing a long jacket, frilled shirt, breeches tied at the waist, and a scarf over his shoulder and under his arm. He is holding a pitcher on his right shoulder with his left hand. A spaniel sits at his feet. To the other side is a small fence.
There is a pair to this figure. Fig. 2139B has been reserved for it.
HEIGHT: 7 Inches
PRICE: Pair: F, Singles: G.

Fig. 2139E
A figure of a boy standing with his legs crossed, wearing a hat with feather, shirt with collar, jacket, kilt with sporran, and socks and shoes. He holds a spaniel in his arms. To his right on rockwork a large pitches rests, below which a streams flows. **There is a pair to this figure. Fig. 2139F has been reserved for it.**
HEIGHT: 9.75 Inches
PRICE: G.

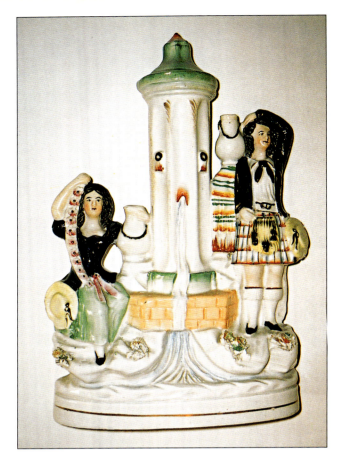

Fig. 2139G

A group figure of a boy and girl, she seated, he standing on either side of a water fountain. She is bareheaded and wears a jacket and long skirt. Her hat rests at her side. She holds a garland aloft with her right hand and her left rests on a pitcher. He wears a shirt with tie, short jacket, kilt with sporran, and a scarf over his right shoulder. His left hand holds a pitcher on his right shoulder. A stream of water pours from the fountain through brickwork to the ground below. HEIGHT: 12 Inches
PRICE: E.

Fig. 2141B

A standing figure of a man with one foot raised onto a water fountain that has a lion's head ornament on it. He wears a plumed hat and highland attire. His left hand is on his hip and his right is around a water pitcher that he holds on his leg. **There is a pair to this figure (they are probably the finest of the water fountain figures). Fig. 2241A has been reserved for it**.
HEIGHT: 9.25 Inches
PRICE: Pair: E, Singles: F.

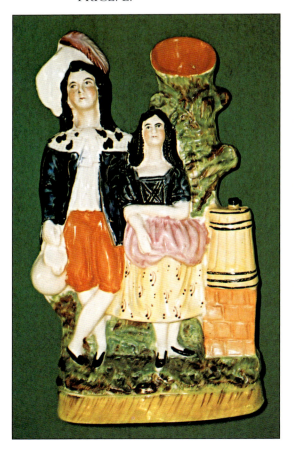

Fig. 2139H

A group spill vase figure of a man and woman standing side by side; he wears a hat with feather, ermine edged cloak, jacket, shirt, and knee breeches. He holds a jug in his right hand and his left is around the woman. She wears a blouse and long skirt with an apron. By her side on a brick pillar a cask rests.
HEIGHT: 8.5 Inches
PRICE: F

Figs. 2141C/2141D

A pair of figures of a man and woman standing by water fountains. To his right and her left a large pot of flowers stands on a plinth. Both adults wear plumed hats, he a shirt, waistcoat, jacket, breeches, and a scarf over his left shoulder. He holds a spade in his left hand and a watering can rests on the bottom of the fountain. She wears a bodice and long skirt with knickers showing and holds a watering can in her right hand; a rake rests against the fountain.
HEIGHT: 8.5 Inches
PRICE: Pair: E, Singles: F.

Fig. 2142D
A spill vase figure of a girl standing, wearing a plumed hat, blouse with sash, and skirt with knickers. She holds a watering can in her left hand and pours water onto the ground below. **There is a pair to this figure. Fig. 2142E has been reserved for it.**
HEIGHT: 7.25 Inches
PRICE: Pair: G, Singles: H.

Fig. 2142A
A group figure of a man standing, wearing a turban, shirt, long jacket, and knee breeches tied at the waist with a scarf. He holds a pail in his right hand and a bird is perched on his left. The woman is seated, wearing a turban, jacket, and long skirt. She holds a pail on her lap and her right hand is upon the handle of a well that is between them.
This is a finely modelled and coloured group, but unfortunately it has been damaged and badly restored. The top of the well has been lost.
Not having a figure to copy from, the restorer has used his imagination and the wellhead now bears little resemblance to the one the potter originally created.
HEIGHT: 8.5 Inches
PRICE: (As is) H.

Fig. 2142B
A figure of a boy standing by a water pump with the handle in both hands; he wears a cap, tie, smock, short trousers, and socks. At the bottom of the pump a jug stands and flowers grow up the pump. **There is a pair to this figure. Fig. 2142C has been reserved for it.**
HEIGHT: 7.5 Inches
PRICE: Pair: F, Singles: G.

Figs. 2143/2143A
A pair of figures of a boy and girl seated on rockwork; both children are bareheaded and barefooted. He wears an open necked shirt, short jacket, and trousers turned up to the knee. His hat is by his left hand. Two streams flow from the rock-work, one by his foot, the other by his side. A string handled pitcher stands by the stream. She wears a jacket buttoned at the neck and long skirt. To her left on top of the rockwork stands a large pitcher. A stream flows from the rockwork. HEIGHT: 8.75 Inches
PRICE: Pair: F, Singles: G.

Figs. 2145A/2145B
A pair of figures of a man and woman, both holding bottles on their shoulders with one hand, the other is on the waist. To his left and her right is a small picket fence. He wears a short jacket, shirt with tie, knee length trousers with boots, and a scarf tied around his waist. A goat is standing on its hind legs with its forehooves on his waist. She wears a short jacket, blouse, and long-skirt. A sheep stands on its hind legs at her side with its forehooves on her waist.
This pair is an adaptation of Figs. 2145/2146 Book Two. The male figure is identical other than a goat replaces the dog and a picket fence replaces the brick well. She is also very similar, other than her dress has been altered and a fence replaces the brick well.
Which pair was made first and why they were altered is impossible to say with certainty; they are both by the same modeller. Possibly he adapted them and supplied the second pair to a different potter.
HEIGHT: 9 Inches
PRICE: Pair: E, Singles: F.

Fig. 2150E
A standing figure of a girl who is bare-headed and wearing a blouse and skirt tied at the waist with a sash. In her left hand she holds a jug and her right hand leans on rockwork below which water flows.
There is a pair to this figure. Fig. 2150D has been reserved for it.
HEIGHT: 11 Inches
PRICE: G.

Figs. 2149G/2149H
A pair of figures of a woman and man standing on a brick arch under which a swan swims. They both lean on rock-work, and she wears a bodice, blouse, and skirt with an apron. She holds a jug in her right hand. He wears a shirt, jacket, and knee length trousers tied at the waist with a scarf and holds a jug in his left hand.
HEIGHT: 8.75 Inches
PRICE: Pair: F, Singles: G

Fig. 2154A
A spill vase group of a girl and boy standing on either side of a tree trunk that has a brick built well beneath. She wears a scarf over her head, bodice, and skirt with an apron. He wears a hat, jacket, shirt, scarf around his waist, and knee length breeches. Both children lean on the top of the well. HEIGHT: 8 Inches
PRICE: H.

Fig. 2155B
A spill vase group of a boy and girl standing on either side of a well; he wears a jacket, open necked shirt, and knee breeches. His hat hangs from his right arm and he holds a cup. His left hand rests on a bucket. She wears a bodice and long skirt with an apron. Her hat is over her arm and she holds a bird in her left hand. Her right hand rests on the bucket. From the well a stream flows.
HEIGHT: 10.75 Inches
PRICE: H.

Fig. 2154B
An arbour group figure of a man standing and a woman seated; he wears highland garb of cap, shirt, tunic, kilt, boots, and a large scarf across his chest and over his shoulder. His left foot is raised and rests on a brick built well from which a stream runs. He holds a jug in his left hand. She wears a blouse and jacket with a long skirt with an apron; her hands rest in her lap. A jug rests against the arbour.
HEIGHT: 10.5 Inches
PRICE: G.

Fig. 2155C
A group figure of a woman and man on either side of a well; she wears a headdress, bodice, and skirt with an apron. Her left hand rests on a bucket that sits on the well. He wears a hat, shirt, waistcoat, and trousers. His left hand is in his pocket and his right rests on her headdress.
HEIGHT: 8 Inches
PRICE: F.

Fig. 2156D
A group figure of a man and woman standing side by side, he with his arm around her. Both adults are barefooted and she wears a long dress with an apron. Her arm rests on a sheaf of wheat that stands on a well at the bottom from which a jug fills with water. He wears a shirt with large collar, jacket, and short trousers, and holds a jug by its handle in his left hand. HEIGHT: 10 Inches
PRICE: F.

Fig. 2156C
A spill vase group figure of a man and woman standing on either side of a tree below, which is a well with a jug on top. She wears a headscarf tied at the neck, blouse, and long skirt with an apron. Her left hand is held to her chest and her right holds a jug by its handle. He wears a brimmed hat, shirt with tie, jacket, and knee breeches and has a bundle under his left arm.
HEIGHT: 12 Inches
PRICE: G.

Fig. 2156E
A figure of a woman standing, wearing a flowing robe. Her left hand holds a basket of grapes on her shoulder; her right hand is by her side.
There is a pair to this large and imposing figure, which might have a religious source. Fig. 2156F has been reserved for it.
HEIGHT: 14 Inches.
PRICE: G.

Fig. 2158D
A figure of a boy standing; he has long hair and wears a tunic, frilled skirt, knickers, shoes and socks. A satchel is at his waist secured by a sash across his chest. In his right hand he holds a string, which secures a sheaf of wheat. He holds a jug on his head with his left hand.
There is no doubt a pair to this figure. Fig. 2158D has been reserved for it.
HEIGHT: 9 Inches
PRICE: G.

Fig. 2163C
A group figure of a man and woman standing, he with his arm around her waist, she with her arm on his chest. She holds a jug in her left hand and wears a hat, blouse, and skirt with an apron. He is long haired and wears a frilled shirt, jacket, and knee breeches. His left hand holds the handle of a well that is to his left, a bucket and chain is to the front, and flowers grow up the side of the well.
HEIGHT: 10 Inches
PRICE: F.

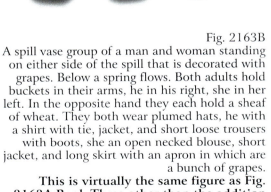

Fig. 2161A
A standing figure of a boy wearing a brimmed hat, shirt with tie, long jacket, and knee breeches. His right hand is on his waist and his left holds a yoke. Two milk pails stand on a platform by his feet, all on a rococo base.
There is a pair to this very rare figure. Fig. 2161B has been reserved for it.
HEIGHT: 9 Inches
PRICE: G.

Fig. 2163B
A spill vase group of a man and woman standing on either side of the spill that is decorated with grapes. Below a spring flows. Both adults hold buckets in their arms, he in his right, she in her left. In the opposite hand they each hold a sheaf of wheat. They both wear plumed hats, he with a shirt with tie, jacket, and short loose trousers with boots, she an open necked blouse, short jacket, and long skirt with an apron in which are a bunch of grapes.
This is virtually the same figure as Fig. 2163A Book Three other than the addition of a spill vase.
HEIGHT: 11.75 Inches
PRICE: F.

Fig. 2167B
A standing figure of a woman wearing a hat with a brim, bodice, and skirt with an apron. She is barefooted and stands on the edge of a stream. She holds a large empty basket over her left shoulder. Her right hand rests on rockwork to her side.
It is not clear as to what this figure signifies; she may be a washerwoman, but no clothes are evident. It is probable that there is a pair. Fig. 2167A has been reserved for it.
HEIGHT: 7 Inches
PRICE: G.

Figs. 2171A/2171B
A pair of mounted figures of a Gypsy man and woman facing left and right who both hold a child on their lap. She wears a long skirt and a large shawl is draped over both her and the child. He wears a top hat, scarf tied around his neck, jacket, waistcoat, and trousers with boots. He holds a basket of fruit in his right hand.
TITLE: 'GYPSYS' (sic)
HEIGHT: 13.5 Inches
PRICE: Pair: E, Singles: F.

Figs. 2173A/2173B
A pair of figures of a man and woman seated on horses; he wears a brimmed hat, shirt with tie, jacket, and trousers. His right hand is on his hip and his left holds the reins. A basket of fruit is in his lap. She wears a brimmed hat, jacket, and long dress. Her right hand is on the horse's neck and her left holds the reins. A basket of fruit is on her lap.
A finely modelled pair, probably a version of 'Going to market and returning home'.
HEIGHT: 10.25 Inches
PRICE: Pair: E, Singles: F.

Fig. 2177A
A spill vase group of a boy standing in a tree wearing Scottish attire of Tam o' Shanter, shirt, tunic, kilt, and tartan stockings. Below, a girl stands with one hand on the neck of a mule that is standing eating with panniers on its back. **This figure is a product of 'The Green factory'. There is probably a pair to this figure. Fig. 2177B has been reserved for it.**
HEIGHT: 10 Inches
PRICE: F.

Figs. 2177C/2177D
A pair of spill vase figures of a donkey standing with panniers filled with flowers. To his left a man sits wearing a hat, jacket, shirt, and knee breeches. His left hand holds the donkey's reins and over his right arm is a basket of flowers. The pair is almost a mirror image with a girl replacing the man.
HEIGHT: 9 Inches
PRICE: Pair: F, Singles: G.

Fig. 2179A
A figure of a girl standing, wearing a brimmed hat, shawl, blouse, and long skirt. To her side she has one arm around a pile of faggotts.
There is probably a pair to this figure. Fig. 2179B has been reserved for it.
HEIGHT: 7 Inches
PRICE: G.

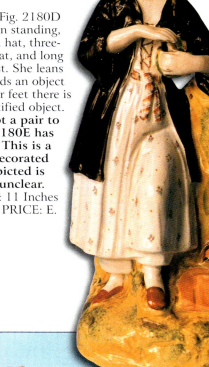

Fig. 2180D
A figure of a woman standing, wearing a brimmed hat, three-quarter length coat, and long dress tied at the waist. She leans on rockwork and holds an object in both hands. At her feet there is another unidentified object.
There is no doubt a pair to this figure. Fig. 2180E has been reserved for it. This is a well modelled and decorated figure. What is depicted is unclear.
HEIGHT: 11 Inches
PRICE: E.

Figs. 2180/2180A
A pair of figures of a man and woman standing, he wears a hat, coat, waistcoat, and knee breeches with leggings. He carries a bundle of faggots on his shoulder and another under his arm. Over his right arm he carries a bag and in his hand a chopper. A dog is seated by his left leg. She wears a bodice, blouse, and a skirt with an apron. Her hat is suspended from her left arm, her right holds a bunch of faggots on her head. To her left, a water barrel stands on a trunk below which a stream issues from brickwork.
A very large and imposing pair, she is previously unrecorded.
HEIGHT: 14.25 Inches
PRICE: Pair: D, Singles: E.

Fig. 2181
A figure of a standing woodchopper, his left foot raised on rockwork. He wears a hat, long coat, shirt with tie, waistcoat, and knee breeches with leggings. A large bound bunch of faggots is carried over his left shoulder and over his right on a sash is suspended a small box. He holds an axe in his left hand. His dog is seated on raised rockwork to his left.
HEIGHT: 13 Inches
PRICE: E.

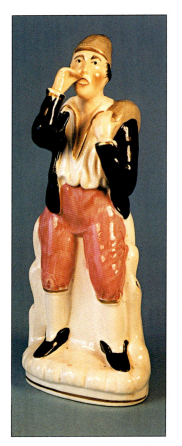

Fig. 2181A
A figure of a man standing, wearing a moleskin cap, open necked shirt, jacket, and breeches. He holds a bag over his left shoulder and his right is held to his mouth. **This figure depicts 'The Mole Man' and he is shown calling. In Victorian times there were many such characters that earned their living touring the countryside catching vermin, often doubling as rat-catchers as well. Their caps were made from moleskins.**
It is possible that this figure is of a pair or series. Each would depict a particular trade or street occupation.
HEIGHT: 8 Inches
PRICE: E.

Fig. 2181C
A figure of a woman seated, wearing a plumed hat with feather, open sleeved blouse, a sash over her left shoulder and across her chest, and an aproned skirt. She is plucking a duck that rests on her lap. **This figure is modelled in the round and was made circa 1835, probably by Lloyd Shelton. There is no doubt a pair to this figure. Fig. 2181D has been reserved for it.**
HEIGHT: 8.25 Inches.
PRICE: G.

Fig. 2181B
A spill vase group figure of a boy chasing a rabbit; he wears a cap, shirt with tie, jacket, and knee breeches. His left hand holds his cap as he leaps over a style. His dog is below, and is chasing a rabbit that is running into a culvert.
This is a very rare and well modelled group and is from the same factory or modeller who made Figs. 2661, 2662 Book Two, and it is possible that there is a pair to this figure, but it is as yet unrecorded.
HEIGHT: 9.75 Inches
PRICE: E.

Fig. 2182B
A group figure of two washerwomen, both have headbands and wear a blouse and long skirt. The one on the left holds her skirt and treads on the clothes in a bucket, the other holds a cloth in both hands.
This is a particularly well-modelled and delicately coloured figure and early from the mould as the delineation of the fingers and toes indicates.
HEIGHT: 11 Inches
PRICE: E.

Fig. 2190A
A group of a standing man wearing a hat with a feather, shirt, waistcoat, jacket, and breeches. In his right hand he holds a dish with coins in; his left arm is around a monkey which sits on a cushioned pillar and wears a hat, coat, and trousers.
This group depicts a circus act or possibly a street entertainer, and there is probably a pair. Fig. 2190B has been reserved for it.
HEIGHT: 6.5 Inches
PRICE: F.

Fig. 2182C
A spill vase group of two women standing in front of an arbour on which two birds are perched. The woman on the left wears a hat and full length coat buttoned to the ground. The woman to the right wears a decorated blouse and long coat and dress. She holds a spray of flowers in her hands.
The authors believe that this rare figure depicts a wedding group of the bride and bridesmaid; if this is so there may well be a companion group of the groom and best man.
HEIGHT: 11 Inches
PRICE: E.

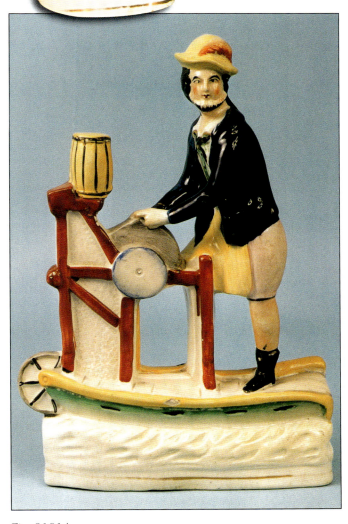

Fig. 2188A
A small figure of a man standing wearing a brimmed hat, jacket, waistcoat, and trousers. He holds a parcel or loaf with his left hand and a joint of meat in his right.
This figure, which is extremely rare, is titled. It is previously unrecorded.
TITLE: FREE TRADE
HEIGHT: 4 Inches
PRICE: E.

Fig. 2191A
A figure of a man standing, working on a knife grinder. He wears a hat with a feather, shirt with tie, jacket, and knee breeches.
This is a quite rare figure and always commands a relatively high price.
The source for this figure is a painting by Tenier that appeared as a print on the front of *The Penny Magazine* **No. 145 in July 1834. A Baxter print was also made using the same source.**
HEIGHT: 10.5 Inches
PRICE: D.

Fig. 2192A
A standing figure of a man wearing the uniform of a policeman and holding a truncheon; there are small holes in the helmet and this figure was made for use as a saltshaker. HEIGHT: 6 Inches
PRICE: H.

Fig. 2195B
A group figure of a boy seated on rockwork, wearing a plumed hat, open necked shirt, jacket, kilt, and a sash over his shoulder and a scarf over his left arm. His right hand rests on the roof of a mill house. A squirrel sits on the roof of the house and is eating a nut.
A quite wonderful figure, and all out of proportion. Clearly the boy is far to large in proportion to the house, and the squirrel far to large in proportion to the boy, but all in all the whole composition is charming and well modelled. A very rare figure and a pair probably exists. Fig. 2195C has been reserved for it.
HEIGHT: 9.5 Inches
PRICE: E.

Figs. 2194A/2194B
A pair of figures of a boy and girl seated on tree stumps, holding spoons in their right hand and holding a bowl on their lap with their left. He wears a shirt with tie, jacket, and long trousers; she wears a bodice and long dress with an apron.
This pair of figures of children eating porridge is extremely rare. They were the product of The Parr factory. The figures illustrated are the only pair known to the authors, and are in pristine condition, having survived intact since they were made in circa 1850. A very charming and attractive pair.
HEIGHT: 7 Inches
PRICE: Pair: E, Singles: F.

Figs. 2195D/2195E
A pair of figures of a girl seated, one wearing a headscarf tied at the neck, bodice, and a long skirt with a slip showing. She has one hand to her chest. On her lap and at her feet is a round flat object. A basket is to her side, partly covered by a cloth. A cat stands on its hind legs with its paws on the object. The other girl is bareheaded and wears a long dress with an apron. A sheet is on her lap and partly in a basket that is on the floor to her right side. A barrel is to her left and a dog sits on its hind legs with its paws in her lap.
These are very rare and extremely well modelled figures. They appear to depict girls either repairing or washing linen.
HEIGHT: 9 Inches
PRICE: Pair: D, Singles: E.

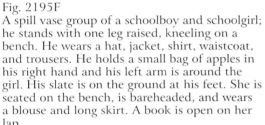

Fig. 2195F
A spill vase group of a schoolboy and schoolgirl; he stands with one leg raised, kneeling on a bench. He wears a hat, jacket, shirt, waistcoat, and trousers. He holds a small bag of apples in his right hand and his left arm is around the girl. His slate is on the ground at his feet. She is seated on the bench, is bareheaded, and wears a blouse and long skirt. A book is open on her lap.
HEIGHT: 7 Inches
PRICE: G.

Fig. 2198F
A spill vase campfire group of a man and woman standing on either side of a suspended cooking pot, she to the left is dressed in highland garb of plumed hat, tunic, ermine edged cloak, and kilt, he to the right wearing a hat, shirt and tie, waistcoat, jacket, and knee breeches. His arms are folded across his chest. A fire burns beneath the cooking pot.
HEIGHT: 9.25 Inches
PRICE: F.

Fig. 2196B
A spill vase arbour campfire group of a man on one side and his wife and child on the other side of a fire over which is suspended a cooking pot. Below is a dead hind and a seated dog. The man wears a hat, shirt with tie, long coat, and trousers. The wife wears a hat, blouse, and long dress, the child a blouse and skirt. **There are a number of these 'campfire' groups and pairs, no doubt meant to portray 'travellers' or gypsies. Some are better modelled and decorated than others. This is quite a poor example.**
HEIGHT: 8.5 Inches
PRICE: G.

Fig. 2198G
A spill vase campfire group of a man seated and woman standing on either side of a fire over which is suspended a cooking pot. She wears a headscarf, blouse, and skirt and holds a bird in her hand; he wears a hat, open necked shirt with tie, jacket, and knee breeches and holds a large hare.
HEIGHT: 9 Inches
PRICE: F.

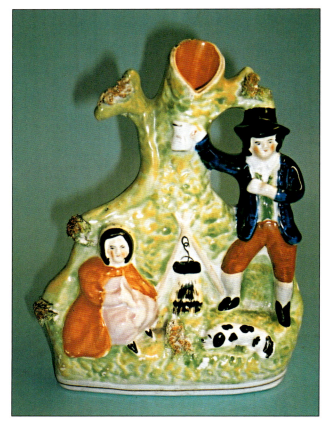

Figs. 2198J/2198K
A pair of spill vase figures of a man and woman seated around a camp fire with one foot on a barrel. He wears a hat, open necked shirt, waistcoat, long coat, and knee breeches. His legs are crossed and one hand is held inside his coat. To his right a cooking pot is suspended over the fire and a girl stands beside it. She wears a cloak over her head, bodice, and long skirt and a boy stands to her left beside the fire over which a cooking pot is suspended.
HEIGHT: 8 Inches
PRICE: Pair: E, Singles: F.

Fig. 2198M
A spill vase group figure of a man standing and a woman seated on either side of a camp fire; he wears a top hat, shirt, waistcoat, jacket, and trousers. He holds a mug aloft in his right hand. A dog lies at his feet. She is seated, wearing a cloak and dress.
HEIGHT: 7.5 Inches
PRICE: H.

Fig. 2198L
A group spill vase figure of two men holding hands and dancing around a campfire; one holds his hand to his hat and wears a hat, waistcoat, long jacket, and breeches, the other wears a short coat, waistcoat, and trousers. A cooking pot is suspended over the fire.
HEIGHT: 5 Inches
PRICE: G.

Fig. 2200E
An arbour group of two women and a man; the arbour is covered with a grapevine and the man stands, wearing a brimmed pointed hat, open necked shirt, jacket, and trousers. Both women are seated and one wears a headdress, scarf, and long dress with bodice, the other wears a brimmed hat and long dress with a scarf over both shoulders. All the figures are holding playing cards to their chests and one has two open cards on her lap.
A very unusual and rare group of three people playing cards.
HEIGHT: 11 Inches
PRICE: E.

Fig. 2200F
A spill vase group of a man climbing a tree and a woman standing by a fence below; she wears a hat with feather, blouse, scarf, and long skirt. Her right hand is on her hip and her left clasped to her chest. He wears a hat with feather, open neck shirt, jacket, and trousers. In his right hand he holds a bird that he has taken from a nest.
HEIGHT: 10 Inches
PRICE: G.

Fig. 2205A
A figure of a seated highlander wearing typical attire of Tam O' Shanter, tunic, shirt, kilt with sporran, and shoes and socks. A bag is strapped over his shoulder. Both his arms and legs are crossed. **Two figures are illustrated, identical apart from decoration. This figure has an unusually shaped base. The authors have not seen a pair; two identical figures could be used as bookends. If they were made for use as bookends these would be the only ones known.**
HEIGHT: 6 Inches
PRICE: G.

Fig. 2201C
A figure of a man seated; he wears a hat, shirt, waistcoat, jacket, and knee breeches. His left arm rests on rockwork and he holds a rifle by its barrel in his left hand.
This figure is very similar to Fig. 2201A Book Three and there is no doubt a pair to this figure. Fig. 2201D has been reserved for it. Fig. 2201A, because of poor modelling of the rifle, has often been described as 'a man with a golf club', on which it sold for an undeserved high price. With the discovery of Fig. 2201C it can with certainly be seen that the figure and its pair has nothing to do with golf.
HEIGHT: 5 Inches
PRICE: H.

Fig. 2207A
A standing figure of a Welsh woman who wears a Welsh hat with headscarf, long jacket, and long skirt with an apron. She holds a bag in her left hand and a filled basket is over her right. **This is a very rare and quite large figure; the one illustrated is the only one recorded. There was probably a pair made and Fig. 2207B has been reserved for it. Welsh figures are all quite rare and sought after.**
HEIGHT: 12.75 Inches
PRICE: D.

Figs. 2208A/2208B
A pair of figures of a Welsh tailor and his wife seated on the back of standing goats; she wears a costume of Welsh hat with bonnet, shawl, and long dress with an apron, and carries a basket in one hand. He also wears Welsh costume of steeple hat, jacket, waistcoat, tie, and breeches. He carries an iron is in his lap and a parcel is on his back.
Welsh costumed figures are highly sought after and desirable. These figures are very rare.
HEIGHT: 11 Inches
PRICE: Pair: D, Singles: E.

Figs. 2209D/2209E
A pair of standing figures of a man and woman dressed in traditional Welsh attire, both wearing Welsh hats, she with a shawl, blouse, and skirt with an apron. Her right hand rests on rockwork and her left is at her waist. He wears a long jacket, shirt with tie, waistcoat, and trousers. He holds a bundle on a stick over his right shoulder.
These are extremely rare figures, the only pair known to the authors. Because of their subject matter they are very collectable.
HEIGHT: 10 Inches
PRICE: Pair: C, Singles: E.

Fig. 2209F
A standing figure of a Welsh woman dressed in typical Welsh costume holding a baby in her arms.
There is probably a pair to this figure. Fig. 2209G has been reserved for it.
TITLE: WELSH COSTUME
HEIGHT: 4.5 Inches
PRICE: F.

Figs. 2209B/2209A
A pair of standing figures of a Welshman and woman dressed in typical Welsh costume, he with brimmed hat, shirt, long coat, and breeches, she with Welsh hat and bonnet, shirt, and long skirt. He holds his lapel with one hand and a basket in the other. She has a basket over her left arm and holds a pot in her right.
She is a rare figure. He is extremely rare. This pair has a centrepiece (see Fig. 2208 Book Two). They depict a Welsh farmer and his wife. The source for this pair is a print of Welsh National Costumes, a copy of which is in The National Museum of Wales.
HEIGHT: 9.5 Inches
PRICE: Pair: D, Singles: E.

Figs. 2211C/2211D

A pair of figures of a woman and man seated in chairs; the woman has a boy standing at her side and her hands are in her lap holding an open book. She wears a mop cap, bodice, and long dress. The boy wears a long coat and knee breeches. The man has a girl standing at his side and has both hands on his thighs. He wears a neckerchief, shirt, waistcoat, long jacket, and knee breeches. The girl is holding an open book and wears a long dress with a ribbon around her waist.
These figures can be found in two sizes, both illustrated.
TITLE: GRANDMAS HOPE - GRANDPAS JOY
HEIGHT: 8.5 & 11 Inches
PRICE: Pair: E, Singles: F.

Figs. 2213A/2213B

A pair of figures of 'Courtship' and 'Marriage'; the group on the right depicts a courting couple seated, he with his arm around her wearing a shirt, cravat, long coat, and trousers. His hat is on the floor by his feet. She wears a long dress and holds an open book in her lap. The group on the left shows them both dressed as before, this time she holds a baby in her lap. A dog is at his feet and a cat at hers. Both figures are on arched, gilt lined bases.
A very rare pair, probably made by John & Rebecca Lloyd. This factory, whilst in existence, continued to make figures in the round with many separate moulds, much in the tradition of pre-Victorian figures. They ceased manufacture in 1852 and are not known to have made 'flatbacks'.
HEIGHT: 6.25 Inches
PRICE: Pair: D, Singles: E.

Figs. 2211E/2211F
A pair of figures of a woman and man seated in chairs; the woman has a boy standing by her side reading a book. She wears a mop cap and dress with an apron. He wears a cap, shirt, waistcoat, jacket, and knee breeches. By his side stands a girl and he has his hand upon her head.
These are earlier than figures 2210/2211 Book Two. These figures were made in the early 1830s.
TITLE: Grandmother – Grandfather
HEIGHT: 7.5 Inches
PRICE: Pair: E, Singles: F.

Fig. 2215A
A group figure of a man seated on a chair and a girl standing by his side; he is bareheaded and wears a shirt, waistcoat, jacket, and trousers. His legs are crossed and he has an open book on his lap. She wears a blouse, skirt with an apron, and knickers.
It is probable that this figure is either another version of 'Grandpas Joy' or it could depict a schoolmaster and pupil. If so, there would be a pair. Fig. 2215B has been reserved for it.
HEIGHT: 7 Inches
PRICE: F.

Fig. 2215C
A group figure of a girl seated in a draped throne wearing a necklace and long tiered dress, reading from an open book to a small child who stands by her side. The child holds a book in her left hand.
There is probably a pair to this figure. Fig. 2215D has been reserved for it.
HEIGHT: 11.5 Inches
PRICE: F.

Chapter 5:
Children with Animals

Children with animals took sentimentality to the extreme and the potters were happy to produce what the public wanted. At one time or another nearly every figure of a child with an animal has been attributed as being of one of the Royal Children. The potters did produce such figures but these have been included in the Portrait Chapter. These attributions were made, usually for commercial reasons. Up until recently portrait figures fetched more than decorative, but that situation has now changed, mainly due to the American market, where collectors are content to collect the figures for their charm and not their personality.

In any event production of figures of children with animals continued well after the Royal children had entered adulthood, so even if the original intention was to portray the Royal children this was lost in time and figures continued to be produced.

As well as the potteries making children with dogs, they also made figures of children with lambs, goats, and a whole host of animals, even including rats!

We have also included in this chapter milkmen and maids.

Listings highlighted in bold type contain additions and alterations which will be found in this addendum. All other Portraits will be found in *Books One and Three, Victorian Staffordshire Figures 1835-1875*.

This chapter is divided into the following sections:

i. Children with Dogs
ii. Children with Birds
iii. Children with Cows
iv. Children with Deer/Fawn
v. Children with Foxes
vi. Children with Goats
vii. Children with Horses/Donkeys/Ponies/ Mules
viii. Children with Lions
ix. Children with Rabbits
x. Children with Rats
xi. Children with Sheep
xii. Children with Zebras

i. Children with Dogs
See Figures 2221 - 2305A Books Two and Three

Figs. 2226C/2226D
A pair of figures of scantily dressed children seated on the backs of red and white spaniels; both children hold bows in one hand and arrows in the other, all on underglaze blue gilt lined bases.
HEIGHT: 6.25 Inches
PRICE: Pair: D, Singles: E.

Figs. 2226E/2226F
A pair of spill vase groups of a boy and girl seated next to a tree trunk in which there is a bird's nest; she wears a brimmed hat, coat, and long dress. He wears a hat, coat with collar, and trousers. A dog lies at their feet.
HEIGHT: 4.5 Inches
PRICE: Pair: F, Singles: G.

Figs. 2227/2228
A pair of spill vase figures of a girl and boy asleep beside a tree in which a large snake is entwined. At their feet are two sheep and, to her right and his left, a large dog stands with one paw raised, protecting the children from the snake.
A very attractive pair of figures, quite rare and very sought after.
HEIGHT: 11.25 Inches
PRICE: Pair: C, Singles: E.

Figs. 2238C/2238D
A pair of figures of a boy and girl standing to either side of a kennel; both wear plumed hats, she a bodice and dress with an apron in which there are flowers, he wears a shirt and kilt with a scarf over his shoulder and through his arm. On top of the kennel beside her a rabbit sits on its haunches. On the kennel beside him a dog sits on its hind legs. He has one arm around it.
HEIGHT: 7 Inches
PRICE: Pair: E, Singles: F.

Figs. 2230/2229
A pair of figures of a boy and girl seated above clock faces, which are encircled by flowers and foliage. To their sides two dogs sit, by her spaniels, by him poodles, both with flags above them. They both hold a feeding bowl in both hands. She wears a blouse and long skirt. He sits cross-legged with a drum at his feet and wears a shirt and skirt.
A matched pair, he is illustrated in the white, she in full colour.
HEIGHT: 11.5 Inches
PRICE: Pair: D, Singles: E.

Figs. 2239/2240
A pair of figures of a boy and girl seated on the backs of spaniels; each child has a drum suspended at the waist by a strap over the shoulders. Both children wear plumed hats, he a shirt with tie, jacket, and trousers, she a bodice and long skirt. Both hold the chain lead of the spaniels that face left and right. By their side is a small table on which is a bowl, each on a shaped gilt lined base.
HEIGHT: 9.5 Inches
PRICE: Pair: D, Singles: E.

Figs. 2240F/2240G
A pair of spill vase figures of a boy and girl seated in trees; both children wear similar clothes of bodice/tunic and skirt/kilt and each hold a hat in their hands. Below each is a kennel outside of which two spaniels are recumbent.
HEIGHT: 8 Inches
PRICE: Pair: E, Singles: F.

Fig. 2240J
A spill vase group figure of a girl seated, wearing a plumed hat, short jacket, long skirt, and a scarf over her arm. She holds her hat in her left hand. To her side is a tree and below a kennel on which a spaniel stands with his hind legs on the top of the kennel and his forepaws against the tree. **There is a pair to this figure. Fig. 2240K has been reserved for it.**
HEIGHT: 7.5 Inches
PRICE: F.

Fig. 2240H
A group figure of a girl standing beside and a boy seated on a kennel; he wears a plumed hat, open necked shirt, jacket, and trousers. She wears a hat, bodice, jacket, skirt, and a scarf over her shoulder and through her arm. Below and to the right of the kennel two dogs sit.
HEIGHT: 7.5 Inches
PRICE: G.

Fig. 2240L
A spill vase figure of a girl seated in front of a tree stump, wearing a fur edged coat, long skirt, and knickers. A whippet lies on rockwork beside her with its forepaws in her lap. She has her left hand on the dog's back and her right rests on its neck. **There is possibly a pair to this figure. Fig. 2240M has been reserved for it.**
HEIGHT: 9 Inches
PRICE: G.

Figs. 2242G/2242H
A pair of spill vase groups of a boy and girl seated in a tree above a kennel; both children wear plumed hats, tunic/bodice, kilt/skirt, and have a scarf over their shoulder. A dog sits in their laps. Beside the kennel a large spaniel sits and a smaller one is recumbent in the kennel.
HEIGHT: 8 Inches
PRICE: Pair: D, Singles: E.

Figs. 2243A/2244A
A pair of figures of a boy and girl seated on the back of a standing dog, the girl with one hand in her lap and the other resting on the head of the dog. She is wearing a plumed hat, blouse, and a skirt with an apron. The boy wears a plumed hat, jacket, and kilt; he also has one hand on the head of the dog and the other in his lap. **This pair is a variant of Figures 2243/2244 Book Two, the main difference being that they are sitting rather than lying on the dog. These are extremely rare figures. They are a matched pair as the dog in one is red and white and in the other black and white. There are only three figures of her recorded and only the one of him.**
HEIGHT: 9 Inches
PRICE: Pair: C, Singles: D.

Figs. 2242L/2242M
A pair of figures of a boy and girl seated on a brick built rabbit hutch. To his left and her right a spaniel is standing on its hind legs with its paws on their laps. They both wear hats, tunic/blouse, and kilt/skirt. Below and at the entrance to the hutch a rabbit sits, and she holds in her arms another rabbit. HEIGHT: 8 Inches
PRICE: Pair: D, Singles: E.

Fig. 2244D
A spill vase figure of a girl seated on rockwork wearing a bodice and long skirt. On her right hand, which is raised to her shoulder, a bird is perched. To her left a dog sits and she has her left hand on its back. The base is rococo and covered in large leaves. **A very rare figure that the authors have not seen before. There must have existed a pair and Fig. 2244E has been reserved for it. The price given is for the figure in the white as illustrated. Should a coloured version be found, it would command approximately three times the price.**
HEIGHT: 6 Inches
PRICE: G.

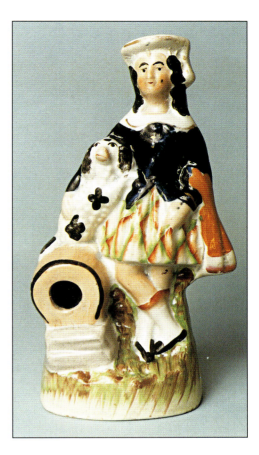

Figs. 2246E/2246F
A pair of figures of a boy and girl standing; he wears a plumed hat, frilled shirt, jacket, knee breeches, and a scarf over his shoulder. She wears a plumed hat, bodice, a skirt with an apron, and a large scarf over her shoulder. To one side of them a poodle sits on a barrel with its forepaws on their waist.
HEIGHT: 8 Inches
PRICE: Pair: E, Singles: F.

Fig. 2246I/2246J
A pair of figures of a boy and girl standing, he cross-legged wearing a hat, shirt with collar, tunic, and kilt with a scarf through his arm. To his right on steps is a barrel on which a dog sits on its haunches with its forepaws on the boys waist. The boy has an arm around the dog. She wears a hat with feather, blouse, skirt with an apron, and knickers. To her left is a barrel, which rests on steps. A dog sits on the barrel with its forepaws on her waist. Her arm is around the dog. HEIGHT: 8 Inches
PRICE: Pair: E, Singles: F.

Fig. 2246G
A figure of a boy seated on a barrel wearing a plumed hat, frilled shirt, tunic, kilt, and a scarf over his shoulder. His hands are in his lap and there is a drum to his side. To the right of the barrel a large dog sits on its haunches with its forepaws on the barrel.
There is a pair to this figure. Fig. 2246H has been reserved for it.
HEIGHT: 9.5 Inches
PRICE: Pair: E, Singles: F.

Figs. 2250/2249
A pair of figures of a girl and boy seated with their arms around a seated spaniel, which is to her right and his left. She wears a hat with feather, blouse, and long skirt; he wears a cap with feather, tunic, kilt, and socks.
HEIGHT: 6 Inches
PRICE: Pair: F, Singles: G.

Fig. 2256B
A group figure of a boy and girl seated on rockwork; both children wear similar clothing of a brimmed hat, jacket, and kilt/dress. Laying below with its head raised is a large dog.
HEIGHT: 6.5 Inches
PRICE: E.

Figs. 2251/2252
A pair of figures of a boy and girl seated on recumbent dogs; he wears a frilled shirt and long tunic and she wears a blouse and long dress.
HEIGHT: 4.5 Inches
PRICE: Pair: E, Singles: F.

Fig. 2253
A figure of a boy standing on a cushion with his legs crossed and leaning on a large seated hound.
There is a pair to this figure that is almost a mirror image with a girl replacing the boy. Fig. 2254 has been reserved for it.
HEIGHT: 8 Inches
PRICE: Pair: E, Singles: F.

Fig. 2257C
A group figure of a girl standing and a boy sitting on a fence; she wears a bodice, dress, and a scarf over her shoulder. A plumed hat is held in her right hand; her left hand is held out holding a bone to a dog that stands at her side. The boy wears a plumed hat, jacket, and kilt and holds a filled basket in both hands.
HEIGHT: 8.5 Inches
PRICE: G.

Fig. 2259F
A figure of a girl seated in a chair with her feet on a cushion; she wears a long dress with an apron. A bird is perched on the back of the chair and a spaniel sits on another cushion to her right side.
There is a pair to this figure. Fig. 2259E has been reserved for it.
HEIGHT: 6 Inches
PRICE: Pair: E, Singles: F.

Figs. 2259A/2259B
A pair of standing figures of a boy and girl dressed in highland attire of plumed hat, tunic/blouse with shirt, and kilt/skirt with a sash over his shoulder and around her waist. Perched on his left shoulder and her right is a bird. He holds a bowl in his right hand. To his left and her right a dog sits begging. Behind the dog's head each hold an open book.
This pair is of Circus or theatrical inspiration and no doubt portrays a Circus act.
HEIGHT: 8 Inches
PRICE: Pair: E, Singles: F.

Figs. 2259C/2259D
A pair of arbour figures of a boy and girl seated, both wearing plumed hats, he with a frilled shirt, jacket, knee breeches, and boots, she with a bodice and long skirt. In his right hand he holds a cockerel and his left is on the head of a dog that stands on its hind legs. She holds a chicken in her left hand and her right is on the head of a dog that stands on its hind legs. Below both children is a bridge under which a stream runs.
The authors have never seen this pair before. They are very well modelled and constructed. The price given is for them is as illustrated in the white; should a coloured pair exist, the price would be considerably more.
HEIGHT: 10.25 Inches
PRICE: Pair: F, Singles: F.

Figs. 2261A/2261B
A pair of figures of a girl and boy seated in chairs, both bareheaded with long hair. She wears a blouse and long skirt. Her right hand is in her lap and her left holds a bird aloft. To her right side a spaniel sits on a cushioned stool. The boy is a mirror image.
HEIGHT: 8.5 Inches
PRICE: Pair: F, Singles: G.

Fig. 2262
A group of a girl seated in a high backed chair, dressed in plumed hat, bodice, and long skirt, pouring from a teapot into a cup that is on a table to her side. A dog sits begging in a chair.
There is probably a pair to this figure, but is as yet unrecorded. Fig. 2262A has been reserved for it.
This figure can be found in two sizes; the larger size is illustrated, being a much finer figure.
HEIGHT: 7 Inches, 5.25 Inches
PRICE: 7 Inch: E, 5.25 Inch: F.

Figs. 2261C/2261D
A pair of spill vase figures of a boy and girl seated on a bank; she wears a hat, blouse, scarf, and skirt, holding fruit in her lap. A dog stands on its hind legs with its forepaws in her lap and a bird is perched in a tree. He is a mirror image and wears a plumed hat, scarf, and long tunic.
HEIGHT: 8 Inches
PRICE: Pair: F, Singles: G.

Fig. 2262B
A figure of a boy seated, wearing a short jacket, kilt with sporran, and a scarf over his right shoulder and across his chest. He holds an open book in his left hand and his right rests on a begging dog that wears a plumed hat and stands on a cushion. **This figure, whilst mainly in the white, is very early from the mould; white and coloured figures were made simultaneously to serve two markets. There is a pair to this figure, a girl replaces the boy. Fig. 2262C has been reserved for it.**
HEIGHT: 6 Inches
PRICE: E.

Fig. 2262D
A figure of a girl standing on a cushion, wearing a large plumed hat, blouse, and short skirt. She holds what appears to be a musical instrument in both hands. To her left is a chair, on the seat of which a dog stands begging and a bird sits on the back.
There is a pair to this figure, with a boy replacing the girl. Fig. 2262E has been reserved for it.
HEIGHT: 8 Inches
PRICE: Pair: E, Singles: F.

Figs. 2267C/2267D
A pair of groups of children seated on the backs of spaniels; both wear plumed hats, she with a blouse and long dress, he a short jacket and trousers. The spaniels have two separate front legs and are all on high rococo bases with two quill holder holes in each.
A very rare pair of figures previously unrecorded.
HEIGHT: 6.25 Inches
PRICE: Pair: D, Singles: E.

Fig. 2265A
A group figure of a boy seated above a bridge under which a swan swims; he wears a plumed hat, frilled shirt, jacket, and breeches. To his right are two large flower pots filled with flowers. To his left a dog sits begging with a dunce's cap on its head. In the boy's lap there is an open book. **The significance of the dog with a dunce's cap would have to do with the open book on the boy's lap, but what the significance is exactly remains a mystery. It is possible that there is a pair to this very rare figure.**
HEIGHT: 8 Inches
PRICE: F.

Figs. 2267E/2267F
A pair of figures of a boy and girl seated on rockwork; he wears a hat with feather, tunic, skirt, and a scarf draped over his shoulder and across his arm. There is a fish in his lap and he holds a walking stick in his left hand. By his side a dog sits above a brick arch. She is almost a mirror image; she wears a hat, blouse, and skirt with an apron and holds a basket of fish in her right hand. A dog sits to her left above a brick arch. HEIGHT: 6.5 Inches
PRICE: Pair: F, Singles: G.

Figs. 2279/2280
A pair of figures of a girl and boy seated on the backs of standing dogs; she wears a blouse and long skirt, he a shirt, short jacket, and trousers. She is seated sidesaddle; he sits astride.
HEIGHT: 5.5 Inches
PRICE: Pair: E, Singles: F.

Figs. 2277C/2277D
A pair of spill vase figures of a boy and girl wearing highland attire of plumed hats, cloak, bodice/tunic, skirt/kilt, he with boots and she with shoes. They both hold a bird aloft. At their feet to the side a spaniel sits.
HEIGHT: 9.5 Inches
PRICE: Pair: E, Singles: F.

Fig. 2277E
A figure of a boy standing, wearing a frilled shirt with tie, jacket, and kilt with a scarf over his shoulder. He holds a hat in his right hand and a rabbit aloft in his left. To his right a dog stands on its hind legs on a cushion. **The boy is standing in a dancing pose. It is probable that this figure depicts a circus act; there is a pair to this figure. Fig. 2277F has been reserved for it.**
HEIGHT: 9 Inches
PRICE: F.

Figs. 2282C/2282D
A pair of spill vase figures of a boy and girl standing with one foot raised onto rockwork; both children are bareheaded with long hair. He wears a long tunic and trousers, she a bodice and long skirt. To their side on a covered table a dog stands on its hind legs begging.
HEIGHT: 7.5 Inches
PRICE: Pair: E, Singles: F.

Fig. 2278C
An arbour figure of a girl seated between two pillars, wearing a blouse and long skirt, holding a bird in her right hand.
Against one of the pillars a dog sits.
There is a pair to this figure. Fig. 2278D has been reserved for it.
HEIGHT: 6.25 Inches
PRICE: Pair: F, Singles: G.

Fig. 2282E
A seated figure of a girl who is bareheaded and wearing a blouse and long skirt with her knickers showing. She holds a dog on her lap with both hands. **There is a pair to this figure that was made be the 'Alpha' factory. Fig. 2282F has been reserved for it.**
HEIGHT: 6.5 Inches
PRICE: Pair: F, Singles: G.

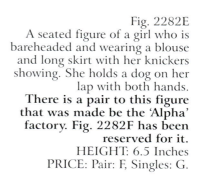

Figs. 2283/2284
A pair of figures of girls standing on cushions with baskets in their hands, wearing a brimmed hat and dress. A spaniel is seated on a cushion to each girl's side.
These figures can be found in two sizes; an 8 inch white pair is illustrated.
HEIGHT: 8 Inches, 6.5 Inches
PRICE: Pair: E, Singles: F.

Figs. 2287/2288
A pair of figures of a boy and girl standing with a bird on their shoulders; to her left and his right is a kennel resting on rockwork on which a spaniel is recumbent. Both the boy and girl are similarly dressed, wearing a blouse/tunic and kilt/skirt.
HEIGHT: 6.75 Inches
PRICE: Pair: F, Singles: G.

Figs. 2284A/2284B
A pair of figures of a girl and boy standing with one foot raised, both wearing a hat, jacket, and skirt/kilt with socks. She holds a garland in her right hand, he in his left, and her left and his right rests on a dog, which stands begging on a covered table.
This pair can be found in two sizes; a 6.5 inch pair and a single 8 inch figure are illustrated.
HEIGHT: 6.5 & 8 Inches
PRICE: Pair: F, Singles: G.

Fig. 2287C
A figure of a girl standing, wearing a large brimmed hat, blouse, skirt, shoes and socks, and a scarf draped over her right arm. A whippet stands on its hind legs on rockwork to her side with its forepaws on her left arm.
There is a pair to this figure. Fig. 2287D has been reserved for it.
HEIGHT: 9 Inches
PRICE: G.

Figs. 2287E/2287F
A pair of figures of a boy and girl standing, both wearing a hat with feather, she with a jacket and dress. She holds a garland in her right hand. To her left side a spaniel stands on its hind legs around which she has her left hand. He wears a jacket, open necked shirt, short trousers tied with a scarf, and knee boots. A dog stands begging at his left side.
HEIGHT: 9 Inches
PRICE: Pair: F, Singles: G.

285

Figs. 2288A/2288B
A pair of figures of a boy and girl standing to either side of shaped pillars; he wears highland attire of cap, tunic with sash, and sporran. A dog is seated on top of the pillar with its forepaws on the boy's chest and he has his arm around the dog. She wears a plumed hat, bodice, long dress, and a scarf over her arm. On the pillar by her side is a pot of flowers on which a bird is perched.
It is possible that these figures portray The Royal Children.
HEIGHT: 6.5 Inches
PRICE: Pair: F, Singles: G.

Figs. 2288E/2288F
A pair of figures of a girl and boy, both seated on rockwork. They are dressed similarly with a blouse and a skirt/kilt. A bird sits on her right shoulder and another sits on his left shoulder. A dog is standing on its hind legs with its forepaws in their laps.
HEIGHT: 6.5 Inches
PRICE: Pair: F, Singles: G.

Fig. 2288G
A spill vase figure of a boy and girl seated on a grassy bank; she wears a tunic and skirt and has one arm around and the other rests on the boy's knee. He wears a hat, open neck shirt, jacket, and trousers. He holds a bird in his right hand and a dog lies to his side with its paws in his lap.
This figure was made by 'The Green Factory'.
HEIGHT: 7.5 Inches
PRICE: G.

Figs. 2288C/2288D
A pair of spill vase figures of a girl and boy, both wearing plumed hats, she with a blouse, skirt tied with a sash, and long trousers, he with a tunic with a sash and trousers. They hold a bird in one hand and a basket of flowers in the other. A dog stands on its hind legs at their feet.
HEIGHT: 7.5 Inches
PRICE: Pair: F, Singles: G.

Fig. 2292A
A small quill holder figure of a girl seated, wearing a long dress with her left arm around a spaniel. Both girl and dog are seated on an over large cushion that forms the holder.
There is a pair to this figure that is almost a mirror image with a boy replacing the girl. Fig. 2292B has been reserved for it. It is possible that this pair portrays the Royal Children.
HEIGHT: 4 Inches
PRICE: Pair: G, Singles: H.

Fig. 2292C
A small quill holder group of a boy and girl seated on a large cushion; he holds a rose in one hand and she has one hand in her lap and the other across her chest. **This figure would appear to be the centrepiece for Figs. 2292A/2292B.**
HEIGHT: 4 Inches
PRICE: G.

Fig. 2292D
A figure of a girl wearing a hat, dress with an apron, and long skirt. She is standing in front of a standing dog. **There is a pair to this figure. Fig. 2292E has been reserved for it.**
HEIGHT: 6 Inches
PRICE: F.

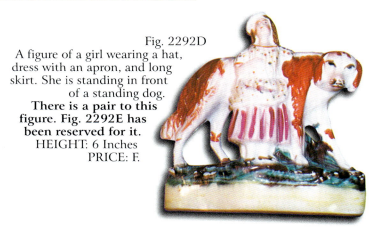

Figs. 2299A/2299B
A pair of spill vase figures of a boy and girl seated with small dogs in their laps; both children wear plumed hats and trousers, he with a long coat and she a blouse. He holds a trumpet in his left hand and she a violin in her right. These figures have a quill hole in the base.
HEIGHT: 6.75 Inches
PRICE: Pair: G, Singles: H.

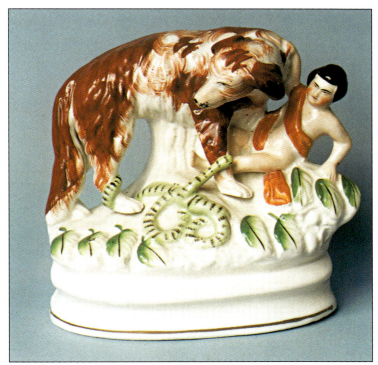

Fig. 2297A
A figure of a dog protecting a child from a snake; the dog stands with the snake wrapped around its legs. A child wearing only a scarf lays on the ground with one hand on the dog's back. **There is a pair to this figure. Fig. 2297B has been reserved for it.**
HEIGHT: 7.5 Inches
PRICE: Pair: E, Singles: F.

Fig. 2299D
A figure of a child dressed in a robe, lying asleep, resting against a recumbent dog, all on a rococo base. **There is probably a pair to this figure. Fig. 2299C has been reserved for it.**
HEIGHT: 3.5 Inches
PRICE: F.

Fig. 2299F
A figure of a boy laying asleep on the back of a
seated dog; he wears a short jacket, open necked
shirt, waistcoat, and knee breeches. A large hat
and two objects are by his feet, all on a shaped,
scrolled, and gilded base.
**This is an extremely finely modelled figure
and also bears similarities with the Landseer
print. It is possible that a pair exists for it.
Fig. 2299G has been reserved for it.**
HEIGHT: 8 Inches
PRICE: E.

Fig. 2299D/F. SO
**A newly discovered print titled 'Saved' from a painting by Sir
Edwin Landseer; whilst not identical to the figures, it is near
enough to be considered the inspiration. These heroic dog
rescue scenes were frequently portrayed in Victorian genre
paintings and it is probable that they inspired the potters to
produce similar figures.**

Fig. 2301B
A figure of a girl stand-
ing, wearing a brimmed
hat, blouse, and skirt
with an apron. Her
knickers show below the
skirt and in her apron
there are bunches of
grapes. She holds in her
left hand a tambourine
that rests on the back of
a seated dog.
**There is a pair to this
figure. Fig. 2301C has
been reserved for it.**
HEIGHT: 6 Inches
PRICE: Pair: F, Singles:
G.

Figs. 2302B/2302C
A pair of figures of a boy and girl seated on the back of
a dog; she wears a blouse and long skirt and holds her
hat in her left hand. Her right rests on the dog's head.
He wears a cap, shirt, waistcoat, jacket, and trousers.
His right arm is at his waist and he carries a basket over
his left.
HEIGHT: 6 Inches
PRICE: Pair: F, Singles: G.

Figs. 2304C/2304D
A pair of spill vase figures of a boy and girl standing,
dressed in highland attire, she with a hat, bodice, and
skirt with an apron. She holds a large flowered scarf
in both hands. He wears a plumed hat, frilled shirt,
jacket, kilt with sporran, and a scarf across his chest. A
water bottle is by his left hand. To his left and her right,
beyond a spill, a large spaniel sits. On the base of each
figure a sheep is recumbent.
**A very well coloured and
modelled pair of figures and
very desirable.**
HEIGHT: 12 Inches
PRICE Pair D, Singles: E.

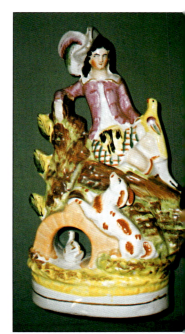

Fig. 2304E
A group figure of a boy seated, wearing highland attire of plumed hat,
open neck shirt, tunic, and kilt with
sporran. He holds a bird in his left
hand and his right arm rests on rockwork. Below him is a bridge under
which a bird swims. His dog stands
on its hind legs with its forepaws on
the bridge.
**There is probably a pair to this
figure. Fig. 2304F has been
reserved for it. This figure could
have been included in a number
of other chapters, i.e. Children
with Birds or Pastoral.**
HEIGHT: 9 Inches
PRICE: F.

ii. Children with Birds
See Figures 2306 - 2310g Books Two and Three

Fig. 2306B
A figure of a girl standing, wearing a plumed hat, blouse, long skirt with her knickers showing, and a scarf draped over both shoulders. She holds a basket in her left hand and a dead bird by its feet in her right. Other birds lay dead by her feet on a brick wall.
There is a pair to this figure. Fig. 2306C has been reserved for it.
HEIGHT: 9.25 Inches
PRICE: Pair: F, Singles: G.

Figs. 2307G/2307H
A pair of figures of a standing boy and girl, he with his legs crossed wearing a round hat with plume, frilled shirt, tie, jacket, panta-loons tied with a sash, and boots; she wears a plumed hat, bodice, and skirt with an apron. Both children rest one hand on the top of a bird coop that stands on a pillar. On top of the coop a bird is perched.
HEIGHT: 7.5 Inches
PRICE: Pair: E, Singles: F.

Fig. 2306D
A figure of a girl standing with legs crossed, wearing a bodice, ermine edged jacket, and multi-layered skirt. She holds a bird in her left hand.
There is a pair to this figure. Fig. 2306E has been reserved for it.
HEIGHT: 7 Inches
PRICE: Pair: F, Singles: G.

Figs. 2308D/2308E
A pair of figures of a child facing left and right, wearing only a sash, and kneeling on the top of a large swan that swims on an intricate gilded base.
HEIGHT: 8.5 Inches
PRICE: Pair: F, Singles: G.

Figs. 2307E/2307F
A pair of figures of a boy and girl seated, both wear-ing plumed hats, jacket/ bodice, kilt/skirt, a scarf over their shoulders, and a shopping basket over one arm. To their side is a large hen house on top of which a chicken stands. They each have one hand held up to the chicken.
HEIGHT: 6 Inches
PRICE: Pair: F, Singles: G.

Fig. 2309C
A clock face group of a boy seated on a grassy mound, wearing a plumed hat, long jacket, and knee breeches. He holds a pipe in both hands. On either side of him a large bird is perched. **It is possible that a pair exists for this figure. Fig. 2309D has been reserved for it.** HEIGHT: 12 Inches PRICE: E.

Fig. 2308G
A spill vase figure of a girl standing, wearing a blouse, skirt, and boots. By her side a cockerel stands. Above and to the side of the spill vase a fox looks down on the bird. **There is probably a pair to this figure. Fig. 2308F has been reserved for it.** HEIGHT: 6 Inches PRICE: H.

Figs. 2309E/2309F
A pair of figures of a standing boy and girl, each wearing a plumed hat, he with a long jacket, cloak, knee trousers, and boots, she with a bodice, cloak, and skirt with an apron. Both children hold a bird with a large tail, she in her left hand and he in his right. The other hand is held to the bird's mouth. HEIGHT: 10 Inches PRICE: Pair: F, Singles: G.

Fig. 2308H
A spill vase figure of a girl seated, wearing a blouse and skirt. To her right side a large hat is on the ground. Above and to either side in the tree an oversized bird is perched. **In the figure illustrated both birds' tails have been restored. There is probably a pair to this figure. Fig. 2308I has been reserved for it.** HEIGHT: 6.5 Inches PRICE: H.

Fig. 2309G
A figure of a man standing; he leans on rockwork to his right and wears a plumed hat, frilled shirt, long jacket, and knee breeches. To his left on a tree trunk a birdcage stands with a bird perched on top. At his feet a spaniel lies.
The modeller was a consummate artist, certainly one of the best in Staffordshire in the 1850s, the time when this figure was made. All of his figures are comparatively rare and much sought after, due to their quality. He was responsible for the figures of The Royal Princes (see Figures 627/628 Book One) and of the boy and girl on deer (see Figures 2332A/2322B Book Three), amongst a number of others. It is possible that this figure also portrays one of The Royal Children. There is a pair to this figure, which is claimed to have been made by the Dudson pottery. Fig. 2309H has been reserved for it. HEIGHT: 9 Inches PRICE: F.

Figs. 2309J/2309K
A pair of figures of a boy and girl standing on a high round base; both children wear a hat with a feather, she with a coat split at the waist showing a skirt and frilled knickerbockers, a large scarf draped over her shoulders, which she holds aloft with her left hand. A cat sits on this arm. She holds a large bird in her right hand. He wears a tunic, kilt, shoes, socks, and a large scarf draped over his shoulders. He holds a dog in his left arm and a bird on his right shoulder.
HEIGHT: 9 Inches
PRICE: Pair: F, Singles: G.

Figs. 2309N/2309P
A pair of group figures of a man and woman seated with a boy and girl standing on rockwork to their side. Both the man and woman have a bird perched on their shoulder. He wears an open neck shirt with a tie, jacket, and trousers; the girl by his side wears a blouse, skirt, and knickers with a scarf over her shoulder. She wears a blouse and skirt with an apron and a scarf over her shoulder; the boy by her side wears a blouse and kilt and a large scarf over his shoulder.
HEIGHT: 7.5 Inches
PRICE: Pair: F, Singles: G.

Fig. 2309R
A figure of a boy standing; he is bareheaded and wears an open neck shirt and long tunic. His left hand is on his hip holding his hat and his right is holding a bird. **There is a pair to this figure. Fig. 2309S has been reserved for it.**
HEIGHT: 7 Inches
PRICE: G.

Figs. 2309L/2309M
A pair of spill vase figures of a boy and girl standing by tree trunks; each child has one hand on a hip and the other holds a bird. They both wear brimmed hats, he with a tunic, jacket, and kilt with a scarf over his shoulder. She wears a bodice and long skirt.
It is possible that this pair were made to portray falconers.
HEIGHT: 8.25
PRICE: Pair: G, Singles: H.

Figs. 2310J/2310K
A pair of figures of a girl and boy dressed in theatrical attire of a headdress with long scarf, blouse/shirt, jacket, and short skirt with pantaloons/kilt with scarf. To her right on rockwork is a birdcage with a bird perched on top. To his left is a similar bird and bird cage.
This pair may well represent a circus act and could have been included in that chapter.
HEIGHT: 9 Inches
PRICE: Pair: F, Singles: G.

iii. Children with Cows
See Figures 2311 - 2325 Books Two and Three

Figs. 2310G/2310H
A pair of figures of a boy and girl standing; she wears a plumed hat, bodice, short skirt, and knickers with a scarf over her shoulder. To her right is a pillar on which is a birdcage with a bird perched on top. She has one hand placed on the cage and the other is at her chest. He is a mirror image and is similarly dressed in plumed hat, tunic, kilt, shoes, and sock with a cape over his shoulder.
These figures were made in two sizes, both illustrated. Usually when a birdcage is included with a figure it denotes Royalty. In this instance, in view of the theatrical nature of their attire, we believe that these figures are depicting performers.
HEIGHT: 9.5 Inches 8 Inches
PRICE: Pair: F, Singles: G.

Fig. 2312E
A spill vase figure of a standing milkmaid wearing a hat, bodice with sash, and skirt with an apron. She holds her right arm aloft against the spill. At her feet is a bucket and to her left a cow stands with its head at her waist.
There is a pair to this figure. Fig. 2312F has been reserved for it.
HEIGHT: 11 Inches
PRICE: Pair: E, Singles: F.

Figs. 2314A/2314B
A pair of figures of a milkmaid and milkman seated before a standing cow and holding buckets in their arms. She wears a hat, bodice, and long dress with an apron; he wears a hat, smock, and trousers.
HEIGHT: 6.5 Inches
PRICE: Pair: E, Singles: F.

Figs. 2318E/2318F
A pair of spill vase figures of a milkmaid and milkman standing in front of cows. She wears a headscarf, blouse, and long skirt. She holds a milk pail in her right hand and her left rests on the back of the cow. He wears a brimmed hat, shirt with tie, jacket, and long trousers. He holds a bucket under his left arm and his right rests on the back of the cow. There are streams on the bases of the figures. Figs. 2323/2323A HEIGHT: 11 Inches
PRICE: Pair: E, Singles: F.

Figs. 2314D/2314C
A pair of figures of a milkman and milkmaid standing before a walking cow; he wears a hat, waistcoat, jacket, and trousers. She wears a hat, blouse, and skirt with an apron and holds a bowl in her left hand.
These figures are well modelled in the round and are in the style of The Parr factory. A number of subsidiary moulds were needed to complete these figures. They were made for a considerable period and late Kent versions decorated with bright gold can be found. A single early Parr 8.75 inch figure of the milkman and a pair of 6.5 inch figures are illustrated.
HEIGHT: 6.5 & 8.75 Inches
PRICE: Pair: F, Singles: G.

Fig. 2318G
A spill vase figure of a milkmaid dressed in hat, bodice, and long skirt, standing holding the head of a cow that stands beside her. At her feet is a milk bucket by which a spaniel sits.
There is a pair to this figure. Fig. 2318H has been reserved for it.
HEIGHT: 10 Inches
PRICE: E.

Figs. 2318C/2318D
A pair of spill vase figures of a milkmaid and milkman seated before and milking a standing cow that is eating grass from a mound. She wears a hat, bodice, and long dress with an apron; he wears a hat, shirt, jacket, and knee breeches. HEIGHT: 7.25 Inches
PRICE: Pair: E, Singles: F.

Figs. 2319/2320
A pair of figures of a milkmaid and milkman who are standing to the rear of a cow, she wearing a hat, bodice, and skirt with an apron, he wearing a hat, shirt with tie, and knee breeches.
These figures are creamers. The figures have a hole in the top of their heads, into which cream was poured, using the figure of the maid or man as a handle. The figure could be lifted and used as a jug, the cream pouring from the cow's mouth.
HEIGHT: 7.5 Inches
PRICE: Pair: E, Singles: F.

Fig. 2322A
A group of a boy and girl seated on a grassy mound; he wears a hat, open neck shirt, jacket, and knee breeches with shoes and socks. She wears a hat, blouse, and long skirt. Below them, lying on the base, is a large cow.
HEIGHT: 7.25 Inches
PRICE: F.

Fig. 2319A
A figure of a milkmaid standing at the rear of a cow; she wears a brimmed hat, bodice, and long skirt with an apron. She holds the apron in her left hand and rests her right on the back of the cow. **As with Figures 2319/2320, there is a hole in the top of their hats, into which cream could be poured, and a second hole in the cow's mouth. There is a pair to this figure. Fig. 2319B has been reserved for it. This figure is very similar to Fig. 2319 and is virtually the same as Fig. 2318 without the spill vase. Two figures are illustrated, differently decorated, and having slightly different modelling.**
HEIGHT: 7.25
PRICE: Pair: E, Singles: F.

Figs. 2323/2323A
A pair of spill vase figures of milkmaids kneeling, milking cows facing left and right, on oblong coloured bases.
A very attractive pair, usually a milkman, is paired with a milkmaid; this is one of the few pairs where a mirror image milkmaid is paired.
HEIGHT: 6 Inches
PRICE: Pair: E, Singles: F.

Figs. 2320C/2320D
A pair of figures of a boy and girl seated with legs crossed on the back of a recumbent cow. She wears a hat, bodice, long dress, and a scarf over her shoulder and across her lap. He wears a hat, tunic with sash, and kilt. Below each cow there is a bucket.
HEIGHT: 7 Inches
PRICE: Pair: E, Singles: F.

Fig. 2323C
A figure of a milkmaid standing before a cow; she is wearing a scarf over her head, blouse, and skirt with an apron. The cow stands in a stream and there is a milking bowl on the base.
There is a pair to this figure. Fig. 2323B has been reserved for it.
HEIGHT: 6.5 Inches
PRICE: Pair: E, Singles: F.

Fig. 2325A
A spill vase figure of a woman standing, dressed in bodice, jacket, and a skirt with an apron. She holds the head of a cow that stands beside her. Below a goat is recumbent by a bridged stream. **There is probably a pair to this figure. Fig. 2325B has been reserved for it.**
HEIGHT: 8.5 Inches
PRICE: E.

Fig. 2328D
A spill vase group of a girl and boy seated to either side of a tree trunk that forms the spill. She wears a hat, jacket, long skirt, and a scarf over her right arm. He wears a hat, shirt, tunic, and kilt. Both of his hands are on his knees. Below them a large stag is at rest.
HEIGHT: 8.75 Inches
PRICE: G.

iv. Children with Deer/Fawn
See Figures 2327 - 2330C Books Two and Three

Fig. 2329 SO
A newly discovered print titled 'My Pets'. The print is very similar to Fig. 2329 and, whilst not identical, it is probable that this print was the inspiration for that figure. The potter then decided to make a matching pair.

Figs. 2326B/2326C
A pair of spill vase figures of a boy and girl standing behind a fawn; he wears a blouse and kilt and is feeding the fawn from a container which he holds in his left hand. She wears a blouse, skirt, and trousers. Her hat is suspended from the spill and she has both hands around the neck of the fawn that has a garland around its neck.
HEIGHT: 6 Inches
PRICE: Pair: E, Singles: F.

Fig. 2328C
A spill vase group figure of a boy and girl, both similarly dressed in plumed hat, tunic/bodice, and kilt/skirt. Both children lean against the spill and look down upon a deer that is at rest below. **This figure is a product of the 'Green' factory.**
HEIGHT: 10 Inches
PRICE: F.

Fig. 2330D
An arbour group figure of a boy and girl standing; he wears a cap, long jacket, shirt, and knee breeches. He holds a deer by its forelegs in his right hand. The other hand rests on the deer's head. She stands to the side with her hands on her hips, wearing a blouse, bodice, and skirt. The deer is between them and rests on its hind legs.
HEIGHT: 9 Inches
PRICE: G.

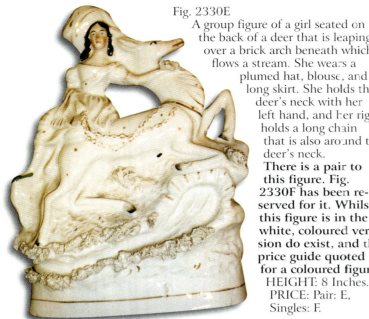

Fig. 2330E

A group figure of a girl seated on the back of a deer that is leaping over a brick arch beneath which flows a stream. She wears a plumed hat, blouse, and long skirt. She holds the deer's neck with her left hand, and her right holds a long chain that is also around the deer's neck.

There is a pair to this figure. Fig. 2330F has been reserved for it. Whilst this figure is in the white, coloured version do exist, and the price guide quoted is for a coloured figure.
HEIGHT: 8 Inches.
PRICE: Pair: E,
Singles: F.

Fig. 2332C

A figure of a boy wearing a large plumed hat and dress with socks, kneeling on the back of a standing deer. He holds the ends of a scarf that is tied around the deer's neck.

There is a pair to this figure. Fig. 2332D has been reserved for it.
HEIGHT: 10 Inches
PRICE: Pair: D, Singles: E.

Fig. 2330G

A figure of a girl standing, wearing a hat with feather, blouse, and long skirt. She is barefooted and a small deer stands on its hind legs with its forehooves on her skirt.

There is probably a pair to this figure, but the authors have never seen this figure or its pair before, and therefore are unaware as to whether its pair has a deer or other animal standing with its forelegs resting on a boy.
HEIGHT: 10.5 Inches
PRICE: F.

Figs. 2332A/2332B

A pair of figures of children seated on the backs of standing deer; he wears a plumed hat, tunic with a collar, skirt, and a scarf over his right arm. She is similarly attired but with a cape over her left shoulder. Both children have a hand resting on the deer's horns and the other holds a garland which serve as reins. Each deer has one leg raised and on the base a flowering plant grows.

These are very finely modelled and decorated figures and extremely rare. The pair illustrated is the only pair recorded. In view of they way the children are dressed they were probably meant to portray The Royal children.
HEIGHT: 7.5 Inches
PRICE: Pair: D, Singles: E.

Fig. 2332F

A spill vase figure of a girl standing, wearing a large hat, blouse, and short skirt. A basket is over her right arm and her left holds a garland that is around the neck of a standing doe.

There is a pair to this figure. Fig. 2332E has been reserved for it. The modeller of this pair also made Figs. 2059C/D.
HEIGHT: 8.5 Inches
PRICE: Pair: E, Singles: F.

v. Children with Foxes
See Figures 2336 - 2337 Book Two

vi. Children with Goats
See Figures 2338 - 2366C Books Two and Three

Figs. 2347A/2347B
A pair of figures of a boy and girl seated to the front of standing goats, each with one arm around the goat's neck. She wears a brimmed hat, bodice, jacket, and skirt with long trousers; he wears a brimmed hat, open necked shirt, waistcoat, jacket, knee breeches, leggings, and boots. He holds a small piece of greenery in his hand.
These figures have never been recorded before and are extremely rare. They were made by The 'Alpha' factory.
HEIGHT: 7.75 Inches
PRICE: Pair: D, Singles: E.

Figs. 2338B/2338C
A pair of figures of a boy and girl seated on standing goats, he astride, she sidesaddle. Both children are wearing plumed hats, he with a tunic and she a dress, both with ermine edged capes.
In view of their attire, these figures could be portraits of The Royal Children. There are many pairs of children on goats, all varying very little from each other. They were clearly a very popular subject as so many were made.
HEIGHT: 6.5 Inches
PRICE: Pair: F, Singles: G.

Figs. 2349A/2349B
A pair of spill vase figures of children standing with goats to their sides; he wears a flat cap, smock, and knee boots. His right arm is on and around the goat, which stands to his right. She wears a flowered hat, blouse, and long skirt. Her left arm is on and around the goat that stands to her left.
These figures were made by The 'Alpha' factory.
HEIGHT: 7 Inches
PRICE: Pair: E, Singles: F.

Figs. 2339B/2339C
A pair of figures of a boy and girl seated on the back of a doe and a stag; she wears a feathered hat, puff sleeved blouse, long dress, and a scarf around her shoulders. He wears a hat with feathers, tunic, kilt, and a scarf around his shoulders.
These figures are porcelaneous and date from the late 1830s or early 1840s. It is possible that they are portraits of the Royal children.
HEIGHT: 5.5 Inches
PRICE: Pair: F, Singles: G.

Fig. 2340B
A group figure of a girl wearing a plumed hat, shirt, bodice, skirt, and long scarf over her shoulder. She is seated on the back of a large seated goat. Beneath the goat on raised rock-work is a bucket.
There is a pair to this extremely rare figure. Fig. 2340C has been reserved for it.
TITLE: WELCH GOAT
HEIGHT: 10.5 Inches
PRICE: Pair: C, Singles: E.

Fig. 2354F
A figure of a man standing with his legs crossed, wearing a hat with feather, shirt, jacket, and knee breeches. A goat stands on its hind legs with its forelegs on his shoulder. He holds a garland in his right hand, which is around the goat's neck. A bridge is below, from which a stream flows.
There is a pair to this figure. Fig. 2354G has been reserved for it.
HEIGHT: 7.25 Inches
PRICE: G.

Figs. 2349C/2349D
A pair of spill vase group figures on scrolled bases of a girl seated on the back of a goat, wearing a plumed hat, bodice, and long skirt. To the front of the goat a boy stands wearing a tunic with a scarf over his shoulder. In his hand he holds his hat, from which the goat is eating. The other figure is a virtual mirror image, with the girl feeding the goat and the boy kneeling on its back.
These figures are the products of The 'Green' factory.
HEIGHT: 7.5 Inches
PRICE: Pair: E, Singles: F.

Figs. 2354B/2354C
A pair of figures of a boy and girl standing in front of seated goats; he is bare-headed and wears an open necked shirt, long coat, and trousers. She wears a plumed hat, blouse, and long skirt.
These figures could be of the Royal children. The head of the boy in particular is very similar to titled figures of The Prince of Wales.
HEIGHT: 5.75 Inches
PRICE: Pair: E, Singles: G.

Figs. 2355/2356
A pair of group figures of a girl seated above a bridge from which a stream flows; she wears a plumed hat, blouse, and a skirt with an apron in which there are flowers. A dog is by her right side with its paws on her lap. A large goat stands on its hind legs with its hooves on her shoulder. The pair is almost a mirror image, other than a boy replaces the girl. He wears a plumed hat, shirt, tunic, and kilt with a sporran. A large scarf is over his left shoulder and across his chest.
HEIGHT: 7.75 Inches
PRICE: Pair: E, Singles: F.

Figs. 2354D/2354E
A pair of figures of a boy and girl standing; both children wear plumed hats, he with an open neck shirt, jacket, kilt, and boots, she a blouse, tunic, and long skirt. A goat stands on its hind legs. To his left and her right, it has its forelegs on their laps and they have their arms around it.
HEIGHT: 9.75 Inches
PRICE: Pair: F, Singles: G.

Figs. 2356A/2356B
A pair of figures of a boy and girl seated on rockwork above a stream. A goat stands on its hind legs to the side with its forelegs resting on their shoulders. They each have one hand on the goat's back and the other in their lap. There is a bucket to her right and his left side, resting on the rockwork. He wears brimmed hat, open necked shirt, waistcoat, jacket, and trousers. She wears a brimmed hat, bodice with a large scarf over her shoulder, and skirt with an apron. Each figure is a mirror image of the other.
HEIGHT: 8 Inches
PRICE: Pair: E, Singles: F.

Figs. 2358E/2358F
A pair of pen holder figures of a cherub mounted on a rearing goat above thistle sprays. Each cherub with an arm raised holding grapes. Each figure is a mirror image of the other, all on round concave bases.
HEIGHT: 9.25 Inches
PRICE: Pair: F, Singles: G.

Figs. 2356C/2356D
A pair of figures of a boy and girl mounted on goats; both children wear a shirt/blouse and kilt/skirt and hold their hats in their hand. The goat is half seated, half standing on a high grassy mound.
HEIGHT: 6 Inches
PRICE: Pair: F, Singles: G.

Figs. 2356E/2356F
A pair of figures of a boy and girl seated on standing goats; she wears a blouse and skirt with an apron and holds a basket in her right hand. Her left hand is on the goat's head. He wears a smock with a tied scarf at the waist. He holds a basket of fruit in his lap and his right hand is on the goat's head, all on a rococo base.
This pair was made by the Parr/Kent pottery. These examples are late versions made towards the end of the nineteenth/early twentieth century. Earlier versions do exist and would be priced accordingly.
HEIGHT: 6.5 Inches
PRICE: Pair: F, Singles: G.

Figs. 2359/2360
A pair of figures on scrolled bases of a girl wearing a brimmed hat, bodice, and long skirt, with a goat sitting to her right with its hooves on her lap and a boy seated wearing a jacket, shirt, and knee breeches with one hand on the back of a dog, which lies to his left.
The discovery of the pair to the girl, of a boy with dog, means that this pair should have been included in the chapter containing shepherds. There is also illustrated Fig. 2359 with a different base. This figure appears to have been made by The Parr/Kent Pottery and it is probable that it was made from moulds acquired by them when another pottery closed down.
HEIGHT: 5.25 Inches
PRICE: Pair: E, Singles: F.

Figs. 2358D/2358C
A pair of spill vase figures of a boy and a girl seated on recumbent goats; she wears a blouse and long skirt and he wears a jacket with sash and a skirt.
HEIGHT: 8.5 Inches
PRICE: Pair: E, Singles: F.

Figs. 2360C/2360D
A pair of figures of a boy and girl seated on rockwork, she is bareheaded, wearing a long dress, and holds a goat that stands on its hind legs to her side. Her hat is on the ground at her feet. He wears a cap, tunic belted across his chest, and kilt with shoes and socks. He holds an object aloft in his left hand and a goat stands on its hind legs with its forelegs on his lap. A large stick is on the ground at his feet.
These figures are a product of The Parr factory.
HEIGHT: 6 Inches
PRICE: Pair: E, Singles: F.

Fig. 2362C
A group figure of a boy seated on the back of a goat and a girl standing at the head of the goat. He wears a hat, blouse, jacket, and knee breeches. His left hand is around the goat's neck. She is leaning with her arm around him and wears a blouse and skirt with an apron. She holds a small barrel in her left hand, all on a rococo base.
HEIGHT: 7 Inches
PRICE: G.

Figs. 2360E/2360F
A pair of figures of a boy and girl seated, dressed in highland attire. He wears a cap, shirt with tie, jacket, kilt with sporran, socks, and shoes. A scarf is over his shoulder. His left leg rests on rockwork and a goat stands on its hind legs with its forelegs on his lap. She wears a hat, tunic, long dress, and a scarf over her shoulder. She has her left arm around a goat, which stands on its hind legs with its forelegs in her lap.
HEIGHT: 6.25 Inches
PRICE: Pair: F, Singles: G.

Fig. 2360G
A figure of a boy standing, dressed in theatrical costume of plumed hat, ermine edged cloak, tunic, and kilt. He holds a garland in his right hand and a goat stands on rockwork to his side with its forelegs on his waist.
There is a pair to this figure. Fig. 2360H has been reserved for it.
HEIGHT: 8.5 Inches
PRICE: G.

Fig. 2365A
A figure of a boy seated on the back of a standing goat.
There are a number of versions of these figures that were always made in pairs and they vary in size, quality, and minor modelling differences. On some occasions the boy is on the right and the girl on the left, on other occasions the positions are reversed.
HEIGHT: 5.5 Inches
PRICE: Pair: F, Singles: G.

vii. Children with Horses/Ponies/Donkeys/Mules

See Figures 2367 - 2384C Books Two and Three

Figs. 2368A/2368B
A pair of figures of a boy and girl seated on the backs of standing mules on titled gilt lined bases; he wears a cap, smock, and trousers. His right hand holds the reins and pails of milk are strung over the saddle. She is seated sidesaddle and wears a hat, long dress, and a scarf around her neck. She holds the reins in both hands. There are also pails of milk strung over the saddle.
TITLE: MILK
HEIGHT: 8.5 Inches
PRICE: Pair: D, Singles: E.

Figs. 2369/2369A
A pair of figures of a boy and girl seated on the backs of standing mules on gilt lined bases. He wears a cap, smock, and socks. She is seated sidesaddle and wears a hat, long dress, and a shawl around her neck. There are baskets of fruit strung over the saddles. Between the feet of the mules is a small fence and a stream runs below.
HEIGHT: 13 Inches
PRICE: Pair: D, Singles: E.

Figs. 2375A/2375B
A pair of figures of a boy and girl mounted on ponies; each child wears a plumed hat and holds a flag in one hand and the reins in the other. He wears a shirt, split jacket, and kilt. He holds a drum in his lap. She is similarly dressed with a skirt rather than a kilt; a tambourine is suspended from her waist.
HEIGHT: 7 Inches
PRICE: Pair: F, Singles: G.

Figs. 2376C/2376D
A pair of figures of a boy and girl seated in an arbour; to her right and his left is a mule with panniers on its back. A steam runs below. She wears a brimmed hat, a blouse with sash across her chest, and short skirt. He wears a hat, tunic, kilt, and a sash across his chest.
HEIGHT: 7 Inches
PRICE: Pair: F, Singles: G.

Figs. 2376E/2376F
A pair of spill vase figures of a boy and girl seated in front of standing mules, both holding their hands up to the reins. The mules have panniers of fruit across their saddles and both the boy and girl hold baskets of fruit under their arms. She wears a hat, long jacket, and long dress; he wears a hat, long jacket, and knee breeches, all on shaped gilt lined bases.
A very rare pair and very well modelled.
HEIGHT: 9.5 Inches
PRICE: Pair: E, Singles: F.

Fig. 2378F
A figure of a boy wearing a plumed hat, smock, and trousers, seated on a standing pony with one front leg raised. A sash is through the boy's arms and around his back.
This figure is previously unrecorded and no doubt there is a pair. Fig. 2378E has been reserved for it. It is very similar to portraits of the Royal Children.
HEIGHT: 7.5 Inches
PRICE: Pair: F, Singles: G.

Fig. 2378G
A figure of a girl standing, wearing a hat with feather, blouse, long skirt, and a large scarf over both shoulders. Her right hand is on the head of a dog that sits by her side. **There is a pair to this figure. Fig. 2378H has been reserved for it.**
HEIGHT: 10.5 Inches
PRICE: G.

Figs. 2383/2383A
A pair of figures of a boy and girl standing in front of a donkey or mule; his right arm rests on its back and his left holds feed for the animal. He wears a shirt with neckerchief, long jacket, and trousers. There is a covered basket beneath the animal. She wears a long dress and holds feed in her hand. A covered basket is beneath the animal.
This pair is decorated in the manner of the Parr factory.
HEIGHT: 8 Inches
PRICE: Pair: E, Singles: F.

Fig. 2378J
A figure of a boy standing, wearing a plumed hat, long tunic with a sporran, and a sash over his shoulder. He holds an object in his right hand and his left is on the head of a dog that sits at his feet. **There is a pair to this figure. Fig. 2378K has been reserved for it.**
HEIGHT: 7.5 Inches
PRICE: G.

Figs. 2384/2384A
A pair of figures of a boy and girl seated on the backs of donkeys, she sidesaddle, he with one foot on the back of the donkey. She wears a hat, blouse, long skirt, and a scarf over her shoulder. A basket of fruit is on her lap. He wears a cap, shirt with tie, waistcoat, jacket, and trousers. One arm is on his knee and the other held to his cap. There is a basket of fruit and leaves on the back of the donkey.
On occasion the boy is titled in gilt script on the base 'If I had a donkey that would not go'. The authors have not seen a titled figure of the girl, although one may exist. The modeller that made these figures also made the figures of Gilpin and Tam O' Shanter (see Figures 989 – 992 Book One).
HEIGHT: 6.5 Inches
PRICE: Pair: F, Singles: G.

Figs. 2381/2381A
A pair of figures of a girl and boy standing in front of a horse; she has her left hand holding the reins, her right on her waist. She is wearing a plumed hat, bodice, short jacket, and dress with an apron; he holds the reins in his right hand and wears a plumed hat, tunic with sash, and kilt.
HEIGHT: 7 Inches
PRICE: Pair: D, Singles: F.

Figs. 2384B/2384C
A pair of figures of boy sweeps sitting back to front on donkeys; each boy wears a cap, shirt, jacket, and trousers and each is a mirror image of the other. They hold the donkey's tail in one hand and a brush over their shoulder in the other. The donkeys are kicking up their rear legs.
A superb pair of figures and extremely rare. One other similar pair of sweeps on donkeys is known. They are different in so far as the sweep is sitting the right way around on the donkey and holds a brush to his head. Figs. 2384D/2384E have been reserved for them.
HEIGHT: 9 Inches
PRICE: Pair: C, Singles: D.

viii. Children with Lions
See Figures 2385 - 2386 Book Two

Figs. 2386A/2386B
A pair of group figures, each of two semi-naked children, one standing and the other kneeling on the back of a walking tiger/lion. A large arbour decorated with a fruiting grape vine contains them. One of the children has his arm raised holding a floral garland.
HEIGHT: 11 Inches
PRICE: Pair: B, Singles: C.

ix. Children with Rabbits
See Figures 2387 - 2393 Book Two and Three

Figs. 2387B/2387C
A pair of figures of a boy and girl standing in front of rock-work holding rabbits in both hands. He wears a shirt, jacket, and trousers; she wears a jacket, skirt, and scarf across her waist. Both children are barefooted and both have their hats to their sides.
HEIGHT: 9 Inches
PRICE: Pair: E, Singles: F.

Fig. 2391A
A group figure of a girl standing, wearing a blouse and knee length skirt. Her right hand is on her hip and her left holds a basket of flowers. To her left is a rabbit hutch on which a rabbit and boy sit. The boy wears a jacket, open neck shirt, and knee length trousers. His right hand rests on the back of the rabbit and his left feeds the rabbit with lettuce. Below there are steps leading to the hutch.
HEIGHT: 7.75 Inches
PRICE: F.

Fig. 2391B
A figure of a girl standing by the side of a rabbit hutch wearing a plumed hat, cloak, blouse, and skirt with knickers showing. Both hands are clasped to her chest. One rabbit sits on top of the hutch and another below. **There is a pair to this figure. Fig. 2391C has been reserved for it.**
HEIGHT: 6.5 Inches
PRICE: G.

Fig. 2393D
A double quill holder figure of a girl standing behind a fence, in front of which is a rabbit hutch with one rabbit on the roof and another two on the ground. **This is an early figure, probably made in the early 1830s, and there may well be a pair for it.**
HEIGHT: 4.25 Inches
PRICE: H.

Fig. 2392B
A figure of a girl standing, wearing a bodice with brooch and a dress with an apron. Her left hand is around a rabbit that sits on its hind legs on top of a hutch. Below the hutch on the ground another rabbit sits.
There is a pair to this figure. Fig. 2392C has been reserved for it.
HEIGHT: 9 Inches
PRICE: Pair: E, Singles: F.

x. Children with Rats
See Figures 2394 - 2396 Book Two

xi. Children with Sheep
See Figures 2397 - 2410 Book Two and Three

Fig. 2393C
A figure of a standing boy, wearing a long jacket, shirt, and knee breeches with his hat held under his left arm. He is resting his right arm on a multi-storied rabbit hutch. A rabbit sits on top of the hutch and another sits below. **There is a pair to this figure. Fig. 2393B has been reserved for it.**
HEIGHT: 6.5 Inches
PRICE: Pair: E, Singles: F.

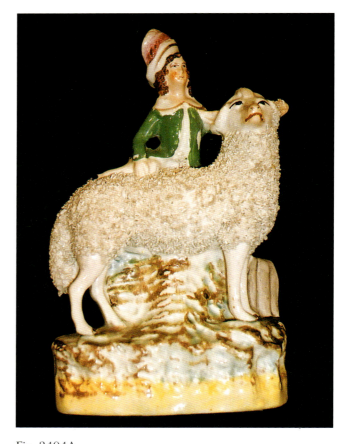

Fig. 2404A
A figure of a boy wearing a plumed hat, large collared shirt, jacket, and breeches, sitting on the back of a standing sheep
There is a pair to this figure. Fig. 2404B has been reserved for it.
HEIGHT: 6.25 Inches
PRICE: Pair: F, Singles: G.

Figs. 2410A/2410B
A pair of figures of seated children, both wearing brimmed hats, he with an open necked blouse and loose skirt, she with a jacket, bodice, and long skirt. A sheep stands beside them on its hind legs with its forelegs in their laps.
HEIGHT: 7.5 Inches
PRICE: Pair: E, Singles: F.

Figs. 2410C/2410D
A pair of figures of a boy and girl seated on the backs of sheep under an arbour that is covered with a grapevine. Both children wear a hat, tunic/blouse with sash, and kilt/skirt. Each child has one hand on the head of the sheep and the other in his or her lap. The base is covered in flowers. HEIGHT: 7.5 Inches
PRICE: Pair: E, Singles: F.

xii. Children with Zebras
See Figures 2411 - 2415A Books Two and Three

Figs. 2415/2415A
A pair of figures of boys dressed in Eastern style costume mounted on zebras; each figures is a mirror image of the other. **These figures were made by The Parr factory.**
HEIGHT: 7.75 Inches
PRICE: Pair: D, Singles: E.

305

Chapter 6:
Dogs

It is the spaniel dog that most people view as typical Staffordshire. They were known in England as Comforters, and in Scotland as Wally Dugs. They sat on either side of the mantelpiece and viewed the world with unconcern. Their origin or inspiration is thought to be the pet King Charles Spaniel 'Dash' that was kept by Queen Victoria and that she had owned since she was a young girl. When she became Queen, Dash was her constant companion and became well known, he himself being the subject of many prints and wool work pictures. There is not however any figure of her with Dash recorded.

The first Comforters appeared at the beginning of the 1840s and they continued to be made well into the 1900s. By the 1880s, like most Staffordshire, the quality of the figures had deteriorated and the bulk of the production consisted of white, badly modelled dogs decorated in bright gold and the previously painted eyes replaced in many instances with glass ones.

The potters, realising that they were onto a commercial success, produced these animals in amazing variety, quantity, and in many sizes. They did not restrict their production to spaniels, producing figures of many other breeds. One of the most popular of these breeds was the whippet, a small greyhound, kept by many in rural areas. Let loose on the land whippets were able to catch rabbits for the pot, the dog being able to venture where the owner might either be shot or fall foul of a man trap. Other breeds were potted, but none so popular as the spaniel and whippet, which appear in this chapter. We have, where possible, identified the breed, but many defy identification as some were not pure bred.

Listings highlighted in bold type contain additions and alterations which will be found in this addendum, all other Portraits will be found in *Books One and Three, Victorian Staffordshire Figures 1835-1875*.

This chapter is divided into eight sections, the two most prolific models, Spaniels and Whippets first, followed by an alphabetical listing of the rest.

i. Spaniels
See Figures 2416 - 2598 Books Two and Three

Fig. 2417A
A seated spaniel with collar, locket, and chain. An unusual example, it is almost identical to Fig. 2417, but is smaller and has an oblong round cornered base. **There is a pair to this figure. Fig. 2416A has been reserved for it.**
HEIGHT: 10 Inches
PRICE: Pair: E, Singles: F.

Figs. 2432/2433
A pair of white and gilt seated spaniels.
As with many of the spaniel pairs, examples can be found in red and white, black and white, and white and gilt and lustre.
HEIGHT: 9.5 Inches
PRICE: Pair: F, Singles: G.

Figs. 2435A/2435B
A pair of red and white seated spaniels.
These dogs are very similar to Figs. 2434/2435 Book Two with the exception that they have collars and no chain. The dogs illustrated have over the years 'flaked', the enamel red has been lost in patches. In the hands of a good restorer they can very easily be returned to their original condition.
HEIGHT: 11 Inches
PRICE: Pair: E, Singles: F.

Figs. 2447A/2447B
A pair of red and white seated spaniels with collars and lockets.
HEIGHT: 6.75
PRICE: Pair: E, Single: F.

Figs. 2441A/2441B
A pair of red and white seated spaniels with collars, chains, and lockets.
This pair is very similar to Figs. 2441/2 Book Two.
HEIGHT: 9 Inches
PRICE: Pair: E, Singles: F.

Figs. 2466/2467
A pair of red and white spaniels.
HEIGHT: 7.5 Inches
PRICE: Pair: F, Singles: G.

Figs. 2441C/2441D
A pair of red and white seated spaniels with collars and chains.
HEIGHT: 6.5 Inches
PRICE: Pair: E., Singles: F.
It is not known how many potters made comforter dogs; it would be surprising if a particular potter made a number of versions that differed slightly.

It is probable that different potters were responsible for the enormous number of variants that are to be found. Pairs differ in size, decoration, and colouring as well as being modelled with and without chains and lockets. Examples can be found with tails curled to the side, erect or in front. That is why the prospect of finding a matching pair, should one have been lost, is so difficult.

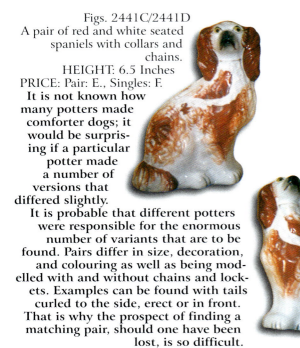

Figs. 2468/2469
A pair of red and white spaniels with locket and chain.
HEIGHT: 9.75 Inches
PRICE: Pair: E, Singles: F.

The following versions, unlike Figures 2416-2469F, have more complex moulds, thus taking the potters longer to design and produce. The time taken in this process can now be appreciated, as these figures portray some of the finest spaniels to have been made. As with their simpler counterparts, these dogs may also be found in the same range of colours, although underglaze black is not generally used.

Figs. 2474A/2474B
A pair of red and white seated spaniels with a collar and locket with a separate front leg.
These figures are similar to Figs. 2474/2475 Book Two, other than size and lack of chain.
HEIGHT: 6.75 Inches
PRICE: Pair: E, Singles: F.

Figs. 2477A/2477B
A pair of figures of red and white spaniels seated with lockets, collars, and chains, and two separate front legs.
HEIGHT: 6 Inches
PRICE: Pair: E, Singles: F.

Figs. 2477C/2477D
A pair of figures of seated spaniels with collars, lockets, and two separate front legs.
These dogs are quite late as all the colours, including the yellow collars, are underglaze. The red is a darker red than that used on earlier dogs.
HEIGHT: 7.5 Inches
PRICE: Pair: F, Singles: G.

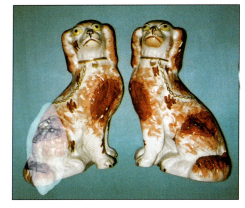

Figs. 2479A/2479B
A pair of red and white spaniels with collars, lockets, hains, and separate front legs.
HEIGHT: 9 Inches
PRICE: Pair: E, Singles: F.

Fig. 2481A
A figure of a seated spaniel with a separate leg and its coat clipped.
The figure illustrated is in the white; coloured examples can be found, the colouring raises their price considerably. This applies to all pairs of dogs.
There is a pair to this figure. Fig. 2481B has been reserved for it.
HEIGHT: 6 Inches
PRICE: Pair: F, Singles: G.

Figs. 2483A/2483B
A pair of figures of seated spaniels with a separate front leg and a collar with a locket.
These figures are very similar to Figs. 2482/2483 Book Two. There are modelling differences, mainly in the shape of the head and tail. They are also smaller. Right hand side figure, Fig. 2483B, is not illustrated.
HEIGHT: 6.25 Inches
PRICE: Pair: D, Singles: F.

Figs. 2495A/2495B
A pair of figures of seated spaniels with separate front legs, collar, and locket.
These figures are decorated all over with underglaze black. The collar and locket are in best gold and the eyes in overglaze enamel. Most of the dogs that are completely covered in overglaze black were made after 1875 and have come to be known as 'Jackfield' dogs. The company of Craven Dunhill & Co. was in existence from 1872 until 1951; before this they were known as Hargreaves and Craven. Their premises were in Jackfield Shropshire, so technically they were not a Staffordshire potter. They marked many of their wares with their place name 'Jackfield', hence the name became attached to the dogs. The body of clay used by them was a dark red. These types of dogs subsequently were copied by many Staffordshire potters and examples have been found marked 'Sadler'.
HEIGHT: 6.5 Inches
PRICE: Pair: F, Singles: G.

Figs. 2496/2497
A pair of figures of seated spaniels with lockets, collars, chains, and two separate front legs.
These figures are early; the lustre is very fine and the modelling extremely good. At the moment dogs decorated with gold lustre fetch much less than if they were decorated in red or black. In view of the quality of many of the early lustre dogs, this situation is unlikely to continue.
HEIGHT: 11.5 Inches
PRICE: Pair: D, Singles: F.

Figs. 2498/2499
A pair of red and white spaniels with chains. They hold flower baskets in their mouths.
These dogs are very similar to Figs. 2504/2505 Book Two and are probably the same, varying only in size and minor modelling differences.
HEIGHT: 7.5 Inches
PRICE: Pair: D, Singles: E.

Figs. 2527C/2527D
A pair of seated red and white spaniels with collars and chains, with their tails curling behind.
These are the same spaniels from the same pottery as Figs. 2527A/2527B Book Three, but without the spill vases. This is an extremely rare pair.
HEIGHT: 11.5 Inches
PRICE: Pair: E, Singles: G.

Figs. 2500/2501
A pair of red and white spaniels with baskets in their mouths.
HEIGHT: 3.5 Inches
PRICE: Pair: G, Singles: H.

Figs. 2533A/2533B
A pair of figures of spaniels seated with collars, locket, and chain, on cobalt blue bases.
Fig. 2533A not illustrated but is a mirror image.
HEIGHT: 6 Inches
PRICE: Pair: E, Singles: F.

Figs. 2520/2521
A pair of 'Disraeli' spaniels decorated in black and white with flower baskets in their mouths.
The black enamel used on these dogs is underglaze and therefore cannot flake. They look as fresh as when they were made.
HEIGHT: 8.5 Inches
PRICE: Pair: D, Singles: F.

Figs. 2534A/2535A An extremely fine pair of seated spaniels with separate front legs and collars and lockets around their necks.
These figures are identical to Figs. 2534/2535 Book Two, other than colouring and shape of base.
HEIGHT: 9.5 Inches
PRICE: Pair: D, Singles: E.

Fig. 2560
A group of two spaniels and a puppy on an arched, cobalt blue, gilt lined base.
This figure was made as a pen holder. The holes for the two quills or pens can be seen on the base. This group can be found in two sizes, both illustrated.
HEIGHT: 6.5 & 5.5 Inches
PRICE: E.

Figs. 2557C/2557D
A pair of group figures of a seated spaniel and its two puppies, one at its feet and the other on its back. The base is shaped and gilt lined.
A very rare and sought after pair of figures; a pair in red and white and a single in black and white are illustrated.
HEIGHT: 5.5 Inches
PRICE: Pair: D, Singles: F.

Fig. 2560B
A penholder group of two spaniels with collars and lockets; a puppy standing on its hind legs is between them, all on a cobalt blue base.
HEIGHT: 5.5 Inches
PRICE: E.

Fig. 2568A
A group figure of a spaniel with two puppies, both standing on their hind legs with their front paws on the spaniel.
A porcelaneous group very similar in modelling to the spaniel in Fig. 2567/2568 Book Two. There may be a pair to this group. Fig. 2568B has been reserved for it.
HEIGHT: 4 Inches
PRICE: E.

Figs. 2559A/2559B
A pair of groups of recumbent spaniels with their pups; these groups are in the form of trinket boxes. They can also be found with a normal oblong base or a decorated shaped base.
A pair with trinket box bases and singles with normal and shaped bases are illustrated.
It is rare to find these pairs intact. Very often the bases are broken and lost.
HEIGHT: 3.75 Inches
PRICE: Pair: E, Singles: F.

Figs. 2571/2572
A pair of seated spaniels with separate front legs.
These dogs were sold either with or without a base; their tails can also vary. Usually they have a 'pom pom' tail, but a more flattened version can be found.
HEIGHT: 4 Inches
PRICE: Pair: E, Singles: F.

Figs. 2576A/2576B
A pair of spaniels seated on tasselled cushions; in the pair illustrated one dog is over half an inch larger than the other and has different coloured tassels.
These are therefore a matched pair for each, which can be found in the two sizes.
HEIGHT: 4.5. and 4.75 Inches
PRICE: Pair: E, Singles: F.

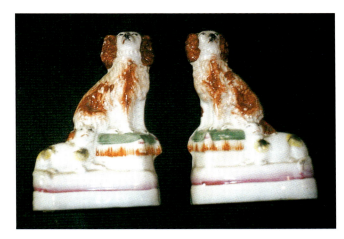

Figs. 2582A/2582B
A pair of figures of spaniels seated on cushions. Below the spaniel a cat is recumbent. A very rare pair of figures.
HEIGHT: 6 Inches
PRICE: Pair: D, Singles: E.

Figs. 2578A/2578B
A pair of standing black and white spaniels; these figures are unusual in so far as both dogs have their tongues hanging out. Why dogs should have been portrayed thus is a mystery.
HEIGHT: 5 Inches
PRICE: Pair: F, Singles: G.

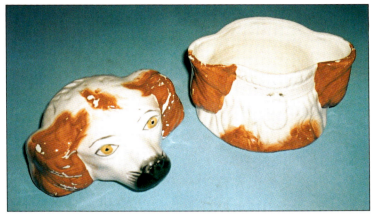

Fig. 2585A
A spaniel's head tobacco jar in two pieces.
HEIGHT: 6 Inches
PRICE: F.

Figs. 2580A/2580B
A pair of spaniels seated with two separate front legs and a collar and locket.
Whilst the two figures illustrated are a pair, they are a matched pair. The same dog was made with two different bases, the blue base being the more attractive of the two.
HEIGHT: 6 Inches
PRICE: Pair: E, Singles: F.

Fig. 2586
A group figure of three spaniels seated around a barrel.
This is a very rare figure; the one illustrated is the only one known to the authors.
HEIGHT: 6.5 Inches
PRICE: E.

ii. Whippets
See Figures 2606 - 2674 Books Two and Three

There is another dog that is also a possible candidate for the origin or inspiration of many of the whippet figures. A size smaller than a Greyhound but larger than the Whippet is the 'Lurcher'. Usually somewhat longer haired he is however very similar to both, other than size, and was kept for the same practical reasons as the Whippet.

Figs. 2632A/2632B
A pair of figures of recumbent Whippets on shaped and scrolled bases. There are many variations of this pair; this pair is very fine, the modelling is superb, and the dog's ribs are delineated. These figures were used as quill holders.
HEIGHT: 4.75 Inches
PRICE: Pair: E, Singles: G.

Figs. 2600/2601
A pair of standing whippets, each with three separately moulded legs.
The base decoration on this pair is of a lemon, turquoise, and brown colour that is applied in a particular way. It was also used on many other figures which would also have been made in the same, as yet unknown, factory.
HEIGHT: 6 Inches
PRICE: Pair: E, Singles: F.

Figs. 2667/2668
A pair of groups of Whippets, both seated, one with the whippet looking down at a dead rabbit that lies on the base, the other with its head erect and a spaniel lies at its feet on the base.
HEIGHT: 6 Inches
PRICE: Pair: D, Singles: F.

Figs. 2602/2603
A pair of figures of recumbent whippets with a dead rabbit at their feet on shaped and scrolled gilt lined bases.
HEIGHT: 7 Inches
PRICE: Pair: E, Singles: F.

Figs. 2675/2676
A pair of spill vase figures of standing whippets, one with a dead rabbit in its mouth, the other with the rabbit laying on the base. Both spills are adorned with flowers and leaves, all on a cobalt blue base.
HEIGHT: 9 Inches
PRICE: Pair: D, Singles: F.

Figs. 2604/2605
A pair of spill vase figures of standing whippets with a dead rabbit on the base.
A matched pair is illustrated.
HEIGHT: 8.5 Inches
PRICE: Pair: E, Singles: F.

Fig. 2677
A spill vase figure of a whippet standing with a rabbit in its mouth; the base to the top of the spill is decorated with a trailing climber.
There is a pair to this figure. Fig. 2677A has been reserved for it.
HEIGHT: 6 Inches
PRICE: Pair: E, Singles: F.

Figs. 2704A/2705A
A pair of spill vase figures of standing pointers with four separate legs. **These dogs are identical to Figs. 2704/2705 Book Two other than the dead birds and the clumps of clay that have been omitted.**
HEIGHT: 6 Inches
PRICE: Pair: D, Singles: E.

iii. Bull Mastiff
See Figures 2678 - 2679 Book Two

iv. Dalmatians
See Figures 2680 - 2691 Book Two

vi. Game Dogs
See Figures 2692 - 2741 Books Two and Three

Figs. 2707A/2707B
A pair of spill vase figures of standing game dogs.
An extremely rare pair of dogs, Fig. 2707A is not illustrated.
HEIGHT: 7.5 Inches
PRICE: Pair: D, Singles: E.

The authors have subsequently examined thoroughly a pair of these figures and are of the opinion that they are twentieth century reproductions; similar pairs can be found without the dogs seated behind that are by the same hand. Both pairs were first seen in the 1970s and some have impressed numbers on the bottom. That is not seen on nineteenth century Staffordshire. It is possible that they are being made on the Continent. They have to date fooled many into believing that they are genuine nineteenth century Staffordshire.

Figs. 2709A/2709B
A pair of spill vase figures of standing game dogs with a bird in their mouths, the spill being decorated with a spray of flowers. **Figure 2709A is not illustrated.**
HEIGHT: 9.5 Inches
PRICE: Pair: E, Singles: F.

Figs. 2733A/2733B
A pair of figures of seated hounds, one upright with his head turned to the left with a collar and chain that is attached to the base, the pair crouching with its chain lead also attached to the base. Both figures are on inverted cobalt blue and gilded bases. There are bowls on the bases.
HEIGHT: 5.5 Inches
PRICE: Pair: D, Singles: F.

Figs. 2718/2719
A pair of group figures of an Irish setter and a King Charles spaniel on coloured arched bases, one seated, the other recumbent. **These figures can be found in two sizes.**
HEIGHT: 10 Inches, 8.25 Inches
PRICE: Pair: D, Singles: E.

Figs. 2733C/2733D
A pair of figures of seated hounds, one upright with his head turned to the left with a collar and chain that is attached to the base, the pair crouching with its chain lead also attached to the base. Both figures are on inverted cobalt blue and gilded bases. **This pair is virtually identical to Figs. 2733A/2733B other than there is no bowl on the base.**
HEIGHT: 4.5 Inches
PRICE: Pair: D, Singles: F.

Figs. 2722B/2722C
A pair of spill vase groups of dogs seated to the side of the spill on which are large decorated leaves. Below two sheep are recumbent. **An extremely rare and very attractive pair of figures**
HEIGHT: 9.5 Inches
PRICE: Pair: C, Singles: E.

Fig. 2735B
A figure of a dog recumbent on an oblong gilt lined base with its head in its forepaws. A large chain that overlaps the base is around the dog's neck. **There is a pair to this figure, Fig. 2735A has been reserved for it.**
HEIGHT: 4 Inches
PRICE: Pair: E, Singles: F.

Figs. 2731C/2731D
A pair of figures of recumbent dogs on gilded, scrolled cobalt blue bases. These figures can also be found with footed bases, the feet shaped like shells.
HEIGHT: 6 Inches
PRICE: Pair: D, Singles: E.

Fig. 2741A
A figure of a dog recumbent on a grassy mound with leaves and flowers; the figure is in the form of a tureen, the base of which is moulded in basket weave.
This is a very unusual figure. These tureens can be found with hens and other birds on the lid and there is a very rare series with wild animals; but, the authors have not seen one with a dog on before. This figure may well be unique.
HEIGHT: 9 Inches
PRICE: D.

Figs. 2746A/2746B
A pair of groups of a seated poodle and a puppy recumbent between its front paws. The poodle has a separate front leg and all are on cobalt blue gilt lined bases.
This pair is similar to Figs. 2745/2746 Book Two, other than there is one puppy less.
HEIGHT: 6.75
PRICE: Pair: E, Singles: F.

vi. Poodles
See Figures 2742 - 2774C Books Two and Three

Fig. 2762B
A group figure of a seated poodle with its paw raised and placed on a covered table on which a cat sits with a bowl in front of it.
There is a pair to this figure. Fig. 2762A has been reserved for it.
HEIGHT: 4 Inches
PRICE: Pair: E, Singles: F.

Figs. 2745/2746
These figures can be found in at least three sizes. The 'fur' on the dogs illustrated was made by passing the clay through a sieve and applying it to the dog's body. These figures may also be found without such decoration, the fur being moulded into the figure. There are illustrated a pair of 7 Inch figures without applied fur, a pair of 6 Inch, and a single 8 Inch with fur applied.
HEIGHT: 8 Inches, 7 Inches, 6 Inches
PRICE: Pair: E, Singles: F.

Fig. 2768A
A group figure of a seated poodle and three pups on a gilt scrolled base.
This figure is very similar to Fig. 2767 Book Two with the addition of the puppies. There is no doubt a pair to it. Fig. 2768B has been reserved for it.
HEIGHT: 5.5 Inches
PRICE: F.

Figs. 2770A/2770B
A pair of figures of standing poodles, each with four separate legs, facing left and right, with their tails curled, each on a shaped base and both decorated with shredded clay to simulate fur. **These figures are porcelaneous and were made in the 1830s.**
HEIGHT: 5 Inches
PRICE: Pair: E, Singles: F.

Figs. 2774D/2774E
A pair of quill holder figures of poodles standing on cobalt blue bases with flower baskets in their mouths. **These figures are very similar to Figures 2774B/2774C other than the addition of holes to the bases and the replacement of dead birds with flower baskets.**
HEIGHT: 6 Inches
PRICE: Pair: E, Singles: F.

Figs. 2772A/2772B
A pair of standing figures of poodles with bags in their mouths and shells on the base.
HEIGHT: 3.5 Inches
PRICE: Pair: D, Singles: F.

vii. Pugs
See Figures 2775 - 2788 Books Two and Three

Figs. 2780A/2780B
A pair of seated Pugs, these figures have no bases and are late. They appear to be a smaller version of Figures 2779/2780 but are not so well modelled.
HEIGHT: 10 Inches
PRICE: Pair: E, Singles: F.

viii. Unidentified Breeds
See Figures 2789 - 2814 Books Two and Three

Figs. 2792A/2792B
A pair of figures of seated dogs on underglaze blue
bases, both smoking pipes with two separate front legs
and upright curly tail.
Figure 2792B not illustrated.
These are probably small versions of Figs.
2791/2792
Book Two.
HEIGHT: 8 Inches
PRICE: Pair: D, Singles: E.

Figs. 2815/2815A
A pair of figures of 'Wolf dogs' seated on rocky
bases; these figures are porcelaneous and very well
modelled.
HEIGHT: 9.5 Inches
PRICE: Pair: E, Singles: F.

Fig. 2816
A figure of a seated dog, probably a Collie, with a separate front
leg on a raised gilt lined base.
There is a pair to this figure. Fig. 2816A has been reserved
for it.
HEIGHT: 6 Inches
PRICE: Pair: E, Singles: F.

Chapter 7:
Animals

After the domesticated and farm animals, the potters turned their attention to wild animals. From the 1840s onwards, these creatures were being brought back from Africa, India, and elsewhere, and were kept in appalling conditions in the travelling menageries.

Overlooked by collectors for many years, these figures are now very much sought after. Considering the scant knowledge that the potters had of these subjects, their modelling is quite superb.

What is even more surprising is how rare models of domestic cats are when compared to the enormous numbers of dog figures.

Listings highlighted in bold type contain additions and alterations which will be found in this addendum, all other Portraits will be found in *Books One and Three, Victorian Staffordshire Figures 1835-1875*.

This chapter is divided into twenty three sections the animals are listed alphabetically:

i. Birds
See Figures 2821 - 2858 Books Two and Three

Figs. 2817/2818
A pair of figures of long tailed birds with wings outspread perched in a tree above nests filled with eggs.
A very attractive pair, quite delicately modelled and very rare.
HEIGHT: 8.5 Inches
PRICE: Pair: E, Singles: F.

Fig. 2818A
A figure of a bird with its wings spread, perched on a stump with a flower on, all on a round base.
There is probably a pair to this figure. Fig. 2818B has been reserved for it.
HEIGHT: 6 Inches
PRICE: G.

Figs. 2819/2820
A pair of groups of figures of birds perched below which are nests of eggs. A poodle stands below one and a spaniel below the other, both looking up.
HEIGHT: 5 Inches
PRICE: Pair: F, Singles: G.

Fig. 2831E
A figure of a duck with a chick in the form of an egg dish.
This is a very well modelled figure.
HEIGHT: 9 Inches
PRICE: E.

Fig. 2828
A figure of a hen dish in two parts used for keeping eggs in.
These dishes were made in many sizes. There are illustrated five of varying sizes from 7 to 11 Inches. The authors have seen them as small as 4 inches and as large as 12 Inches. They were also decorated in varying colours, sometimes just white with gilding.
PRICE: Small 4 to 7 Inches: E, Large 8 to 12 Inches: D.

Fig. 2831F
A figure of a swan in the form of an egg dish.
Illustrated with this figure is a figure of 2831G, an egg dish in the form of a duck. As the bases on these two figure are identical, it is probable that they were sold as pairs.
HEIGHT 7 Inches
PRICE: E (Each).

Fig. 2831B
Two figures of a crested dove in the form of a two-part dish.
Any two of these figures will pair each other.
HEIGHT: 8 Inches
PRICE: D.

Fig. 2831G
A figure of a duck in the form of an egg dish.
Two figures are illustrated, any two will pair each other.
HEIGHT: 7 Inches
PRICE: E.

Fig. 2831D
A figure of a duck in the form of a two-part dish, to be used for the storage of eggs, in this case presumably duck eggs.

This is quite a rare figure. Two figures are illustrated, each identical; any two will pair with each other.
LENGTH: 9 Inches
PRICE: E.

Figs. 2844A/2844B
A pair of figures of birds perched on rockwork, each is a mirror image of the other.
These figures are similar to Figs. 2843/2844 Book Two. There are, however, differences in the modelling of the head and wings.
HEIGHT: 10 Inches
PRICE: Pair: E, Singles: F.

Figs. 2833/2833A
A pair of spill vase figures that are also quill or pen holders of a bird perched on a branch next to a nest containing eggs.
This pair of figures may be found with either a gilt lined or coloured base.
HEIGHT: 7.5 Inches
PRICE: Pair: E, Singles: F.

Figs. 2857/2857A
A pair of figures of exotic birds perched on rockwork above a stream, facing to the left and right.
HEIGHT: 9.25 Inches
PRICE: Pair: E, Singles: F.

Fig. 2833B
A spill vase figure of two doves on either side of a nest in which there are four eggs. A snake is curled around the base and is attacking the eggs. All of this is on a rococo style base. HEIGHT: 8.5 Inches
PRICE: F.

Fig. 2858A
A spill vase figure of a bird perched on a branch adjacent to which is a nest; the base is decorated with trailing greenery. HEIGHT: 7.75 Inches
PRICE: E.

320

Fig. 2859
A double quill holder figure of a bird perched in a tree above a nest of eggs which is en-circled by a snake. Another bird lies dead on the base, which is rococo. **This is also a spill vase holder, but on this particular figure the spill has been filled in.**
HEIGHT: 9 Inches
PRICE: E.

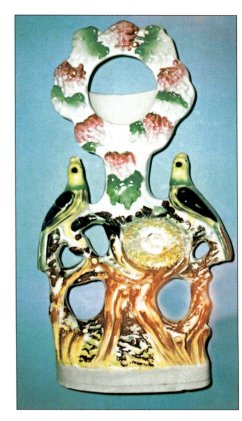

Fig. 2859C
A watch holder figure of two birds perched on either side of a nest, in which there are three eggs. The watch holder is decorated with grapes and leaves.
HEIGHT: 12 Inches
PRICE: F.

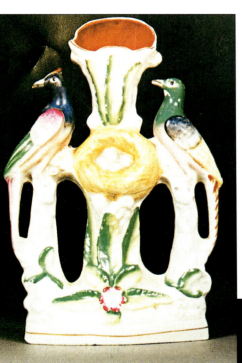

Fig. 2859A
A spill vase group figure of two exotic birds perched on either side of the spill. A nest with eggs is on the spill and flowers are on the base.
HEIGHT: 9.5 Inches
PRICE: E.

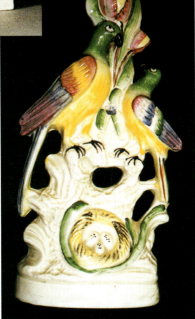

Fig. 2859B
A group figure of two exotic birds perched one above the other on rockwork; between them is a large flower, the head of which form's a candleholder. Below and on the base is a nest filled with three eggs.
HEIGHT: 9 Inches
PRICE: E.

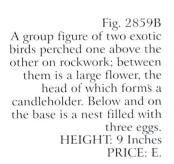

Fig. 2860
A double quill holder group of a bird with its wings outstretched clutching a snake in its talons. Three chicks are in a nest below.
HEIGHT: 5.25 Inches
PRICE: F.

ii. Camels
See Figures 2861 - 2866 Books Two and Three

iii. Cats
See Figures 2867 - 2890 Books Two and Three

Figs. 2886A/2886B
A pair of figures of seated cats with separate front legs decorated to resemble tortoiseshell.
HEIGHT: 6 Inches
PRICE: Pair: D, Singles: F.

iv. Cows
See Figures 2891 - 2903 Books Two and Three

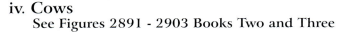

Figs. 2896A/2896BB
A pair of spill vase figures of a standing cow facing left and right. The spill is decorated with leaves.
These are very rare figures and the pair illustrated are 'matched', i.e. they did not start off life together.
HEIGHT: 10 Inches
PRICE: Pair: D, Single: E.

Fig. 2896C
A spill vase figure of a standing cow, the spill decorated with shredded clay.
This figure is very similar to Fig. 2896A; they are, however, different models. The spill, position of the tail, and horns are all different. They are a smaller, untitled version of 'Milk Sold Here'. There is a pair to this figure. Fig. 2896D has been reserved for it.
HEIGHT: 9.5
PRICE: F.

Fig. 2896E
A spill vase figure of a standing cow; a bucket of milk is on the ground by her forelegs.
There is a pair to this figure. Fig. 2896F has been reserved for it.
HEIGHT: 8.5 Inches
PRICE: F.

Figs. 2900/2901
A pair of spill vase figures of cows standing with recumbent sheep below.
The pair illustrated are a 'matched pair', as a 'true' pair would both have the same coloured decoration.
HEIGHT: 7 Inches
PRICE: Pair: D, Singles: F.

Fig. 2903B
A figure of a recumbent cow on a shaped gilt lined base. This figure could be used either as a spill vase or a creamer; the cream could be poured into the spill and out through the cow's mouth, the tail being the handle.
There is a pair to this figure. Fig. 2903A has been reserved for it.
HEIGHT: 5 Inches
PRICE: Pair: D, Singles: F.

v. Deer
See Figures 2905 - 2926 Books Two and Three

Fig. 2922B
A spill vase figure of a standing deer with a snake coiled around it.
There is a pair to this figure. Fig. 2922A has been reserved for it. This figure is from the same factory as Fig. 2922 Book Two and is a derivation of that figure.
HEIGHT: 7.5 Inches
PRICE: E.

Fig. 2922C
A spill vase figure of a standing deer with four separate legs, a front leg raised.
There is a pair to this figure. Fig. 2922D has been reserved for it.
HEIGHT: 8.5 Inches
PRICE: Pair: E, Singles: F.

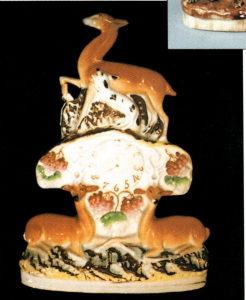

Figs. 2910A/2910B
A pair of spill vase figures of a stag and doe standing with one leg raised; each figure has a hind reclining between their legs.
This pair can be found in two sizes; a pair of the smaller and a single of the larger size are illustrated. This pair is very similar to Figs. 2909/2910 Book Two, the main difference being the decoration to the spill vase.
HEIGHT: 6.75 7 9.5 Inches
PRICE: Pair: E, Singles: F.

Fig. 2916B
A figure of a leaping deer with a tree trunk behind on a gilt lined base.
There is a pair to this figure. Fig. 2916A has been reserved for it.
HEIGHT: 6 Inches
PRICE: Pair: E, Singles: F.

Fig. 2922E
A clock face group of three deer, one on top of the figure is standing and is being brought down by a dog. Below is the clock face that is surrounded by a grapevine and on the base two deer are seated facing each other.
HEIGHT: 9 Inches
PRICE: F.

vi. Donkeys/Mules.
See Figures 2927 - 2936A Books Two and Three

Fig. 2935B
A pair of spill vase figures of a donkey standing before a tree trunk. At his feet a foal is recumbent. A stream runs between the donkey's legs. The pair is a mirror image.
HEIGHT: 12 Inches
PRICE: Pair: E, Singles: F.

vii. Elephants.
See Figures 2937 - 2949 Books Two and Three

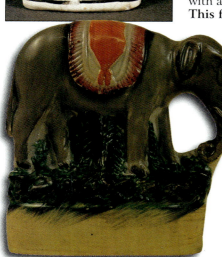

Fig. 2939C
A figure of a standing elephant with a saddlecloth.
This figure can be found in two sizes, both illustrated. There is a pair to this figure. Fig. 2939D has been reserved for it.
HEIGHT: 7 Inches.
3 Inches.
PRICE: 7 Inches Pair: D, Singles: E, 3 Inches Pair: E, Singles: F.

viii. Fish
See Figure 2951 Book Two

ix. Foxes
See Figures 2952 - 2971 Books Two and Three

Figs. 2953A/2953B
A pair of figures of foxes standing with one foot raised; a very finely modelled pair with all legs separated.
HEIGHT: 8 Inches
PRICE: Pair: E, Singles: F.

Figs. 2963/2964
A pair of spill vase figures of standing foxes with a bird in their mouths; the spills are decorated with flowers.
HEIGHT: 9 Inches
PRICE: Pair: E, Singles: F.

324

Fig. 2968A
A spill vase group of a fleeing fox being chased by a dog that is leaping over a bridge. Under the bridge a swan swims.
There is probably a pair to this figure. Fig. 2968B has been reserved for it.
HEIGHT: 12 Inches
PRICE: E.

Fig. 2978A
A spill vase figure of a standing giraffe and its keeper.
There is a pair to this very rare figure. Fig. 2978 has been reserved for it. This is another version of Fig. 2973 Book Two; this figure does, however, have the size of the giraffe more in keeping to the size of the keeper.
HEIGHT: 10 Inches
PRICE: D.

Fig. 2969B
A group of a fox crouching in undergrowth to the right of a tree stump; below that are two rabbits.
HEIGHT: 5.5 Inches
PRICE: E.

x. Giraffes
See Figures 2972 - 2977 Books Two and Three

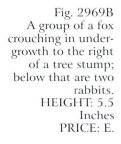

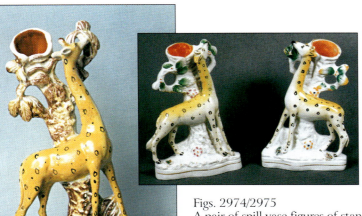

Figs. 2974/2975
A pair of spill vase figures of standing giraffes. The spill is in the form of a tree from which the giraffes are eating.
These very rare figures can be found in two sizes; a large pair one in the white, the other in colour, and a pair of 7.25 inch figures are illustrated.
HEIGHT: 13 Inches, 7.25 Inches
PRICE: 13 Inch Pair: A, Singles: C, 7.25 inch Pair: B, Singles: D.

Fig. 2978SO
Illustrated is a coloured print of a painting by Laurent Agasse, titled 'The Nubian Giraffe' that is the source or inspiration for Figs. 2972/2973 and 2978/2978A.

xi. Goats
See Figures 2979 - 2982 Books Two and Three

Figs. 2982A/2982B
A pair of spill vase figures of goats standing on rockwork; below and between their feet a kid is reclining.
HEIGHT: 5.5 Inches
PRICE: Pair: F, Singles: G.

xii. Gorillas, Monkeys
See Figures 2983 - 2986 Books Two and Three

i. Horses
See Figures 2987 - 3001B Books Two and Three

Figs. 2987/2988
These figures can also be found decorated as zebra's, see Figs. 3106/3107.

Figs. 2998C/2998D
A pair of spill vase figures of recumbent horses on coloured shaped bases.
This potter made a number of similar figures, all with different animals below the spill. See Figs. 2971 Fox, 2813 Dog, 3077C Rabbit, Book Three.
HEIGHT: 6 Inches
PRICE Pair: F, Singles: G.

xiv. Leopards
See Figures 3002 - 3011 Books Two and Three

Figs. 3009A/3009B
A pair of figures of a reclining leopard and a reclining tiger with leaves on the base.
These figures can be found decorated as either a leopard or a tiger. The authors have seen pairs of tigers and pairs of leopards and, as illustrated, a mixed pair.
HEIGHT: 4 Inches
PRICE: Pair: E, Single: F.

xv. Lions
See Figures 3012 - 3035 Books Two and Three

Figs. 3027/3028
A pair of recumbent lions with a sheep at their feet, on waisted shaped bases. An uncoloured pair and a coloured single are illustrated. These figures are modelled in the round and were made in the early 1830s.
They may either be biblical in inspiration, or more likely theatrical, as part of Van Amburgh's act was to make a lion lay down with a lamb.
HEIGHT: 4 Inches
PRICE: Pair: B, Singles: E.

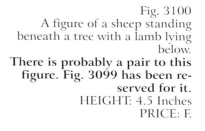

Fig. 3100
A figure of a sheep standing beneath a tree with a lamb lying below.
There is probably a pair to this figure. Fig. 3099 has been reserved for it.
HEIGHT: 4.5 Inches
PRICE: F.

Figs. 3035/3036
A pair of standing lions with lambs at their feet; these are very small figures and were made cheaply as fairings to be given away as prizes at fairs. The lambs have not been decorated at all and no gilding has been used.
HEIGHT: 3.5 Inches
PRICE: Pair: F, Singles: G.

xvi. Pigs.
See Figures 3066 - 3067 Book Two

xvii. Rabbits
See Figures 3069 - 3077C Books Two and Three

xx. Squirrels
See Figures 3101 - 3103 Books Two and Three

xxi. Tigers
See Figures 3104 - 3105 Book Two

xxii. Zebras
See Figures 3108 - 3126 Books Two and Three

Figs. 3070/3070A
A pair of figures of seated floppy eared rabbits.
HEIGHT: 6 Inches
PRICE: Pair: C Singles: E.

Figs. 3106/3107
A pair of spill vase figures of standing zebra's with one front leg raised.
These figures are identical to Figs. 2987/2988, other than they are decorated as horses. The potters used the same moulds for the two different animals.
HEIGHT: 12 Inches
PRICE: Pair: D, Singles: E.

xviii. Rhinoceri
See Figure 3078 Book Two

xix. Sheep
See Figures 3080 - 3098 Books Two and Three

Figs. 3081/3082
A pair of spill vase figures of a standing ewe and ram.
These figures can be found in two sizes. The 5.5. Inch version is illustrated. These figures were made by the Parr pottery; in later Kent versions two ewes are portrayed rather than a ewe and ram.
HEIGHT: 5.5 Inches, 7 Inches
PRICE: Pair: E, Singles: F.

Figs. 3114/3115
A standing pair of zebras on coloured oval bases.
These figures can be found in two sizes.
HEIGHT: 8 Inches, 4 Inches
PRICE: Pair: E, Singles: F (8 Inch); Pair: F, Singles: G (4 Inch).

xxiii. Reptiles

Figs. 3127/3128
A pair of spill vase figures of a zebra being chased by a fox that is jumping over a small bridge under which a stream flows, one being a mirror image of the other.
It is possible that it is not a fox but a hyena that is being portrayed; the zebra is correctly modelled with a brush mane, for otherwise it could have been portraying a dog chasing a horse.
HEIGHT: 10 Inches
PRICE: Pair: D, Singles: E.

Fig. 3130A
An Alligator or Crocodile in the form of a tureen on a bamboo decorated base.
This figure, previously unrecorded, is part of a very rare service that includes other tureens with lids depicting an elephant, a rhinoceros, and a leopard (Figs. 2949, 3078, 3011 Books Two and Three). It is possible that others will come to light.
HEIGHT: 7 Inches
PRICE: C.

Figs. 3129/3130
A pair of figures of standing zebras with four separate legs on oval gilt lined bases.
Although quite small figures, the central support was necessary to prevent the figure collapsing in the kiln.
HEIGHT: 3.25 Inches
PRICE: Pair: E, Singles: F.

Chapter 8:
Houses, Cottages, and Castles

Most of the pre-Victorian figures in this category were made of porcelain, making them expensive to produce and they had a specific use. These figures were not intended for the working classes, but for the middle and upper classes of society. The pastille burners were used to combat the awful odours that were prevalent in the towns and cities at that time. Once sanitary conditions improved, their use became obsolete.

In the 1840s a change occurred and figures were made in pottery, making them cheaper to produce and affordable to a wider section of the public. In this mass production the figures lost their original purpose and became decorative items, or in some cases money boxes.

With this is mind the potters produced figures of houses, castles and buildings connected with Royalty, The Crimean War, and associated with criminals and murderers or their victims. Their imagination also drew them to the making of idealised building, many of which had they ever been built would have promptly fallen down.

This chapter is divided into the following sections:

   i. Titled Buildings
   ii. Untitled Buildings
   iii. Pastille Burners

i. Titled Buildings
See Figures 3131 - 3151 Books Two and Three

ii. Untitled Buildings
See Figures 3155 - 3219 Books Two and Three

Fig. 3154
A double spill vase figure of a castle, with central door below two windows and a clock face. A large plant growing up either side.
HEIGHT: 7.5 Inches
PRICE: G.

Fig. 3160A
A figure of a twin turreted castle with a clock face in the middle. **This figure is very similar to Fig. 3160 Book Two. It has a different configuration of doors and windows.**
HEIGHT: 5.5 Inches
PRICE: H.

Fig. 3160B A figure of a twin turreted castle with a clock face in the middle. **A debased version of Figures 3160/3160A.**
HEIGHT: 3 Inches
PRICE: H.

Fig. 3153
A figure of a castle with a turret at either end a central door flanked by four windows on each side.
HEIGHT: 7 Inches
PRICE: G.

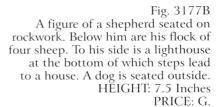

Fig. 3177B
A figure of a shepherd seated on rockwork. Below him are his flock of four sheep. To his side is a lighthouse at the bottom of which steps lead to a house. A dog is seated outside.
HEIGHT: 7.5 Inches
PRICE: G.

Fig. 3178E
A group figure of a boy and girl standing on either side of a windmill with a sheaf of wheat under their arms. **This is a different version of Figure 3178B Book Three.**
HEIGHT: 10 Inches
PRICE: F.

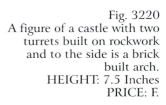

Fig. 3220
A figure of a castle with two turrets built on rockwork and to the side is a brick built arch.
HEIGHT: 7.5 Inches
PRICE: F.

Fig. 3183A
A figure of a turreted building with a sentry to the side.
This figure is an adaptation of Fig. 3183 Book Two, and must have originated from the same modeler. What is interesting is that instead of it being decorated with best gold, Sunderland lustre has been used, which might suggest that this figure was made there.
HEIGHT: 7.5 Inches
PRICE: G.

Fig. 3221
A spill vase figure of a cabin with steps leading to it. Below and to the left a man and woman stand.
HEIGHT: 8.5 Inches
PRICE: F.

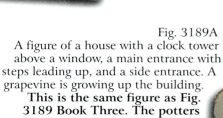

Fig. 3187
A figure of a church with two turrets and three entrances, all surmounted by a cross.
This figure can be found in two versions, either as a clock face figure or as a watch holder. Both versions are illustrated.
HEIGHT: 10.5 Inches
PRICE: G

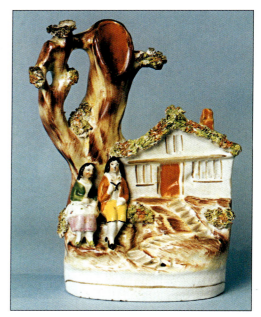

Fig. 3189A
A figure of a house with a clock tower above a window, a main entrance with steps leading up, and a side entrance. A grapevine is growing up the building.
This is the same figure as Fig. 3189 Book Three. The potters have omitted the figure of the dog and have not applied the shredded clay decoration; it was produced more cheaply and no doubt sold more cheaply.
HEIGHT: 9.25 Inches
PRICE: G.

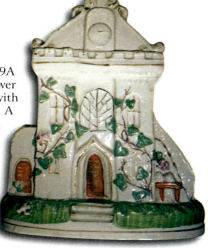

Fig. 3222
A spill vase figure of a cabin with steps leading to it. Below and to the left a man and woman stand.
This figure is similar to the preceding one other than the spill is different and a different model has been used for the man.
HEIGHT: 8 Inches
PRICE: G.

Fig. 3223
A figure of a six sided folly with steps leading to a central door above which are two windows and flanked by three on either side **Typical of a house that would never have been built, it could not be used as either a moneybox or a pastille burner. It has, however, a charm all of its own.**
HEIGHT: 6 Inches
PRICE: F.

Fig. 3225
A figure of a house on an arched base with two doors to the side and five windows over two stories, all decorated with shredded clay. A hole has been pierced in the base and the figure is for use as a quill holder.
HEIGHT: 5 Inches
PRICE: H.

Fig. 3226
A figure of a house on a rococo base with steps leading to a door that is flanked by windows on two levels. One chimney is situated on a sloping roof.
HEIGHT: 4 Inches
PRICE: H.

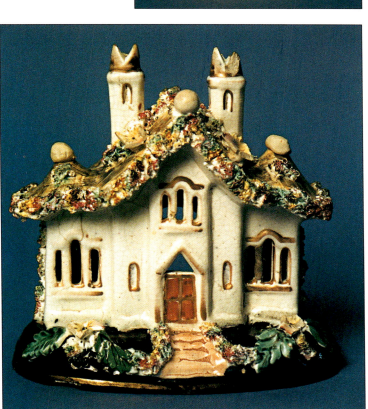

Fig. 3224
A quite elaborate house of two chimneys, three pierced windows, and steps leading to the central door, all on a decorated underglaze blue base.
It is probable that originally this would have had an aperture in the back so that it could be used as a pastille burner.
HEIGHT: 5 Inches
PRICE: F.

Fig. 3227
A very simple house of one chimney under a pitched roof with steps leading to the front door that has a window on both sides and three above.
Made for use as a moneybox.
HEIGHT: 3.75
PRICE: H.

331

Fig. 3228 An Eastern type building of a central door flanked by two towers, the whole decorated with flowers.
HEIGHT: 7 Inches
PRICE: G.

Fig. 3229
A six-sided building with a central chimney, below which are five windows surrounding a central door.
HEIGHT: 4 Inches
PRICE: G.

Fig. 3231
A figure of a two-story house with two roofs, on the lower of which a cat sits next to a window, with a water butt to the side. Below and to the right of the front door a dog sits below a window. A large kennel is at the side of the house. HEIGHT: 7.5 Inches
PRICE: G.

Fig. 3230
A figure of a castle with three turrets; below the central turret are steps leading to an entrance.
HEIGHT: 5 Inches
PRICE: H.

Fig. 3232
A figure of a castle with three turrets and barred windows and an entrance door to the right.
HEIGHT: 4 Inches
PRICE: G.

Fig. 3233
A figure of a house that has ornate chimneys and four windows but no door!
HEIGHT: 5 Inches
PRICE: G.

Fig. 3236
A figure of a small house with three chimneys and side projections. A tree grows from the back and above.
HEIGHT: 4 Inches
PRICE: G.

Fig. 3234
A figure of an elaborate house with a central door, six windows, and three towers connected by arches.
HEIGHT: 7 Inches
PRICE: G.

Fig. 3235
A figure of a three-story tower house with two pillars on either side of a central door, seated outside of which is a dog.
HEIGHT: 7.5 Inches
PRICE: G.

Fig. 3237
A figure of a two-story house, with a small tower and steps leading to a central door.
HEIGHT: 5.5 Inches
PRICE: G.

Fig. 3238
A figure of a church or school with one large chimney above a pointed, sloping roof; the centre section has four windows and a door at each side.
HEIGHT: 6 Inches
PRICE: H.

Fig. 3239
A figure of a castle with two turreted side towers and a central section with a sloping roof above a clock.
HEIGHT: 5.25
PRICE: G.

Fig. 3241
A figure of a round house with a central chimney and flowers on the roof and base.
HEIGHT: 4.5 Inches
PRICE: H.

Fig. 3240
A figure of a house covered with flowers surrounding a central door, the whole terminating in a single chimney. A dog sits amongst the flowers at the side.
HEIGHT: 5.5 Inches
PRICE: G.

Fig. 3242
A spill vase figure of a pair of semi-detached houses, one with steps leading to the front door. To the side of the house two dogs are running.
HEIGHT: 6 Inches
PRICE: G.

iii. **Pastille Burners.**
See Figures 3251 - 3297 Books Two and Three

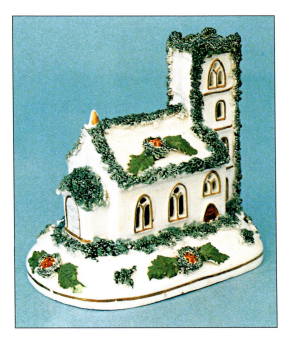

Fig. 3248
A figure of a church with a tower to the side; the unusual decoration of holly on the roof and base might have meant that this was a pastille burner used as a Christmas decoration.
HEIGHT: 5.25
PRICE: G.

Fig. 3243
A figure of a building with a double pitched roof and tower beside, with three entrances and three windows.
There is no doubt as what this building portrays as 'SCHOOL' is on a banner above the entrance.
HEIGHT: 7.75
PRICE: G.

Fig. 3244
A spill vase figure of a thatched roof building with steps leading to the entrance, all surrounded by trees.
HEIGHT: 8.25
PRICE: H.

Fig. 3249
A figure of a gazebo or garden house, the roof supported on five pillars with a small font in the middle.
HEIGHT: 3.75
PRICE: G.

Fig. 3250
A figure of a two-piece house with a central door above which is a window; there are four other windows on either side. The roof and base are flower covered.
HEIGHT: 5 Inches
PRICE: F.

Fig. 3276A
A figure of a six-sided building with a central door and a window on either side.
HEIGHT: 3.5 Inches
PRICE: H.

Fig. 3299
A very elaborate two-piece figure of a house with arched entrance below a window; two other windows are either side. The roof and base is covered with fruit and flowers.
HEIGHT: 5.75
PRICE: F.

Fig. 3300
A lilac coloured castle in two pieces; both turrets, the walls and base are covered with flowers.
Lilac coloured pastille burners are the most sought after and are usually very elaborate.
HEIGHT: 7 Inches
PRICE: E.

Fig. 3298
A two-piece figure of a castle with two entrances and steps leading to a high door with a tower above.
The building is separate from the base.
HEIGHT: 4 Inches
PRICE: F.

Chapter 9:
Sport and Miscellaneous

Included in this chapter are the wrestlers, cricketers, and jockeys who are unidentified. It is also used to include other figures which do not sit happily in the preceding chapters. It is in fact somewhat of a clearing house for all those figures which we do not know where else to put.

Figs. 3316/3317
A pair of figures of mounted jockeys, both dressed in cap, shirt with tie, and riding breeches; one hand is on the saddle-cloth and the other holds the reins on the horse's flank. Each figure is a mirror image of the other.
HEIGHT: 8.5 Inches
PRICE: Pair: E, Singles: F.

Fig. 3307A
A standing figure of a boy wearing a Scot's hat, open necked shirt, waistcoat, jacket, and kilt. He holds a bat in his right hand and a ball in his left.
There is probably a pair to this figure; it is not known why a Scottish child should be portrayed with a cricket bat and ball. If the pair comes to light, the reason may become clear. It is possible that this figure and its pair depict children's games.
HEIGHT: 7 Inches
PRICE: F.

Figs. 3321A/3321B
A pair of figures of women seated sidesaddle on horseback with jockeys to their side. Those jockeys are holding the head of a rearing horse. Each woman is dressed in riding habit of hat, blouse, and long skirt. The jockeys are dressed in cap, shirt with tie, and breeches.
A very rare pair and much sought after.
HEIGHT: 8 Inches
PRICE: Pair: D, Singles: E.

Fig. 3326
A figure of a man sitting astride a beer barrel, wearing a tricorn hat that is decorated with grapes and grape leaves, long coat, waistcoat, and knee breeches, holding a jug in one hand and a cup in the other. **This figure is in the form of a jug and has a detachable lid that is usually missing. Early Parr figures as illustrated are rare; later Kent versions are much more common. This figure can be found in three sizes; the 8 Inch version is illustrated.**
HEIGHT: 9.5 Inches, 8 Inches, 7 Inches
PRICE: E.

Fig. 3328B
A head only figure of a bearded man wearing a turban; it is probable that there should be a lid for this figure that would have served as a tobacco jar.
HEIGHT: 7 Inches
PRICE: G.

Fig. 3326A
A bust of a man wearing a tricorn hat, shirt, waistcoat, and jacket. He is longhaired and bearded. He holds a basket in front of him on the top of which is a dead rabbit. **This figure is in the form of a jug; two figures are illustrated, in one the title has been obliterated.**
TITLE: MERRY CHRISTMAS
HEIGHT: 8.25 Inches
PRICE: F.

Fig. 3328A
A figure of a seated man with his legs crossed holding objects in his hands. **This figure is in the form of a tobacco or snuff jar.**
HEIGHT: 8 Inches
PRICE: F.

Figs. 3335A/3335B
A pair of standing figures of a man and woman, both dressed in flowing robes and both holding a spaniel in one hand to their waist, he with his left arm resting on a pillar. A large scarf is draped over his shoulders across his leg and over his wrist. **These figures have defied identification. He appears to have only one leg, but this is probably due to the figures composition. Without the spaniels they could be taken for religious figures. They are possibly of theatrical or classical inspiration.**
HEIGHT: 15 Inches
PRICE: Pair: F, Singles: G.

Figs. 3336/3336A
A pair of figures of a boy and girl reclining, he is dressed in open neck shirt, waistcoat, jacket, and knee breeches. His right elbow rests on rockwork and his legs are crossed. The girl is seated, her left hand resting on rockwork. She is bareheaded and wears a blouse and long dress. Her right arm is held across her waist.
The figure of the girl was made as a balancing pair to Fig. 3336, 'The Red Boy'.
HEIGHT 5.5 Inches
PRICE: Pair: F, Singles: G.

Fig. 3336B
A figure of a boy reclining, dressed in frilled shirt, waistcoat, jacket, and knee breeches; one elbow rests on rockwork and the other arm is around a small dog, which sits on his lap.
This figure is an adaptation of Fig. 3336, 'The Red Boy'.
HEIGHT: 5 Inches
PRICE: F.

Figs. 3345B/3345C
A pair of figures of a dog seated on a tasselled bench, standing guard over a child who kneels on a cushion beside him. Below a wolf lies dead. Each figure is a mirror image of the other, the only difference being that a girl replaces the boy.
The boy is a portrayal of Gelert and Prince Llewellyn's son. The girl was made as a balancing figure to make a pair. Both figures are extremely rare.
HEIGHT: 9.5 Inches
PRICE: Pair: D, Singles: E.

Fig. 3344A
A standing figure of a woman dressed in a flowing garb over a suit of armour. On her chest is a cross and she holds a large sword in both hands.
This figure is another version of Joan of Arc.
HEIGHT: 14 Inches
PRICE: E.

Fig. 3344B
A standing figure of a woman dressed in a flowing garb over a suit of armour. On her chest is a cross and she holds a short sword in both hands.
This figure is an adaptation of Fig. 3344A, Joan of Arc. It has also been mistakenly titled 'St. JOHN'. It is not a portrayal of St. John; it is possible that the potters meant to title the figure either 'St. JEAN' or 'St. JOAN', but due to illiteracy the title was misspelled.
HEIGHT: 14 Inches
PRICE: E.

Figs. 3346D/3346E
A pair of spill vase figures of a stork standing and a fox seated on gilt lined rococo style bases. One vase features the two seated on either side of a plate; the other has them seated to either side of a long-necked jar.
These figures are a portrayal of an Aesop's fable, 'The Stork and the Fox'. At one time the fox and the stork were good friends, so the Fox invited the Stork to dinner, and for a joke put nothing before her but some soup in a very shallow dish. This the Fox could easily lap up, but the Stork could only wet the end of her long bill in it, and left the meal as hungry as she began. 'I am sorry the soup is not to your liking', said the Fox. 'Pray do not apologise', said the Stork. 'I hope you will return this visit and come and dine with me soon'. So a day was arranged when the Fox should visit the Stork; but when they were seated at the table, all that was for their dinner was contained in a very long-necked jar with a narrow mouth, into which the Stork could put her bill, but the Fox could not insert his snout. All the Fox could manage was to lick the outside of the jar. 'I will not apologise for this dinner', said the Stork, 'one bad turn deserves another'.
HEIGHT: 7 Inches
PRICE: Pair: E, Singles: F.

Fig. 3346F
A spill vase figure of 'The fox and the stork'. The stork is perched above the fox that holds a necked vase. A nest of eggs is on the base.
There will be a pair to this. Fig. 3346G has been reserved for it.
This is another version of the Aesop fable, 'The fox and the stork' (see also figures 3346C/D/E).
HEIGHT: 7 Inches
PRICE: F.

Fig. 3355D
A figure of a boy standing, wearing an off the shoulder garment and short trousers. He holds a sickle in his left hand and his right rests on a sheaf of wheat.
This figure is emblematic of autumn and there would have been another three to complete the set. Figs. 3355E, F, G are reserved for them.
HEIGHT: 8.5 Inches
PRICE: F.

Fig. 3359B
A spill vase group figure of two naked children standing on either side of a tree stump on which a large flowering plant grows. Each of the children are holding a scarf that is draped decorously over them.
HEIGHT: 8 Inches
PRICE: G.

Figs. 3354A/3354B/3354C/3354D
A standing titled set of the Four Seasons.
Summer – A girl holding a basket of fruit. Autumn – A boy holding a sheaf of wheat. Winter – A boy ice skating holding his coat. Spring – A girl with a garland of flowers.
A number of variations of these figures can be found, and pre-Victorian versions with square bases were also made.
HEIGHT: 10 Inches
PRICE: Set: E, Singles: F.

Fig. 3355A
A figure of a girl standing holding a basket under her arm; she is wearing a dress with a skirt beneath.
This figure is emblematic of 'Summer' and was probably made by Lloyd Shelton; the colouring identifies this as part of the series of which Fig. 3355 is 'Winter'.
HEIGHT: 9.5 Inches
PRICE: F.

Figs. 3361/3361A
A pair of figures of cherubs standing, holding a basket of grapes in one hand and a bunch of grapes in the other. Both cherubs are scantily dressed in a loin cloth with a wreath of grape leaves on their heads.
These figures were made in The Parr factory and are both on gilded rococo bases.
HEIGHT: 9.75 Inches
PRICE: Pair: F, Singles: G.

Fig. 3361H
A group figure of three cherubs surrounding a clock face that is mounted on a pedestal. The two cherubs standing on either side hold large ribbons, the one at the top holds a bunch of grapes, and the whole is adorned with a fruiting grapevine.
HEIGHT: 11.25 Inches
PRICE: G.

Fig. 3362
A group of a man and a woman standing arm in arm under an umbrella; he is wearing a hat, waistcoat, jacket, and trousers. She is wearing a hat and long dress, holding a bag in her left hand. **This figure can be found in at least two sizes, both illustrated. This figure is a copy of a Pre-Victorian figure which is sometimes titled 'The Dandies'.**
HEIGHT: 8.25 & 6 Inches
PRICE: H.

Fig. 3384
A figure of a man seated on a barrel dressed in a waistcoat, open necked shirt, and breeches. He wears a headdress of grapes and leaves and holds a cup in his right hand. **This figure portrays 'Bacchus' and is a product of The Parr factory.**
HEIGHT: 6.75
PRICE: H.

Figs. 3362A/3362B
A pair of figures of a man and woman dressed in eighteenth century attire, he wearing a jacket and knee breeches with his right hand behind his back. She wears a bodice and long skirt and holds a fan to her face. Both figures are on arched and scrolled bases. **These figures are not at all typical of nineteenth century Staffordshire and appear to be copying earlier French or Continental porcelain figures.**
HEIGHT: 6.75
PRICE: Pair: F, Singles: G.

Fig. 3385
A figure of a girl/woman
standing holding her
nightgown,
with a cloak to the side.
**A somewhat 'risqué'
figure for, as can be
seen, she is not wear-
ing any underwear.**
HEIGHT: 4 Inches
PRICE: F.

Fig. 3388
A spill vase group of two figures standing on
either side of a tree, one is handing a bird's
nest – in which there is a sheep's head – to the
other.
**This group is quite an oddity; it would
appear that a modeller made this from a
number of quite separate parts. It is clearly
a 'one off' and was probably made for his
amusement. All the parts are genuine, as is
the title. The main part of the group is of
Abraham and Isaac (Fig. 1671 Book One),
the arm holding the nest is from Paul and
Virginia (Fig. 1181 Book One), the odd
hats are from other figures, and beards
have been added – one painted blue. The
whole has then been given the very odd
title 'Jem Crow and Blue Beard'.**
HEIGHT: 11 Inches.
PRICE: When sold at Auction in 2002 it
made £530-00.
When sold at Auction in 2006 it made £506-
00.

Fig. 3386
A figure of a child asleep on a day bed
dressed only in a short nightshirt with his
bottom showing.
HEIGHT: 3.5 Inches
PRICE: H.

Fig. 3387
A very unusual figure of a man's boot and
a lady's shoe on a shaped gilt lined base.
**It is probable that this was designed to
hold quills and ink.**
HEIGHT: 5 Inches
PRICE: F.

Index

NOTE: Included in this index are the indexes for Book One, Book Two, Book Three and Book Four: Book 1 is in Standard text, Book Two, in *Italics* Book Three in **Bold Standard** text. Book Four in **_Bold Italics_**

344

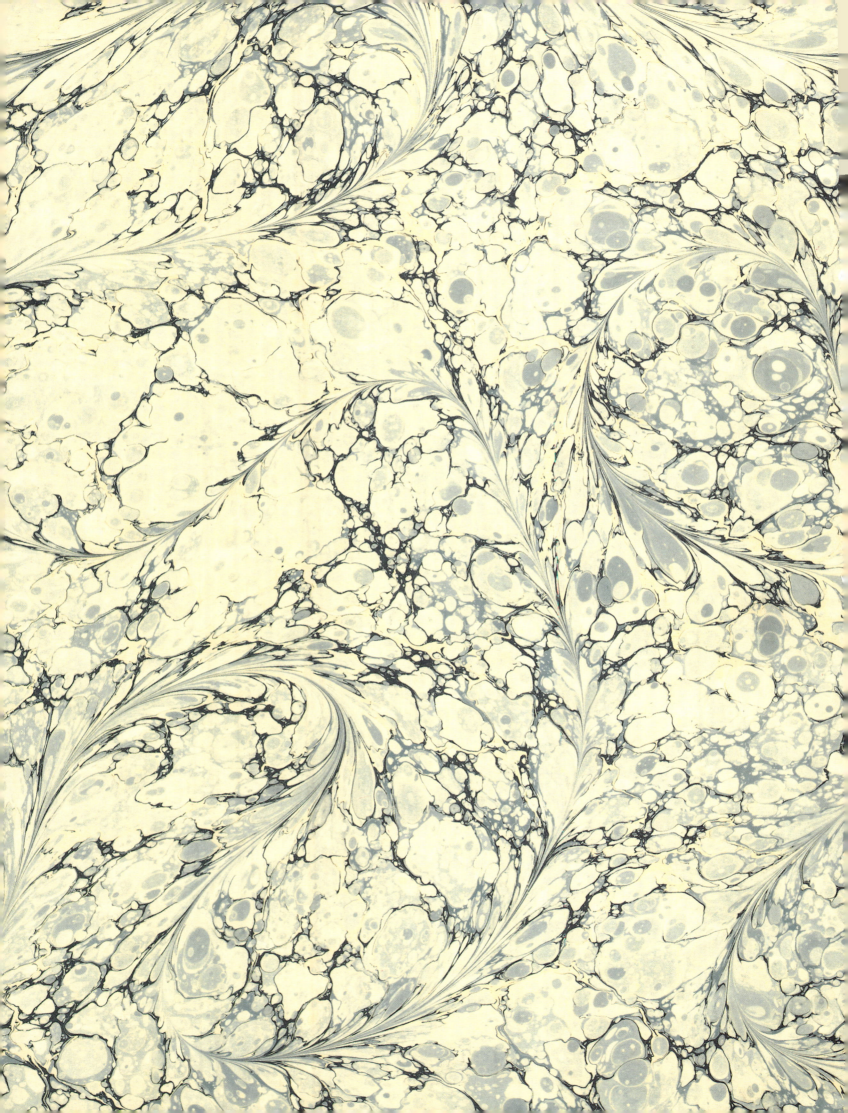